AF342407

THIS SIDE OF PARADISE

**BODY AND LANDSCAPE IN
LOS ANGELES PHOTOGRAPHS**

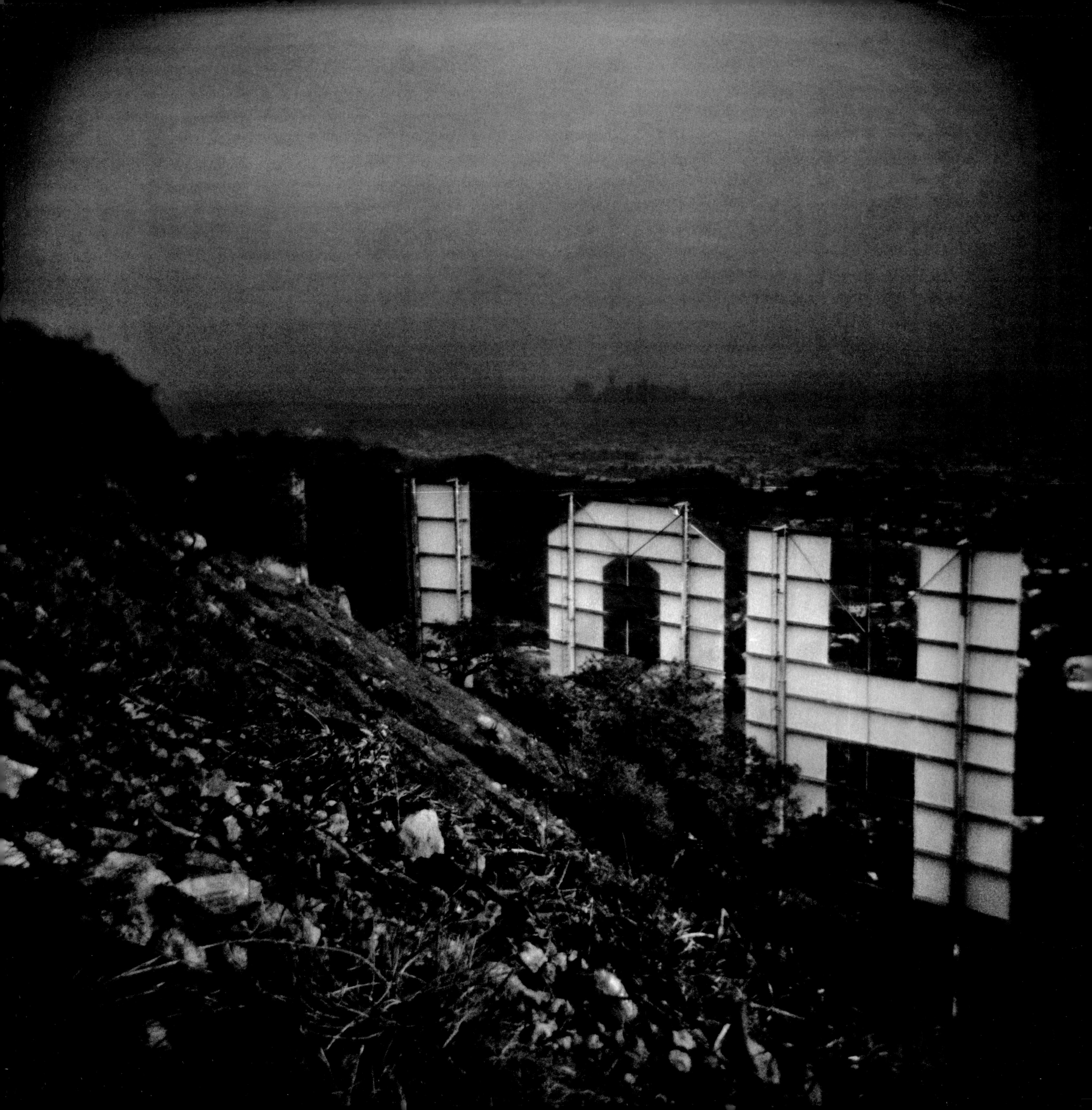

Jennifer A. Watts
Claudia Bohn-Spector

With an introduction by
Douglas R. Nickel

THIS SIDE OF PARADISE

BODY AND LANDSCAPE IN LOS ANGELES PHOTOGRAPHS

THE HUNTINGTON LIBRARY,
ART COLLECTIONS, AND
BOTANICAL GARDENS

MERRELL
LONDON · NEW YORK

ACKNOWLEDGMENTS

This is our third collaboration and, with it, our professional debts continue to grow. Many people have offered their advice and expertise over the several years it has taken us to pull this project together. Early on, Darryl Curran, David Fahey, and Stephen White, among others, supplied innumerable leads. We also benefited from the excellent guidance of our Advisory Committee: Michael Dawson, Bill Deverell, Karen Higa, Greg Hise, Chon Noriega, Sally Stein, and Tim Wride. Dr. Douglas R. Nickel was an enthusiastic supporter of this project from the beginning, and we are grateful for his insightful introduction to this volume.

This project owes its very existence to the generosity of its funders: Bank of America; Daniel Greenberg, Susan Steinhauser, and the Greenberg Foundation, Los Angeles; the Terra Foundation for American Art, Chicago; the Herb Ritts Foundation, Los Angeles; and the Pasadena Art Alliance. We would like to express our deep gratitude for their support.

Several significant grants and fellowships allowed us to research and write this publication, including those from the Arts and Humanities Council of Montgomery County, Maryland; the Center for Creative Photography, University of Arizona (Ansel Adams Fellowship); the J. Paul Getty Trust, Los Angeles (Library Research Grant); and the John Randolph Haynes and Dora Haynes Foundation, Los Angeles (Research Grant). The Haynes Foundation grant enabled us to hire Jason Hill and Rachel Longaker, two superb research assistants who helped with every conceivable aspect of this publication and exhibition.

We have met and spoken with a large group of talented artists, collectors, and dealers who have shown us thousands of photographs and brought new and interesting work to our attention. We particularly want to thank Laura Aguilar; Thomas Alleman; James Baker; Uta Barth; Joseph Bellows, Joseph Bellows Gallery, La Jolla, California; Gusmano Cesaretti; Beverly Feldman and Stephen Cohen, Stephen Cohen Gallery, Los Angeles; Eileen Cowin; Lou D'Elia; John Divola; Susan Ehrens and Leland Rice; Rebecca Beltrán and David Fahey, Fahey/Klein Gallery, Los Angeles; Christina Fernandez; Robbert Flick; Robin Blackman, Fototeka, Los Angeles; Jeffrey Fraenkel, Fraenkel Gallery, San Francisco; Harry Gamboa, Jr.; Ken Gonzales-Day; Todd Gray; Nancee Jaffe, Christopher Grimes Gallery, Santa Monica, California; Karen Halverson; Anthony Hernandez; Miyo Hernandez; John Humble; Jan Kesner, Jan Kesner Gallery, Los Angeles; Colleen Donaghe and Craig Krull, Craig Krull Gallery, Santa Monica, California; Margo Leavin and Sarah Nichols, Margo Leavin Gallery, Los Angeles; Gary Leonard; Timothy Buggs, Karyn Lovegrove Gallery, Los Angeles; Theresa Luisotti, Gallery Luisotti, Santa Monica, California; Benjamin Trigano, M + B, Los Angeles; Jerry McMillan; Willie Middlebrook; Don Normark; Ken Ohara; Catherine Opie; Dennis Reed; Tanya Brodsky, Regen Projects, Los Angeles; Hannah Sloan, RoseGallery, Santa Monica, California; Andy Schwartz; Allan Sekula; John Sonsini; Larry Sultan; Miriam Y. Katz, the Marjorie and Leonard Vernon Collection, Los Angeles; Gosia Wojas, Susanne Vielmetter Los Angeles Projects, Culver City, California; Nils Vidstrand; Devik Wiener; and Julie Casemore, Stephen Wirtz Gallery, San Francisco. Janet Fireman, Jim Heimann, Lisa Henry, Nancy Troy, Sam Watters, and Gloria Williams also proved instrumental in opening doors for us, and we wish to thank them as well.

Likewise, the staff at many institutions and archives made an extraordinary breadth of materials available. Deserving of special mention are Kent Kirkton, Black Photographers of California Archive/California State University Northridge; Leslie Calmes, Denise Gosé, Trinity Parker, Amy Rule, Britt Salvesen, and Marcia Tiede, Center for Creative Photography, University of Arizona; Anne Blecksmith and Wim DeWit, the Getty Research Institute, Los Angeles; Weston Naef, Virginia Heckert, Anne Lyden, Brett Abbott, Karen Hellman, and Jacklyn Burns, the J. Paul Getty Museum, Los Angeles; Cristine Noriko Paschild and Jane Nakasako, Japanese American National Museum, Los Angeles; Eve Schillo, Los Angeles County Museum of Art; Kevin Maiberger, Los Angeles Police Department; Carolyn Kozo Cole, Los Angeles Public Library; Lynda Bunting and George Davis, the Museum of Contemporary Art, Los Angeles; Mark McKenna and Brian English, the Herb Ritts Foundation, Los Angeles; Genie Guerard and Octavio Olvera, Department of Special Collections, Charles E. Young Research Library, University of California, Los Angeles; and Dace Taube, Regional History Center, University of Southern California.

Huntington Library colleagues have been an unwavering source of support. Steven Koblik, President; David Zeidberg, Avery Director of the Library; Robert C. Ritchie, W.M. Keck Foundation Director of Research; and Alan Jutzi, Avery Chief Curator of Rare Books championed the project at every turn. Manuel Flores, Ava Moeller, Marlyn Musicant, Susan Rogers, Randy Shulman, Jessica Todd Smith, Laurie Sowd, Donna Stromberg, John Sullivan, Devonne Tice, and Susan Turner-Lowe supplied vital on-the-ground support in many arenas. Jane Tsong and Gregg Bayne were key in bringing the exhibition design and installation to fruition. Erin Chase deserves special mention for her incomparable assistance and support.

The innovative exhibition design was the brainchild of the architecture firm Daly Genik, Santa Monica, California, especially Kevin Daly, David Pakshong, and Hannes Willroth. It is a pleasure to work with the editorial, design, and production staff at Merrell Publishers. We want especially to recognize Hugh Merrell, Claire Chandler, Mark Ralph, Nicola Bailey, Paul Arnot, and Michelle Draycott. Graham Howe and Robin McCarthy of Curatorial Assistance, Inc. worked closely with us to make the touring component of this show possible.

Our personal debts have grown with this project as well. We are particularly grateful to Antonia Bryan, Christiane Riederer von Paar, Dan Meinwald, and Joan Weinstein for their valuable feedback, expertise, and friendship. We are truly fortunate to have supportive spouses who have cheered us on every step of the way. Abundant thanks to Howard and Bill, for the editing, the intellectual and moral support, and the many, many hours of homework and childcare.

Jennifer A. Watts and Claudia Bohn-Spector

DIRECTOR'S FOREWORD

Sprawling, complex, and diverse, Los Angeles has for a very long time conjured up imagery as seductive and contradictory as the place itself. Over the past one hundred and fifty years, potent relationships between glamour and catastrophe, sunshine and noir, between lives ended and lives begun anew have fascinated photographers trying to explain the nearly inexplicable about Los Angeles. *This Side of Paradise: Body and Landscape in Los Angeles Photographs* examines the dynamic relationship between the city and the art of photography from the 1850s to the present. This catalog (and the exhibition from which it is drawn) focuses on the rich history of Los Angeles photography as it documents, explains, and mythologizes this fascinating city and region. Featuring over two hundred historic and contemporary images drawn from the Huntington Library's superb photographic holdings, as well as from other important lenders, *This Side of Paradise* will undoubtedly prompt new readings and interpretations of the visual culture of Southern California. At the same time, the catalog and exhibition will bring this remarkable visual legacy to new audiences of curious viewers.

A photograph—any photograph—blurs the line between the real and the imagined. Even a photograph at its most utilitarian obscures as much as it reveals. If one accepts this premise, then surely Los Angeles is one of photography's most seductive urban subjects, both as a place of fact—a population of 4 million people living within jurisdictional boundaries of some 470 sq. miles (1220 sq. km); 300 days of sunshine a year; $9\frac{1}{2}$ in. (24.1 cm) of annual rainfall; over two hundred languages in everyday use—and as a place of myth and stereotype—Los Angeles as a "city of dreams," "a semi-tropical paradise," "the nightmare at the terminus of American history," "a city without a center."

Los Angeles's imagery bears this out. Amateur and professional photographers alike have tried to capture Los Angeles and the people within it through myriad prisms. They have produced a far-flung archive of enduring photographs that continue to inspire, even as the place itself undergoes radical transformation. This long, graceful look at more than a century's worth of artistry offers a compelling journey through the very biography of Los Angeles and its people.

Henry Huntington, this institution's founder, believed Los Angeles to be the city of the future. He settled here, far from his native New York, and began at once to make his mark, first establishing the contours of the city with his rail lines, which stretched out to extensive real estate interests, and then, in 1919, building a world-class research library and botanical gardens on prime ranchland north-east of Los Angeles. He demonstrated his belief in Southern California by collecting items relating to its history and formation. One result of this prescient acquisition policy is an impressive photograph collection unparalleled in its visual documentation of the rapid and explosive transition of Los Angeles from pastoral landscape to thriving metropolis. Out of this great collection arose the idea for this exhibition.

With this show and catalog, the curatorial team of Jennifer A. Watts and Claudia Bohn-Spector, who have previously collaborated on aspects of Los Angeles imagery and the greater American West, reunite with equal parts imagination and ambition. For the very first time they bring together two themes that have always captivated photographers in Los Angeles—body and landscape—and point to the rich and visually compelling overlap between the two. Through their judicious curatorial skills, they have ensured that the photographs they have gathered—each captivating and arresting in its own right—add up to a visual sum of even greater intellectual magnitude than their many individually brilliant parts.

David Zeidberg
Avery Director, Huntington Library, San Marino, California

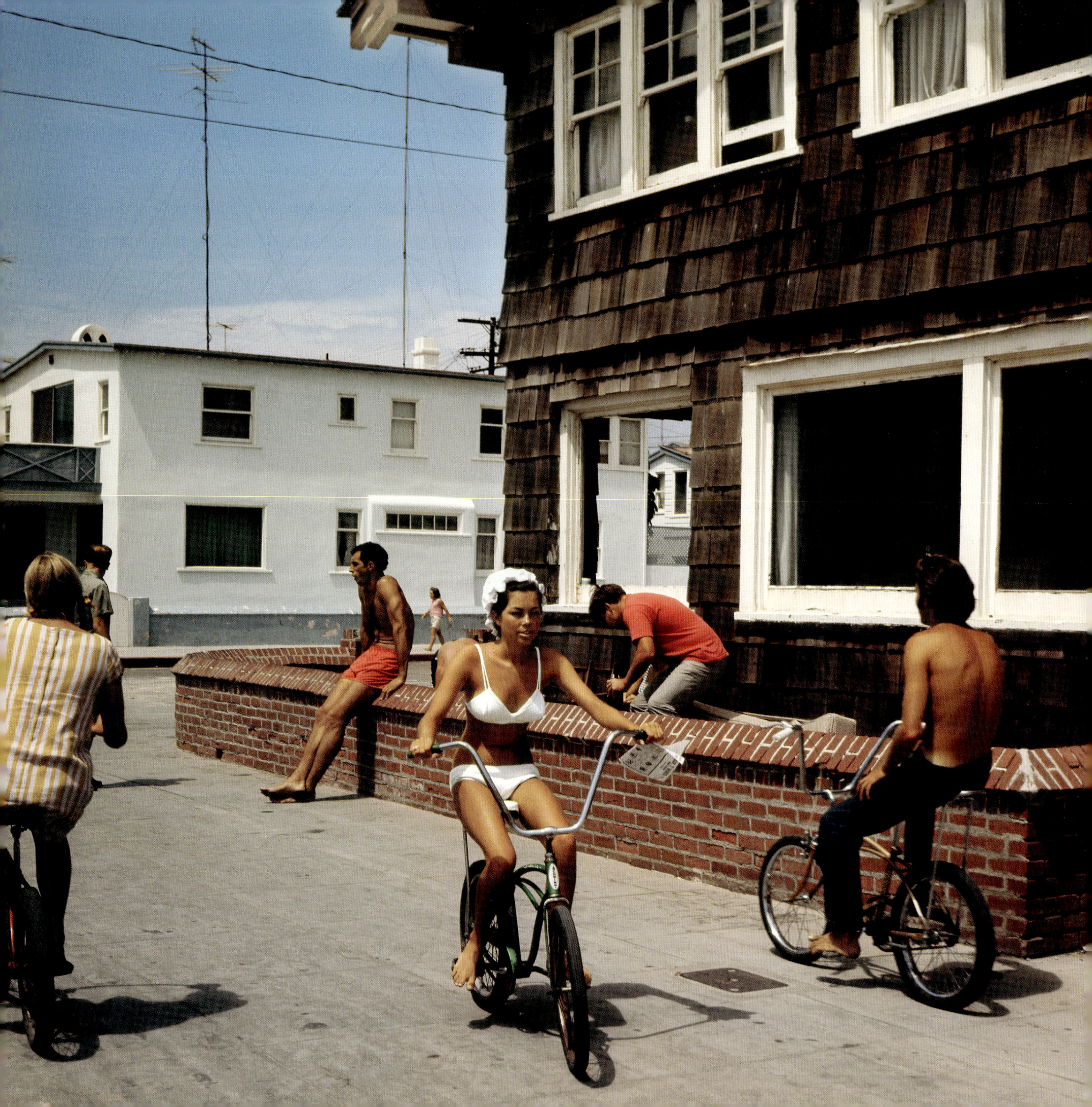

INTRODUCTION

Douglas R. Nickel

The hypothesis is this: a landscape photograph does not merely depict its subject, but always stands in some kind of reciprocal relation to it. For each of us, a location will attain a certain visual identity through our lived experience of the place: our memory collapses this experience into a set of mental images that, taken together, stand (for us) for the meaning of the place. But often we find we can recognize the look and feel of a place we have never visited, or have visited only cursorily—a recognition born not of direct encounter, but through the experience of images or descriptions of that place. Photographs, especially, appear to perform a kind of cognitive reduction to visual essence that makes them seem like memories of their subjects; indeed, they sometimes displace actual memories. We might call the special way the photograph transmutes object into image its "idealization" of its subject. This, more than its specificity or its putative resemblance to direct encounter, may be what makes the photograph such a potent carrier of meaning in Western society.

Such reduction feeds what Jean-Paul Sartre called the *imaginaire*: the "imaginary," that vast complex of mental images and associated beliefs and ideologies that construct for the individual (and, by extension, society) what we take to be our reality. The hypothesis, then, derives from the fact that image-makers are as subject to this process of influence as anyone else. They are trained to carry around in their heads a set of conventions for distilling perceptions into pictures. However, once they view one or more existing images of a place they wish to depict, they lose all innocence of it. The picture-maker can no longer see or represent that landscape without also inscribing into the resulting work the previous images and conventions that have infected his or her sense of the place; whether aware of it or not, he or she will be looking at the landscape through the filter of the imaginary. This is true even when the intended goal is to make something entirely new: the artist's rejection of the old is invariably mirrored in the alternative to it he or she seeks and finds. His or her representation, if then seen by others, will itself infect, modify, and become absorbed into the body of images it addresses, in an ongoing reciprocal process. The image alters the maker, who accordingly alters the next image, and so on.

No city has functioned more strongly within modern consciousness as a set of images than Los Angeles. The mythic Los Angeles obtains its force from the way its characterizations have tended toward the poles of a continuum. At one end, film and television have made Los Angeles utopian: images of its mild climate, sunshine, beaches, Mediterranean vegetation, boulevards, mansions, luxury hotels, swanky nightclubs and boutiques, shiny cars, swimming pools, and healthy bodies have been stereotyped, through repetition, into our cultural lexicon. At the other, we have urban dystopia: Los Angeles figured as a city of corruption and crime, of alienation and celebrity self-absorption, of racism, gang violence, smog, and freeways; figured as the millennial city, where natural forces (earthquakes, volcanoes) or human inventions (atomic weapons, power-plant meltdowns, nuclear war, viruses, cyborgs from the future)

John Divola
Zuma, #63, 1978

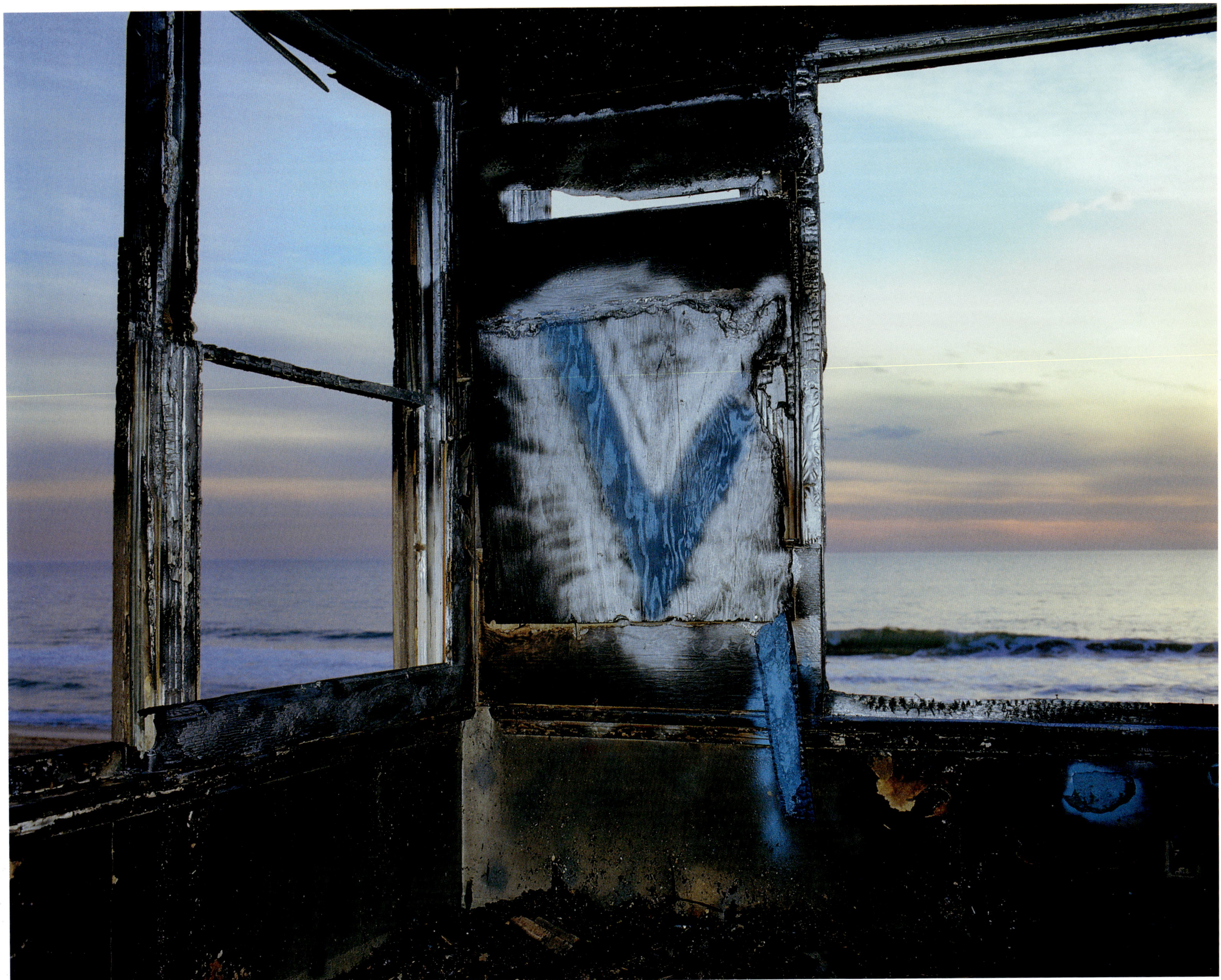

restyle the familiar landscape into a setting for some projected collapse and subsequent social disorder.[1]

As the center of the American movie industry, Los Angeles has provided locations that are always close at hand to filmmakers, but the city's particular attraction as a theme and locus for cinematic production is not explained away by proximity or convenience. It is true that, as backdrop to so much lens-based activity, the ambient look of Southern California found itself mapped into large portions of our vicarious experience. But the cultural construction of Los Angeles as both imagined Eden and apocalyptic ground zero is not the result of accidental forces. Insofar as the photographers represented in *This Side of Paradise* have absorbed, modified, rejected, and reproduced an imaginary place as much as a real one, each might be thought to occupy a position on the continuum that moves from dream to nightmare.

Except for Las Vegas, no other American metropolis has had as little practical reason for being situated where it is as Los Angeles. The five thousand or so Tongva people who lived in the Los Angeles basin before the arrival of the Spanish anticipated the city's modern trend toward decentralization: their scattered villages formed on the alluvial plain wherever a natural spring provided a source of water near food, as the local rivers flowed undependably when they flowed at all. Unlike other cities built upon navigable waterways, ports, or trade routes, Los Angeles was sited by political fiat. The Franciscans founded Mission San Gabriel Arcángel in 1771 near present-day Montebello, but five years later a flash flood destroyed it, compelling the friars to move it to its current location closer to the San Gabriel Mountains. In 1781, eleven civilian families led by Captain Fernando Rivera y Moncada trekked 9 miles (14.5 km) west from the mission and, on orders from Governor Felipe de Neve, founded the pueblo of Nuestra Señora la Reina de Los Angeles del Río de Porciúncula. The soldier and explorer Gaspar de Portolà had visited the place in 1769. His expedition diarist, Father Juan Crespi, wrote of it:

> After traveling about a league we entered a very spacious valley, well grown with cottonwoods and alders, among which ran a beautiful river from the north-northwest, and then, doubling the point of a steep hill, it went on afterward to the south . . . . As soon as we arrived, about eight heathen from a good village came to visit us; they live in this delightful place among the trees on the river.[2]

The expedition witnessed three consecutive earthquakes that day, but this did not deter Crespi from appreciating the beautiful Los Angeles River (which he named the Río de Porciúncula in honor of St. Francis's chapel at Assisi) and suggesting a settlement there. The first written description of what would eventually become Los Angeles thus evokes a setting of friendly natives living in prelapsarian comfort. In Crespi's representation it was already largely a place of the imagination—already related to venerable images and other sacred places. This gave De Neve

the will to build something from nothing. The cow town that soon materialized was miserable to behold, but it was lucrative for the Spanish and then Mexicans who controlled it, and so it grew.

Los Angeles was a city created through investments. After Alta California was ceded to the United States in 1848, the fate of the city fell to real estate men and robber barons. While the northern part of the state expanded dramatically with the Gold Rush (a story that became the creation myth for the entire state), Los Angeles remained a violent backwater. It entered the nation's consciousness through a report of 1861 by traveler J. Ross Browne, published in *Harper's Weekly*. Browne describes being invited by resident vigilantes to participate in the local sport: man-hunting. "Why, you would sit at the breakfast table of the Queen of the Angels and hear the question of going out to shoot men as commonly discussed as would be duck-hunting in any other country. At dinner the question would be, 'Well, how many did they shoot to-day? Who was hanged?'"[3] Invariably, the victims were Mexicans, Chinese, blacks, or Native Americans, who fare little better in the existing legal system than they did at the hands of Browne's sportsmen.

Salvation from this lawless state of affairs appeared in the form of the "Big Four": Collis Huntington, Leland Stanford, Mark Hopkins, and Charles Crocker. Having established the Central Pacific Railroad in 1861 and having connected it to the Union Pacific in 1869, the former Sacramento merchants found it advantageous in the next decade to extend their line down to Los Angeles and points beyond. The estimated 18 million acres (7.3 million ha) of property acquired by the company through federal land grants ultimately proved the most profitable aspect of the initiative. Along the tracks grew stops, then towns, and around them farms. The Southern Pacific was simply infrastructure for a larger scheme: the company needed passengers and freight to make the railroad profitable, and it needed settlers to take advantage of its new landholdings. The massive effort to market California to potential buyers of the railroad's (now greatly inflated) real estate offerings required a bucolic, virtuous image of the region to predominate. Meanwhile, the company invested in water projects along its right-of-ways: the fertile but arid region was made vastly more habitable—which is to say, profitable—by large-scale irrigation. The fuel for this growth was extensive capitalization. The result was modern agribusiness, which soon enough squeezed out the small farmer, as Frank Norris describes in his tale of railroad greed and duplicity, *The Octopus* (1901). The locomotive connected Los Angeles to civilization, tourism to the Southland, and California's bounty to the world.

As a city built on speculation, Los Angeles depended to an inordinate degree upon good salesmanship and well-crafted imagery. From Governor de Neve on, it was a city predicated less on need than on desire, on futurity—what might be possible. The explosive population growth of the region that followed the arrival of the railroad required other bold projects to sustain its momentum: hydroelectric power, highways, the creation of a navigable port, and, above all, fresh water. Few in the history of Los Angeles have demonstrated as much visionary imagination as the self-taught engineer William Mulholland, the builder of the Los Angeles Aqueduct. Born in Ireland, Mulholland made his way to New York and San Francisco, tried his hand at mining in the Arizona Territory, and finally arrived at Los Angeles in 1877. He rose from ditch cleaner for the private Los Angeles Water Company to become its superintendent, and when the city took over the business in 1902 he retained the title at the new Los Angeles Bureau of Water Works and Supply. Mulholland and his former boss, Mayor Frederick Eaton, were convinced that the growth of the city depended on the diversion of water—large amounts of it—from the agricultural uplands of the Owens Valley to the San Fernando Valley and on to the city. Through political machination, the city of Los Angeles then bought or cheated local farmers out of the water rights to the Owens River, and floated a bond measure to subsidize the $24.6 million needed for construction of the 223 miles (359 km) of pipes, tunnels, dams, and sluices of the aqueduct. The measure was backed by speculators quietly investing in the Valley, who enjoyed a real estate bonanza from property they purchased there in advance. The opening of the aqueduct in 1913 was greeted as Mulholland's (and the city's) triumph; it left Owens Lake a dry alkali wash. Mulholland's soaring achievement was met, in almost mythic fashion, with an equally great fall, when in 1928 the St. Francis Dam he had built near Santa Clarita collapsed. The 15 billion gallons (57 billion l) of water released carved a path 2 miles (3.2 km) wide on its way to the sea, burying most of Ventura County under yards of muddy debris. Hundreds of people were killed. Mulholland, who had inspected the dam the morning before the break and declared it safe, was found negligent and forced to resign in disgrace. It was the worst American civil engineering failure of the twentieth century.

The Los Angeles–Owens Valley water wars figure as the centerpiece to Roman Polanski's classic movie *Chinatown* (1974), in which Chief Engineer Hollis Mulwray is something of an anagram for Mulholland. The plot centers on the fabrication of a drought in order to manipulate real estate prices in the Valley. *Chinatown* was, in fact, meant to be the first film of a trilogy by screenwriter Robert Towne, the second of which, *The Two Jakes* (1990), brought back *Chinatown*'s protagonist, J.J. Gittes (played by Jack Nicholson), and took the post-Second World War oil boom as a motif. The never-made *Cloverleaf* would have done the same for freeway construction. Film noir works so well in Los Angeles not simply because of its inversion of sunshine and all that has been made to represent for the city, but also because it has appeared a quintessential site for entertaining fears about alienation, corruption, infidelity, and disillusionment. These are not fears specific to Los Angeles or even to cities, but in the Judeo-Christian tradition the garden always implies expulsion, and hubris and idolatry invite punishment. The cynical Hollywood failures and hangers-on who populate Nathanael West's novel *The Day of the Locust* (1939) are perhaps the best noir subjects drawn to date. The main character

here, an artist who finds work as a scene painter, dreams of painting his masterpiece, *The Burning of Los Angeles*. The story's apocalypse, however, is—consistent with West's world view—more of a whimper than a bang.

Dystopia is not the opposite of utopia, not its mirror image. Both are alternative realities, alternatives that each begin in current social reality and draw out implications in radically different directions. Fictionalized dystopias share common themes: discrimination, the repression of intellectuals and free thought, the denial of privacy and other civil liberties, the repression of democracy. Romantic love is thematized: dystopias are often predicated on state or corporate control of the individual, and any other kind of social affiliation—to the family, to another individual—is considered dangerous. The state is often represented by a figurehead, and his (usual) cult of personality is sustained by an all-pervasive, fully censored media. Southern California's defense industries lurk behind James Cameron's *Terminator* movies, in which a nuclear-decimated, machine-controlled Los Angeles of the year 2029 results from a government project called Skynet, a computer-based defense system that becomes sentient and launches America's entire missile arsenal at Russia. Los Angeles in 2019 is the setting for Ridley Scott's *Blade Runner* (1982). This city—a version of Fritz Lang's *Metropolis*, left behind by those who could afford to flee its pollution, crime, overpopulation, and teeming ethnicity—is likewise under threat from androids who are largely indistinguishable from humans. Scott turned Union Station into his futuristic police station, and the streets of downtown into trash-strewn lanes crowded with noodle shops and disintegrating apartment buildings. Reverse-engineering the message, we realize that the robots in these films act as a foil for the quality of humanity: the cold-blooded Terminator has none, and the Replicants of *Blade Runner* struggle to achieve it. Both films and the dystopian future they depict not only focus on Los Angeles as a location, but also suggest how the intolerance and lack of compassion of, say, road rage prefigures such a future, how the uprising of 1992 sparked by the police's beating of Rodney King predicts worse events still to come.

The Los Angeles of the imagination has shaped the way the city has been physically planned, designed, and built. Its function in our national consciousness requires we view it not for what it is or has become, but for what we need it to be. The photographs found on the following pages could never be considered documents—if that term implies a record of extant reality—as the reality depicted in them is already a representation, and always seen through the lens of desire and projection. There is no neutrality here, only the work of imagination.

NOTES

1. See Mike Davis, *Ecology of Fear: Los Angeles and the Imagination of Disaster*, New York (Metropolitan Books) 1998.

2. Father Juan Crespi, quoted in Ruth E. Baugh, "Site of Early Los Angeles," *Economic Geography*, 18, January 1942, p. 90.

3. J. Ross Browne, quoted in Steven Vincent (ed.), *O California: Nineteenth and Early Twentieth Century California Landscapes and Observations*, San Francisco (Bedford Arts) 1990, p. 21.

GARDEN

Fattest land I ever saw.
Harrison Gray Otis, publisher

When photography reached the United States soon after its invention in 1839, Los Angeles was a Mexican pueblo that hardly invited photographic curiosity. Perched on the edge of the continent in an arid basin, the city grew in part because of water, first supplied by artesian wells and the Los Angeles River, and much later brought from hundreds of miles away. By the late 1880s, thousands rushed to Southern California to seize land invoked by boosters (the region's vociferous pitchmen) as the last American paradise—a place of spectacular beauty, salubrious climate, and unlimited economic potential.

Such early photographers as Carleton E. Watkins and C.C. Pierce affirmed the promoters' hyperbole, depicting undulating landscapes, breathtaking vistas, and scenes of lush pastoral splendor. Later image-makers showed residents in harmonious union with nature—modern-day descendants of Adam and Eve basking in a land of perpetual sunshine.

Others worked in a less exalted vein, conjuring up visions of Los Angeles that challenged prevailing myths. They pictured the city not as a Garden of Eden, but as a concrete jungle of stucco, cars, and freeways blistering under the harsh midday sun. Still others homed in on Los Angeles as a place of masquerade and pretense, exposing Southern California's penchant for dreamy artificiality.

Somewhere between these extremist visions, however, flowered the real Los Angeles, a place where millions steal moments of pleasure and delight from the bustle and tedium of everyday life.

William Mortenson
Torse, c. 1935

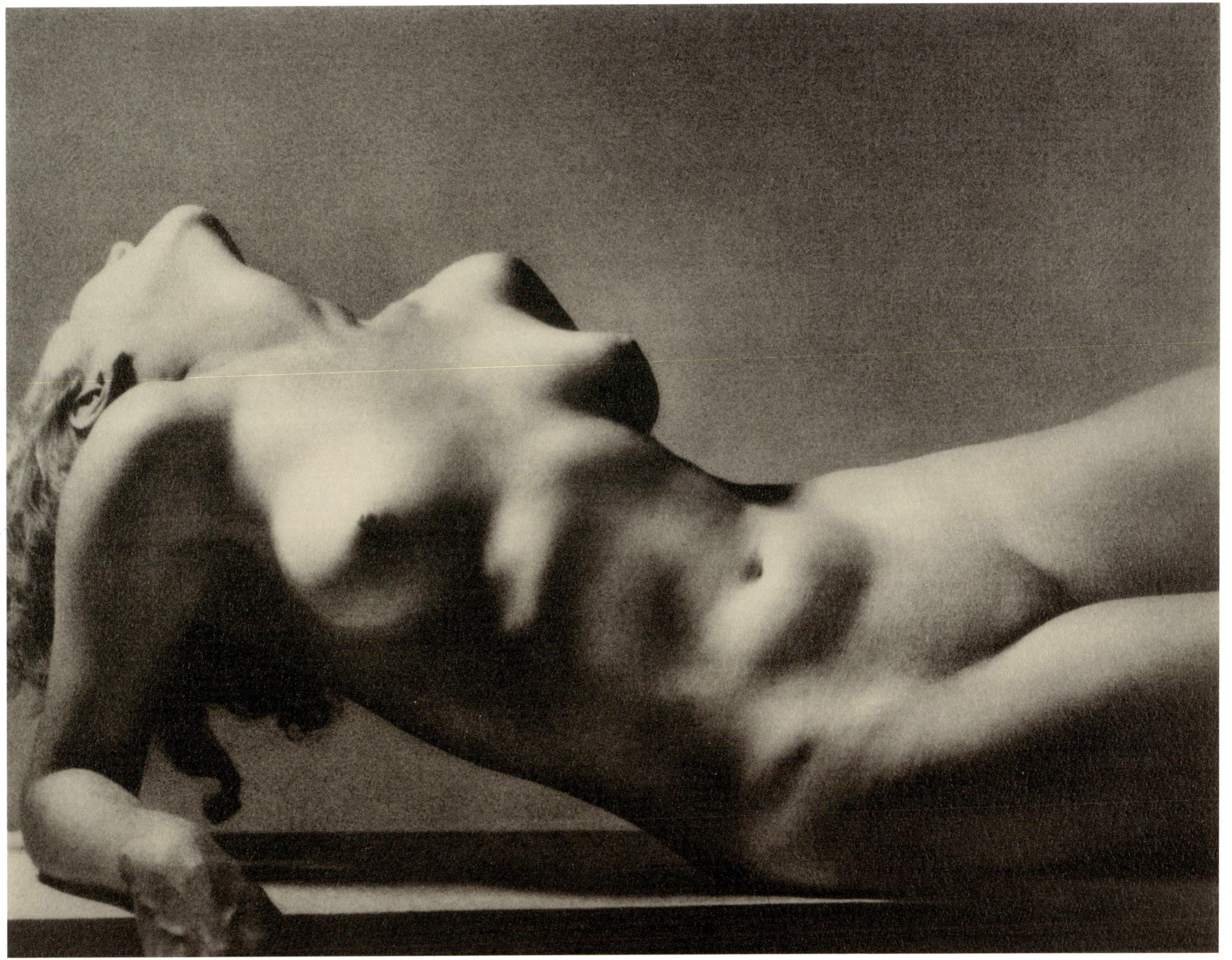

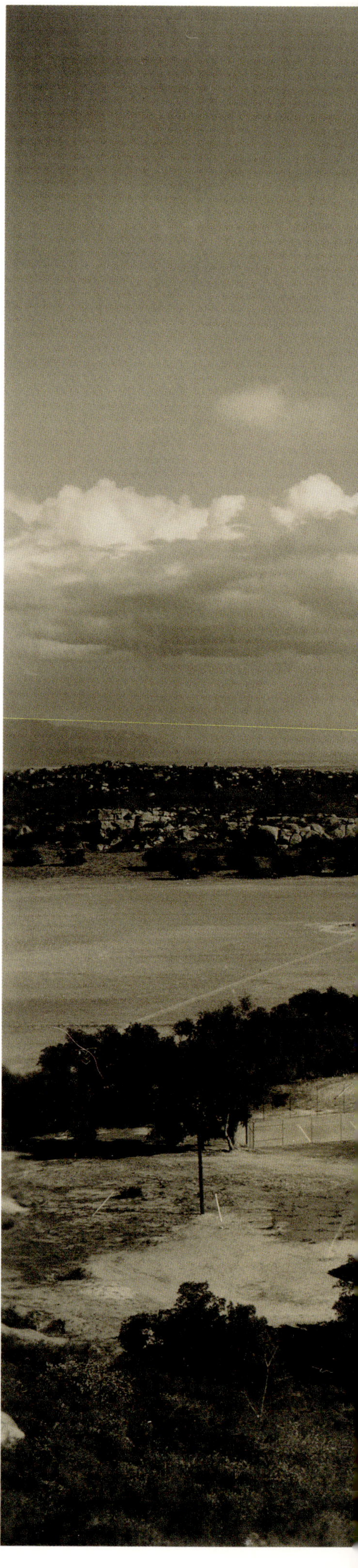

Unknown
*San Fernando Valley from
above Chatsworth, looking
toward Los Angeles with
E. John Brandeis's estate
in the foreground,* n.d.

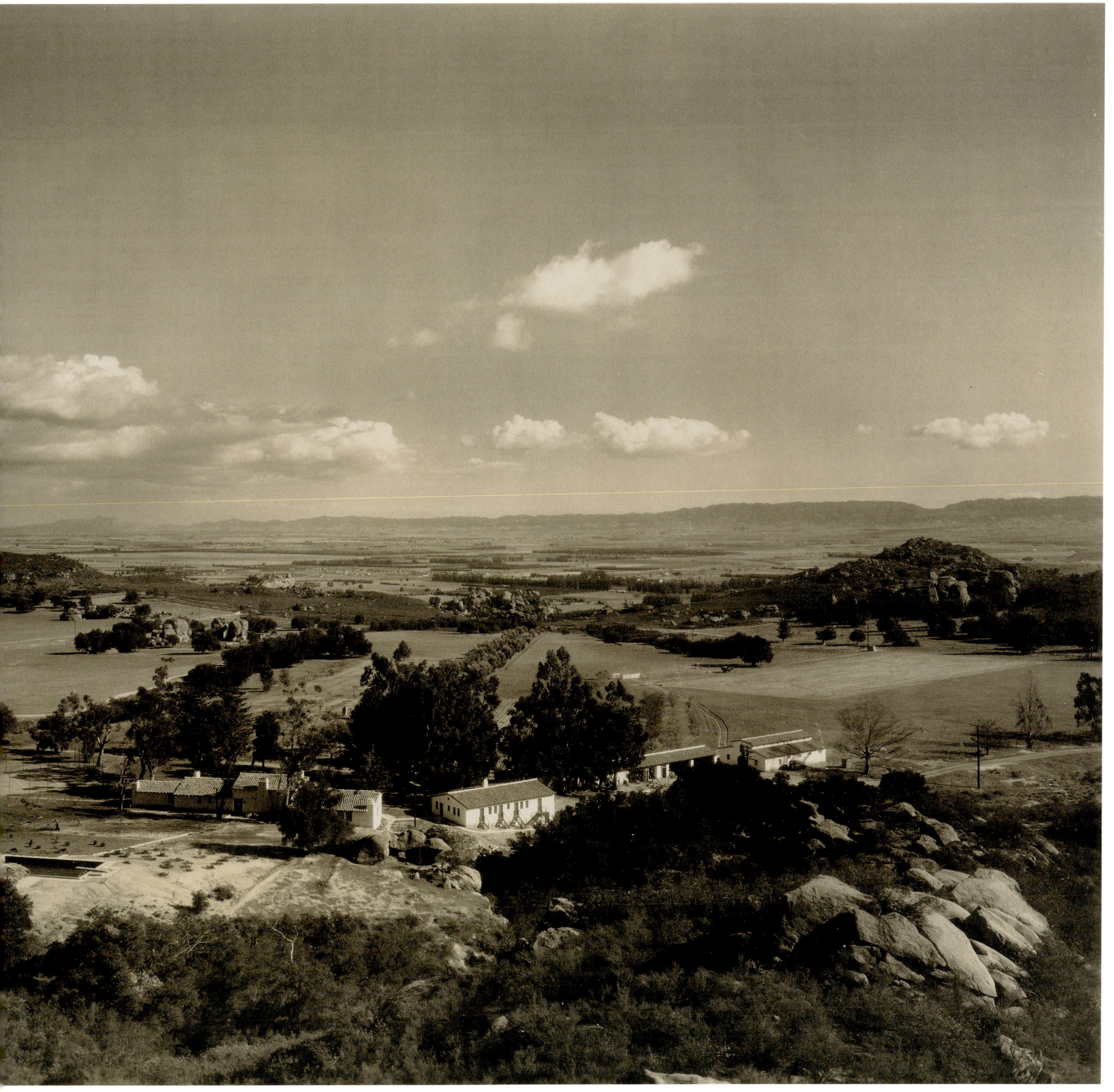

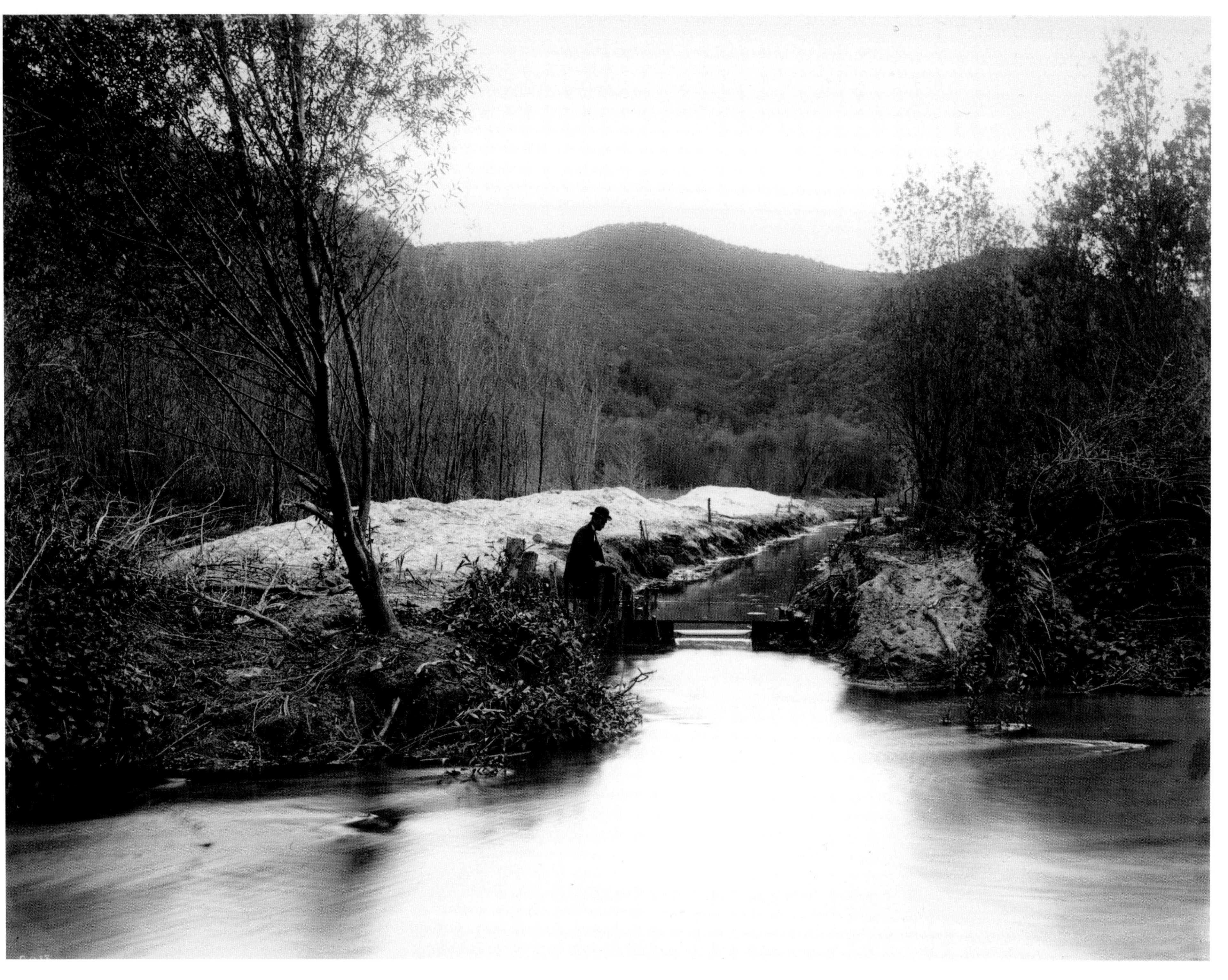

C.C. Pierce
*Griffith Park and Los Angeles
River at the Source*, 1900

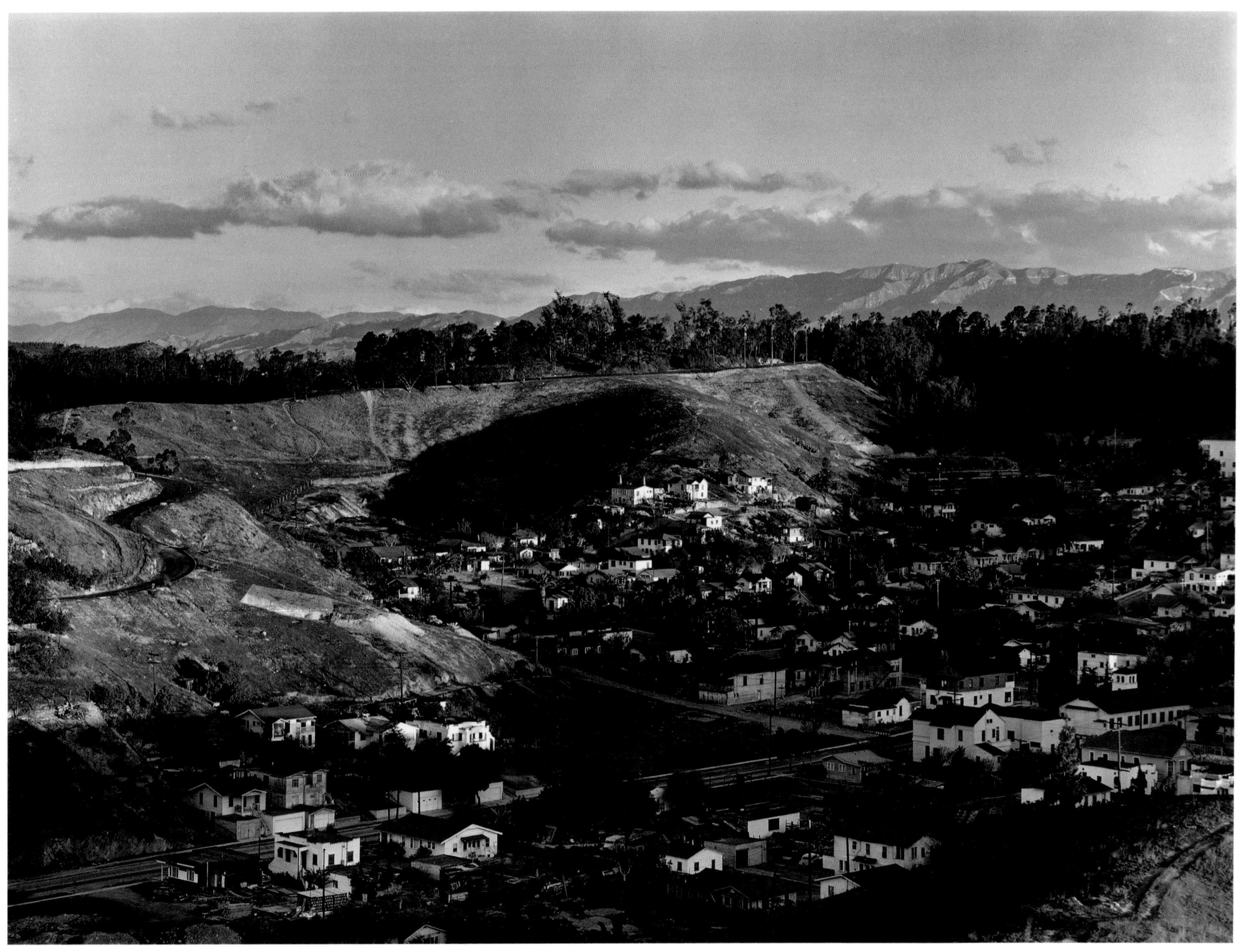

Don Normark
Palo Verde Neighborhood
with Elysian Park Beyond,
1949

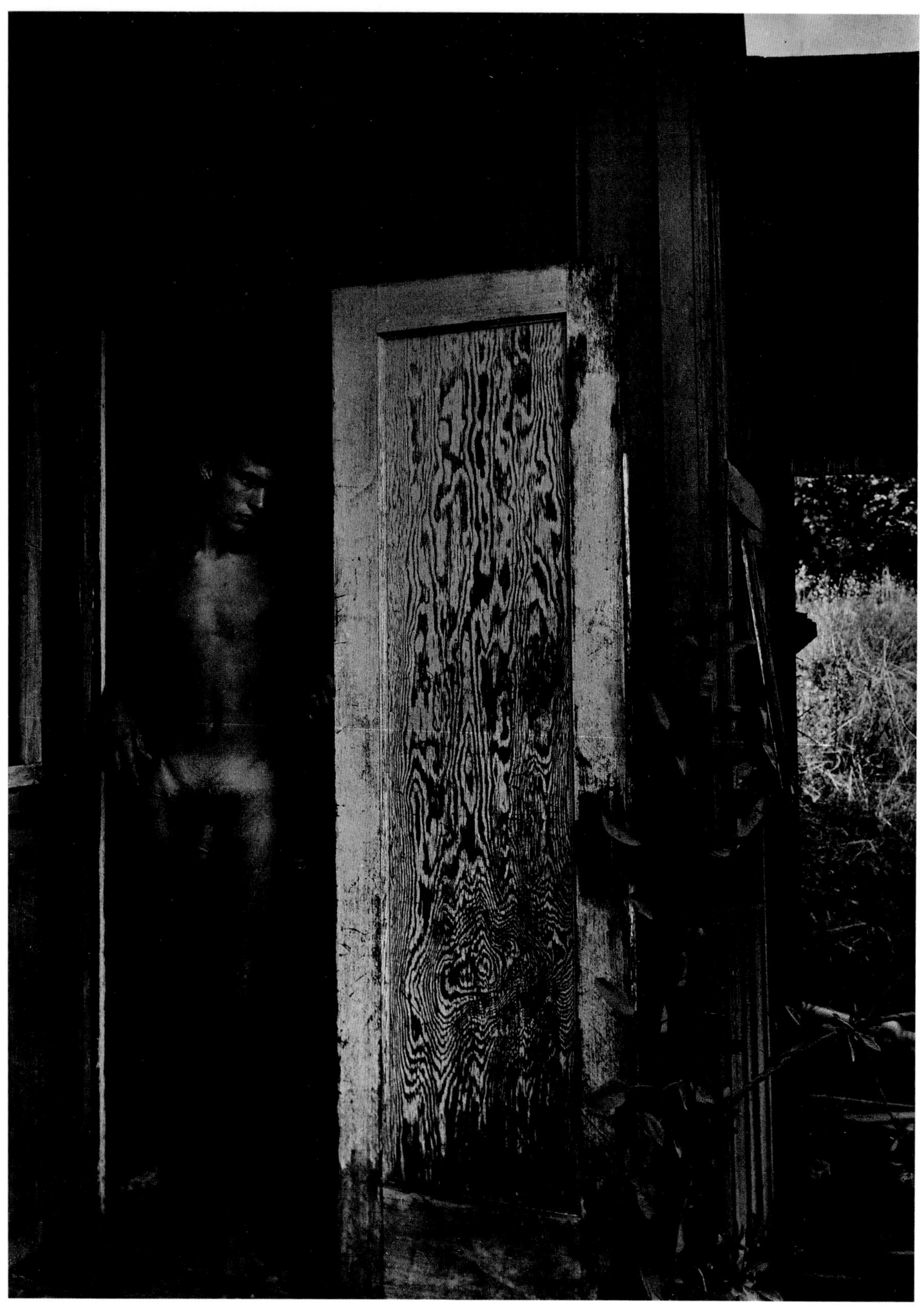

Edmund Teske
[Mark Rambeau], 1962

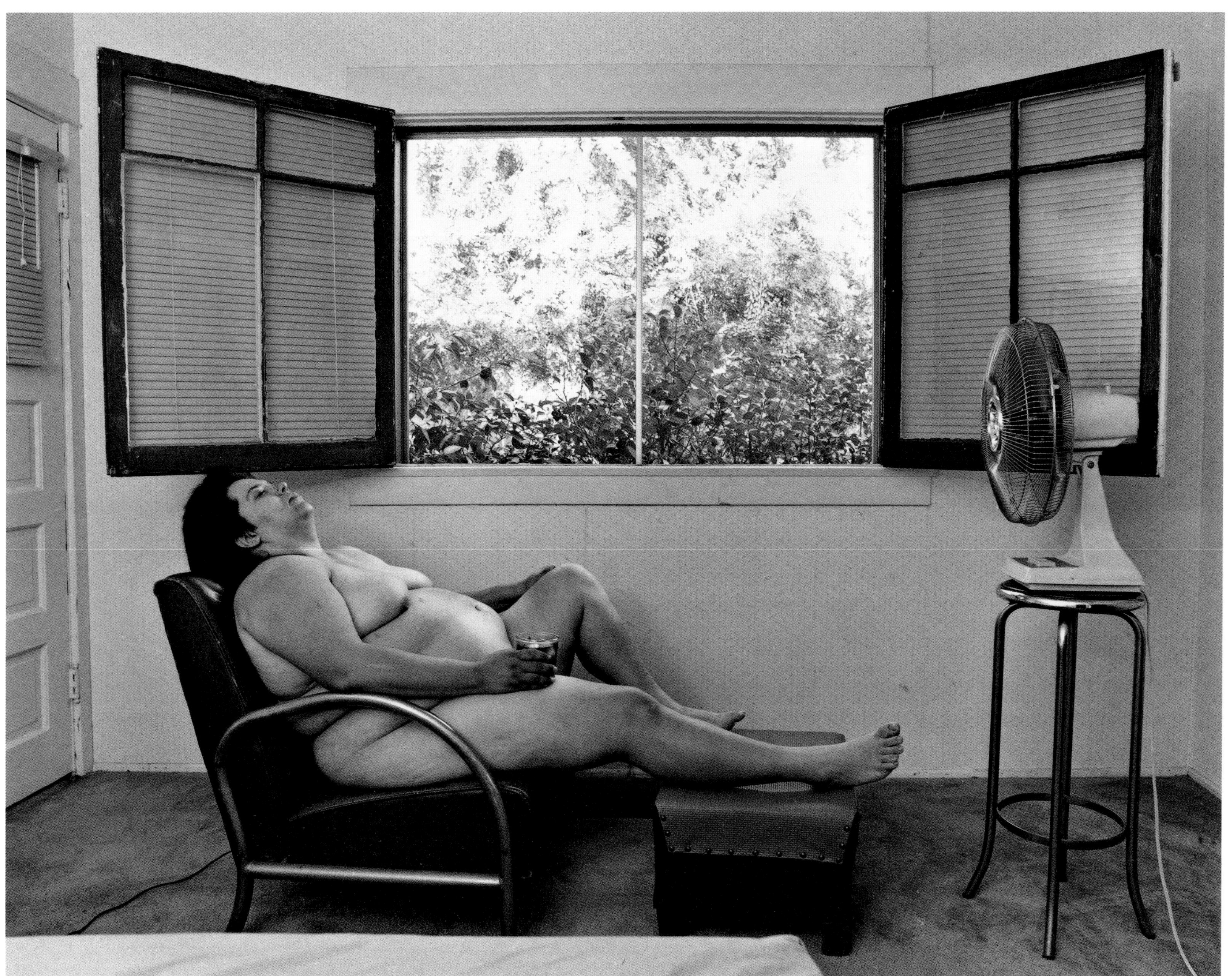

Laura Aguilar
In Sandy's Room, 1990

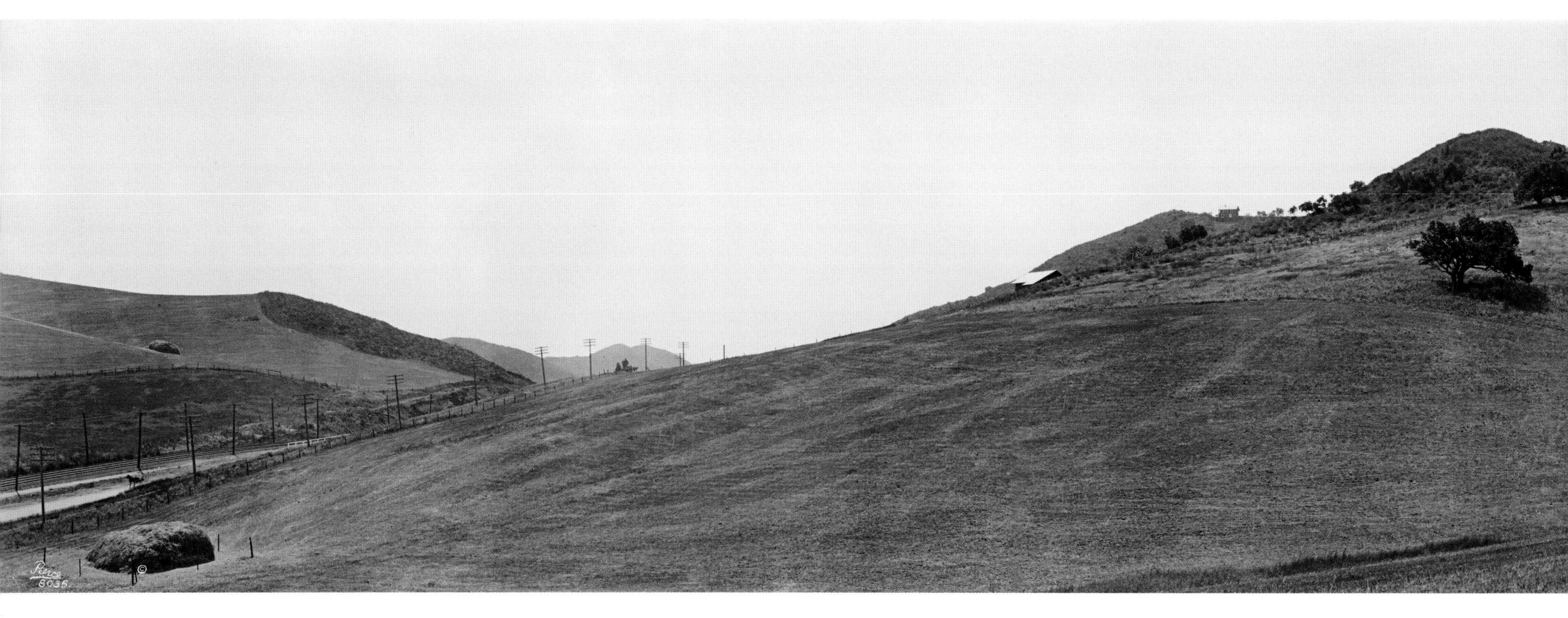

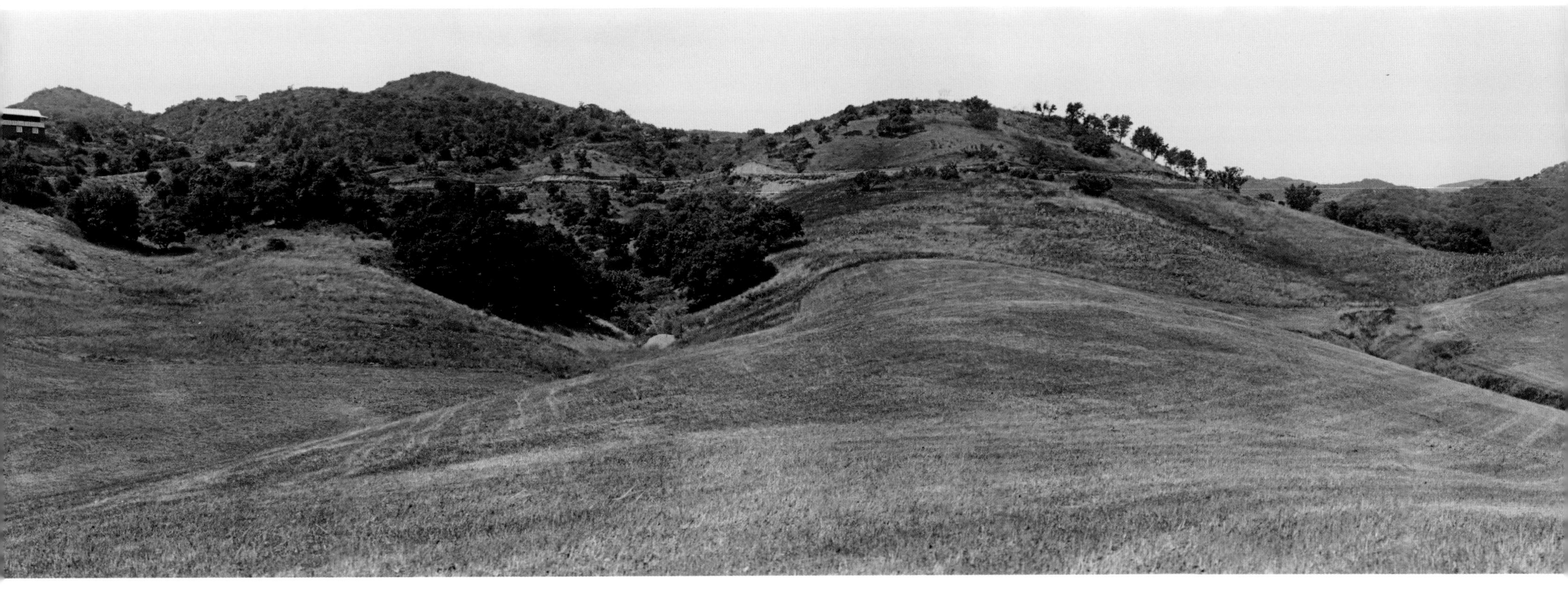

C.C. Pierce
North End of Cahuenga Pass,
Los Angeles, 1910

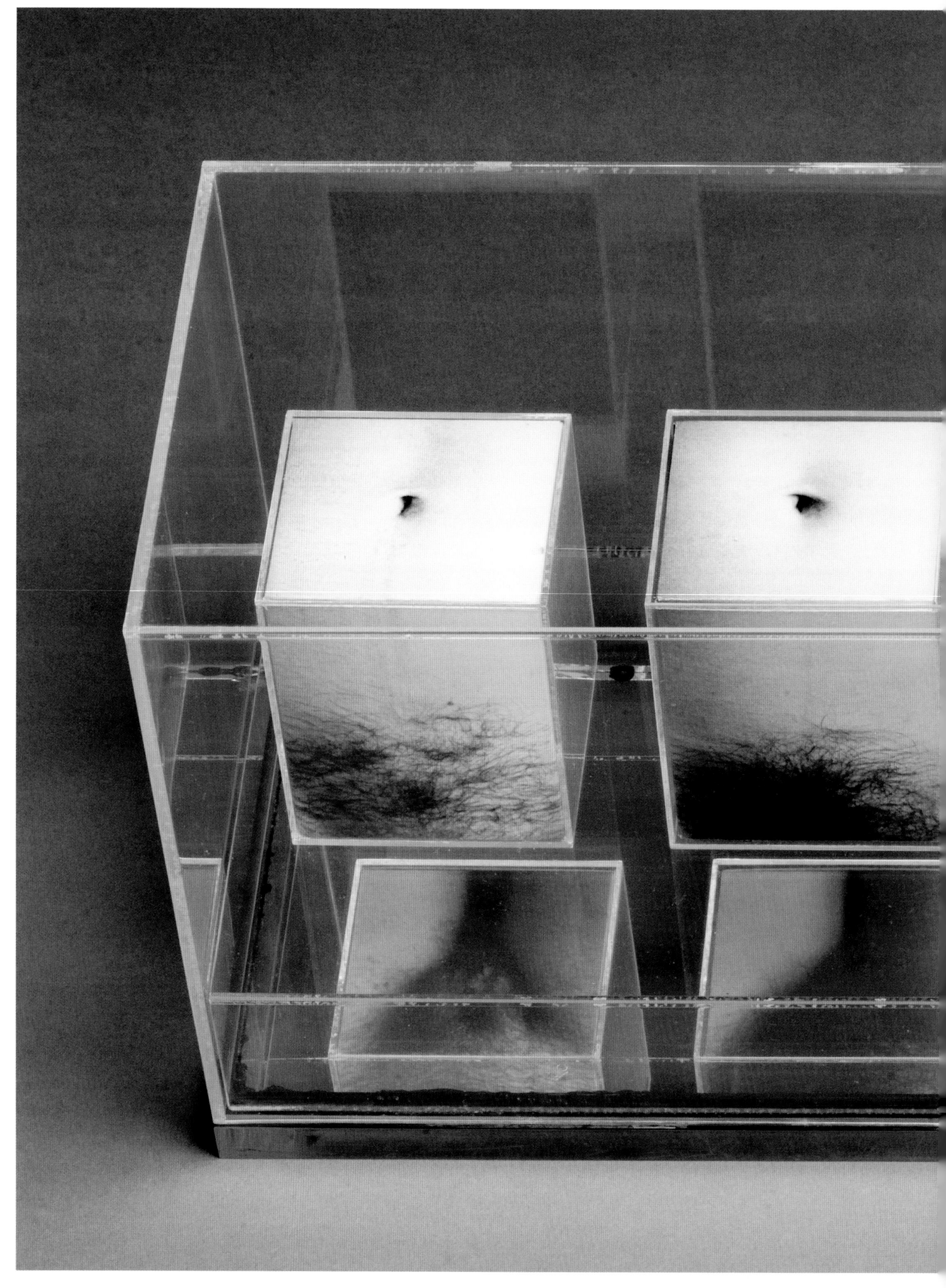

Jerry McMillan
Five Boxes, 1965–67

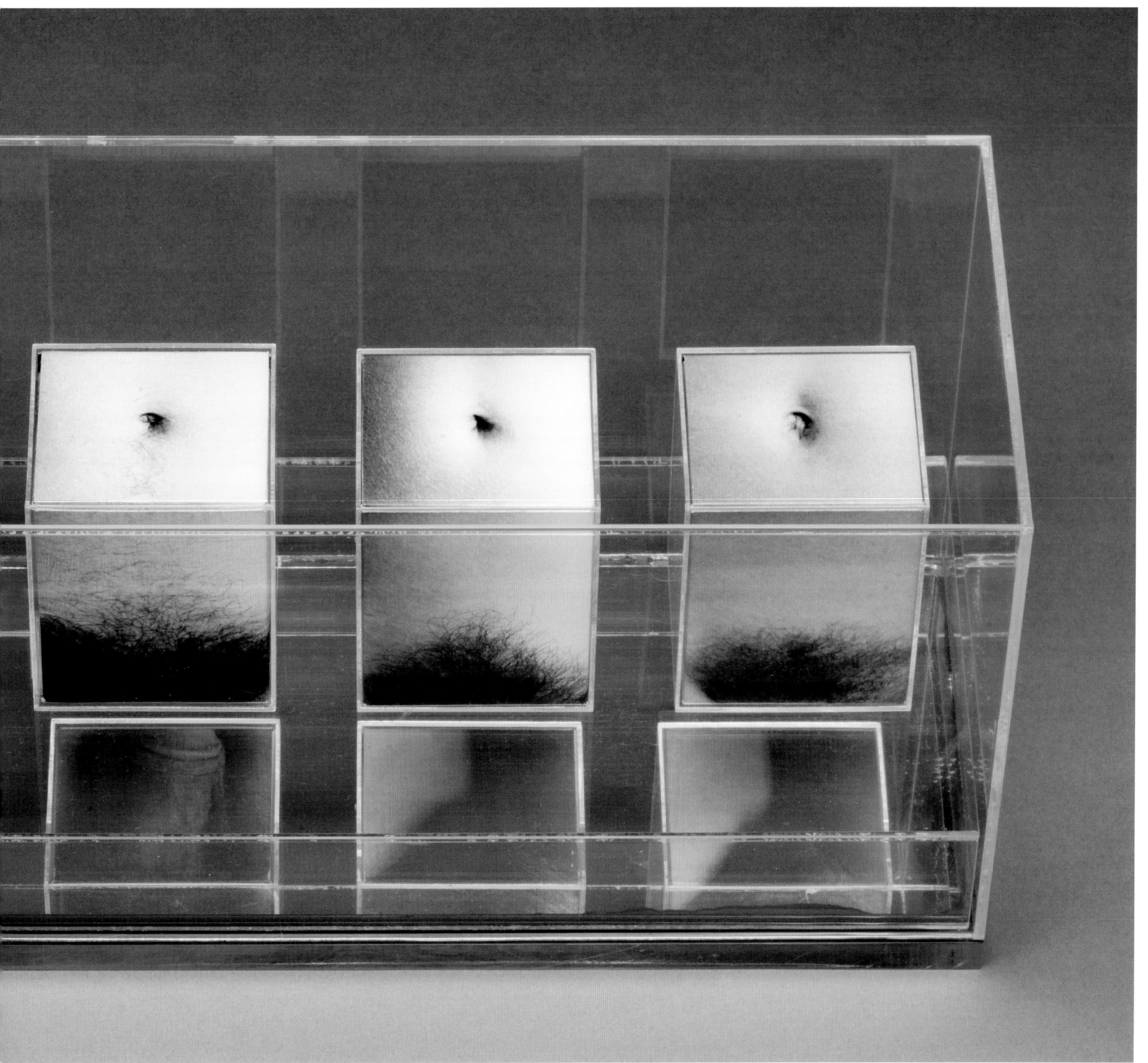

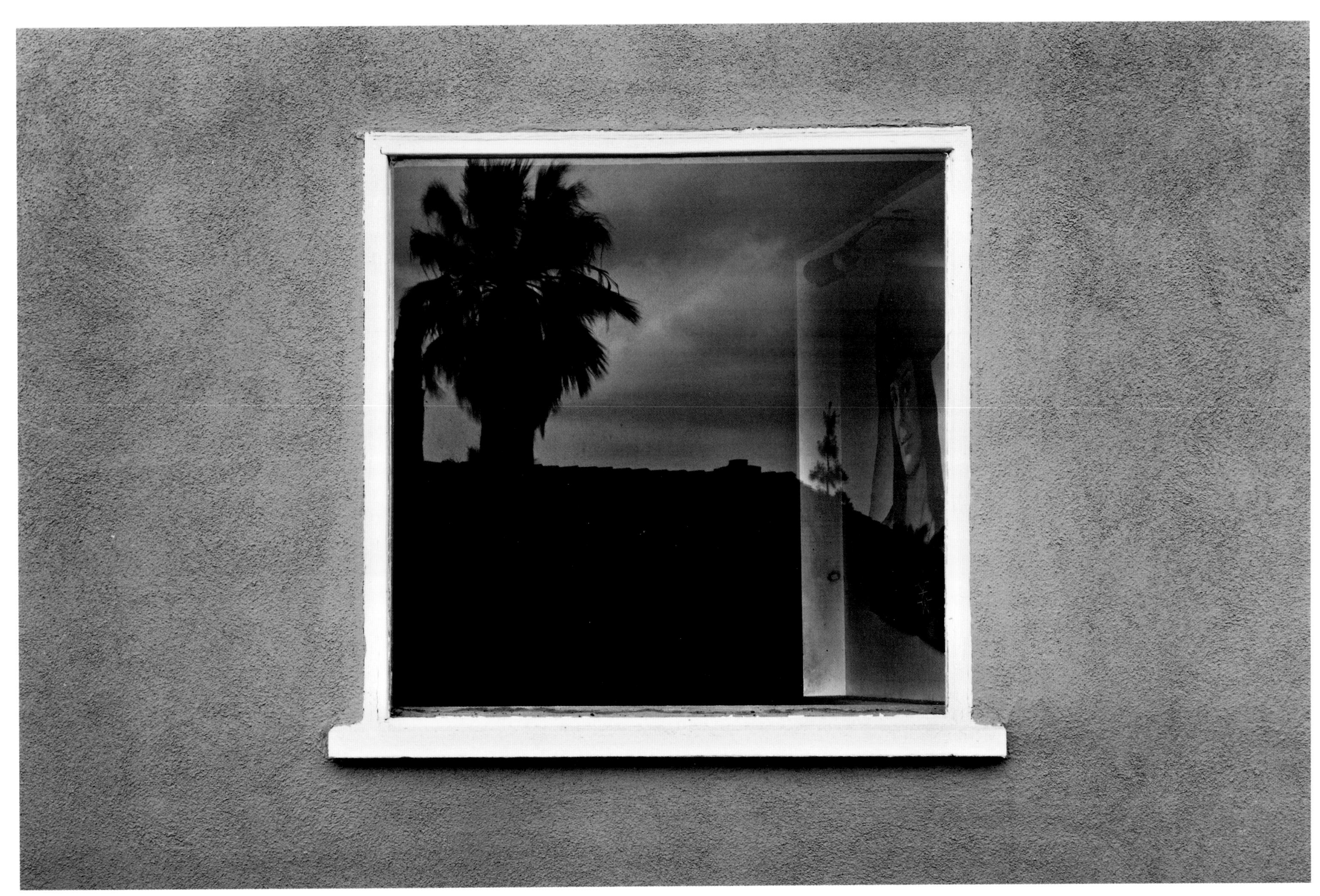

Lewis Baltz
Claremont, 1973

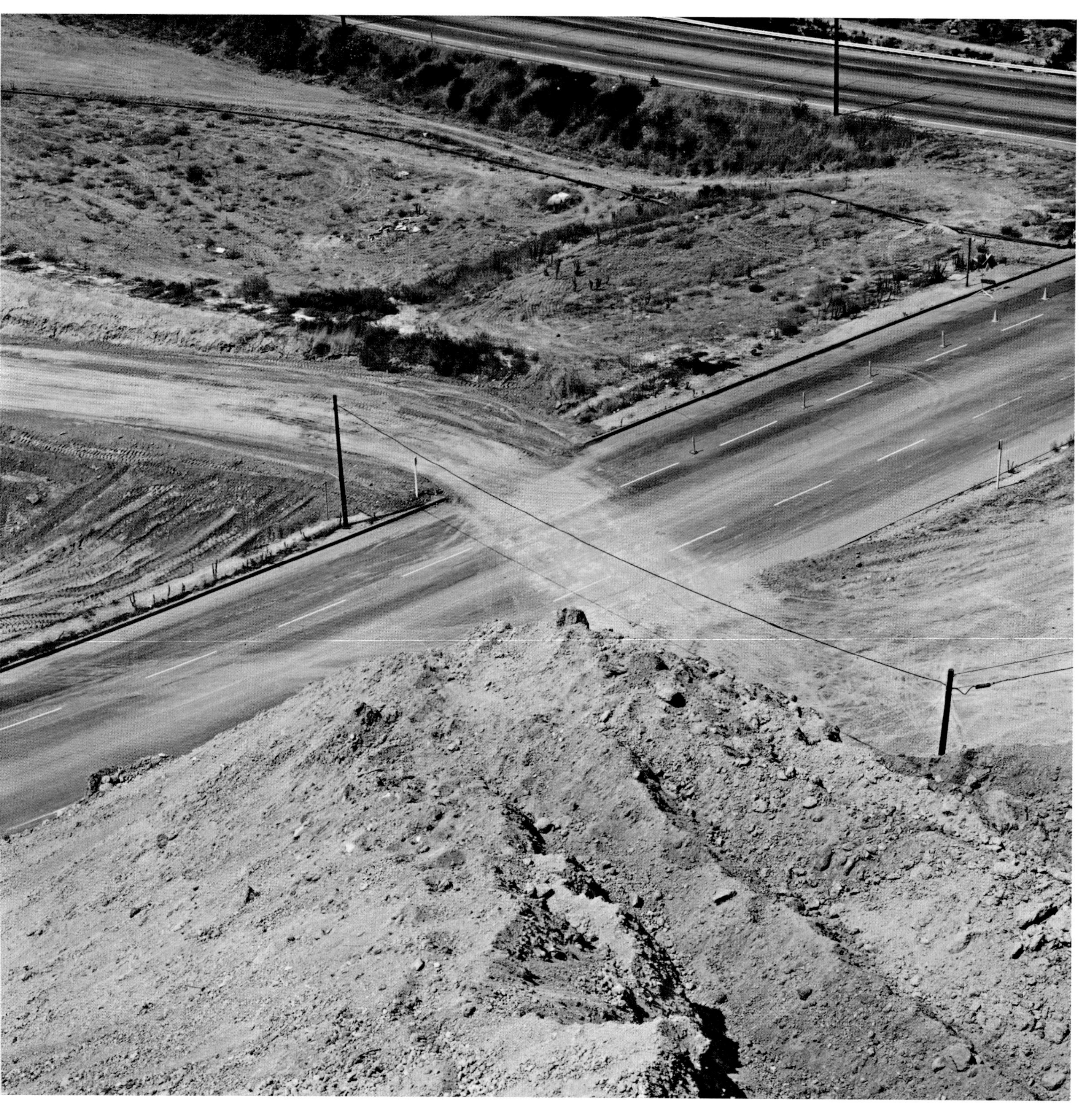

Joe Deal
Inglewood, California, 1979

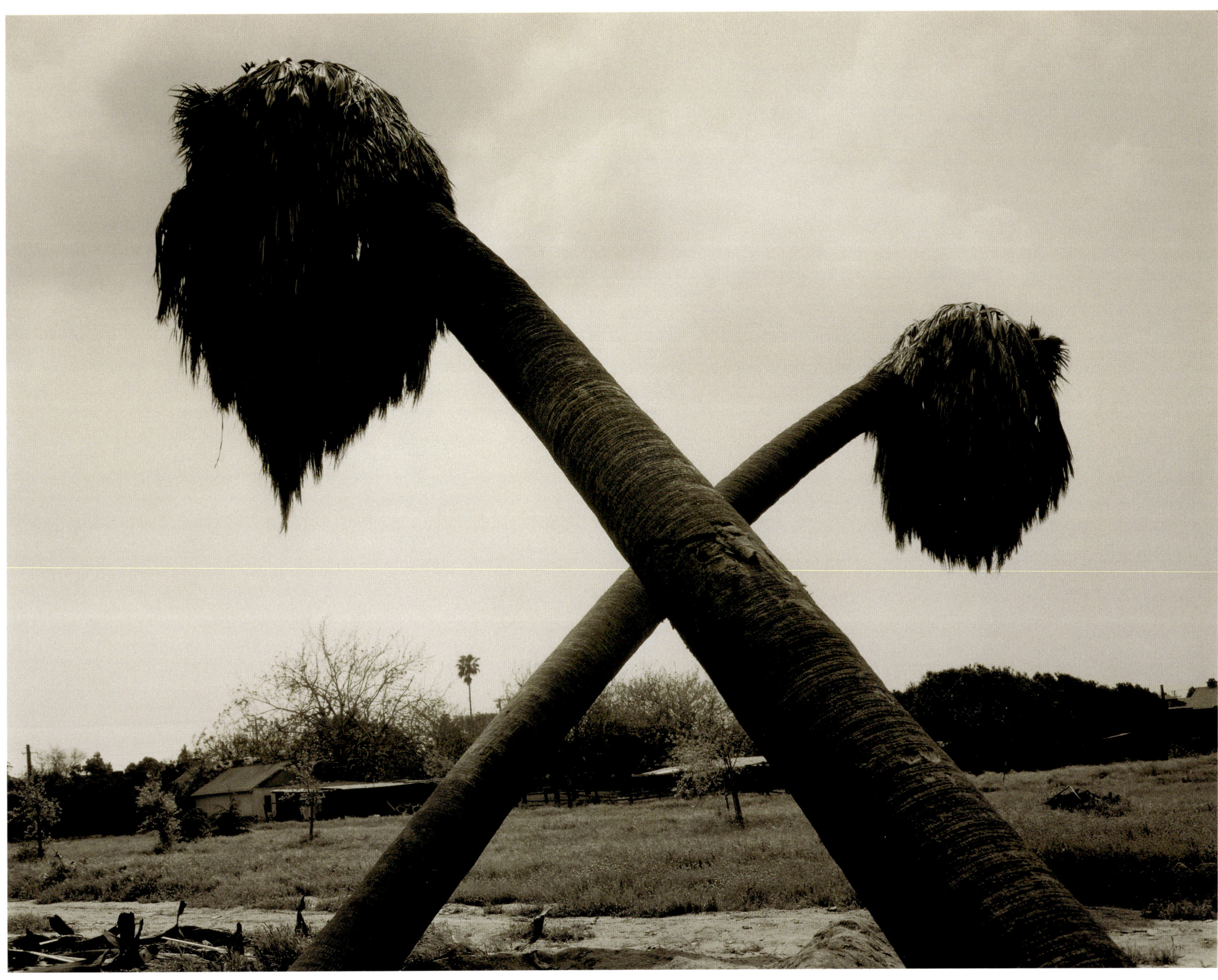

Robert Adams
Ontario, California, 1983

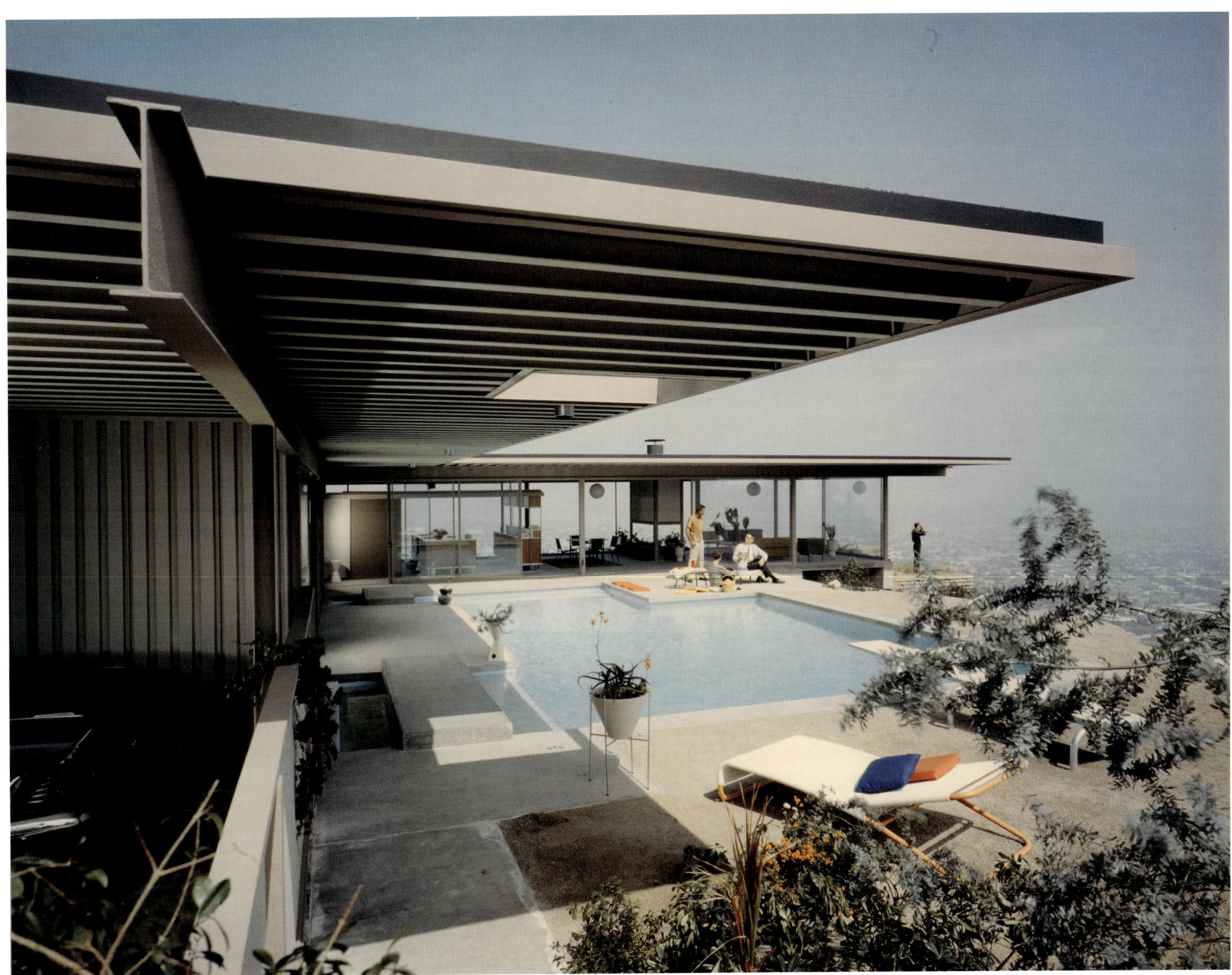

Julius Shulman
Case Study House #22,
West Hollywood, 1960

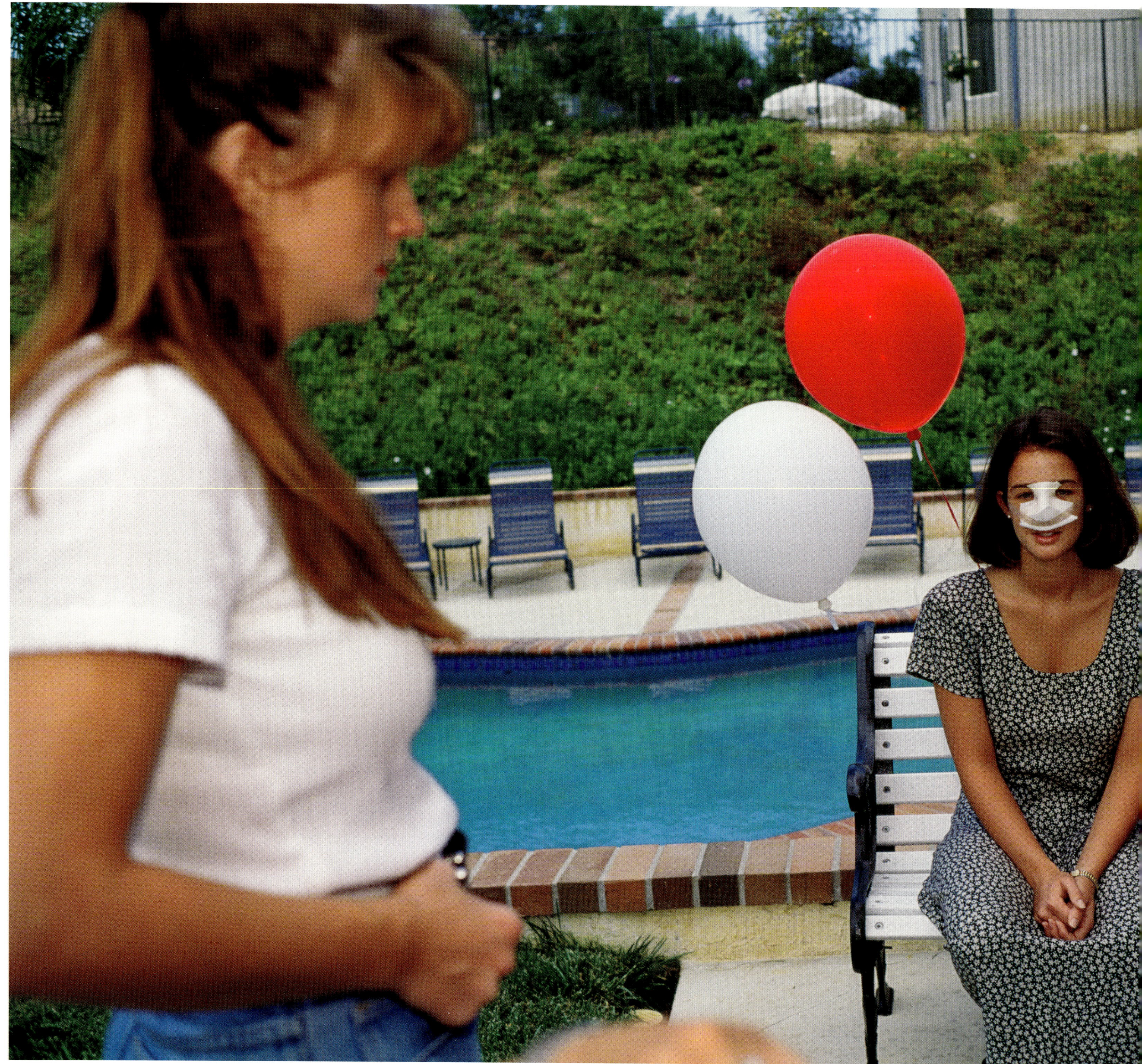

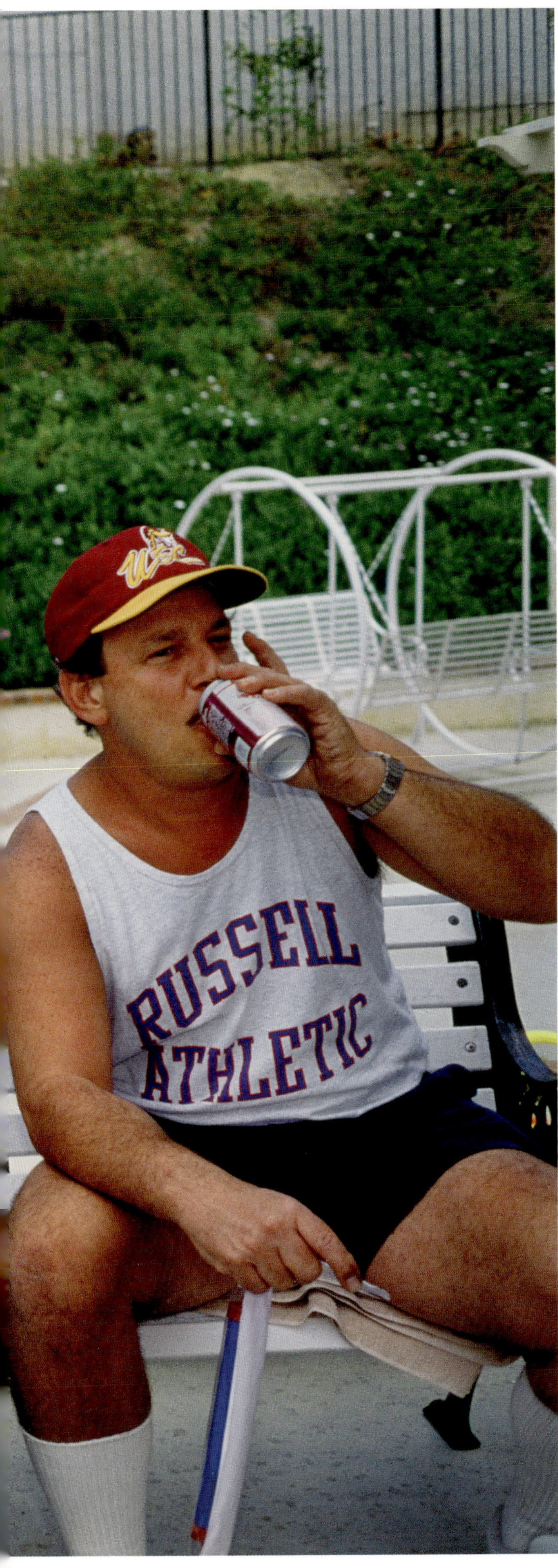

Lauren Greenfield
*Lindsey at a Fourth of July
party three days after the
surgery, Calabasas*, 1933

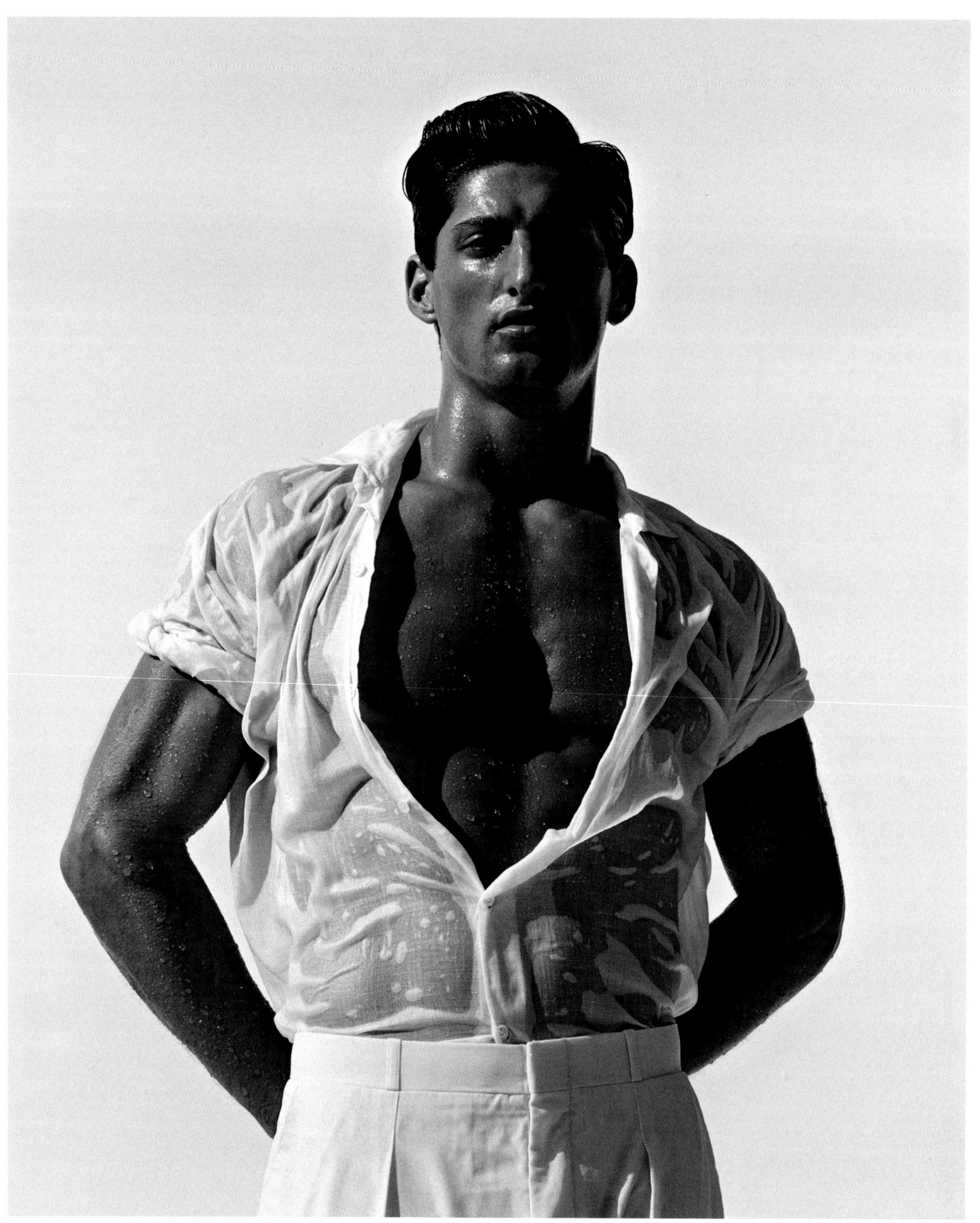

Herb Ritts
Tony in White, Hollywood,
1988

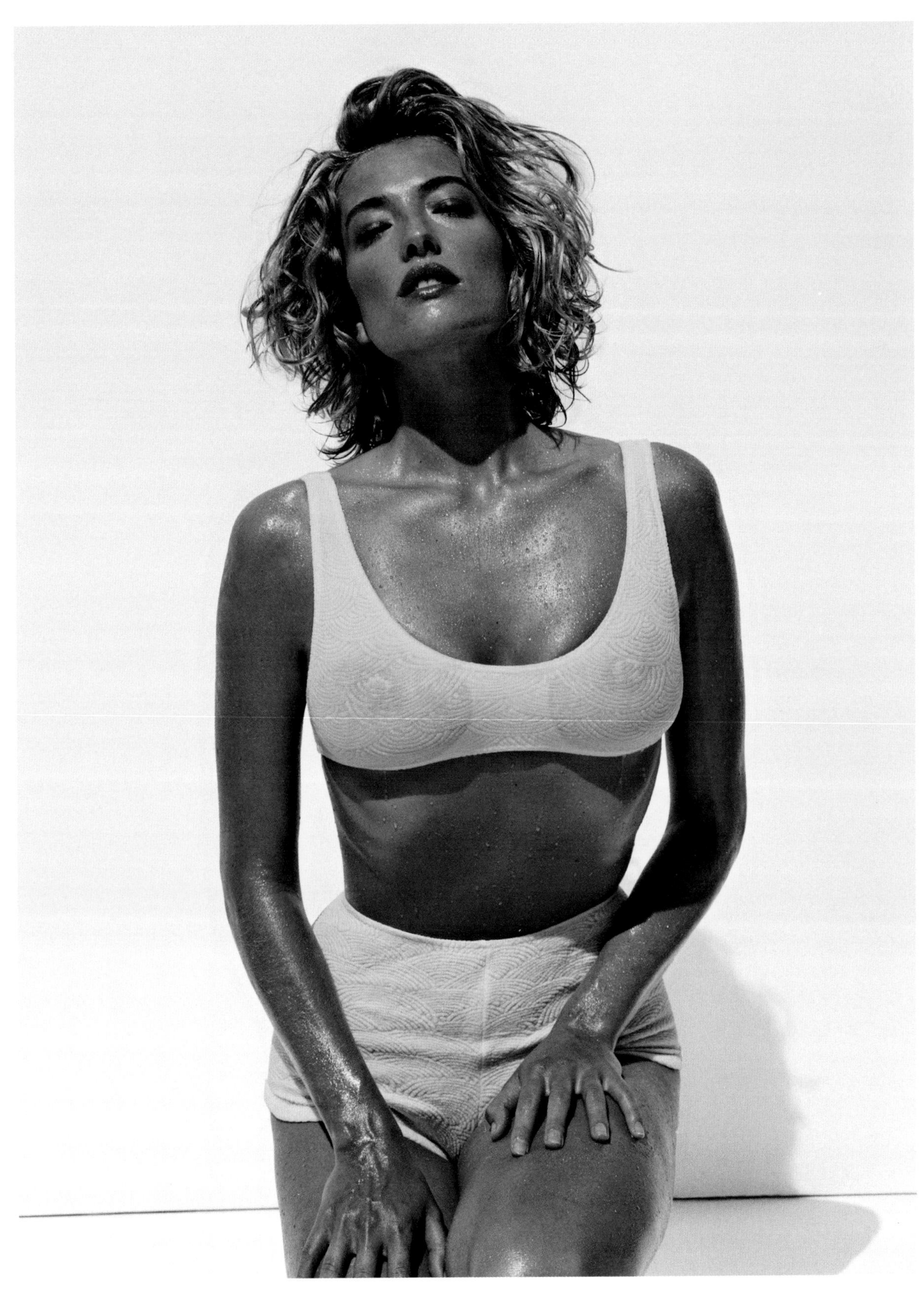

Herb Ritts
Tatjana in Swimsuit, Hollywood,
1989

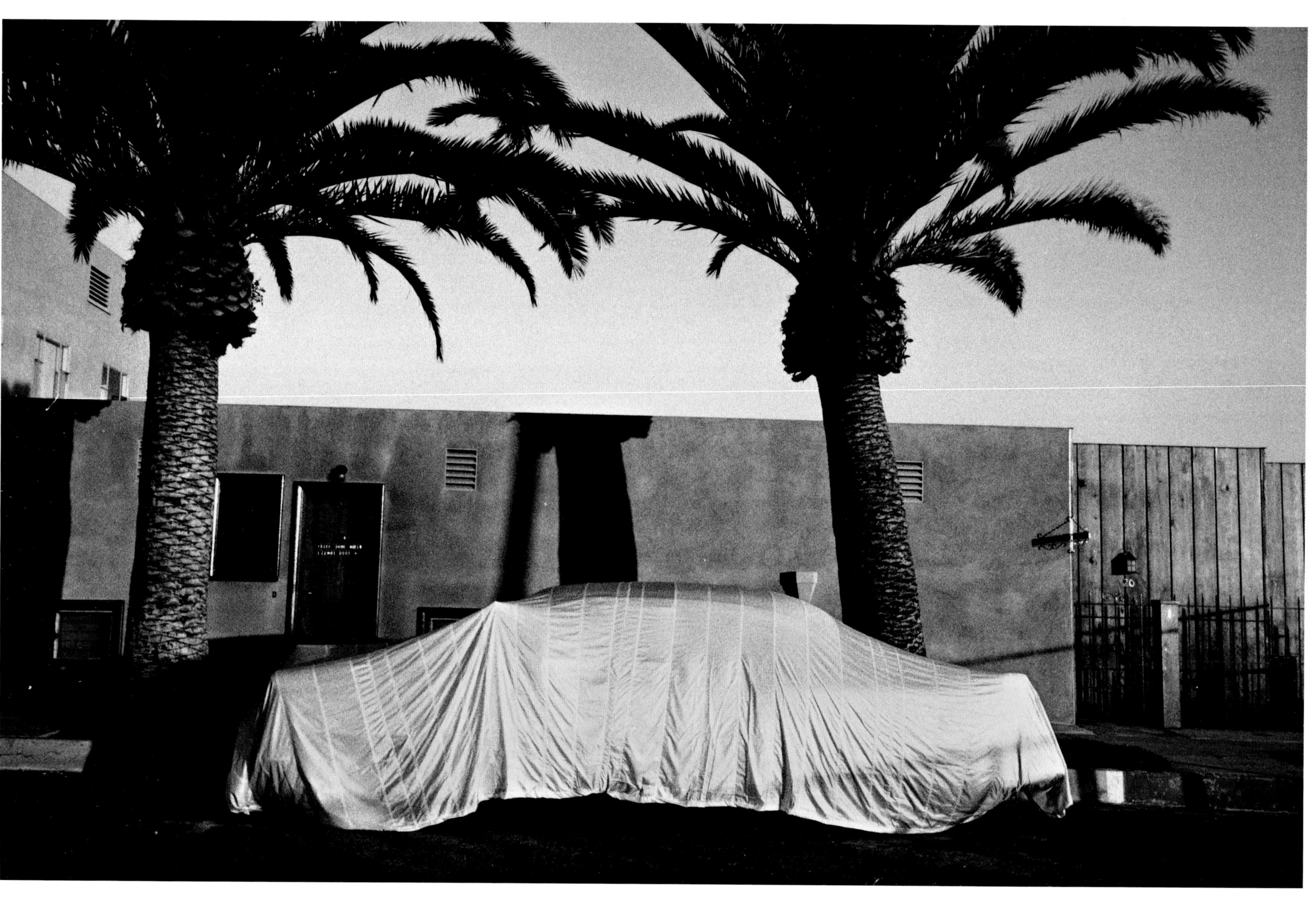

Robert Frank
*Covered Car—Long Beach,
California*, 1956

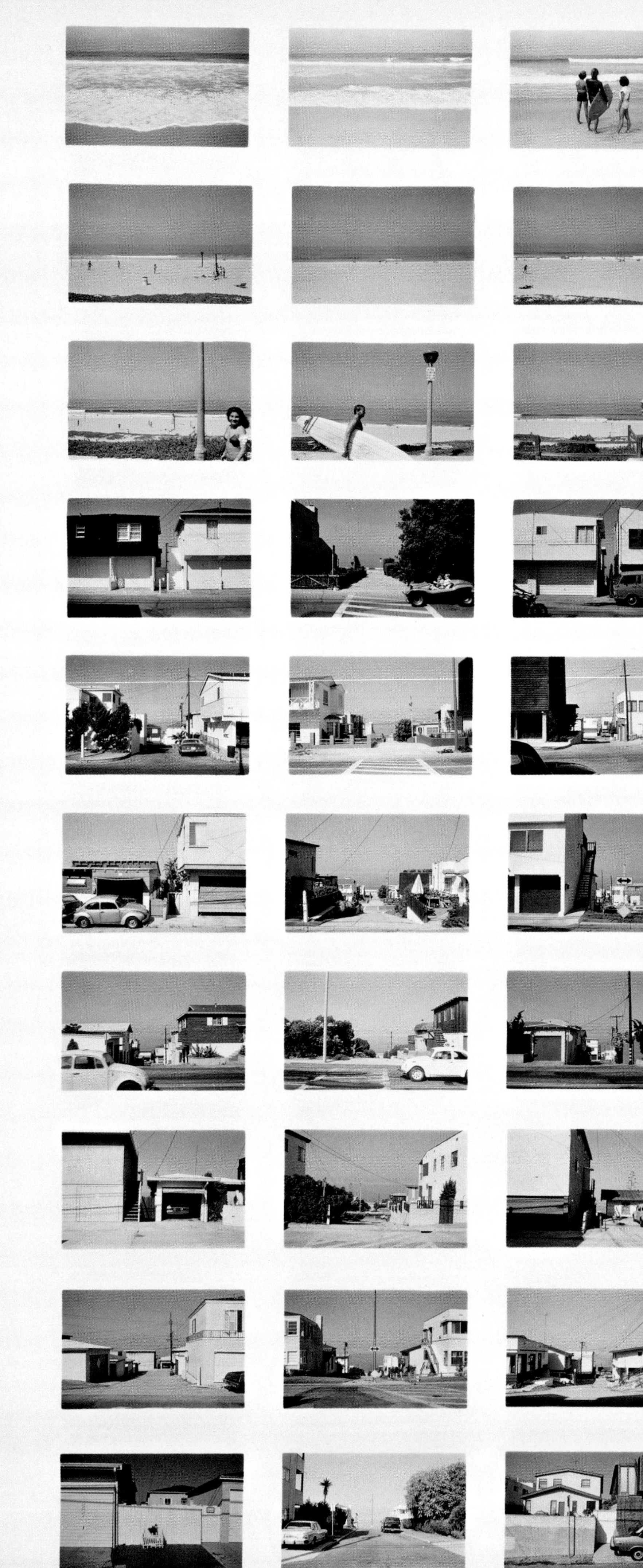

Robbert Flick
*Manhattan Beach, Looking
West from Vista*, 1980

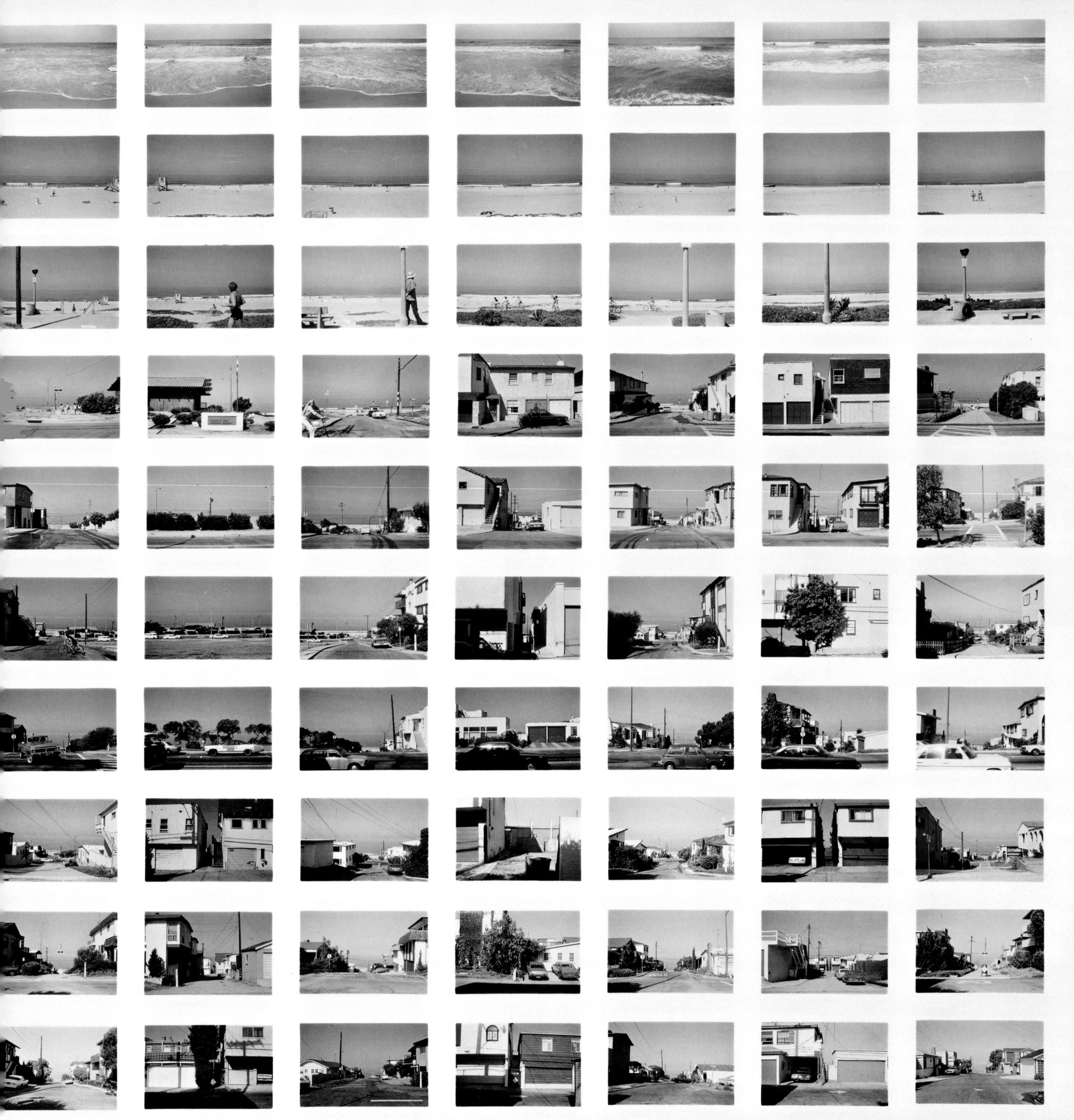

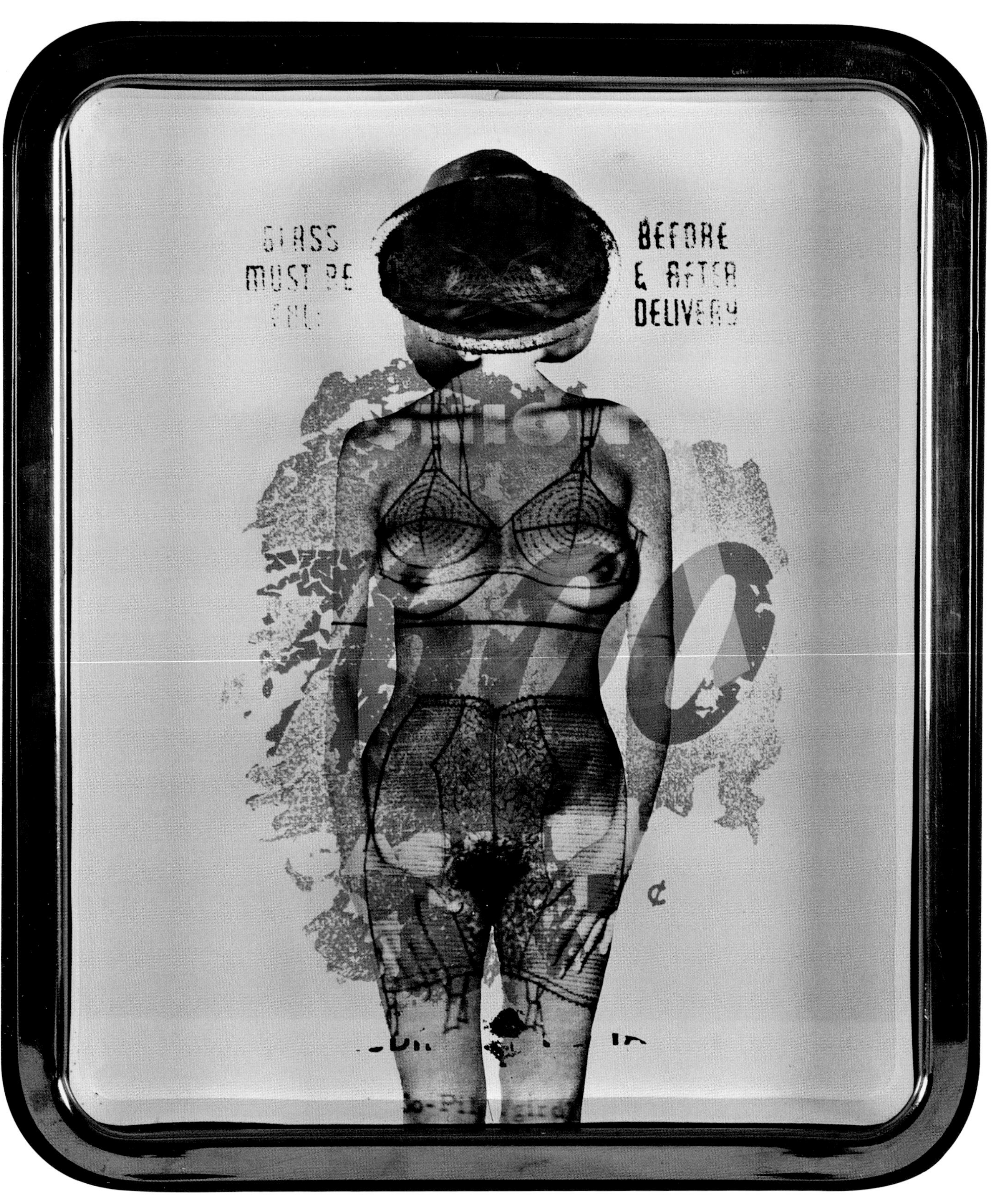

Darryl Curran
Before & After Delivery, 1968

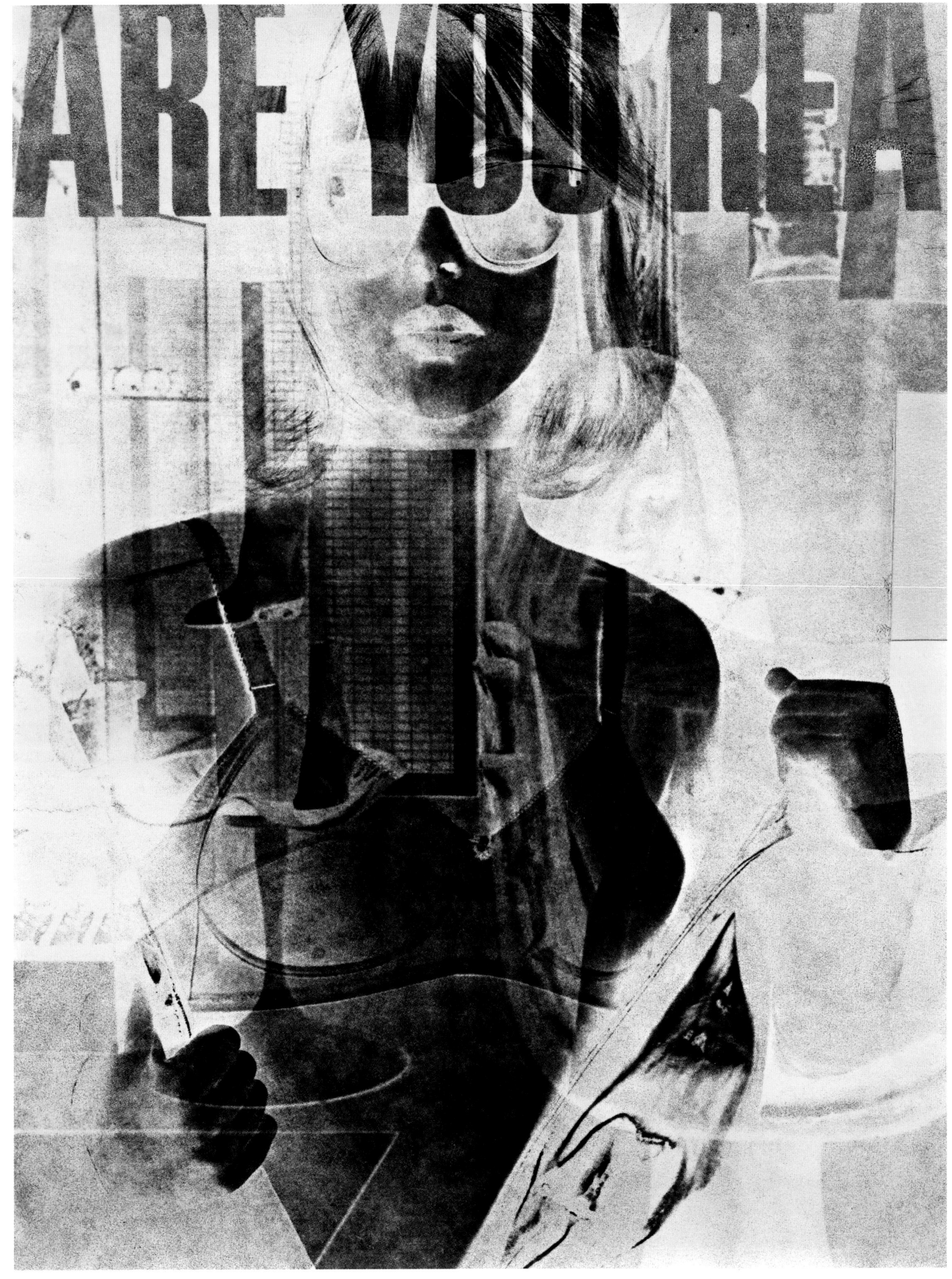

Robert Heinecken
Are You Rea #12, 1966

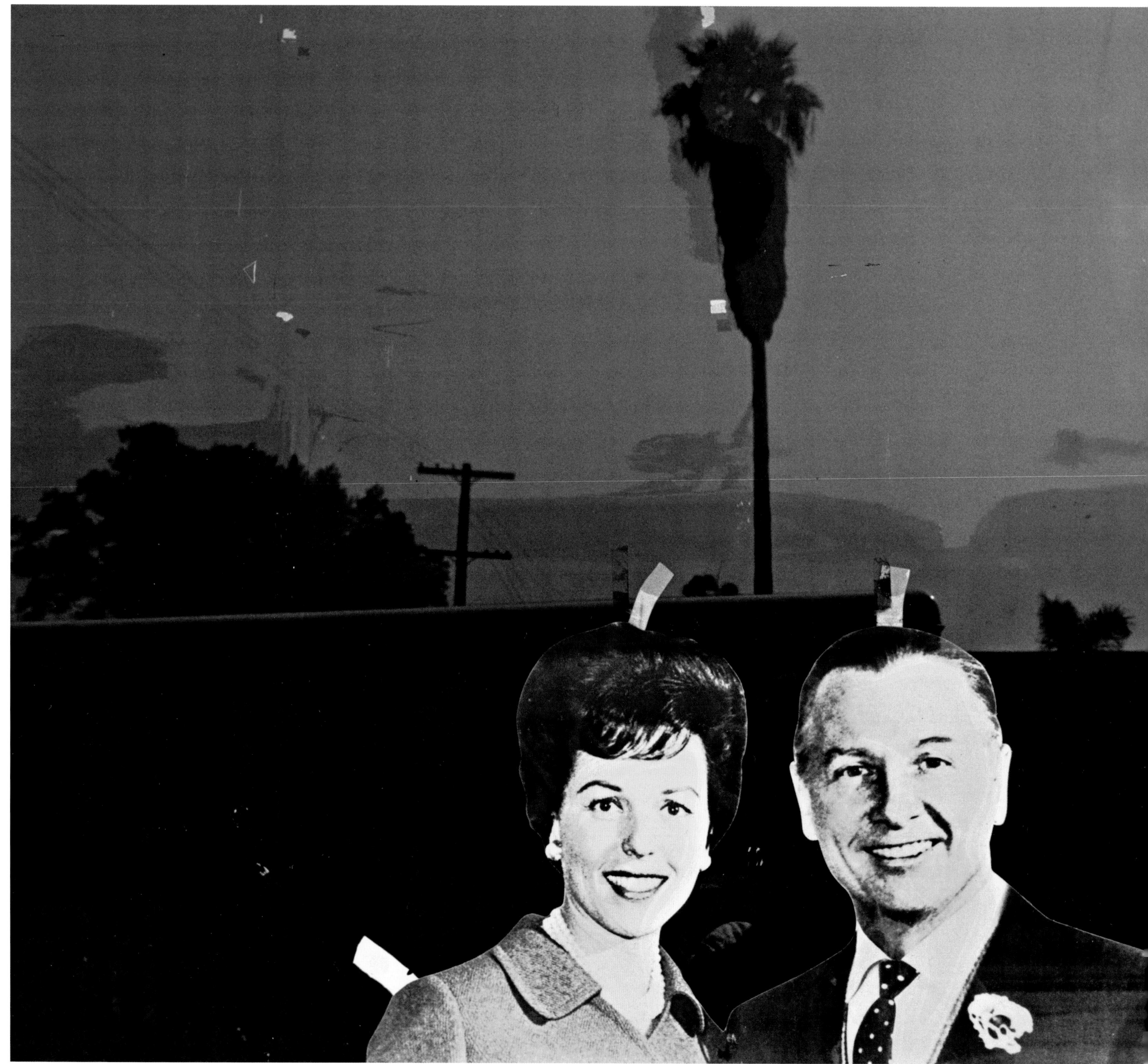

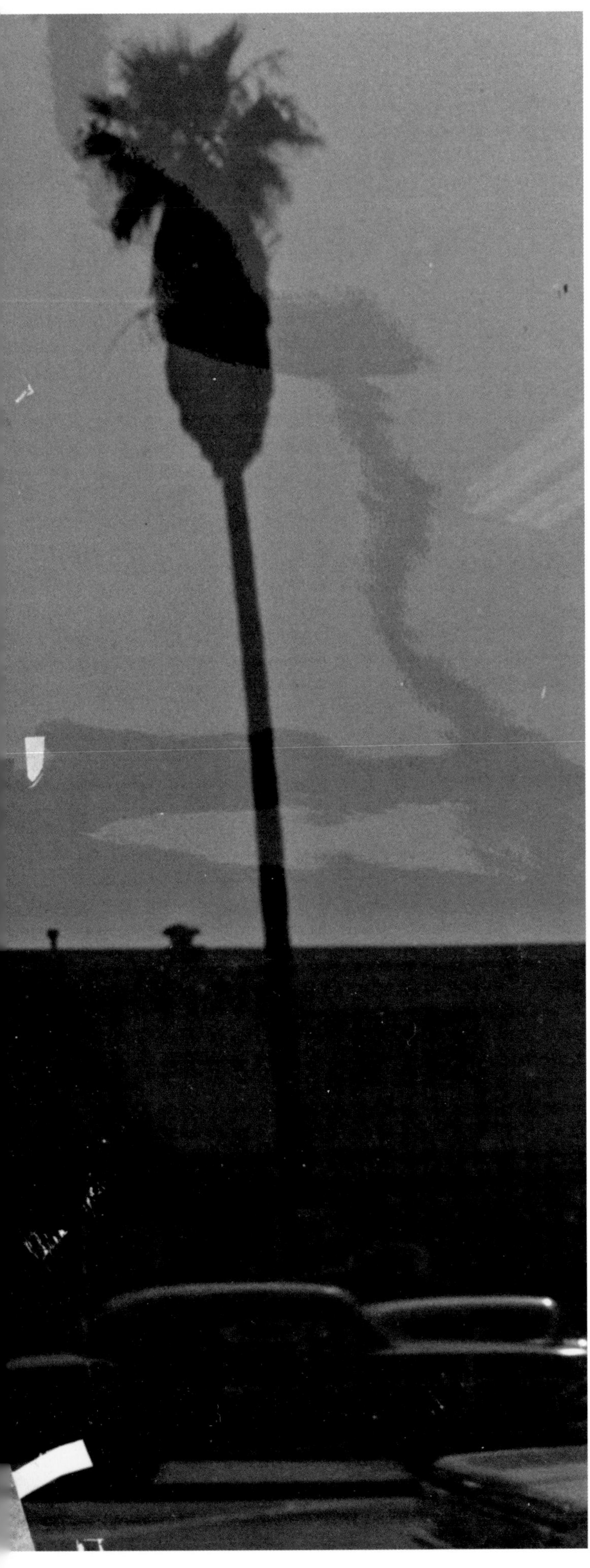

Lee Friedlander
Los Angeles, 1965

MOVING IN PLACE
LOS ANGELES IN PHOTOGRAPHS Jennifer A. Watts

Los Angeles is . . . a fluid . . . "moving" city, not only a city that moves itself—breaks itself down, builds itself up again, displaces and regroups itself—but also a city in which movement, *freedom* of movement, is a strong premise of life.
Cees Nooteboom[1]

Ansel Adams is not the first photographer who comes to mind when one thinks of Los Angeles. Why would the artist synonymous with the landscapes of Yosemite specifically, and with Nature's grandeur more generally, have any affinity with a city legendary for its endless concrete sprawl? But Los Angeles intrigued Adams, who visited the city several times, beginning in the 1940s.[2] In 1942, he put down tentative roots in Los Angeles when the Art Center School, the nation's first art school with a full-time photography curriculum, hired him to teach.[3] Adams felt energized by the city. "Los Angeles is a very exciting place," he wrote. "It is very alive, and very straightforward."[4] Despite his enthusiasm, his tenure was brief.[5] He resigned his position at the Art Center School in March 1943, and thereafter did not return to the city for any but short visits. One year was long enough, however, for the photographer to contemplate what could have been in the City of Angels. "Had the Los Angeles business not turned sour . . . I might have been able to work up into a more lively existence there," he mused to a friend upon his departure.[6]

It is certainly tantalizing to consider Ansel Adams making a creative muse out of Los Angeles. Perhaps a work of 1967 entitled *Interchange, Los Angeles Freeway* provides some insight into one subject that might have preoccupied him had he settled in Southern California (fig. 1). A tight, vertical view from the air highlights serpentine rivers of concrete, with cars and trucks flowing serenely through the picture's center as bright sunlight glints off hoods, windshields, and railings. Here is the freeway system as man-made equivalent of Yosemite's gargantuan Half Dome rock face; here is the "great concrete gesture" of Los Angeles.[7]

More than a century earlier, when Los Angeles was a violent cow town of a few thousand people, photographers also made pictures that tried to explain and describe the place to themselves and others. In the intervening decades, millions upon millions of photographs—taken by tourists, commercial studios, artists, documentarians, and amateurs of every imaginable background and produced for every conceivable reason—represented the tangible, physical Los Angeles. But Los Angeles is nothing if not also idea, symbol, myth, and state of mind—to those within and outside its boundaries—and photographers have had their say in this realm as well.

Yet despite its allure, or because of its sheer complexity, Los Angeles has largely defied attempts to examine its photographic legacy. Writings

Fig. 1
Ansel Adams
Interchange, Los Angeles Freeway, 1967

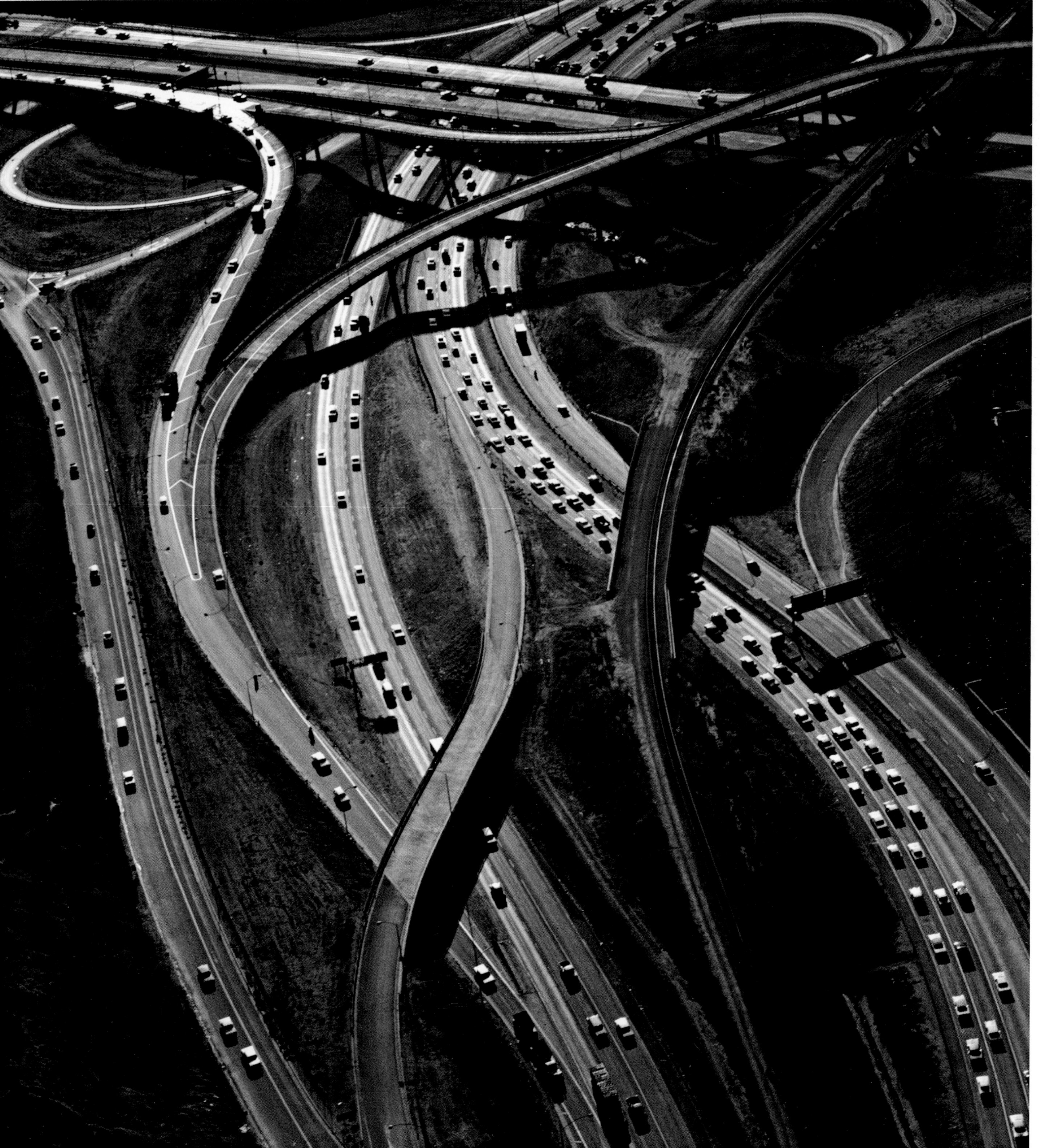

and exhibitions focus on images produced in response to either artistic or documentary impulses, but certainly not on those that bridge the two genres or span the breadth of Los Angeles's history.[8] Like the place itself, the enterprise seems too gigantic, too difficult; the task is altogether improbable and quixotic. Yet, given that this is a city where photography has played such a fundamental role in shaping perceptions for residents and outsiders, it is important to start somewhere.

This essay takes a close look at photographs that respond to the *physical* reality of Los Angeles—its location, topography, climate, light—to evoke a powerful, if often mythic, sense of both place and landscape. These are photographs made in Los Angeles about Los Angeles. As individual works, they hold out glimpses of living, moving, and being in a city characterized as "an extreme among [American cities]"—a place bigger, louder, shinier, more brash, more vulgar, and more precarious than its peers.[9] Taken together, the images offer a lay of the land both real and imagined.

Starting out

Photography's beginnings in Los Angeles were, like the place itself, inauspicious. A motley assortment of low-slung adobe buildings huddled near the banks of a mercurial river, Los Angeles in the 1850s was notable for little save its lawlessness and daily murder rate. Between 1851 and 1858, only eight men tried their hand at photography, none for more than a year. Today, not a single daguerreotype exists that depicts the town in this very early period.[10]

A cock-eyed view taken around 1862 by William M. Godfrey, a former Michigan dentist turned photographer, is Los Angeles's first extant landscape photograph (fig. 4). From his stance on Fort Moore Hill at the western edge of the pueblo, Godfrey looked out over the central plaza's whitewashed adobe buildings to the unseen Los Angeles River and sweep of oak trees and citrus groves beyond. A brick reservoir at center presides over a virtual ghost town, with crisscrossing footpaths the only hints of activity. This is most definitely the "very sleepy town" of early resident Horace Bell's description, albeit one in which "absolute barbarism ruled."[11]

Even this first humble picture, no bigger than a calling card, obscured as much as it revealed about Los Angeles. Early photography's inability to capture movement possibly conspired with the time of day when the view was made to present the city as bucolic and utterly innocuous. Godfrey's Los Angeles is hard to reconcile with the Los Angeles of nine years later, in which an orgy of racial violence left nineteen Chinese dead in the very center of the area seen in the photographer's placid image.[12]

Godfrey is famous mostly for his place at the head of the line; he became the first de facto landscape photographer of the city simply because no one else wanted the job.[13] But perhaps the real legacy of "Godfrey's first" is the impulse, right from the beginning, to let

photography speak for Los Angeles more presumptively than it ought. Certainly the images that followed up to the turn of the century trumpeted a one-dimensional story of the expanding village as idyllic garden spot.

The population of Los Angeles grew to 11,000 in the 1870s, still a relatively modest number, but respectable enough to provide a decent pool of clients for photographers. A new group of image-makers began, at first tentatively, to depict the tableau of city, countryside, and surf for both locals and prospective settlers.[14] But it would take a San Francisco photographer known worldwide for his views of the Yosemite Valley to do aesthetic justice to the place slowly being reshaped into the "semi-tropic paradise" touted by its many promoters.

In the spring of 1877, Carleton E. Watkins arrived by train in Los Angeles and got to work. The linking of the Southern Pacific Railroad with Southern California the previous year (and the later boon of the Santa Fe Railroad lines into Los Angeles) put the region on the map. Watkins arrived just as railroad-initiated population growth, which would become a population explosion, began. The photographer, who had spent peripatetic years finding the "best view," looked out over the infant citrus groves and vineyards, the rugged beachside tent cities, and the newly bustling streets of Los Angeles and made unforgettably beautiful photographs of a place that was on the verge of utter transformation (figs. 2, 3).[15]

By the time of Watkins's first visit, the booster drumbeat had begun reverberating through the land. It cast Los Angeles as a sun-kissed Garden of Eden where anything could, and did, grow beyond one's wildest imaginings. The vocal enthusiasm of the railroad companies was soon joined by a chorus of promoters who insisted that the region's perfect climate was not only a healer of the sick but also a balm to the well, breeding a new, more intelligent, and morally superior (and, not incidentally, all-white) class of people. When Watkins returned to Los Angeles for a second and final time in 1880, photography had already been conscripted for this strident advertising campaign, the likes of which had never before been seen in urban America.[16]

The photographs streaming out of late nineteenth-century Los Angeles and thence around the world anticipated what would follow. Such influential regional journals as *Land of Sunshine* and myriad publications produced by the railroads, chambers of commerce, and real estate interests used photographs to promotional ends. The exotic vegetation produced by the Mediterranean climate, including palms, cacti, oranges, and flowering vines, became totems, the sheer abundance and rapidity of their growth reinforcing ideas of man's mastery over the land. The interplay of climate, fecundity, and history gave birth to what the boosters proudly claimed was a "new and nobler race." Non-white residents were presented in photographs as colorful "types" if Mexican or Chinese, or as "relics" or "ancients" if members of the local Native American population.[17]

Fig. 2
Carleton E. Watkins
Old Santa Monica, 1877

Fig. 3
Carleton E. Watkins
The Pasadena, Near San Gabriel, 1877

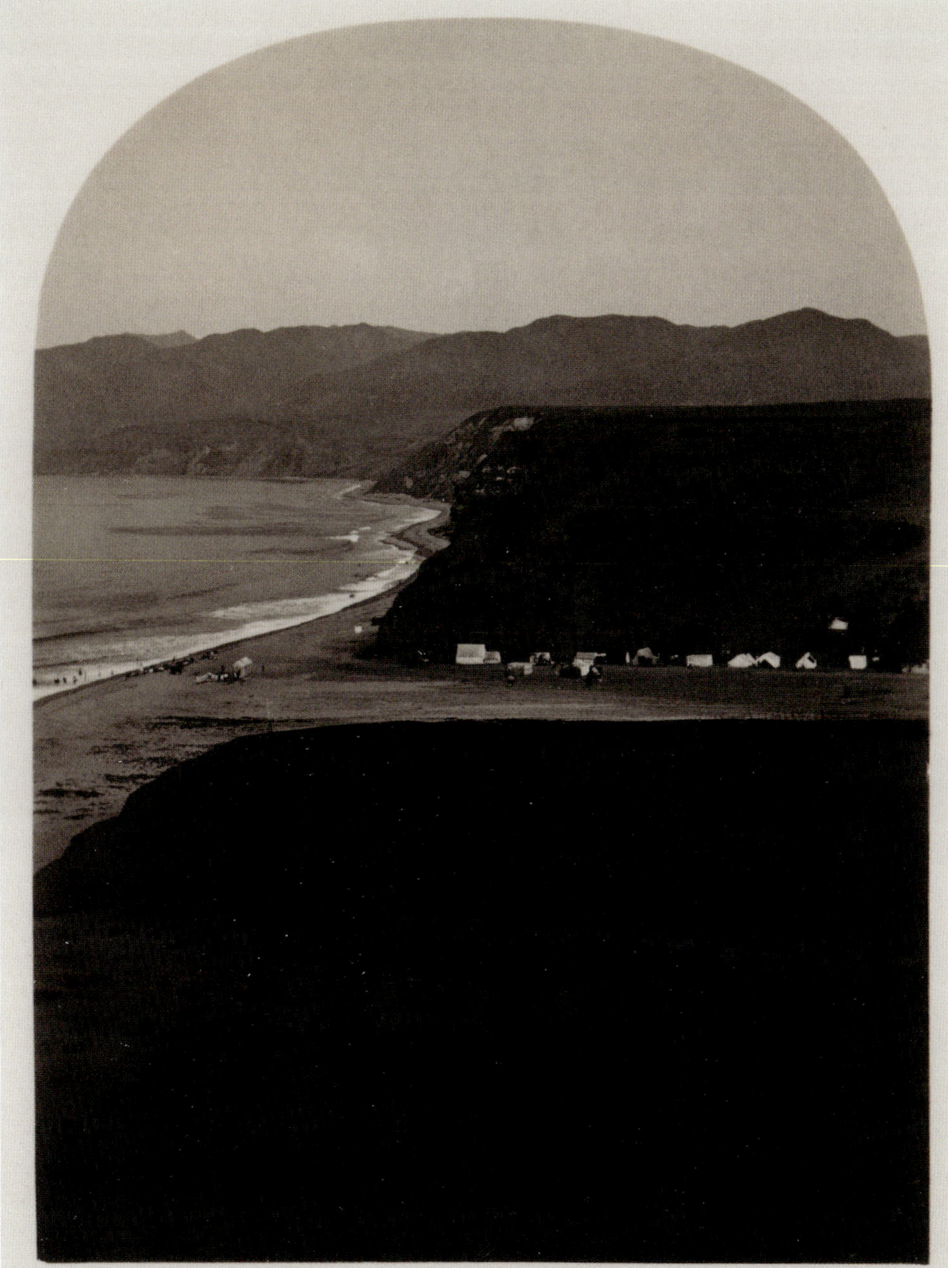

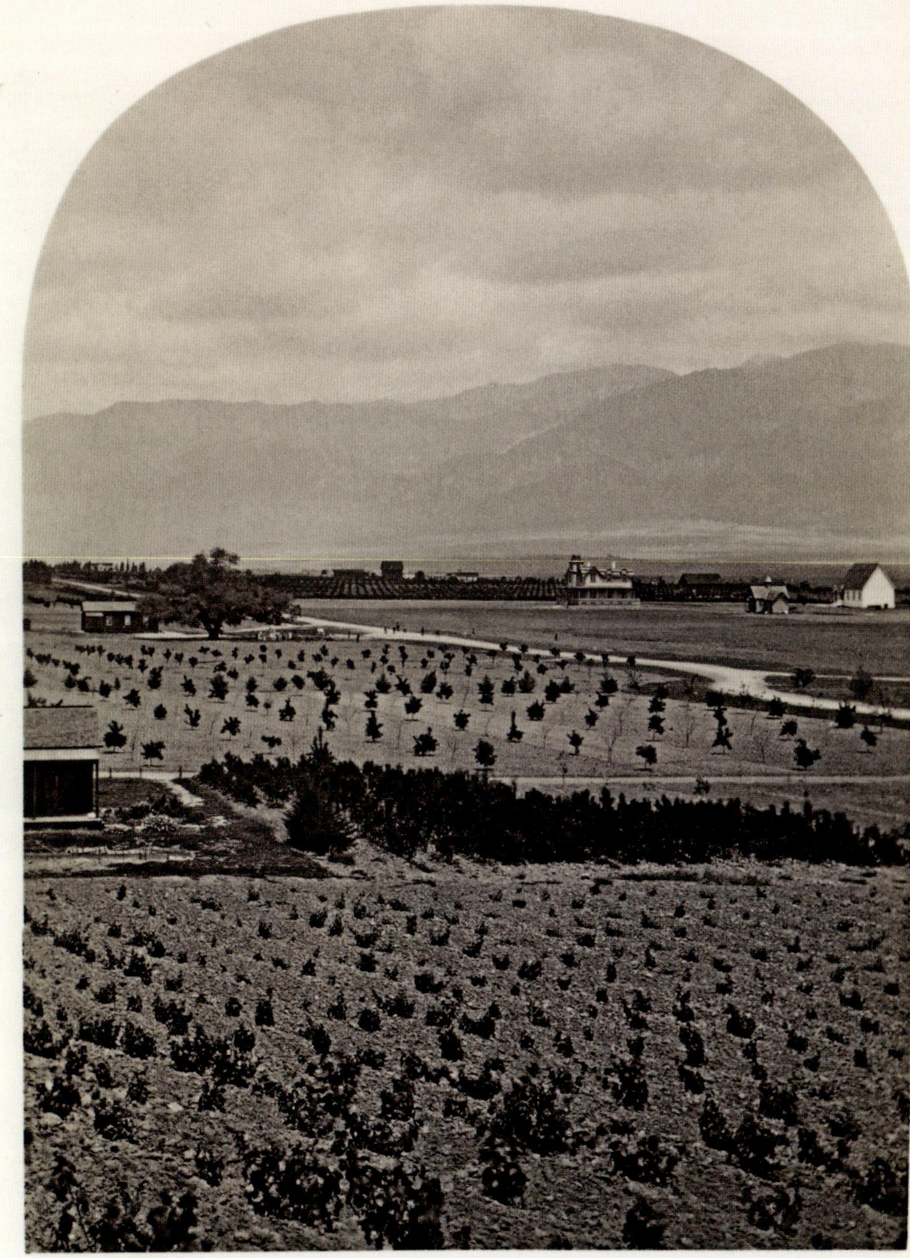

The hurly-burly of downtown, its buzz, busyness, and impressive new buildings, offered innumerable targets for the photographer of Los Angeles seeking proof of the city's cultural and civic attainments in the early twentieth century (see p. 113). And the amateur snap-shooter emboldened by the Kodak revolution followed suit to a remarkable degree, in both what was photographed and how it was photographed.[18] The era's rhetoric, followed in near lockstep by photography, usually ignored the underlying requirements and necessities of Paradise. Rare, for instance, are the pictures that show how a dry region found, stored, and used its water. And, given the lack of pictures representing a workforce that was largely Chinese and Mexican, photographs inevitably perpetuated the paradisiacal ideal of a place that came about with a minimum of toil. Boosters made sure to attribute their garden city to a can-do Yankee ingenuity that had transformed a "quondam Mexican town" into something infinitely more enticing.[19] But the photographs made it appear, like the biblical Eden, effortless, the result of God's abundant favor.

The promotional gambit paid off beyond all expectations. The city's population soared to well over 100,000 by the turn of the century.[20] Between 1887 and 1889 sixty new towns covering 79,000 acres (32,000 ha) cropped up in the region, and the value of real estate transactions in 1887 alone exceeded $200 million.[21] Los Angeles may have been an easy target for the naysayers who saw through booster hokum, but people kept coming, many in response to the powerful lure of photography. The pastoral Los Angeles of William M. Godfrey and Carleton E. Watkins was fast disappearing beneath the tide of Midwestern and East Coast immigrants bent on changing the city to meet their various dreams and desires.

On the move

Most of the people pouring into Los Angeles arrived, like Carleton E. Watkins before them, on the train. The railroad made Los Angeles possible, and no entity better understood the power of photography to sell its wares. William Henry Jackson, the expeditionary photographer famed for his views of Yellowstone National Park, was one of the railroad's most powerful allies, creating stunning large-scale views of western American tourist resorts and attractions.[22] In about 1889, Jackson made a mammoth-plate panorama of the Raymond Hotel, a luxury hostelry on the outskirts of Los Angeles (see pp. 82–83). *The* destination for wealthy Easterners, with its two hundred well-appointed rooms and forty bathrooms, the Raymond dominated the local hillside and offered beautiful views of the San Gabriel Mountains framing the Los Angeles Basin. From his elevated perch, Jackson took in the newly graded hillside and impressive lawns and gardens, chock-full of cacti, cypress trees, fan palms, and other exotic horticultural specimens. Visitors and workers (and even the hotel's horses) heeded the famed photographer's signal to stand

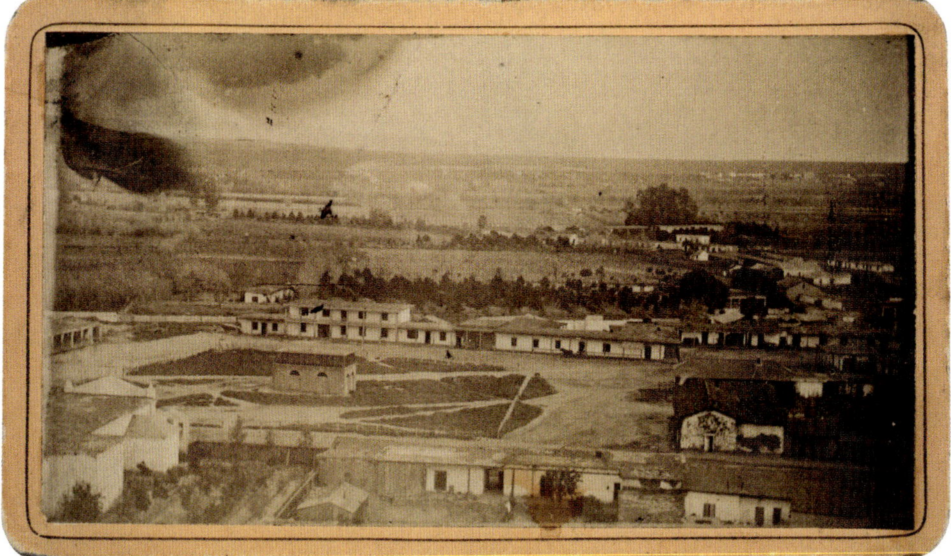

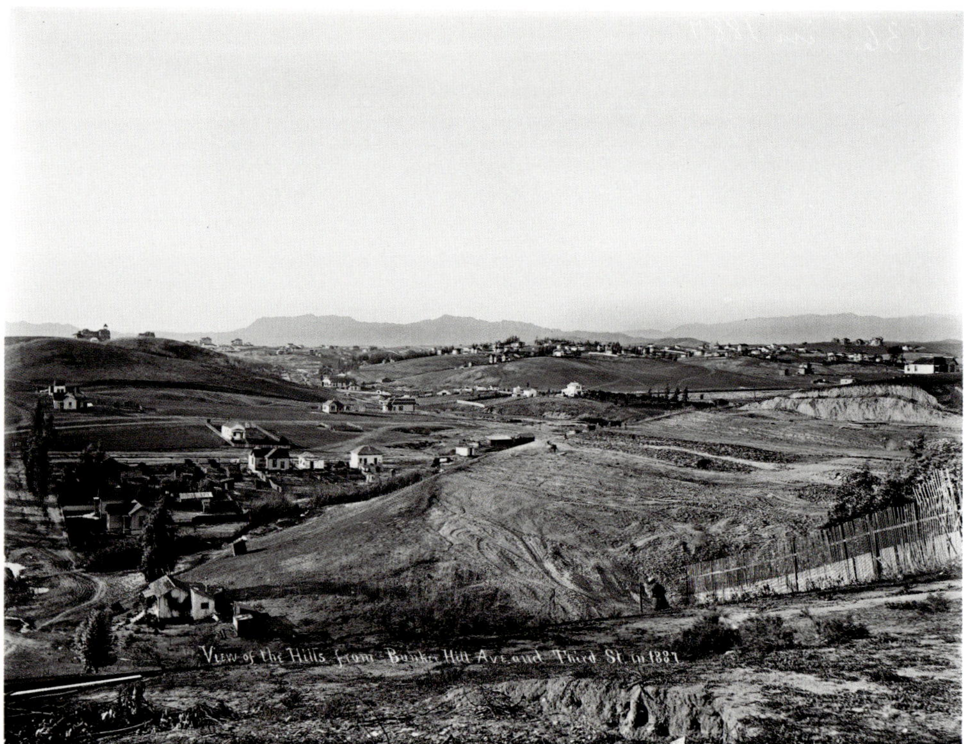

still for the exposure, only a rooftop flag indicating the day's light breeze. This gigantic panorama, seamlessly blending four separate negatives, was a large-as-life advertisement for the Los Angeles good life. Expensive to produce and rare today, the image is the nineteenth-century equivalent of an indoor billboard. It surely hung in a proud realtor's office, a railroad waiting room, or a bank lobby.

Just as the railroad proclaimed humanity's technological dominion over time and space, the travelers disembarking at the Raymond Hotel found a landscape already bent to the will of the region's settlers. Hills had been tamped down and reshaped, plants imported, water and electricity channeled, streets and tracks laid, houses built (fig. 5). "There was nothing tentative or experimental about [the immigrants'] approach to this new and novel environment," writes journalist Carey McWilliams of this raw energy.[23] The hoards of newcomers marshaled vast resources to build an American city that felt familiar to them yet was, at the same time, strikingly different. Los Angeles became America's "gigantic improvisation," where old and new collided in unforeseen and unimagined ways.[24]

How did photography negotiate tensions between the landscapes of the familiar and the strange? If we begin with William McClung's assertion that "photography not only mediates the dialogue between the found . . . and . . . the constructed city" but also "largely establishes its terms and drives its conclusions," what are some of the dominant themes in the Los Angeles of photographs? And what conclusions can be drawn, if any, about the city as seen through the camera's lens?[25]

If nineteenth-century photographs established a largely static vision of Los Angeles as a paradisiacal garden brimming over with palm trees, fruits and flowers, twentieth-century Los Angeles was a city on the move. Largely hemmed in by rugged mountains and ocean, the once wide-open spaces of the Los Angeles Basin began to look like a crazy quilt of lots stitched together by train tracks and roads, all illuminated by the glare of a million electric lights (see p. 181). The many miles of track used by Henry Huntington's Pacific Electric streetcars laid a steel grid over the landscape of the entire region in a centrifugal network of rails that linked a constellation of real estate interests.[26]

Fresh infusions of water boldly imported from 250 miles (400 km) northeast of Los Angeles pushed the city's boundaries farther into the San Fernando Valley, and miles of pavement obediently followed. The muscular expansion of Los Angeles in the 1920s made earlier growth spurts seem anemic. From 1910 to 1930, Los Angeles County grew as much as the rest of the entire American West, while the city added 80 sq. miles (207 sq. km) of annexed land and 600,000 new residents to its territorial and demographic heft. New and mighty industries—oil, motion pictures, and aviation—added economic diversity to the region's agricultural and manufacturing base. By 1930, Los Angeles had more than 1 million residents and could boast that it was the world's largest city in terms of area.[27] Describing Los Angeles as "inexplicable" and

"incongruous," journalist Sarah Comstock noted its "mushroom growth, its sprawling hugeness, its madcap speed, its splurge of lights and noise and color and money." Her breathless depiction of 1928 might well have been a photographic primer, suggesting the ways in which the city was represented in that era's imagery, too.[28]

Photographs of the metropolis on the make emphasized progress, development, and industry, all seasoned by evocative images of the good life in the Southern Californian sunshine. Never before had a major city grown so aggressively outward, so horizontally. The Pacific Electric Red Cars piloted tourists from mountain to ocean ("Possible in a single day!"), and the Pacific Electric Railway Company churned out images of the sybaritic pleasures offered by transit technology (see pp. 66, 69, 156). Residents, too, rode from distant communities to jobs or for a day's shopping in the city's center or pleasure-seeking at the beach. Mechanized transit became inextricably linked with Los Angeles and its people, both fundamentally tied to, and reliant upon, movement. An overriding sense of motion infuses the imagery of the era. As if glimpsed through the windows of a jostling streetcar, the viewer's senses buzzing from the dry air, the smell of orange blossoms and oil rigs, and the sun's glare on palm trees, bungalows, fairytale architecture, and prosperous business blocks, Los Angeles seems impressionistic, ephemeral, a disorienting landscape of striking oppositions.

Los Angeles's hyperactive growth coincided with Angelenos' enthusiastic embrace of the automobile. By 1920, the city claimed one car for every 3.6 residents.[29] This was only the beginning of its unending love affair with the car: "Every family has its automobile; and so frenzied are these people with their own enthusiasm that they must needs leap into the car (which they often do in bathing suits) and drive for sheer ebullience. . . . our insane American lust for hurry, noise, and glare—are here seen in the *nth* degree."[30] The roads followed the electric rail routes and went well beyond them, up hillsides and down canyons, crisscrossing every part of the county. The speed, the convenience, the freedom of driving the open road, with no real weather to spoil the experience, proved perfectly intoxicating to Angelenos. The eventual death of the expansive streetcar trolley system, rather than being due to some conspiracy by nefarious oil and tire companies (one of the most intractable of Los Angeles myths), was about personal choice on a massive scale.[31] Whether a journey was by rail or car, space in Los Angeles telescoped down to the distance between two points, and time warped to fit this distance. The effect was photographic, even cinematic. Los Angeles seen through the rectangular windshield of the automobile, zipping by in narrative leaps, beholden to fast-paced sequencing and visual circumlocutions, resembled motion-picture make-believe.

How to make visual sense of the region's rapid-fire urban growth? How to assimilate, through pictures, the new automotive landscapes in which city and country merged, collided, and overlapped? Los Angeles's commercial photographers seized upon the early suburban-era vogue

Fig. 6
"Dick" Whittington Studio
*View of Castellammare
Subdivision, Pacific Palisades,*
1931

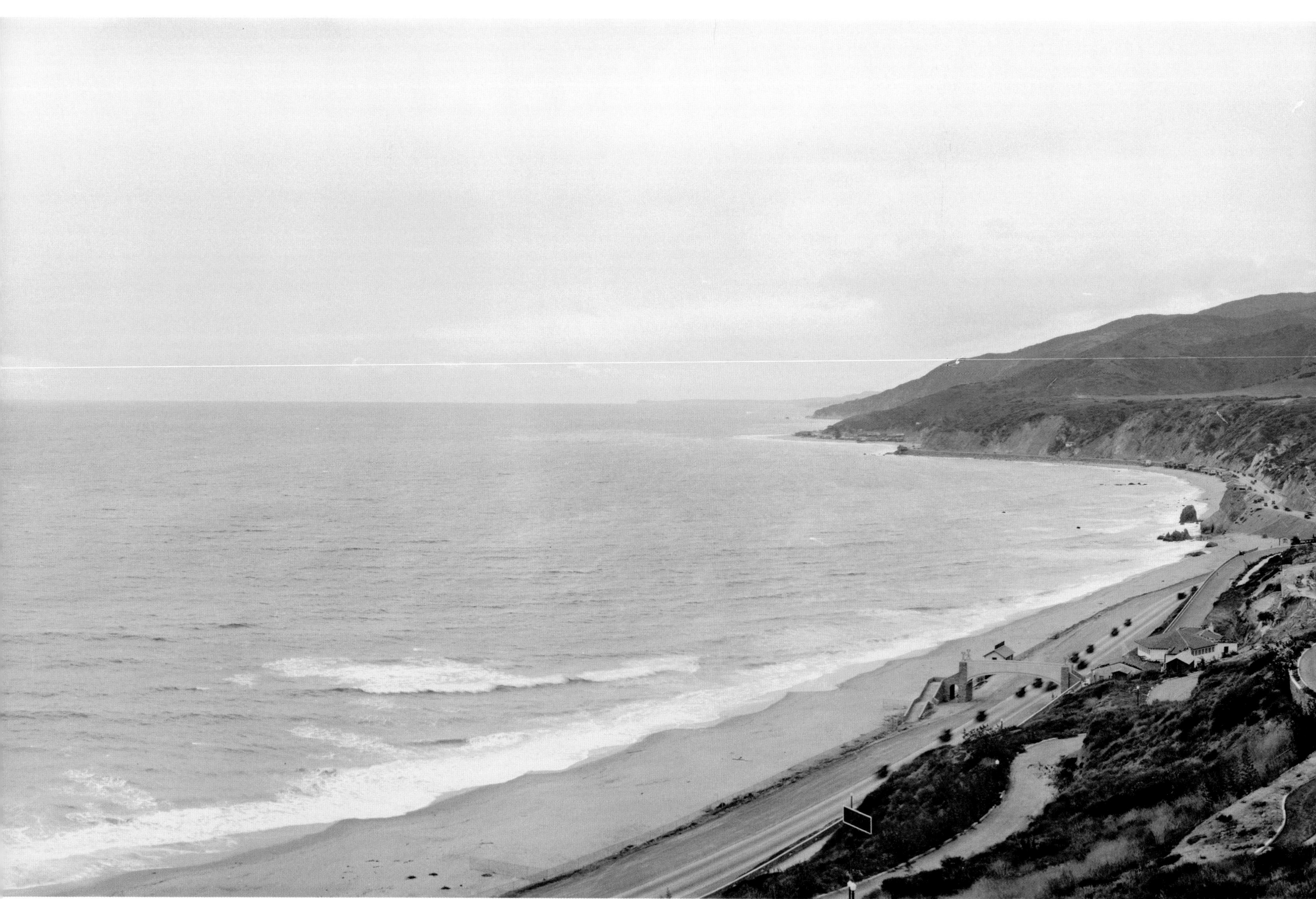

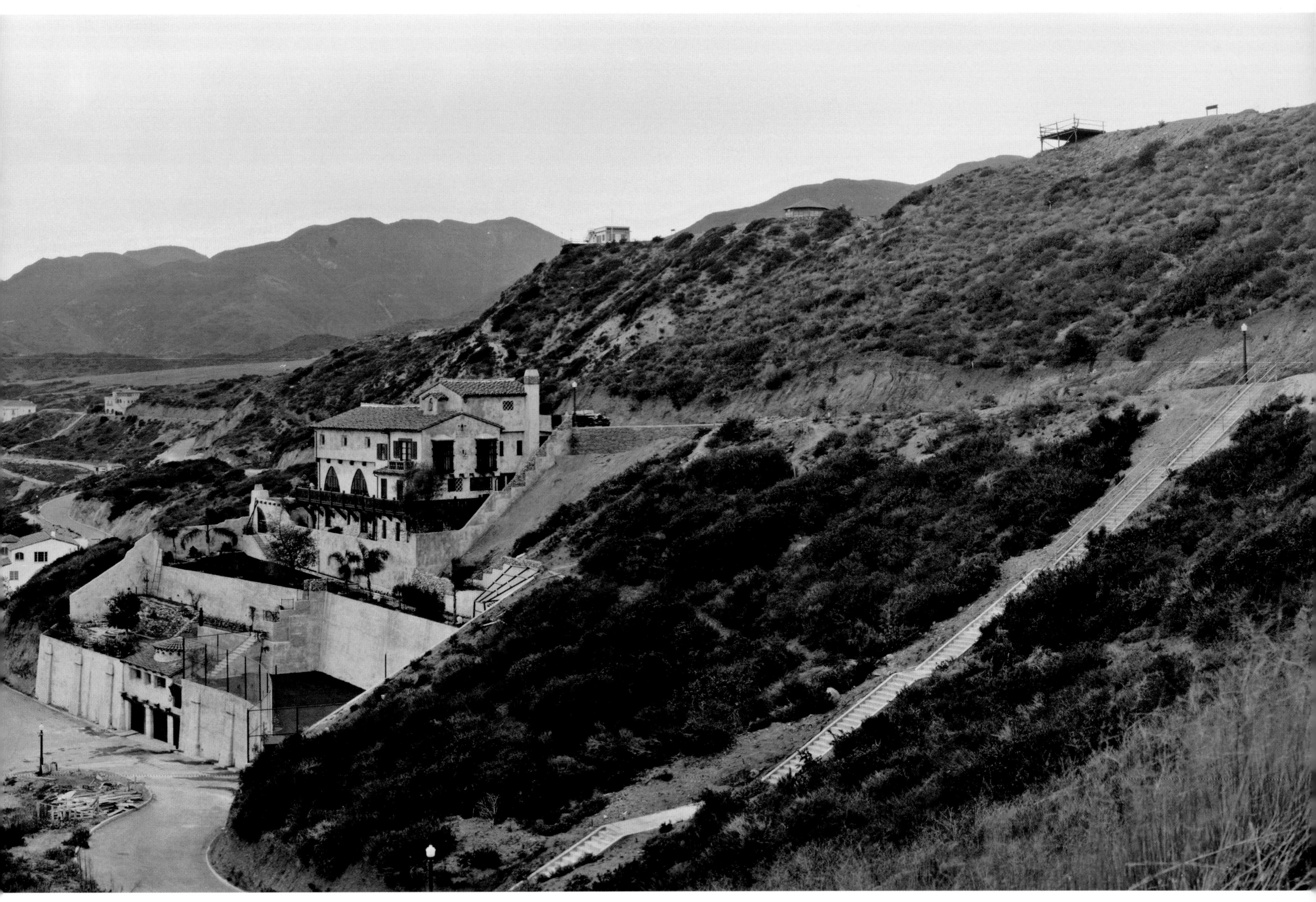

Fig. 7
Dennis Hopper
Double Standard, 1961

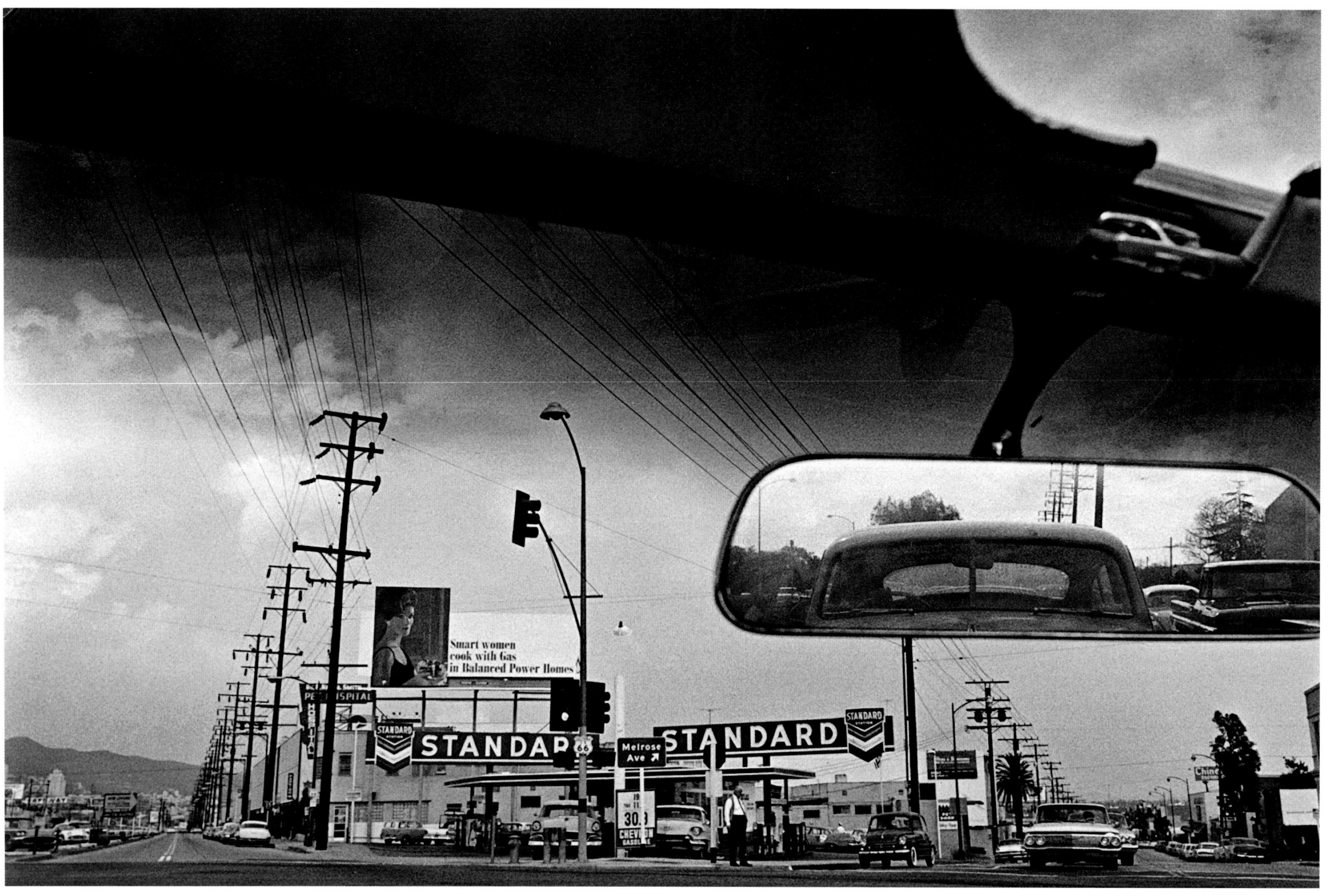

Smart women
cook with Gas
in Balanced Power Homes
STANDARD
STANDARD
Melrose
Ave
30.9
CHEVRON
GASOLINE

for panoramic photography to evoke the city's movement. A negative
5 ft (1.5 m) long spooling through the back of a mechanized Cirkut camera
seemed a perfect mimic for the long, low, unfurling spaces of Los Angeles
(see pp. 118–19).[32] Yet these giant images simultaneously and ironically
gave the city's mushrooming growth decisive boundaries. They offered
a safe measure of containment to its spreading grid. A photograph of the
Castellammare ("Castle by the Sea") subdivision in Pacific Palisades
shows palatial homes spilling down a hillside meticulously carved to
accommodate their gargantuan whims (fig. 6). This dreamlike view
gives traction to city fathers' claims of Los Angeles as the place where
"civilization meets the sea." Cars motoring silently by on the undulating
coastal highway participate in this reverie where nature is improved for
pleasure and the pursuit of the good life. A makeshift lookout is just visible
on the hillside above, with an arrow (surely placed there by a realtor)
beckoning passers-by to step right up and take a look. From this
commanding vantage point, observers can make the scene their own.

By the time Dennis Hopper made *Double Standard* from a convertible
idling at the intersection of Santa Monica Boulevard, Melrose Avenue, and
Doheny Drive, this had become the quintessential view—the driver's-eye
view—of Los Angeles (fig. 7). Like the panoramic photograph, the
rectangle of the windshield contains the scene. Here are the ciphers of
twentieth-century Los Angeles: a cacophony of billboards, telephone
poles, electric wires, traffic lights, signs, arrows and, of course, miles of
pavement and sky, and cars, cars, cars (reflected in the rearview mirror).
Here is the Pop Art city of surfaces, signs, and symbols made famous by
Ed Ruscha and his catalog of buildings lining the Sunset Strip and by
paintings appropriating the ubiquitously bland commercial signage
of Los Angeles's roadways.[33]

The automobile and its literal and cultural by-products—cruising,
smog, congestion, status, speed, freedom, freeways—became the stuff
of both legend and photography. Not just a convenient mode of
transportation for a linear city, the automobile and driving embodied
a way of life, one that Angelenos took to as eager disciples. Southern
California's incessant automobility legitimated the unique urban and
suburban growth patterns of greater Los Angeles. Instead of conforming
to East Coast or European notions of what a city should look like—that is,
a central downtown with teeming streets and abundant services—Los
Angeles took on the mantle of "a city without a center." The roots of this
spatial and developmental logic can be found in the nineteenth century,
but there is no doubting the fact that the automobile soon became the
chromed and enameled icon of how Los Angeles looked, felt, and was
experienced (see p. 120). Movies, food, faith, *everything*, it seemed, was
dispensed for the driver's ease and pleasure (see p. 117; fig. 8).
Boulevards—Wilshire, Sunset, Hollywood, Santa Monica—became as
famous as the movie stars who cruised them. Los Angeles evolved into
a city of structures and symbols for passenger and driver: outsized,
garish, recognizable at any speed. Sleek billboards and hand-painted

signs shouted their wares in competition for drive-by customers
(fig. 9). Architecture responded to a culture of mobility with drive-ins,
drive-throughs, and crazy-looking buildings easy to identify from afar
and while on the move.

Photographers could not resist the larger-than-life architectural
concoctions that became synonymous, like Hollywood movie sets, with
Los Angeles's superficiality. Myra Breckenridge, Gore Vidal's fictional
transsexual heroine, en route to Metro-Goldwyn-Mayer on a bus,
expresses a common familiarity with this streetscape:

> This particular section of town is definitely ratty-looking with
> dingy bungalows and smog-filled air; my eyes burn and water.
> Fortunately elaborate neon signs and an occasional
> eccentrically shaped building make magic of the usual. We
> are now passing a diner in the shape of an enormous brown
> doughnut. I feel better already. Fantasy has that effect on me.[34]

In addition to the doughnut, at one time or another the city sported
a gargantuan papier-mâché sphinx's head (real estate office); windmills
(bakeries); an iceberg, a hand-cranked cooler, an owl (ice cream shops);
a hat, a shoe, a coffee pot, and a hotdog (restaurants); and a shapely
female leg (hosiery store). Though, by day, some of these whimsical
structures may have appeared as tatty as an ageing starlet, the night-
time magic of neon and electric lights transformed them into something
altogether more substantial and surreal, as photographers were quick
to recognize (see p. 180).

Representations of the quirky, pleasurable, and often inane side of
car culture eventually gave way to the scapegoating of the automobile
for society's deepening ills. "No one walks in Los Angeles" became the
anthem of song and image, fueled by the rise of the freeway system in
the 1960s and 1970s. The freeway is, David Brodsley writes, "the city's
great synecdoche, one of the few parts capable of standing for the
whole."[35] Be that as it may, portrayals of freeways are more often than
not sinister, negative, and even imply depravity. The freeway is cast as
a disassociative and center-less (read "soulless") space where people,
cocooned in their cars, have nothing to engage them but their own sorry
thoughts. If the automobile alienated drivers from their surroundings,
the freeway alienated them absolutely. The photographic iconography
as represented by Ansel Adams—black-and-white and shot from high
above—emphasized this alienation in the starkest visual terms. The
freeway system came to prominence in an age of growing skepticism
about large-scale earth-moving projects. A burgeoning conservation
movement questioned the environmental effects of ruthlessly
manipulating nature to satisfy urban growth, and art-trained
photographers of the 1970s turned the spotlight on the "man-altered"
spaces that Los Angeles supplied so promiscuously (see pp. 26, 27, 195).[36]

In one respect, this surge of imagery showing cracked pavement
and stucco, scorched earth and tattered palms, served as a tonic (and

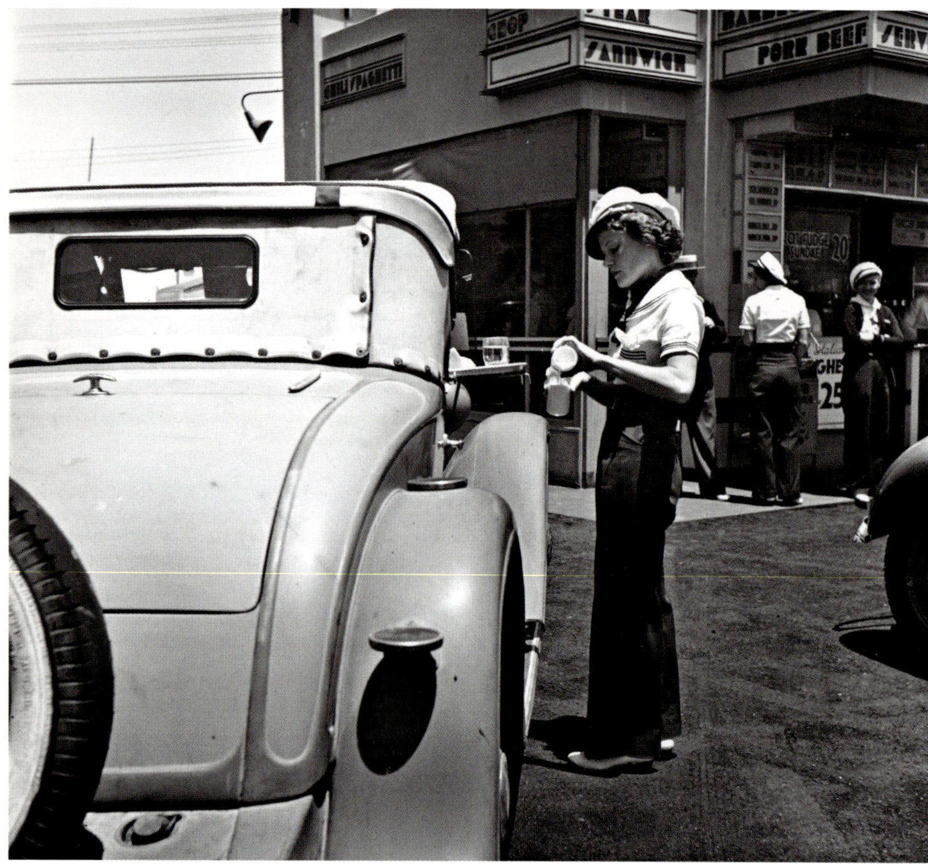

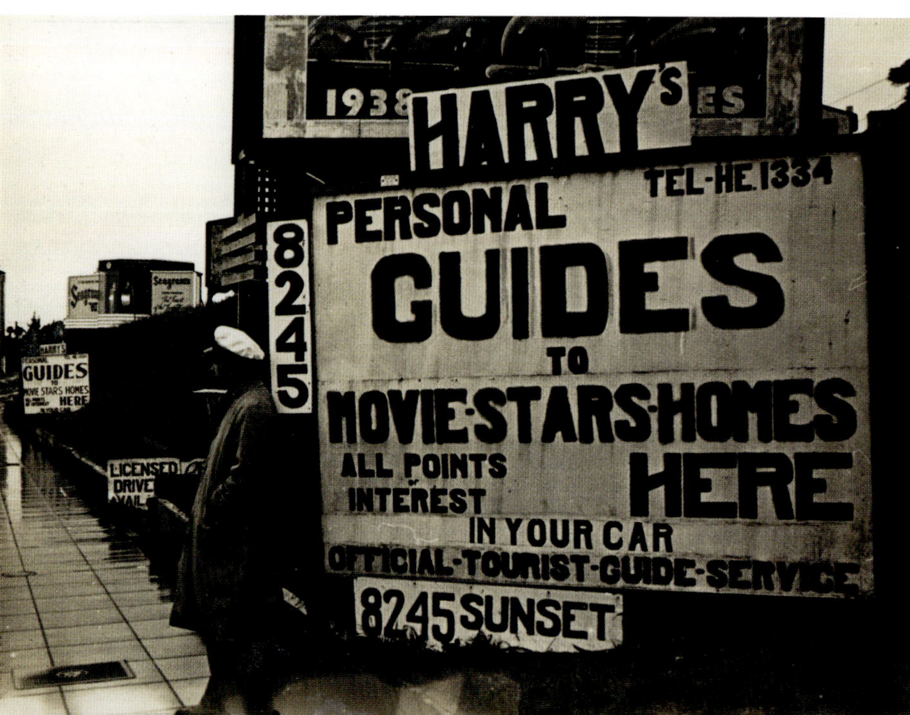

necessary corrective) to the visual indigestion engendered by the boosters' long tradition of beach and "babe" images. Jeff Gates's *In Our Path* series, documenting the construction of the Century (or I-105) Freeway, gets to the heart of the physical displacement that has affected the poor and ethnic minorities in disproportionate numbers (see p. 194).[37] Gates's own childhood feelings of "loss and abandonment" growing up in the San Fernando Valley drew him to the subject, and the black-and-white images narrate the story from its beginnings in 1983. Vacant, boarded-up houses await removal, their surfaces inscribed with profane graffiti, their weed-choked yards littered with the detritus of former inhabitants. A decade later, the end: ribbon-cutting celebrations, the gleaming new freeway empty save for transportation officials, civic leaders, and a bevy of University of Southern California cheerleaders standing beside a perfect layer cake, the freeway inscribed atop in white sugar frosting.

But whose Los Angeles is this car-clogged city of freeways? In one sense, it is almost every resident or visitor's city in the modern era. Yet the well-worn paths and byways seen in Charles Puck's photograph *Buena Vista Street* show another historic reality, one of alternative routes caused by foot traffic, meandering and non-linear (see p. 114). These are the back roads that have always been and are yet there, though they seem to be from another century. They are the routes of those who cannot afford cars or, for any number of reasons, do not drive in a resolutely automotive city. These are sometimes the landscapes of the homeless, as in Anthony Hernandez's series, wild and strangely domesticated all at once, beauty and misery all tangled up together (see p. 93).

Images of cars and freeways may define Los Angeles, but they do so imperfectly. Photographers are allegiant to other tropes as well. Consider the right angles and manicured lawns of suburbia, as in John Divola's photographs of a pretty teenager walking alone, presumably to school, or the ubiquitous scene of a homeowner watering his lawn (see p. 124; fig. 10). Divola is no celebrant of the literally pedestrian in Los Angeles. The lives of his subjects in these pictures seem small, shrunk down to a gridded, homogenized existence of square lots and predetermined routes. Is this their world as they saw and experienced it? Writer D.J. Waldie, a non-driver, meditates on suburban Lakewood. On his daily ambulatory journey to and from work in a place where he has lived his entire life, he muses on the sacramental aspects of suburban Los Angeles: if not exactly a paradise, a salvation of sorts for many seeking a better or even a "good enough" life.[38]

Robbert Flick also evokes Los Angeles by walking it. *Manhattan Beach, Looking West from Vista* is a gridded block of one hundred individual images stacked one atop another (see pp. 36–37). To create this part of his *Sequential Views* series, Flick systematically paced each intersecting street, in this case west from Vista Avenue, making images that use the horizon line as the single thread binding the larger visual tapestry. Reading from top to bottom (navigationally west to east),

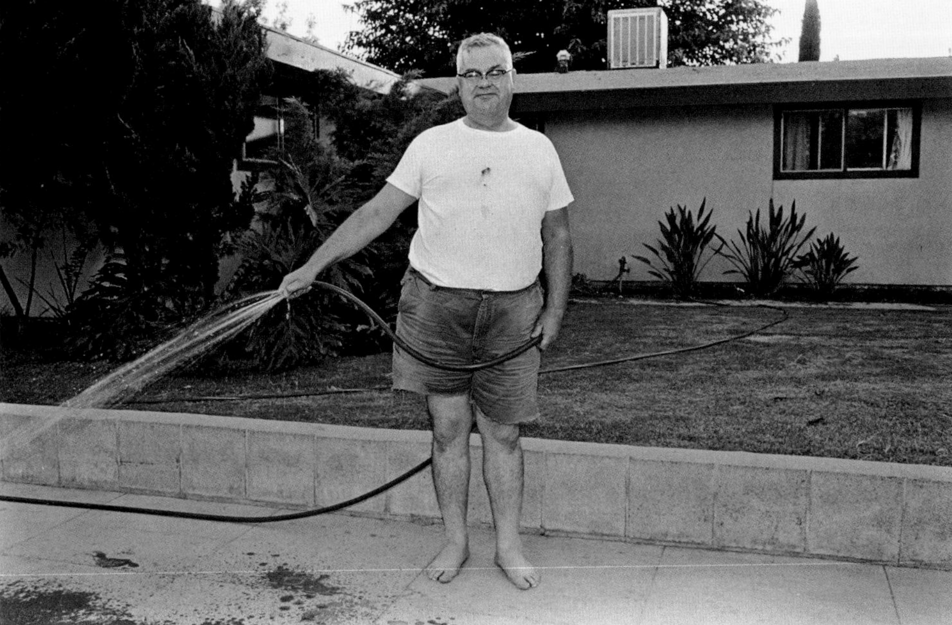

the viewer steps backward from the ocean's edge through rippling surf, monochromatic sand, and sun-baked streets, past surfers, cyclists, duplexes, VWs and dune buggies, runners, sunbathers, crosswalks, and crazy sculpted trees. The total effect is mesmerizing and paradoxical, like Los Angeles itself, capturing movement and stasis, order and chaos, beauty and blight, all in ephemeral, split-second glimpses. A decade later, the ineluctable pull of driving puts Flick behind the wheel of his car for the *L.A. Documents* series. The orderly, even serene, effect of his earlier work is replaced by a jam-packed frenetic blur of color, texture, word, and image (fig. 11). Movement unfurls in fits and starts, the eye scanning the scene for recognizable bits to bring meaning to the whole.[39] "It's as if," writes David Ulin, "Flick is commenting on the impossibility of Los Angeles as a coherent structure, even as he offers us a different kind of coherence, albeit one from which you must step away to see."[40]

Standing still

If the view behind the windshield (or bus window) is the default position for seeing Los Angeles, and the autoscape one of its primary visual metaphors, the sprawling natural landscape is certainly another. Devoted to the acceptance of photography as a legitimate fine art form, Los Angeles's early Pictorialists used hazy effects to soften the harsh light of progress and emphasize the romantic qualities of Southern California's sun and surf (see pp. 212, 213). These photographers tended to look at the city through a scrim of longing and desire, portraying Los Angeles as a place where life slowed down and became far less complex. It was a perspective that emphasized nature and rendered people as secondary subjects in and on the landscape. If the documentary photography of an earlier era responded to the need to depict nature corralled, controlled, and conquered, the Pictorialists were intent upon finding nature resurgent through their moody images of Southern California's landscape and environs.

The Pictorialists found a willing partner in *Touring Topics*, the Automobile Club of Southern California's important popular magazine.[41] *Touring Topics* debuted its "Rotagravure Section" in 1922, using photography to showcase idyllic spots accessible to the motorist. These were scenes observed not from a speeding car but from one parked by the side of the road in sun-dappled shade. Ernest Pratt's *Mulholland Highway* is not about dominion, speed, the triumph of engineering, all things the iconic highway embodied. Rather, it evokes the leisurely sensation of a Sunday drive, downplaying movement to favor sunshine glinting off rock and bush (see p. 110). The automobile merges seamlessly with the landscape as though it were a natural extension of the scene. The distant view minimizes the roadway itself, making little of the massive earth-moving effort that created it at great expense. In a panoramic photograph taken some seventy years later, Karen Halverson reverses the perspective, foregrounding the highway's infrastructure, using the

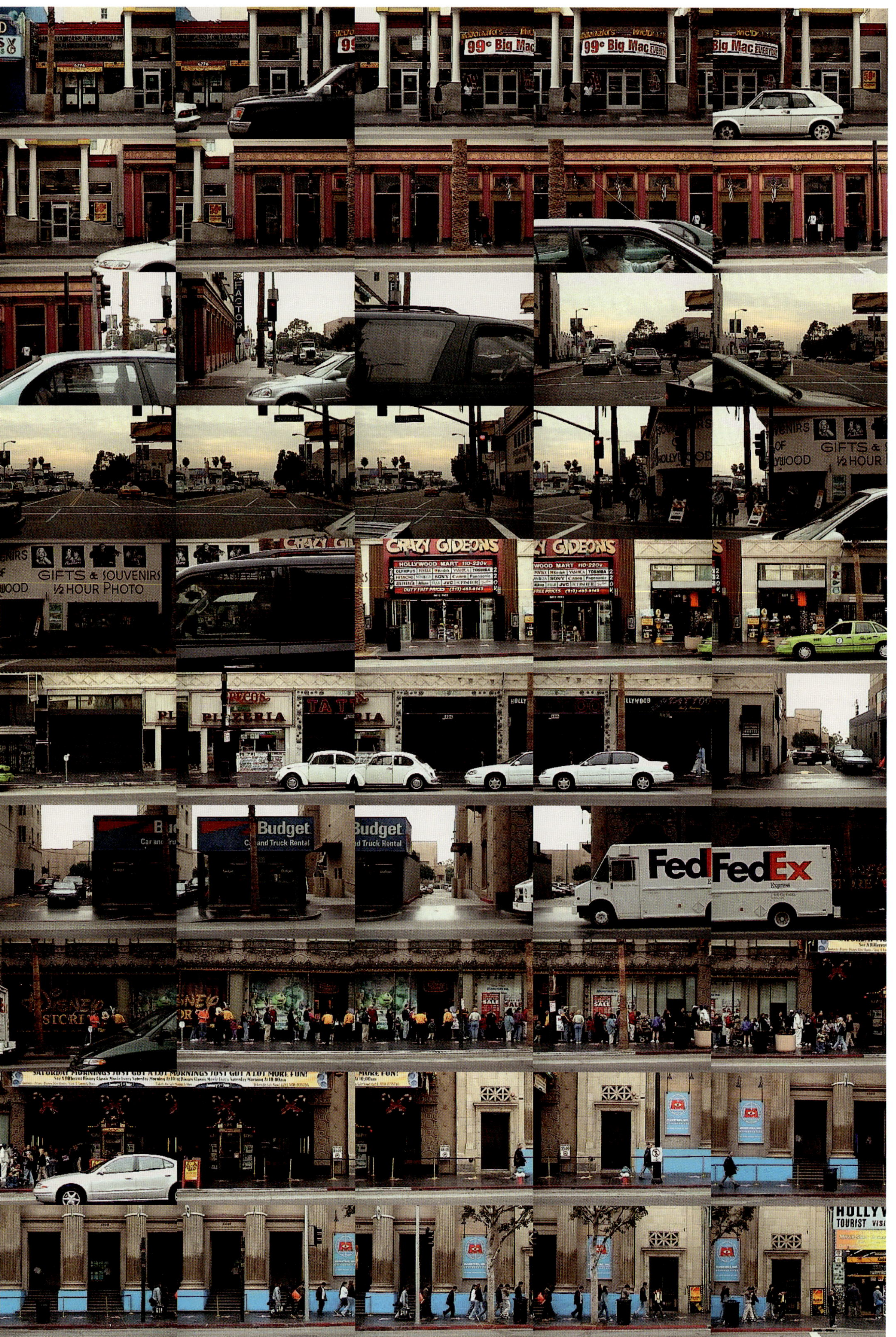

Fig. 11
Robbert Flick
Hollywood Blvd North and South, between La Brea and Cahuenga (detail, looking south at Highland), 2001

telephone pole and wires, asphalt, and painted lines to structure and
delimit tree, hillside, and dramatic sky beyond (see pp. 108–109).

Even the Pictorialists' overtly urban images used the play of light
and shadow to temper textures of concrete and steel. Will Connell's
Study in Diagonals of 1925 is, as *Touring Topics* described it, "a novel
and almost cubistic study" of the entrance to the Third Street Tunnel
(fig. 12).[42] A pedestrian and several cars seem incidental set against
a superstructure rendered heroic by the brilliant light–dark contrast
playing across the tunnel's wall. Only a small group of Japanese
American Pictorialists consistently mined the abstract potential of the
cityscape, experimenting with the city's literal textures and reflective
surfaces (fig. 13).[43] Despite occasional innovations, Pictorialism's
prevailing aesthetic, with its heavy emphasis on nostalgia and
romanticism, was resolutely pre-modern. Given the region's penchant
for myth-making, it seems no accident that the movement lasted far
longer in Southern California than elsewhere.[44]

Los Angeles's best-known early Pictorialist rejected the city that
drew him in. A Midwesterner who arrived in 1906 for a visit that turned
into a seventeen-year stay, Edward Weston settled in rural Tropico on
the city's outskirts. Only the Pacific Electric Red Car line running past
his rustic house and studio augured the future for his country idyll. From
the first, Weston was thoroughly smitten by Southern California's climate
and outdoor lifestyle, and he spent leisurely hours hiking in nearby
Griffith Park, bathing in mountain streams, and stargazing on the banks
of the Los Angeles River. He made poetic use of these natural settings
and the piquant light when commercial or portrait work did not confine
him to the studio. Proximity to Hollywood and a growing circle of
bohemian actors, intellectuals, and artist friends gave him willing sitters
whose creative energies informed and nourished his own (see p. 214).
But as the 1920s brought throngs of people and quaint Tropico rapidly
became suburban Glendale, Weston's vision of Los Angeles soured.
His disintegrating marriage, coupled with disdain for rampant
urbanization (with its "grey people, their grey houses and greyer
minds"), compelled him to flee in 1923 to the pastoral calm and quiet
artistic stimulus of Mexico.[45] Ironically, just as Weston rejected the
quaint nostalgia of Pictorialism in favor of the new, hard-edged
modernism that would come to define his work, he rejected the city
in favor of the country.

On his return to the United States in 1927, Weston's revulsion with
Los Angeles was complete and irreversible. The city seemed one
undifferentiated, somber grid of "smug bungalows," "squat business
blocks," and "stucco and cardboard pretensions" peopled by equally
bland, lifeless residents. "If only there were beautiful places to walk
nearby," Weston lamented from his studio hideaway.[46] Instead, he
retreated inside to make sharp-eyed still lifes of fruits, vegetables, and
nudes.[47] Though he famously never learned to drive, Weston obtained
an automobile from some friends. The financial burden was onerous, but

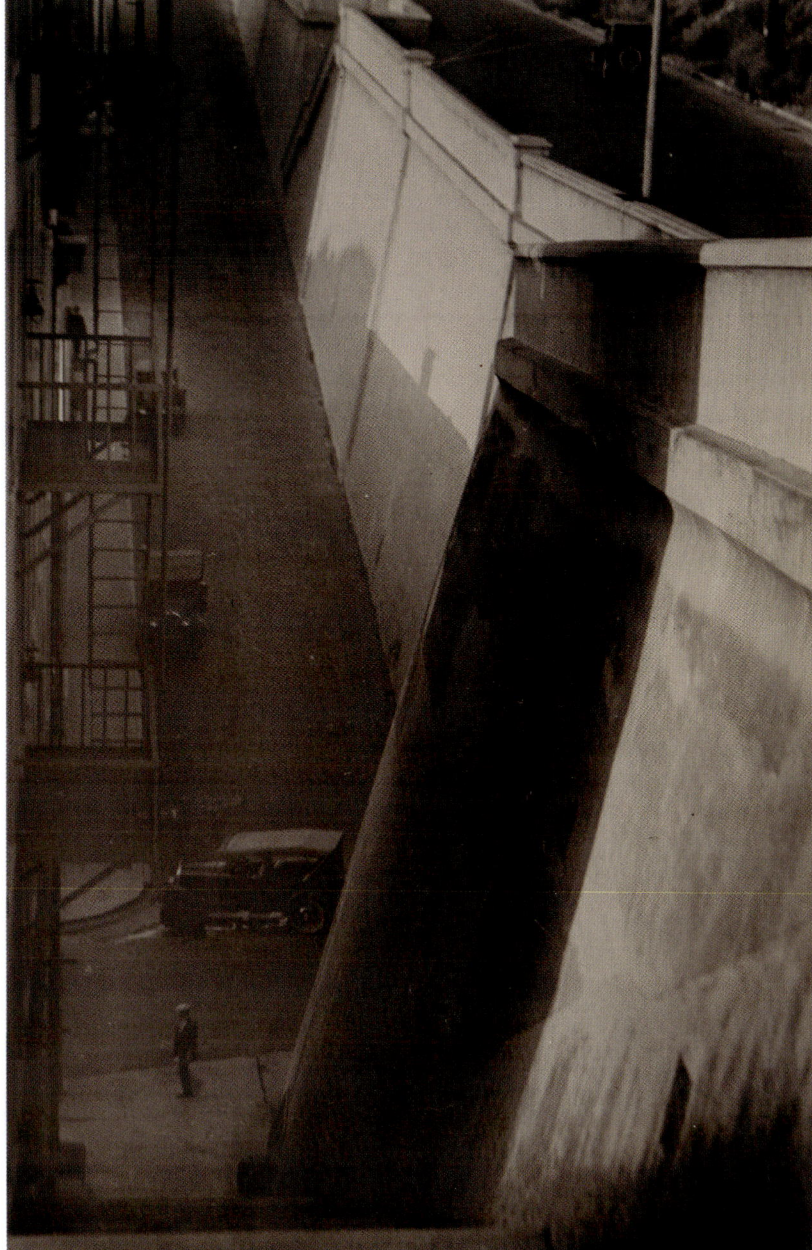

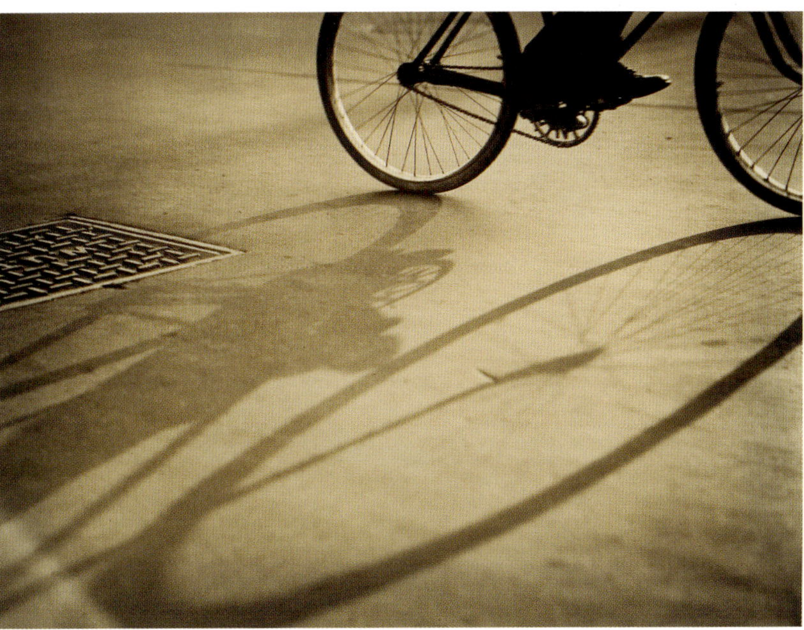

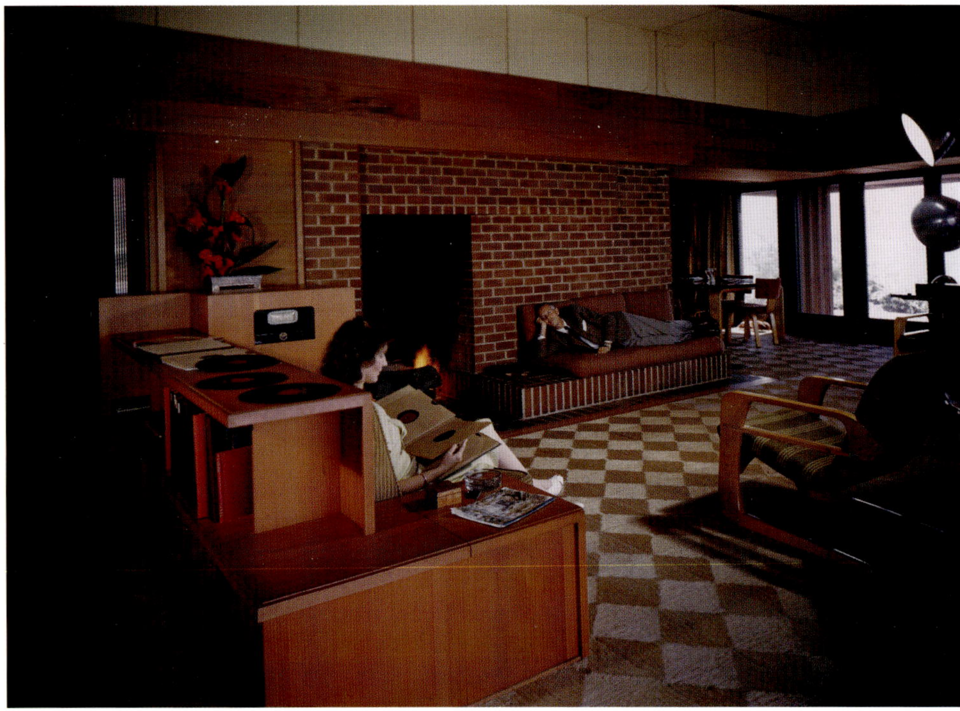

he was a pragmatist. "Business cannot be conducted these days without a car: one must fit into the speed of our time," he wrote in his journal.[48]

Weston's profound disaffection with Los Angeles was complex, partly a result of his thorny familial relations. Yet his isolation in the face of the city's explosive transformation from a rural to an intensely urban environment exacerbated his feelings. Nature as Weston defined it felt increasingly unattainable in 1920s Los Angeles, even by car. He left in 1927 for the remote Northern California village of Carmel and never looked back, save for a two-year period in Santa Monica and some brief, necessary visits. To him, the city was utterly irredeemable, the only aspect of visual interest being the motion-picture-studio back lots. In 1939 and 1940, Weston visited Metro-Goldwyn-Mayer and Twentieth Century Fox to capture the amusing juxtapositions and overt fakery of movie sets and mannequins (see p. 145).[49] These wood-and-stucco masquerades were Weston's metaphors for the fallen city itself.

Weston's vision of Los Angeles as pastoral refuge collided head-on with a city bent on expansion. As the people kept coming—1.2 million in 1930, 1.4 million in 1940, almost 2 million in 1950, 2.5 million in 1960—citrus groves, bean fields, and open lots were plowed over and rapidly subdivided to meet the insatiable hunger for home ownership. Developers refined a golden equation: available land plus assembly-line construction using cheap materials and cheap labor equaled thousands upon thousands of homes (see pp. 96–97, 143). This was an architecture predicated on a mild climate of barely distinguishable seasons in which people moved freely between inside and outside, albeit leisurely. Just as Los Angeles's car culture came to embody a frenetic, continuous movement, the house and its occupants symbolized an opposite perspective upon place: cultivated languor. Whether as seen in photographs of Cliff May's middle-class ranch houses or in the high-brow homes of Richard Neutra, Rudolph Schindler, and their International Style cohorts, these were houses made for lolling about in (see pp. 29, 87; fig. 14). This was weather-induced ennui, perhaps most stereotypically presented in a picture by surf photographer Leroy Grannis. Bronzed and buff youth hang out near shingled beach bungalows with nothing better to do than watch the scene unfold before them (see p. 6).

But the beach bungalow and its leisurely lifestyle popularized by Gidget and her movie star ilk was only one domestic environment among a diverse assortment. The private homes of twentieth-century Los Angeles, like the city's commercial buildings, took on a variety of guises: Spanish Colonial, English Tudor, Alpine, Cape Cod, Airplane Bungalow. This freewheeling domestic architecture did not conform to any conventional rules, its polyglot mix of styles making it ripe for derision. "Turning a corner in the Hollywood hills," wrote Carey McWilliams, "one comes upon . . . an elaborate Norman-French chateau or a monstrous square home, in no style whatever. . . . As much as anything else, it is the lack of a functional relationship between these homes and the land on which they rest that creates the illusion of unreality."[50] Such homes as these were not the offspring of Hollywood fantasy, as is often claimed, but rather their progenitors.[51] Even so, the movies (and later the television programs) of the 1930s through the 1950s took these hybrid settings and made them normative. They were sterile and perfect and utterly unlike the complicated world of their occupants. In *Some Rooms*, artist John Baldessari used production stills of these imaginary spaces (see p. 172). At the center of this amusing work are the imaginary owners, enjoying themselves at a party and still recognizable despite the partial obliteration of their faces. Yet an air of menace intrudes at the margins as gangster types seem to peer into these private spaces with perhaps sinister purpose.

Pushed aside

This darker cinematic undercurrent had its real-life equivalent in the marginalization of Los Angeles's "ethnic others." Race and class had everything to do with where and how Angelenos lived, and photographs reflect that reality. Unlike their more well-to-do counterparts lounging on sun-drenched patios, the poor and marginalized kept, or were kept, moving, their transience less about freedom of choice than lack of options. Early white migrants found the flat-roofed adobe dwellings of their Mexican predecessors entirely too primitive, quaint relics of a fading past (see p. 85). Many Mexicans were pushed into downtown tenements and rural hollows as white migrants moved in and land values rose (fig. 15). Even marginal spaces became contested lands. The tight-knit Mexican–American community of Chavez Ravine, so poignantly documented in the photographs of Don Normark in 1949, fell victim a few years later to the cause of "redevelopment" (see pp. 17, 193). Dodger Stadium stands in its place today. The nineteenth-century Chinese quarter, confined to a few blocks near downtown Los Angeles, was likewise erased (see p. 84). In the late 1930s, the gleaming new Union Passenger Terminal arose in its place, the station's architecture evoking a Mediterranean fantasy past of opulent courtyards and red clay tiles.

Others found themselves forced out of their comfortable existence through different types of erasure. Consider Clem Albers's photograph of Mrs. Nagamine on the porch of her large, Spanish-style residence with its lush, tropically landscaped grounds. This image from 1942 seems a classic pride-of-place picture (see p. 89). But Albers worked for the United States War Relocation Authority.[52] The Nagamine family, owners of the American Produce Company, were soon to be sent off to Manzanar, near Independence, California, or some other internment camp, along with more than 100,000 Japanese and Japanese Americans. This photograph, at its inception, had become a *memento mori* of a prosperous Southern Californian life. Another image by Albers, looking every bit the film still from a make-believe crime scene, depicts the back staircase of the Burlington Hotel in Los Angeles's "Little Tokio." The

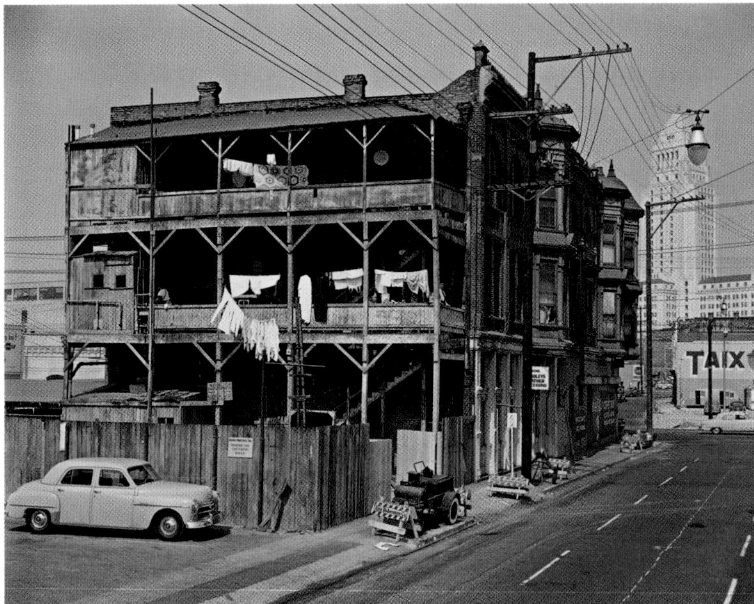

Fig. 15
Leonard Nadel
Commercial and Alameda Streets, June 12, 1952

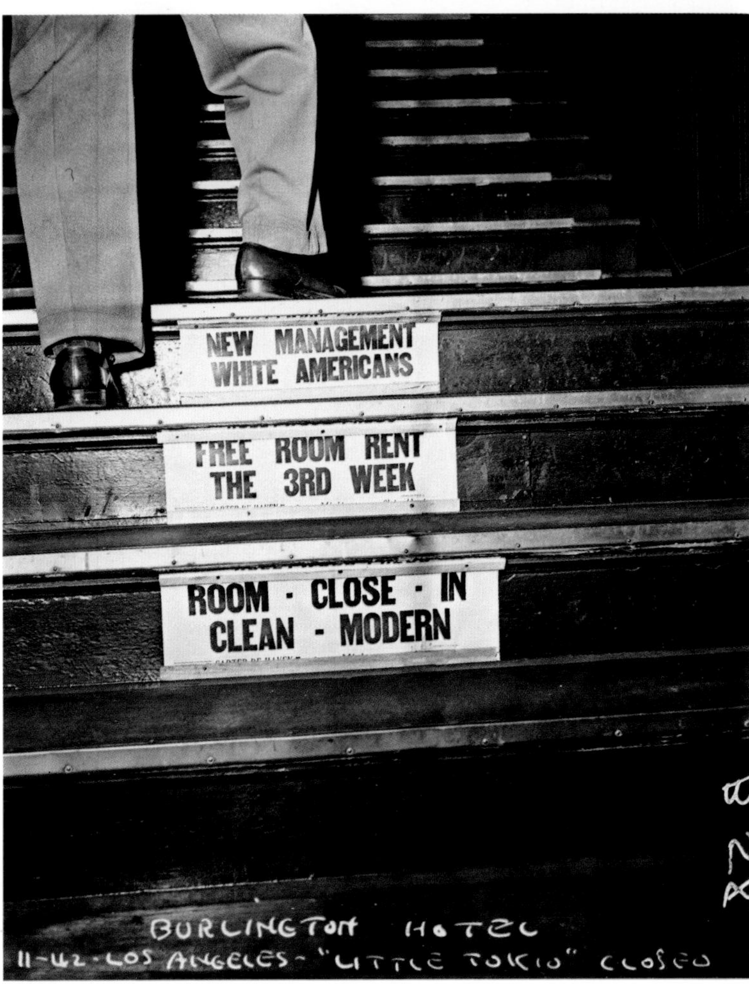

Fig. 16
Clem Albers
Burlington Hotel, "Little Tokio" Closed, Los Angeles, 1942

disembodied legs of a 1940s gumshoe-like figure highlight the bold signage announcing: "New Management White Americans" (fig. 16).

As Little Tokyo cleared out, African Americans moved in. The small neighborhood became known from 1942 to 1945 as "Bronzeville." But it was South Central Los Angeles, with its tidy bungalows, thriving businesses, many churches, and popular Central Avenue nightclubs, that became the beating heart of Los Angeles's African American community (see p. 173).[53]

Any benign representations of domestic normalcy within Los Angeles's racial or ethnic enclaves were obliterated in 1965 by the Watts riots, an explosive response to the long-simmering economic and racial tensions sparked by city housing patterns that sanctioned segregation in housing, work, and life generally. The world now saw only apocalyptic visions of smoldering buildings and streets in chaos, a seeming war zone of tanks, soldiers, and flames (see p. 191). Like a recurring nightmare a quarter-century later, photographs of South Central Los Angeles again on fire in 1992 solidified the city's identity as a flashpoint of racial violence (see p. 196).

Perhaps the most poignant contemporary image of displacement in a car-centric city is Mary Ellen Mark's wrenching photograph of the Damm family, taken in 1987 (see p. 105). Destitute and rootless, the family have made the automobile their home. For the Damms, Los Angeles is truly the "nowhere city," an unending series of streets without destination or purpose.

City of fact, city of mind

Ansel Adams's initial admiration for Los Angeles turned into disdain after he left the city. "Hell we are building here on earth," he wrote with Nancy Newhall in their great conservationist jeremiad *This Is the American Earth* (1960), illustrating the statement with William Garnett's striking aerial views of smog, suburban tracts, and the endless urban grid (figs. 17–19).[54] Los Angeles as a screen upon which a world's fantasies and nightmares are projected is not a new idea. As the historical epicenter of America's movie and television industry, the city's back lots, tracts, and deserts are *the* standard landscapes, as familiar to a Midwesterner as to a German, even if neither has ever set foot in the place. This strange familiarity with a clichéd landscape of beaches, palms, celebrities, and disaster has also bred a strong contempt. It is part of the "tendency of outsiders," writes David Ulin, to come out for a week or two or three, then sniff, as D.H. Lawrence did in 1920, that "Los A. is silly—much motoring, me rather tired and vague with it. California is a queer place—in a way, it has turned its back on the world and looks into the void Pacific."[55] People often find— and see and photograph—what they are looking for. It is a Gordian knot of looking that twines in and back and around on itself. Even so, photographs by outsiders can reveal much. Robert Frank, breezing through Los Angeles on a Guggenheim grant-funded project that

ultimately became *The Americans* (1959), made some of the most resonant views of the city involving its car and celebrity-infused culture (see pp. 34, 176).

Yet how does one comprehend as large and disorienting and, in many ways, exceptional a place as Los Angeles? As Gavin Lambert asked in 1959 in his short story about the city "The Slide Area": "How to grasp something unfinished yet always remodeling itself, changing without a basis for change?"[56] Representing extremes is always easier than visualizing complexity. Extremist renderings of Los Angeles have their photographic roots in the nineteenth century. That potent vision of Los Angeles as an Eden, a pristine garden of gargantuan fruit under perpetually balmy skies, gained currency through the photographs that became part and parcel of the city's civic identity. But extreme calls to extreme, and more cynical generations turned these easy visual formulations back on themselves. To be sure, the palm-tree iconography stuck (see p. 25). But in the city's modern and postmodern invocations it is no longer a booster's symbol of the good life; rather, as in Robert Adams's view of decimated palms falling down against each other, it has become symptomatic of human folly, the Fall in the Garden (see p. 27).

The representational limitations of photography are nowhere more evident than in such a place as Los Angeles, even as we admit that the photographic record is vast. The agendas of its image-makers are, and always have been, varied. It is a city built on image: the image of itself and the one that it projects to the world. As it was for Ansel Adams, making the view from above is tempting (see p. 224). It seems to suggest a God-like measure of control—and judgment. One contemporary photographer's aerial vision defines, for him, a landscape of unremitting social anxiety in a cancerous city "metastasizing ceaselessly." Yet he also admits that "our perceptions are contingent on the positions our bodies occupy in space."[57] In Los Angeles that space is usually not up in the air but down on the ground, often in a vehicle traveling from one place to another. But that ground, and the modes of travel and life upon it, are as diverse as the city itself. Los Angeles is arguably among the least understood and the most photographed cities in the world. Photography can never fully reveal: it can only lift the curtain to suggest. It is in the interstices between the everyday city of fact and the mythic city of mind that the truth of Los Angeles lies.

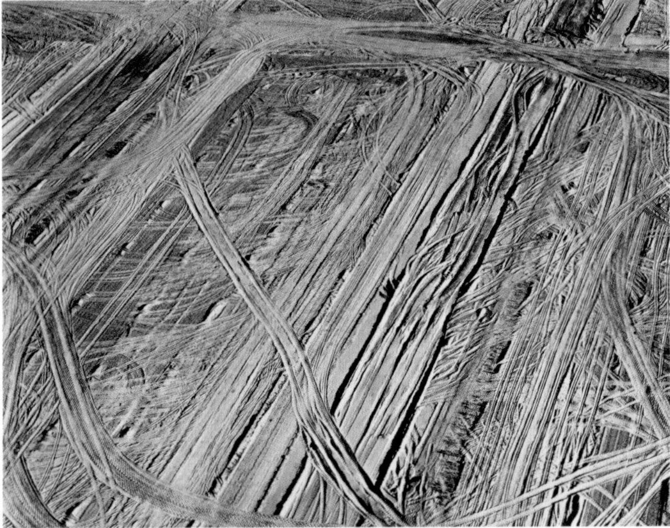

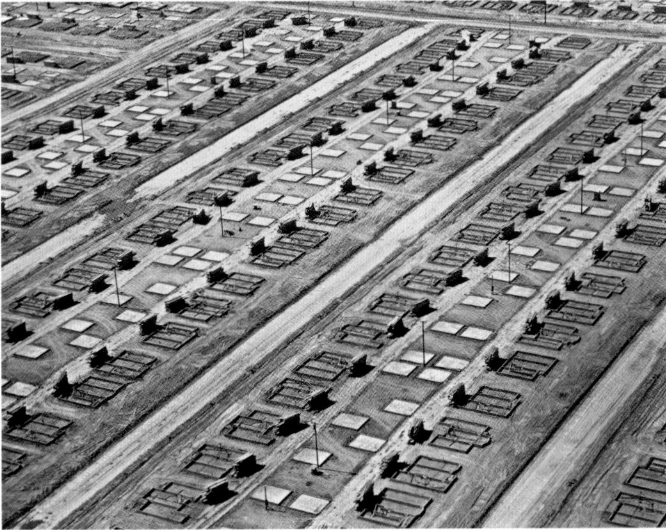

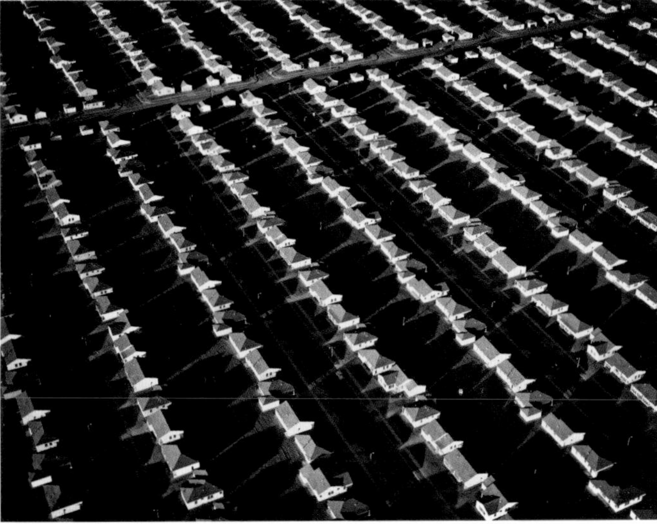

Top to bottom
Figs. 17–19
William A. Garnett
Grading Lakewood, California,
1950; *Foundations and Slabs,*
Lakewood, California, 1950;
Finished Housing, Lakewood,
California, 1950

NOTES

1 Cees Nooteboom, "Autopia," in *Writing Los Angeles: A Literary Anthology*, ed. David L. Ulin, New York (Library of America) 2002, p. 573.

2 Adams visited Los Angeles in 1941 on assignment for *Fortune* magazine. Some of the pictures appeared in "City of Angels," *Fortune*, March 14, 1941, pp. 90–94. One hundred digitized images from the assignment are on the Los Angeles Public Library website, lapl.org. See also Ansel Adams with Mary Street Alinder, *An Autobiography*, Boston (Little, Brown and Company) 1985, p. 164.

3 Adams needed to take commercial assignments in order to support his artistic pursuits. This teaching position started his career as a legendary instructor at Yosemite National Park and elsewhere. For an excellent overview of the photography program at the Art Center School and its historic influence in photography circles, see Michael Dawson, "Art Center School: Photography Comes of Age," in Victoria Dailey *et al.*, *LA's Early Moderns: Art/Architecture/Photography*, Los Angeles (Balcony Press) 2003, pp. 292–93.

4 Ansel Adams to David McAlpin, January 10, 1943, Ansel Adams Archive, Center for Creative Photography, University of Arizona, Tucson (hereafter CCP), AG31:2:1:21 Activity Files: "Diary," 1915–84.

5 Adams's teaching demands limited his own creative endeavors, and few prints exist from his brief period in Los Angeles. These include a photograph of the mannequins on the Columbia Studios back lot (see p. 144), and an image of a cemetery angel foregrounded against the Long Beach oil fields, which Adams liked well enough to include in one of his later portfolios. The Zone System is the most influential aspect of Adams's Los Angeles tenure, developed with fellow instructor Fred Archer to help students determine exposure and development times in order to calibrate the tonal range of the finished print.

6 Ansel Adams to David McAlpin following his resignation as the chair of the Photography Department at the Art Center School, April 16, 1943; Ansel Adams Archive, CCP, AG31:2:1:21 Activity Files: "Diary," 1915–84.

7 Adams referred to Yosemite as the "great earth gesture." Ansel Adams, *Yosemite and the Sierra Nevada*, Boston (Houghton Mifflin Company) 1948, p. xiv.

8 For periodized overviews of Los Angeles's art photography, the following resources are helpful: Michael Dawson, "Photography South of Point Lobos," in Dailey *et al.*, *LA's Early Moderns*, ch. 3; Leland Rice, *Southern California Photography 1900–1965: An Historical Survey*, Los Angeles (The Photography Museum) 1980; Leland Rice, "Los Angeles Photography: c. 1940–1960," *Journal: The Los Angeles Institute of Contemporary Art*, 5, April–May 1975, pp. 28–37; Gloria Williams Sander with Therese Mulligan, *The Collectible Moment: Photographs in the Norton Simon Museum*, Pasadena, Calif. (Norton Simon Art Foundation) 2006. Los Angeles as surveyed in documentary photographs can be found in David Gebhard and Harriette Von Breton, *L.A. in the Thirties: 1931–1941*, Salt Lake City (Peregrine Smith) 1975; Bruce Henstell, *Los Angeles: An Illustrated History*, New York (Alfred A. Knopf) 1980; Los Angeles 200 Committee, *Spectrum/200: Photographs from the History of Los Angeles, 1860–1940*, Los Angeles (Los Angeles 200 Committee) 1983; Jon and Nancy Wilkman, *Picturing Los Angeles*, Salt Lake City (Gibbs Smith) 2006.

9 Sarah Comstock, "The Great American Mirror: Reflections from Los Angeles," *Harper's*, 156, May 1928, p. 715.

10 Dr. William Osborn and Moses Searles made the first daguerreotype of Los Angeles on August 9, 1851. Their choice of subject is unknown, the image long since lost. The eight Los Angeles daguerreotypists working at some point between 1851 and 1858 were H.W. Bartlett, Solomon Nunes Carvalho, William M. Godfrey, A.M. Johnson, J. Lewis, George Reuben, and the aforementioned Osborn and Searles. John S. Craig, *Craig's Daguerreian Registry*, Torrington, Conn. (John S. Craig) 1994, p. 153. Peter Palmquist and Thomas Kailbourn speculate that there may have been two additional daguerreotypists in the city: A. Hallman and T.S. Hereford. Peter E. Palmquist and Thomas R. Kailbourn, *Pioneer Photographers of the Far West: A Biographical Dictionary, 1840–1865*, Stanford, Calif. (Stanford University Press) 2000, pp. 271 and 296.

Reproductions of only two Los Angeles daguerreotypes have been identified: a view of the seaside town of San Pedro by William M. Godfrey, *c*. 1852, and an unattributed daguerreotype of the Abel Stearns adobe "El Palacio," dating to about 1858. Copies of both daguerreotypes are at the Huntington Library, San Marino, California.

11 Horace Bell, *Reminiscences of a Ranger or Early Times in Southern California*, Los Angeles (Yarnell, Caystile & Mathes) 1881, p. 82.

12 A mob of several hundred white residents murdered nineteen Chinese men and boys at Calle de los Negros (or Negro Alley) on October 24, 1871, in a dispute involving the shooting of a white policeman. Leonard Pitt and Dale Pitt, *Los Angeles A to Z: An Encyclopedia of the City and County*, Berkeley (University of California Press) 1997, p. 91.

13 Given the social and economic climate of Los Angeles in the 1860s, few could make a living in the photographic profession, and those who made a go of it had additional jobs as well. Two such were John H. Henfield and Stephen Rendall. Rendall, who partnered with William M. Godfrey sometime in the mid-1860s, made the first photographic panorama of Los Angeles in 1869. Godfrey specialized in landscape work, mostly in the stereographic format. He also made *carte de visite* portraits and worked on commission for such clients as the U.S. Army Corps of Engineers and some powerful local families. Godfrey's output of landscape images appears relatively small—235 distinct views at last count.

14 Important regional photographers of the 1870s, many of whom employed the stereograph for their landscape imagery, included H.T. Payne and A.C. Varela (the son-in-law of musician John Philip Sousa), as well as studio photographers Valentin Wolfenstein, Victor Ponet, Francis Parker, A.S. Addis, and William M. Godfrey, who returned to Los Angeles around 1871 after a brief tenure in the nearby Mormon community of San Bernardino. Godfrey would ultimately settle in San Bernardino, east of Los Angeles, where he continued to photograph as well as trying his hand at mining and the newspaper business.

15 Watkins had a free pass on the Southern Pacific Railroad (SPRR), a significant financial perk provided by company head Collis P. Huntington, his lifelong friend and benefactor. Watkins's trip coincided with the linking of San Francisco to Los Angeles via the SPRR line through the Tehachapi Pass, as well as the photographer's need to rebuild his inventory of images after the devastating loss of his negatives to rival Isaiah Taber in 1875. Watkins may have gone to Los Angeles on his own initiative or possibly at the behest of several landowners who intended to use his images for promotional ends. Peter E. Palmquist, *Carleton Watkins: Photographer of the American West*, Albuquerque (published for the Amon Carter Museum by the University of New Mexico Press) 1983; Douglas R. Nickel, *Carleton Watkins: The Art of Perception*, New York (Harry N. Abrams) 1999; Weston Naef, ed., *Carleton E. Watkins Mammoth Plate Catalog Raisonné Project*, Los Angeles (The J. Paul Getty Museum) forthcoming.

16 Carleton E. Watkins's visit in 1880 was undertaken, in part, to make images that would provide the basis for illustrations in two regional promotional publications, *Semi-Tropic California* and *Thompson & West's Illustrated History of Los Angeles County*. For a fuller treatment of Watkins's two trips to Southern California, see Naef, *Carleton E. Watkins*.

17 Jennifer A. Watts, "Picture Taking in Paradise: Los Angeles and the Creation of Regional Identity, 1880–1920," *History of Photography*, 24, Autumn 2000, pp. 243–50.

18 *Ibid*.

19 Major Ben C. Truman, *Semi-Tropical California: Its Climate, Healthfulness, Productiveness and Scenery*, San Francisco (A.L. Bancroft & Company) 1874, p. 27. See also Glenn S. Dumke, *The Boom of the Eighties in Southern California*, San Marino, Calif. (The Huntington Library) 1944; John E. Baur, *The Health Seekers of Southern California, 1870–1900*, San Marino, Calif. (The Huntington Library) 1959; Carey McWilliams, *Southern California Country: An Island on the Land*, New York (Duell, Sloan & Pearce) 1946, especially ch. 1. For an introduction to regional boosterism, see Kevin Starr, *Material Dreams: Southern California Through the 1920s*, New York (Oxford University Press) 1990.

20 There were approximately 11,000 people in Los Angeles in 1880, a figure that increased to more than 50,000 in a decade. By 1900, the census counted 103,000 people residing in the city and 170,000 in the county.

21 McWilliams, *Southern California Country*, pp. 120–21.

22 Jackson visited Los Angeles briefly in 1867. Between 1885 and 1892, he rode the rails making photographs to promote, among other things, regional hotels. He traveled in California on several occasions, one of which was in the winter of 1889, when he made approximately 750 views, among them a panorama of the famous Hotel del Monte in Monterey. Jackson's visits to Southern California and the resulting output warrant further research. See William Henry Jackson, *Time Exposure: The Autobiography of William Henry Jackson*, New York (G.P. Putnam's Sons) 1940, especially pp. 259 and 324–26. See also Peter B. Hales, *William Henry Jackson and the Transformation of the American Landscape*, Philadelphia (Temple University Press) 1988.

23 McWilliams, *Southern California Country*, p. 350.

24 *Ibid*., p. 12.

25 William Alexander McClung, *Landscapes of Desire: Anglo Mythologies of Los Angeles*, Berkeley (University of California Press) 2000, p. 11.

26 Spencer Crump, *Ride the Big Red Cars: How Trolleys Helped Build Southern California*, Los Angeles (Crest Publications) 1962, pp. 159–60.

27 For an excellent introduction to Los Angeles in the 1920s and its monumental growth, see Jules Tygiel in *Metropolis in the Making: Los Angeles in the 1920s*, ed. Tom Sitton and William Deverell, Berkeley (University of California Press) 2001, pp. 1–10.

28 Comstock, "The Great American Mirror," p. 715.

29 Comparable car ownership statistics were one for every thirty Chicagoans or one in thirteen nationally. Richard Longstreth, *City Center to Regional Mall: Architecture, the Automobile, and Retailing in Los Angeles, 1920–1950*, Cambridge, Mass. (MIT Press) 1997, p. 13.

30 Comstock, "The Great American Mirror," p. 720.

31 For a thorough debunking of the pervasive theory of a Los Angeles transit conspiracy, see Scott L. Bottles, *Los Angeles and the Automobile: The Making of the Modern City*, Berkeley (University of California Press) 1987.

32 The Rochester Panoramic Company patented the Cirkut camera in 1904, but Kodak took it over soon after, marketing it until 1941. Five different models allowed 180–360-degree views ranging in length from 42 in. (107 cm) to 20 ft (6.1 m). The format proved the perfect vehicle to trumpet larger-than-life achievement in the Progressive Era.

33 It is no coincidence that Ferus Gallery used *Double Standard* for its announcement in 1964 of Ruscha's exhibition. See Craig Krull, *Photographing the L.A. Art Scene, 1955–1975*, Santa Monica, Calif. (Smart Art Press) 1996, pp. 11–15. For an excellent and extended discussion of Ruscha and his relationship to Los Angeles, see Whiting, *Pop L.A.*, especially ch. 2, "Cruising Los Angeles," pp. 63–105.

34 Gore Vidal, *Myra Breckenridge/Myron*, New York (Random House) 1986, p. 26.

35 David Brodsley, *L.A. Freeway: An Appreciative Essay*, Berkeley (University of California Press) 1981, p. 51.

36 A group of landscape photographers, many with imagery based in the American West, emerged as part of a so-called "New Topographics" school, a term that arose from an exhibition held in 1975 at the George Eastman House in Rochester, New York. Some of these photographers—Robert Adams, Lewis Baltz, Joe Deal, and Henry Wessel, Jr.—are represented in this publication. See William Jenkins, *New Topographics: Photographs of Man-Altered Landscape*, Rochester, NY (International Museum of Photography) 1975.

37 The literature on freeways and ethnic displacement is sparse, but an excellent redress is Gilbert Estrada, "If You Build It, They Will Move: The Los Angeles Freeway System and the Displacement of Mexican East Los Angeles, 1944–1972," *Southern California Quarterly*, 87, Fall 2005, pp. 287–315.

38 D.J. Waldie, *Holy Land: A Suburban Memoir*, New York and London (W.W. Norton) 1996. Waldie writes: "The grid limited our choices, exactly as urban planners said it would. But the limits weren't paralyzing. The design of this

suburb compelled a conviviality that people got used to and made into a substitute for choices, including not choosing at all. There are an indefinite number of beginnings and endings on the grid, but you are always somewhere" (p. 116).

39 For a retrospective of Robbert Flick's entire Los Angeles œuvre, see *Robbert Flick: Trajectories*, exhib. cat. by Michael Dear *et al.*, Los Angeles County Museum of Art, September 2004–January 2005.

40 *Ibid.*, p. 13.

41 *Touring Topics* editor Phil Townsend Hanna was an enthusiastic amateur photographer who joined the Camera Pictorialists of Los Angeles in 1914 when the group was founded. For a discussion of *Touring Topics*'s use of western American art as part of its regional promotional agenda, see John Ott, "Landscapes of Consumption: Auto Tourism and Visual Culture in California, 1920–1940," in *Reading California: Art, Image, and Identity, 1900–2000*, ed. Stephanie Barron *et al.*, Berkeley and Los Angeles (University of California Press and Los Angeles County Museum of Art) 2000, pp. 51–67.

42 *Touring Topics*, 17, December 1925, "Rotagravure Section," after p. 28.

43 While Dennis Reed argues persuasively that the Pictorialist movement was "a highly diverse and complex phenomenon," and indeed there was both a significant amount of experimentation and a range of subjects presented, the preponderance of imagery of Southern California from the 1910s to 1930s is weighted toward the romantic portrayal of land and sea and sunlight. Dennis Reed, "Southern California Pictorialism: Its Modern Aspects," in *Pictorialism in California: Photographs 1900–1940*, exhib. cat. by Michael G. Wilson and Dennis Reed, Los Angeles, The J. Paul Getty Museum; San Marino, Calif., The Henry E. Huntington Library and Art Gallery, 1994, pp. 67–88, especially pp. 83–86. See also Michael Dawson, "Transitions in Southern California Landscape Photography, 1900–1940," in *Land of Sunshine: An Environmental History of Metropolitan Los Angeles*, ed. William Deverell and Greg Hise, Pittsburgh (University of Pittsburgh Press) 2005, pp. 209–11.

44 For a discussion of the role of the Camera Pictorialists of Los Angeles, see Dawson, "Photography South of Point Lobos," pp. 270–73. See also Reed, "Southern California Pictorialism," pp. 69–74.

45 Edward Weston to his family, August 8, 1923, Edward Weston Papers, Family Correspondence, Outgoing, CCP, AG38:8/3.

46 Nancy Newhall, ed., *The Daybooks of Edward Weston*, vol. 2, New York (Horizon Press in collaboration with The George Eastman House) 1966, p. 40.

47 Weston made very few landscape studies in Los Angeles after 1923. In 1925, on a brief return visit from Mexico, he spent a day in the city's industrial district and made negatives of a plaster works factory building and of the Ready-Cut Homes tower, which he described as "the great phallus of industry—stiffly erect and holding the sperm of a thousand 'ready-cut-homes.'" Additionally, there are several views of his son Neil atop a boat skeleton in Wilmington, a port suburb of Los Angeles, and an image of 1936 of the Hollywood reservoir entitled *Lake Hollywood*. Finally, Weston made one image of a garish and decaying plaster-of-Paris "monument" on the famed Wilshire Boulevard. See Amy Conger, *Edward Weston: Photographs from the Collection of the Center for Creative Photography*, Tucson (Center for Creative Photography, University of Arizona) 1992, figs. 176–77, 877–79, 964, and 967.

48 Edward Weston, quoted in Newhall, *The Daybooks*, vol. 2, p. 41.

49 To see the full Metro-Goldwyn-Mayer and Twentieth Century Fox series of photographs, see Conger, *Edward Weston*, figs. 1428–40 and 1517–25.

50 McWilliams, *Southern California Country*, pp. 362–63.

51 Architectural historian David Gebhard perceptively observes that in such movies as *What a Widow* (1930), starring Gloria Swanson, and in Fred Astaire and Ginger Rogers's *Shall We Dance* (1936), "the architecture depicted . . . solidified current taste rather than leading the way. Sets were derived from the real world of Hollywood and Beverly Hills, not the other way around." Gebhard and Von Breton, *L.A. in the Thirties*, pp. 109–10.

52 Photojournalist Clem Albers documented the round-up of Japanese Americans in Los Angeles and surrounding communities for deportation to Manzanar and other internment camps during the Second World War. He also took photographs showing life in the camps. For more information on Albers's life and career, see Gerald H. Robinson, intro. by Archie Miyatake, *Elusive Truth: Four Photographers at Manzanar*, Nevada City, Calif. (Carl Mautz Publishing) 2002. The U.S. National Archives and Records Administration has 383 photographs by Albers on its website: archives.gov/research/arc.

53 Carolyn Kozo Cole and Kathy Kobayashi, *Shades of L.A.: Pictures from Ethnic Family Albums*, New York (New Press) 1996, is a wonderful sampling of historic images depicting various ethnic and racial groups in Los Angeles.

54 Ansel Adams and Nancy Newhall, *This Is the American Earth*, San Francisco (Sierra Club) 1960, pp. 36–38.

55 Quoted in David L. Ulin, "The Mediated City: Robbert Flick and the Meaning of Los Angeles," in Dear *et al.*, *Robbert Flick*, p. 11.

56 In Ulin, *Writing Los Angeles*, p. 411.

57 David Maisel, *Oblivion*, Portland, Ore. (Nazraeli Press) 2006, p. vii.

LUST IN THE LAND OF SUNSHINE
THE BODY IN LOS ANGELES PHOTOGRAPHS   Claudia Bohn-Spector

It has always seemed to me, ever since I was little, that sex (i.e., inspiring lust) was what L.A. was about. And that the thing to do was inspire lust so mighty that it would overcome those who might inspire lust in you.
Eve Babitz[1]

Man is a creation of desire, not a creation of need.
Gaston Bachelard[2]

Contrary to popular belief, Los Angeles does not defy description so much as provoke it. Literary representations of the city as an "earthly paradise," a "huge desert encampment," a "city of dreadful joy," and, more recently, a "city of quartz" are among the best-known in a seemingly endless stream of identifiers.[3] Almost from the beginning, Los Angeles engendered an imagery steeped in lust and desire. It has been described as "either a harlot or a virgin . . . a God forsaken desert or a garden of Eden—filled with newlyweds or nearly-deads."[4] It was a place at once raw and compelling—the "great Joy City of the West," where balmy climes, constant sunshine, and cheap real estate fueled the dreams of millions.[5]

Since the mid-nineteenth century, Southern California has seduced America's imagination with images celebrating its stunning location and topography: vast open spaces, monumental scenery, fertile lands, and outsized crops rarely failed to impress audiences back east. It was a region of prodigious endowments and even bigger appetites—for the spoils of Western expansion, for empire building, for power, wealth, and physical well-being. Such hyperbole soon encompassed descriptions of the region's inhabitants, pouring in by the thousands after the Gold Rush of 1848. Invigorated by the salubrious climate and scenic beauty, Californians were extolled as progenitors of a new race that harkened back to the roots of ancient civilization.[6]

The exaltation of Southern California's physicality, with all its attendant racial and ethnic prejudice, helped spawn a pervasive body culture that firmly took root in Los Angeles in the 1920s, aided by the camera as its promulgator and eager amanuensis.[7] Over time, gorgeous physiques, bronzed skin, and an infectious sex appeal became virtually synonymous with Southern California, fostering increasingly lustful interpretations of both the city and the landscape itself:

> Imagine Marilyn Monroe, fifty miles long, lying on her side, half-buried on a ridge of crumbling rock, the crest of the Santa Monica Mountains, with chaparral, flowers and snakes writhing over her body, and mists, smog or dreams gathering in every curve. You'd need a certain height to recognize that intricate course as a body. But that's Mulholland . . . . It's about as long as an old movie, and as full of scents and half-grasped fears and splendors as Marilyn's drowsy state.[8]

For writer David Thomson, Mulholland Drive, that 21-mile (34-km) stretch of asphalt and gravel overlooking Los Angeles, embodies the "grace and

Fig. 1
Larry Sultan
Backyard, Woodland Hills,
2002

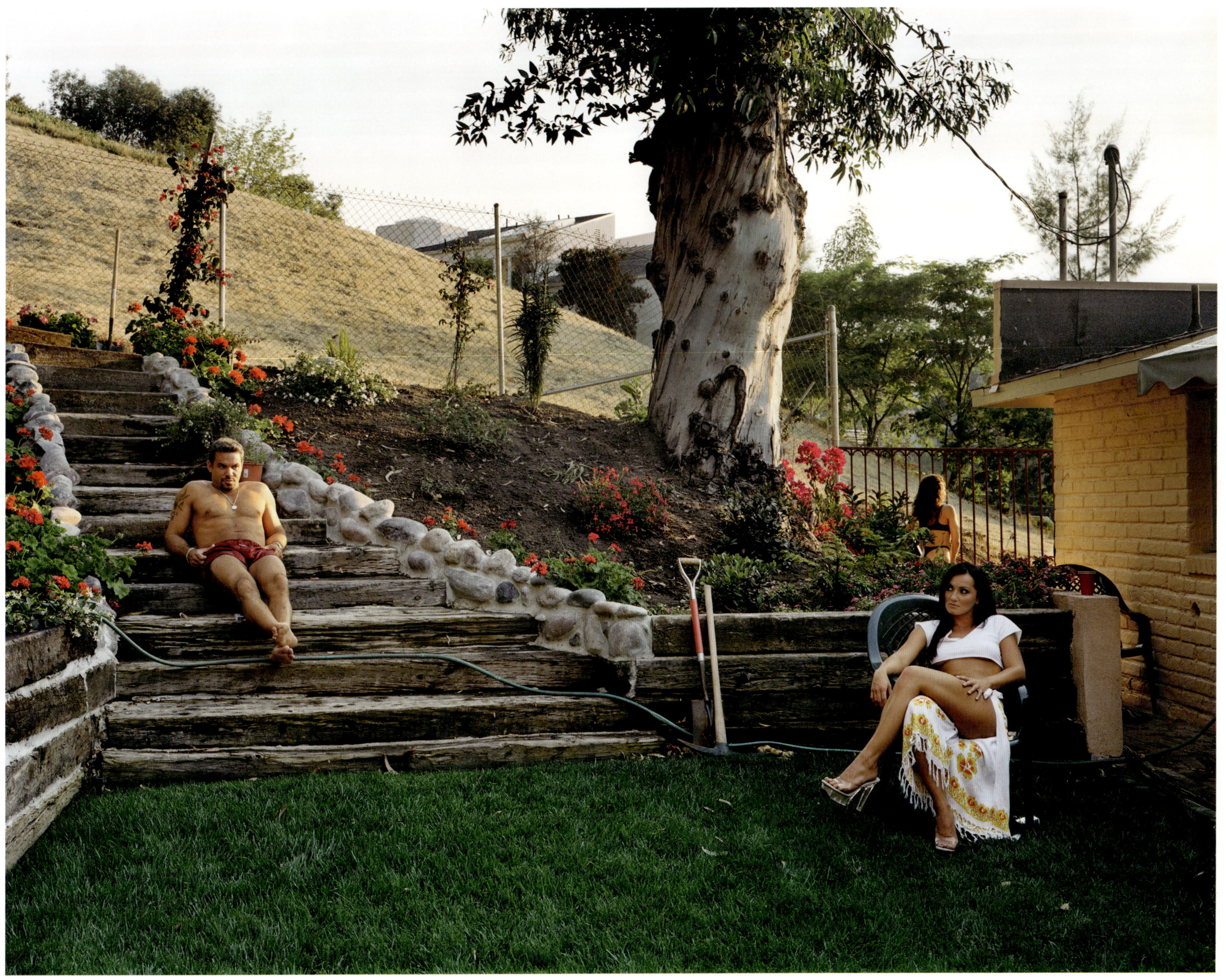

dread" at the heart of the city.[9] It's "a pin-up and an idea . . . a highway made for narcissism and envy, an example of privilege, luxury and airy superiority that whispers: 'Look at me—take me, if you can.'"[10] The Hollywood sign rising at Mulholland's eastern end is both a come-on and a warning: "It's there to tell us the landscape is a kept woman as well as a collapsing topography."[11]

This essay focuses on the emergence of physical culture in Los Angeles, proposing a contextual narrative through which to view the photographs in this exhibition. It examines how Los Angeles bodies have been seen by the camera since the late nineteenth century, and how the medium has helped in constructing the city as a "sunny refuge for White Protestant America"—a place fixated on youth, fitness, and spectacular bodies.[12] Darker takes on Los Angeles have challenged such upbeat celebrations, interpreting bodies not as sites of pleasure but as places wounded by empire, racism, sickness, and death. Los Angeles bodies, as they emerge from the photographic record, are variously emblematic of a city that "brings it all together" (Los Angeles's official slogan) or of a city that is a nightmare at the terminus of American history, as Mike Davis has noted. Drawing on the region's disjunctive spaces, unique light, and Mediterranean pretensions, they encapsulate both the glories and the unrealized dreams of the great American enterprise.

Inspiring lust

Just north of Mulholland Drive, spread out between the Santa Monica, San Gabriel, and Santa Susana mountains, lies the San Fernando Valley. Once an arid flatland with a Franciscan mission and a handful of *ranchos*, the Valley is now "fertile, flush-friendly, and be-pooled."[13] Its dramatic transformation from wasteland to oasis was made possible by water from the eastern Sierra Nevada, brought to the Southland by the Los Angeles Aqueduct in 1913. When water first gushed down the spillway at 400 cubic ft (11.3 cubic m) per second, the aqueduct's chief engineer, William Mulholland, captured the spirit of an age by exclaiming: "There it is—Take it!"[14]

Today, the San Fernando Valley is a densely populated grid of middle- and upper-class homes, shopping malls, and car dealerships. It is also the epicenter of the U.S. adult film industry, which places its erotic fantasies in local settings. Virtually all American triple-X movies are shot and distributed here, infusing both landscape and local economy with the faint aroma of illicit sex. Photographer Larry Sultan's documentary project *The Valley* began inconspicuously, with an editorial assignment to cover a day in the life of a porn star. A long-time resident of the San Francisco Bay Area, Sultan flew down to Burbank and drove to a home near to where he had grown up:

> I walked into this dentist's house that, not unusually, had all his family pictures on display. I noticed pictures of children and his wife, and then I noticed a tangle of bodies in the middle of the room. The friction

between the reality of that familial setting and the fantasy that was being played out was so close to what I had grappled with in a lot of my prior work that I knew I had to explore it further.[15]

The one-day assignment turned into a five-year project covering the strange fictions and behind-the-scenes tedium of porn sets from Van Nuys to Woodland Hills. Rented out for two or three days—the time it takes to shoot an X-rated film—these ordinary homes become the symbolically charged backdrops on which the sexual fantasies of millions are projected. Here, on the "Plains of Id," as Reyner Banham called Los Angeles's sprawling flatlands, beats the heart of the city. It is "where the crudest urban lusts and most fundamental aspirations are created, manipulated and, with luck, satisfied."[16]

Yet naked flesh is only the surface lure that draws us deeper into Sultan's mysterious yet familiar landscapes. In *Backyard, Woodland Hills* (fig. 1), a semi-clad couple lounges outdoors, their smooth, sun-tanned bodies as flawless as the impossibly verdant lawn. Lost in thought, they display a dreamy *ennui*—two actors passing time between takes. A plastic garden hose snakes languidly past a shovel and pickax, suggesting that this backyard Eden is filled with both labor and nature's temptations. The weathered steps at the left draw the gaze to the parched hillside beyond, underscoring the artifice of this sultry suburban enclave. The image is at once seductive and unnerving, redolent with the mystique and unfulfilled promise of Southern California.

It is also Sultan's reckoning with his own native Valley, with an adolescence spent daydreaming on irrigated lawns and flesh-toned Naugahyde sofas.[17] He recalls that when his parents bought a new home in Woodland Hills in 1961, they turned it into a virtual pleasure zone, with plastic grapes dangling from painted tendrils, a green shag rug, and a sparkling pool complete with waterfall.[18] There, cocooned by palm fronds, spruce, and eucalyptus trees, they lounged and sipped Martinis, listening to the music of Louis Prima, the "King of Swingers." For Sultan, the particular smells, sounds, and rhythms of the San Fernando Valley triggered infinite carnal imaginings, fueled by budding manhood, smog, and heat. The Valley is a place, he said, "where in the middle of the day, everyone stops work and has a great time together."[19] Big, sensual, and inviting, the landscape once conquered by man had in turn conquered him, spawning an entire culture predicated on the arousal of pleasure and lust. How did this happen? What are the keys to a visual language that documents, hails, and, ultimately, debunks Los Angeles as an "earthly paradise" and "golden land," a place of vast animal feeling, "meaty and raw, untempered by any mental sauce"?[20]

When British writer Nathan Silver first came to Los Angeles in 1969, he said that he "was conveniently prepared for almost anything except for what it really looked like—a quite beautiful place."[21] Today's visitors might be equally surprised, though they would hardly recognize the city as boosters envisioned it over a century ago. Aided by artists and image-makers, Los Angeles's champions painted the region as a lush,

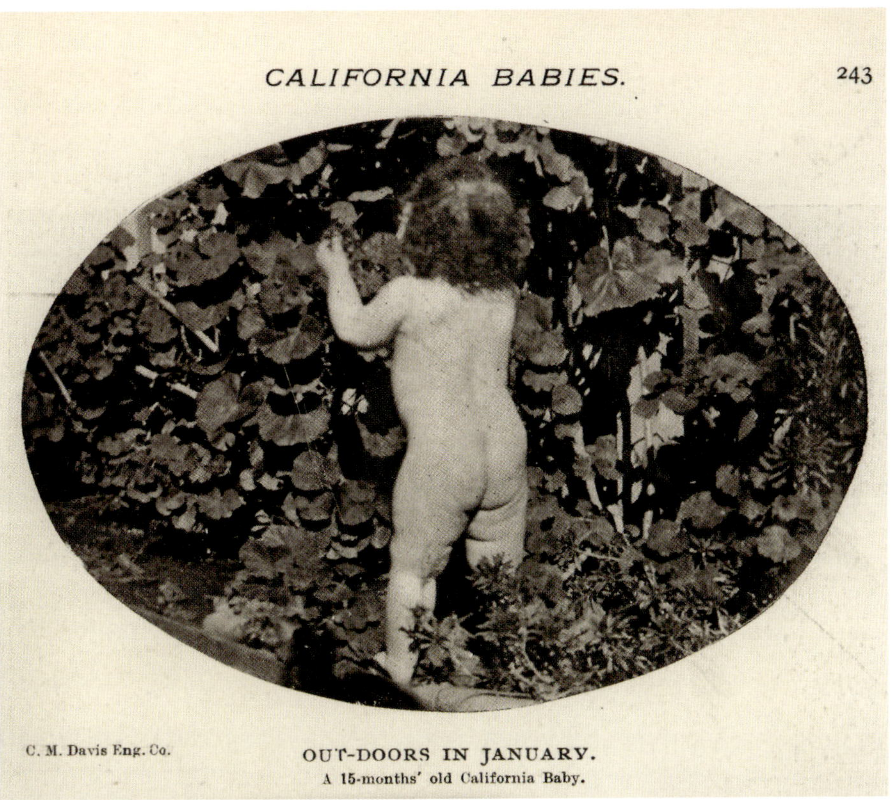

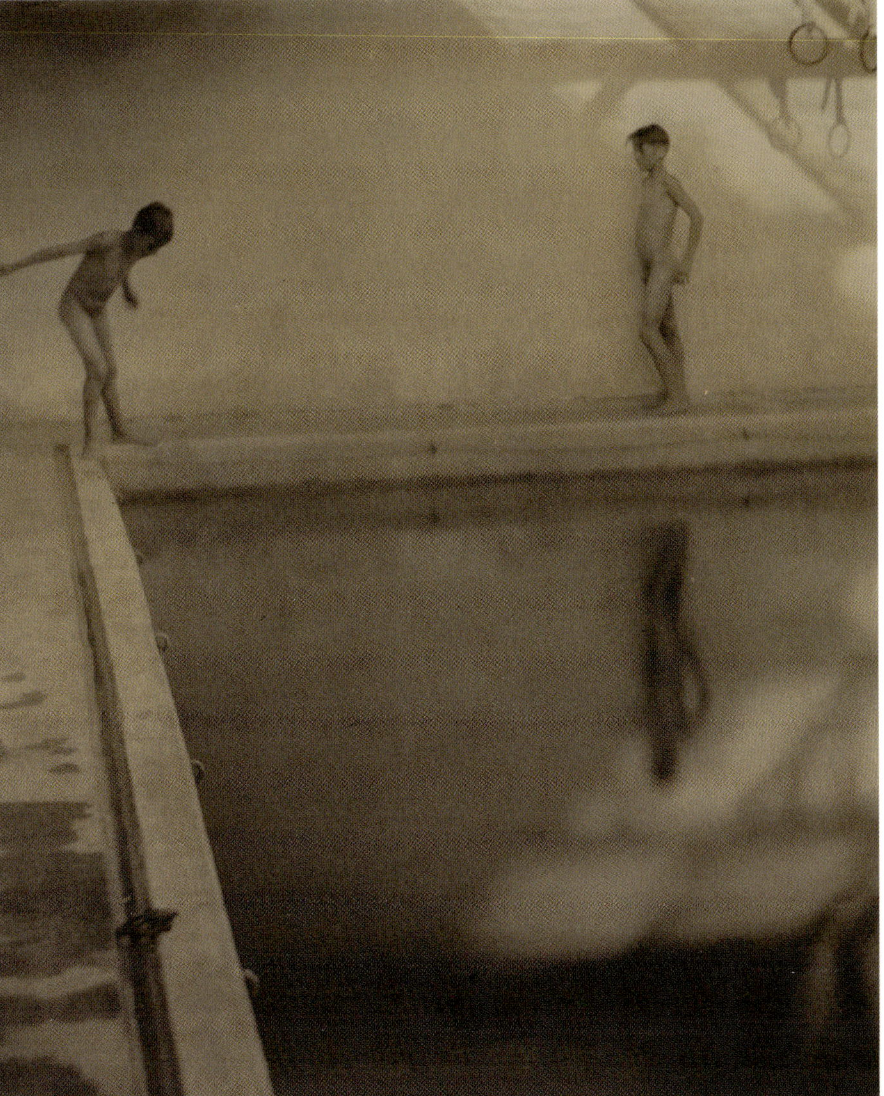

semi-tropical oasis, a mythical "Island on the Land," overflowing with nature's bounty.[22] With California's entry into the Union in 1850 and the arrival of the first transcontinental railroad in Los Angeles less than a generation later, thousands flocked to seize this Promised Land. The building boom of the 1880s, the parallel rise of the oil and motion-picture industries in the early 1900s, and the completion of Mulholland's aqueduct cemented Los Angeles's reputation as a virtual lotus land of opportunity.

Southern California's promoters were equally quick to exploit new scientific claims that warm, dry weather benefited health, and multitudes came to harness the restorative powers of sunshine.[23] Health seekers included the flamboyant Charles Fletcher Lummis, a "malarial journalist from Chillicothe, Ohio," who arrived in Los Angeles in 1884—on foot.[24] Together with Harrison Gray Otis, the mercurial publisher of the *Los Angeles Times*, he became one of the titans of the city's booster era. Their bold and imaginative project required, as Mike Davis has noted, "the continuous interaction of myth-making and literary invention with the crude promotion of land values and health cures."[25] When Lummis became editor of the illustrated monthly *Land of Sunshine* in 1895, he used both pen and camera to articulate his interest in physical culture and the American West. For him, children were the true flowers of the Southland, stunning "products" of the region, much like its giant fruits and vegetables.[26] "It is climate," he wrote, "which turns out on one side of the continent consumptives and nervous-exhaustion-victims, and children runted by imprisonment in poison air for four months at a time; and on the other side health and joy of life and children like infant gods."[27] To prove his point, he published pictures of vigorous youngsters frolicking in the buff amid lush vegetation with such captions as "Don't Need Much Clothes Here" and "Out-Doors in January" to underscore the benefits that climate had wrought (fig. 2). "Nowhere else in the world do English-speaking children average so high in physique as California," he claimed in 1899. "And while it is too early in evolution to state the case as flatfootedly with regard to mentality, all logic tends to show that the same advantages will accrue."[28]

Other boosters echoed Lummis's racial metaphysics, attesting to the power of sunshine to galvanize Anglo-Saxon energies.[29] Often, they summoned photography to support their claims. Don Milton's *Cyclists in Sunset Park* from the early 1920s (fig. 4) and *Hikers Near Alpine Tavern, Mt. Lowe* from 1932 by an unknown photographer working for the Pacific Electric Railway Company (fig. 5) glorify the beauty and vigor of young Californians. They appear fresh-faced and smiling as they bask in the Southland's Mediterranean climate. In quieter niches of photographic expression, Edward Weston captured two of his sons by an indoor pool, focusing his lens on their graceful athleticism (fig. 3). Responding to the ambient light and exotic drama of early Hollywood films, he and other art photographers, such as Ernest M. Pratt (see p. 213), Marjorie Bentley (see p. 212), and William Mortenson, frequently echoed Los Angeles's booster language, bolstered by the Pictorialist vision then holding sway.[30]

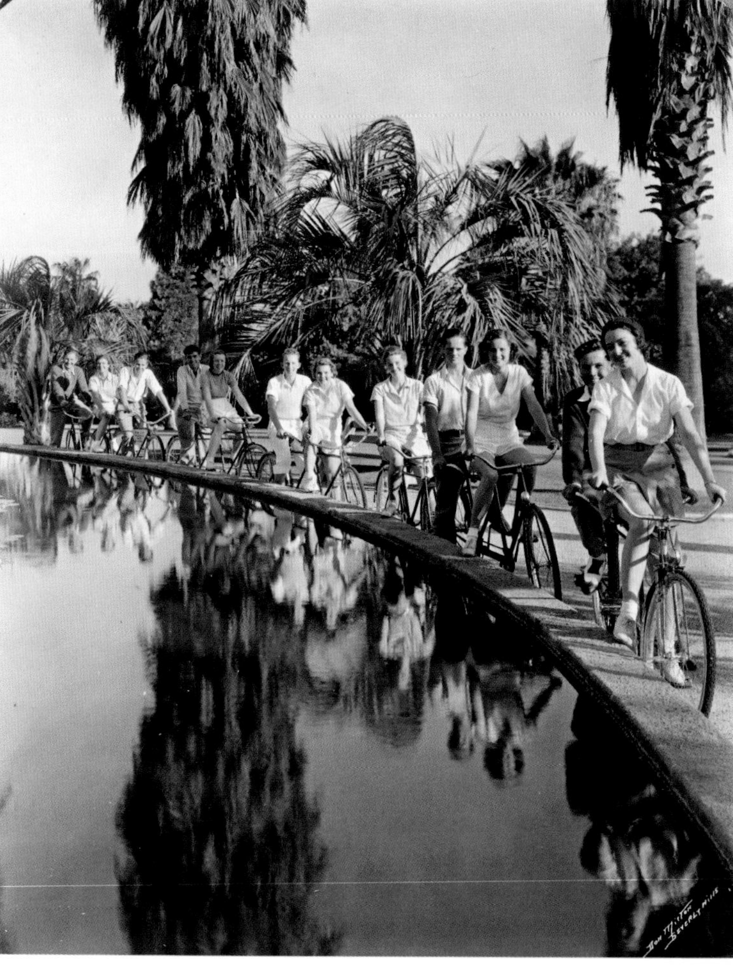

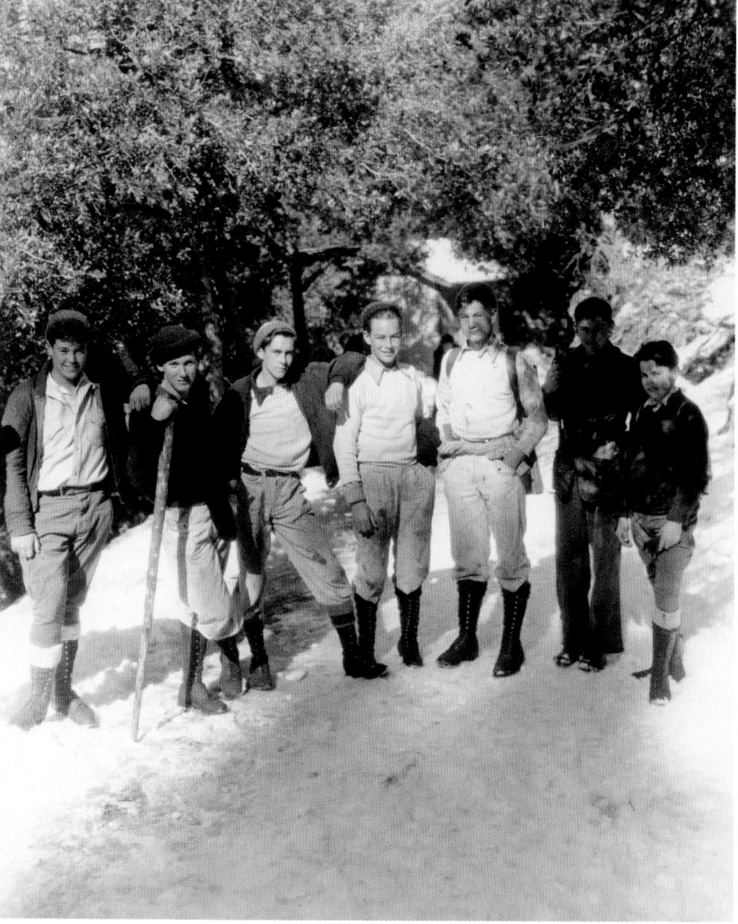

The celebration of Californian youth persisted well into the 1950s and 1960s, when *Cosmopolitan* magazine proclaimed that "in California the boys and girls grow bigger and more beautiful. They are longer of leg, deeper of chest, better muscled than other American youngsters. Even their feet are bigger."[31] California's young women, immortalized in such motion pictures as *Gidget* and the *Beach Party* series, are the "prettiest, biggest, lithest, tannest, most luscious girls this side of the international date line."[32] Even Richard Avedon, photographing on the beach in Santa Monica in 1963, succumbed to the infectious trope of the Californian *Übermensch*, depicting a radiant young boy perched high on his father's outstretched hand (fig. 6). Suffused in hazy evening twilight, the youngster appears as an infant idol, the happy avatar of a new civilization.

The twentieth century, with its extraordinary contradictions and complexities, rendered the Los Angeles booster project at once trite and persuasive. On the one hand, the city was, in the words of social critic Morrow Mayo, a commodity, "something to be advertised and sold to the people of the United States like automobiles, cigarettes, and mouth wash."[33] On the other, it was a real place, home to increasing multitudes, who embraced an imagery created to convince them of the region's glorious future. By the 1920s, health and physical culture had become inextricably linked to the promotion of Southern California. The economic boom of that decade, the rapid modernization of broad sectors of American society, a pervasive consumer culture, new fashions and sexual mores, and the rise of the entertainment industry—all focused on the body as the site of leisure and consumption.[34] The body was increasingly seen as an "instrument of pleasure" whose value was determined by how closely it matched the idealized images of beauty and youth romulgated by the new mass media.[35] As hemlines rose and bathing suits shrank, bodies became ever more public, satisfying the voyeuristic demands of an era intoxicated with modernity and the politics of display. Such bodies found a luxuriant playground in the balmy, sun-drenched terrain of Southern California, where beaches and outdoor activities beckoned year round. In an article from 1936 in *Westways*, one of the region's premier booster magazines, Los Angeles journalist Farnsworth Crowder remarked:

> The influence of the sun, land, and climate on physical growth, on the incidence of maturity, on the color of the skin, on the rate of metabolism, on the resistance to disease and senility, on the phenomena of sex and sexual periodicity—these things would serve, if known, to emphasize the fact that the body, its appearance, its functions and senses is *central* to California life and psychology. . . . There is an inevitable, intrinsic sub-tropical drive, backed by the authority of the land itself, physiologically to 'go native.'[36]

Naturally, Hollywood, this powerful fantasy industry that had settled in Los Angeles in the early 1900s, capitalized on these cultural propensities. It entered into a symbiotic relationship with the region, churning out

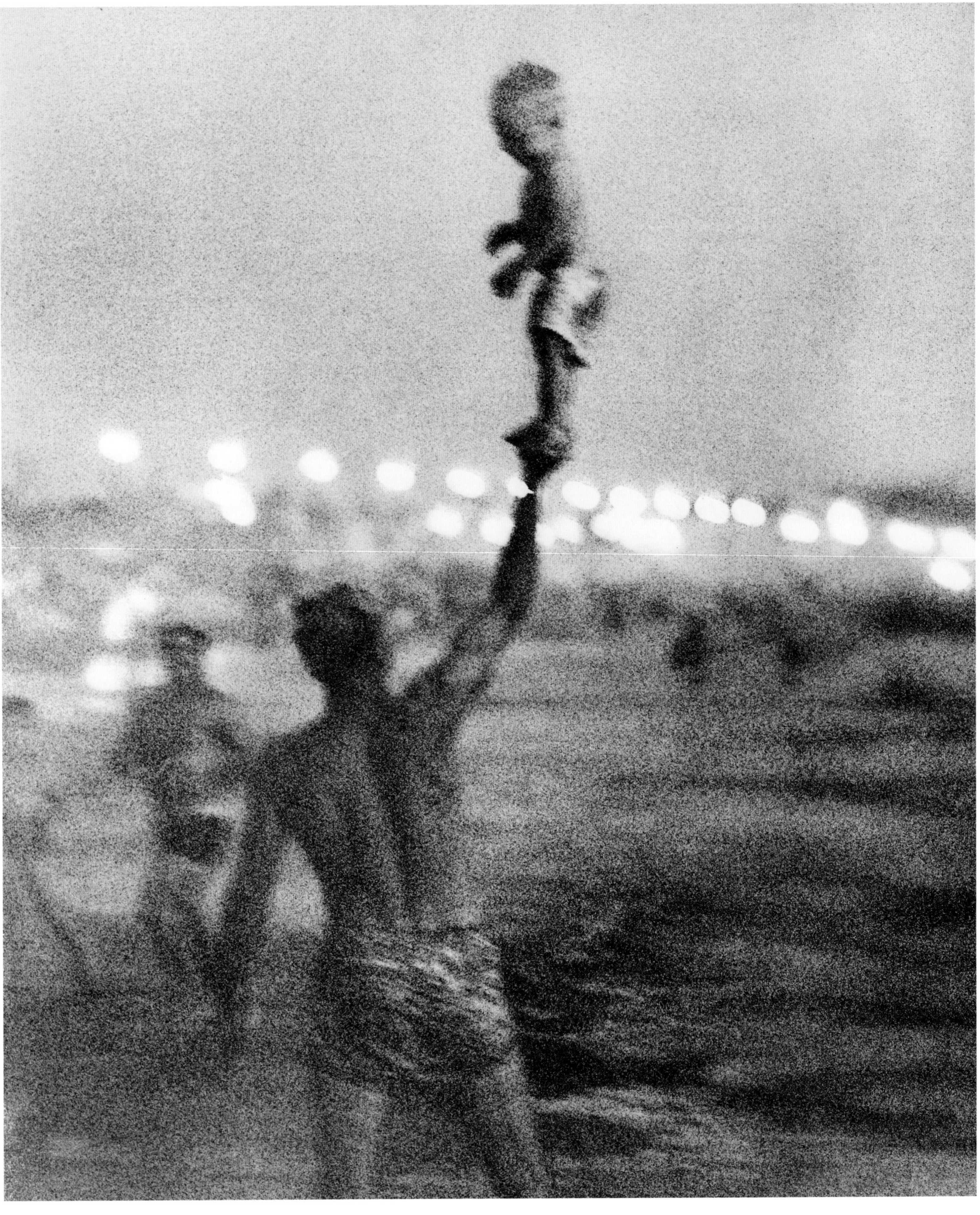

Fig. 6
Richard Avedon
Santa Monica Beach #4,
September 30, 1963, Santa
Monica, California, 1963

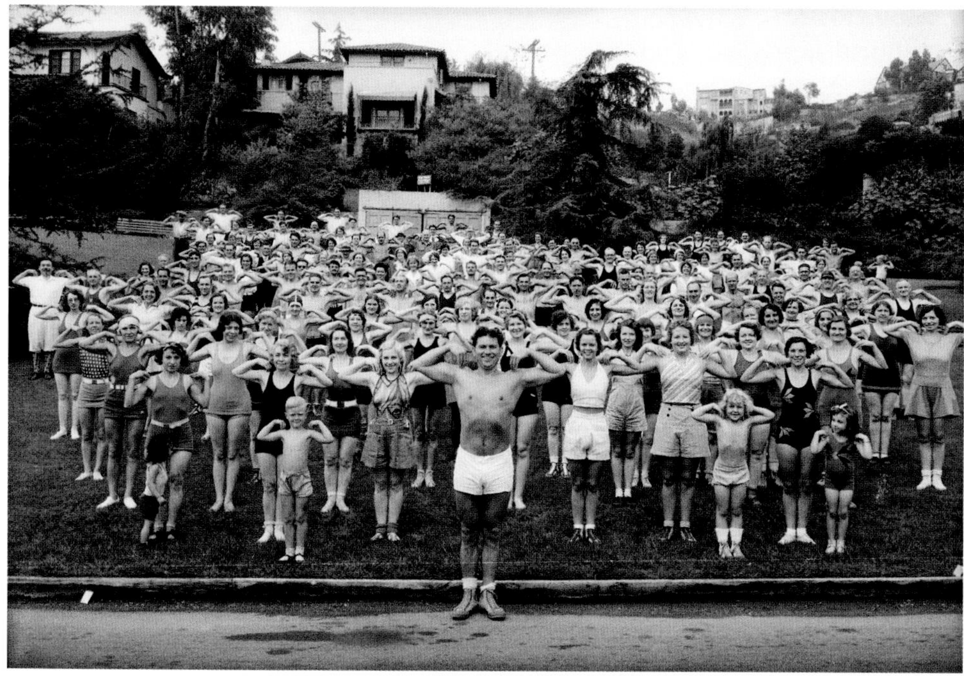

images that intensified and spread Los Angeles's lust-driven lifestyle. Early Hollywood films titillated their audience with salacious tales of "neckers, petters, white kisses, red kisses, pleasure-mad daughters, [and] sensation-craving mothers."[37] Others promised "brilliant men, beautiful jazz babies, champagne baths, midnight revels, petting parties in the purple dawn, all ending in one terrific smashing climax that makes you gasp."[38] Then, as now, sex sold movies, and nowhere was this more evident than in Los Angeles. The landscape was awash with signs of Hollywood's ubiquitous presence, from sprawling studios and fantastical architecture to outsized billboards hawking everything from the latest exercise machines to diet pills. In 1929, one writer bemoaned that establishments catering to the insatiable demands of beauty-seekers had literally overrun the city:

> Beauty farms, rejuvenation palaces and plastic surgery emporiums . . . have sprung up around the movie center like mushrooms in a shady glen. . . . They vary in type from the almost secrecy-guarded clinic-farms in outlying suburbs . . . to the elaborate mansions along Wilshire Boulevard that advertise youth of face and form with electric-lighted billboards of semi-nude women.[39]

Beauty had become a major Los Angeles industry, proclaiming its libertine lifestyle and sun-kissed good looks. Photographers of all persuasions dazzled viewers with images centered on beauty, youth, and movie-land glamour.[40] In the 1930s and 1940s, Hollywood photographer George Hurrell helped shape the image of practically every major screen star of the day, manipulating their image to perfection. His portrait of Carole Lombard (see p. 149) shows the actor in dramatic lighting that brilliantly echoes the dazzling Los Angeles sunlight outside. Louise Dahl-Wolfe, one of the era's leading fashion photographers, worked in an equally glamorous vein, pioneering fashion shoots in natural daylight. From the 1930s to the 1960s, she took pictures of Hollywood luminaries for *Harper's* and *Vogue*, including a portrait from 1938 of Dolores del Rio luxuriating in the late-afternoon sun (see p. 147). Dahl-Wolfe captured the actor in California's unique sparkling light, which writer Don Waldie described as "clear as stone-dry champagne after a full day of rain." "Everything in this light is somehow simultaneously particularized and idealized," he continued, "and that's the light that breaks hearts in L.A."[41] In her pressed-cotton pantsuit, flip-flops, and heavy gold bracelet, Del Rio is the very embodiment of Los Angeles's relaxed, elegant style.

Hollywood photography changed over the years. With the arrival of *Life* magazine in 1936 and the death of the studio system, fashion greats including Irving Penn, Richard Avedon, and Herb Ritts elaborated upon Dahl-Wolfe's "environmental" style. Ritts's portraits of models Tony Ward (see p. 32) and Tatjana Patitz (see p. 33) were shot in the late 1980s, on the roof of the photographer's Hollywood studio. The models pose against a stark white background, their chiseled, tanned physiques glistening with oil and tiny droplets of water. Tony is shot from slightly below, making him appear larger than life, long-limbed and beautiful, like an ancient Athenian. Tatjana faces the viewer, her head thrown back in sultry adoration of the sun. "Coming from California and growing up where I did, I've always had a fondness for and innate sensitivity to light, texture, and warmth," Ritts said in an interview in 2000. "I abstract it in my photographs: I like large planes and spaces, areas of texture and light, like deserts or oceans or monumental places."[42]

Other artists took a subtler, if no less sensuous, approach, honing in on the young screen stars' magnetic allure and easy-going physicality. William Claxton's portrait of 1955 of jazz icon Chet Baker and his wife Halima (see p. 175) is a case in point. Like many photographers before and after him, Claxton was enamored of the lush Southern California landscape, posing his subjects outdoors, on the beach or in their open convertibles.[43] Here, Chet and Halima perch on a windowsill in an empty Redondo Beach home. Lit from behind by a stream of hazy daylight, the couple radiate an affectionate intimacy that belies Baker's descent into alcohol and drug abuse less than a year later. Claxton highlights the trumpeter's passions by placing his instrument in the center of the composition. A jazzman's horn, Claxton said, is like "an extra appendage"—a humorous metaphor that only enhances the erotic appeal of this picture.[44]

Such celebrity photographers as Claxton, Dahl-Wolfe, and Ritts impressed upon the American public the importance of "looking good." This was especially true in Los Angeles, where sprawling beaches and "endless summers" mandated year-round public display. As Farnsworth Crowder pointed out, "sun-bathing, nudity, bare heads, open-neck shirts are not imposed by cranks; they are *dictated* by the sun. Health consciousness is extreme and . . . the climate so entirely congenial to the American athletics mania that sports flourish and 'champions' are a major product."[45] "Dick" Whittington's image of fitness guru Paul Bragg, *Paul Bragg and Hikers in Hollywood Hills*, from around 1930 (fig. 7) and Julius Shulman's *Sunday Trekkers on Mount Hollywood* from 1933 (fig. 8) provide ample evidence that outdoor athleticism was "in." Surfing had been introduced to the Southland in 1907, and early imitators of the sport braved the waves soon after (fig. 9), spawning an entire subculture that became virtually synonymous with Southern California.[46] "Bathing Beauty" spectaculars, such as the one captured by photographer Miles Weaver in 1920 (see pp. 158–59), provided titillating waterfront entertainment.[47] In later years, Hollywood stuntmen, wrestlers, weightlifters, high-school gymnasts, and members of the downtown Los Angeles Athletic Club showed off their skills at Santa Monica's famed Muscle Beach.[48]

Founded by amateur athletes after the 1932 Olympics in Los Angeles, Muscle Beach reached the height of its international renown in the boom years that followed the Second World War, when Los Angeles photographer Max Yavno took his famous image of acrobats and bikini-clad onlookers (see p. 157). Sensational feats, a vaudeville atmosphere, and near-naked crowds made Muscle Beach a mythic Los Angeles

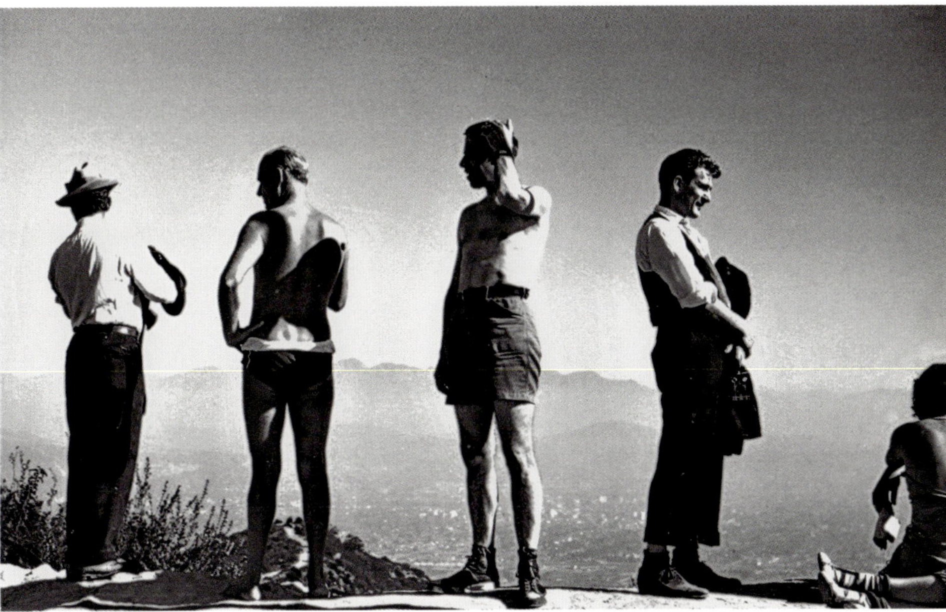

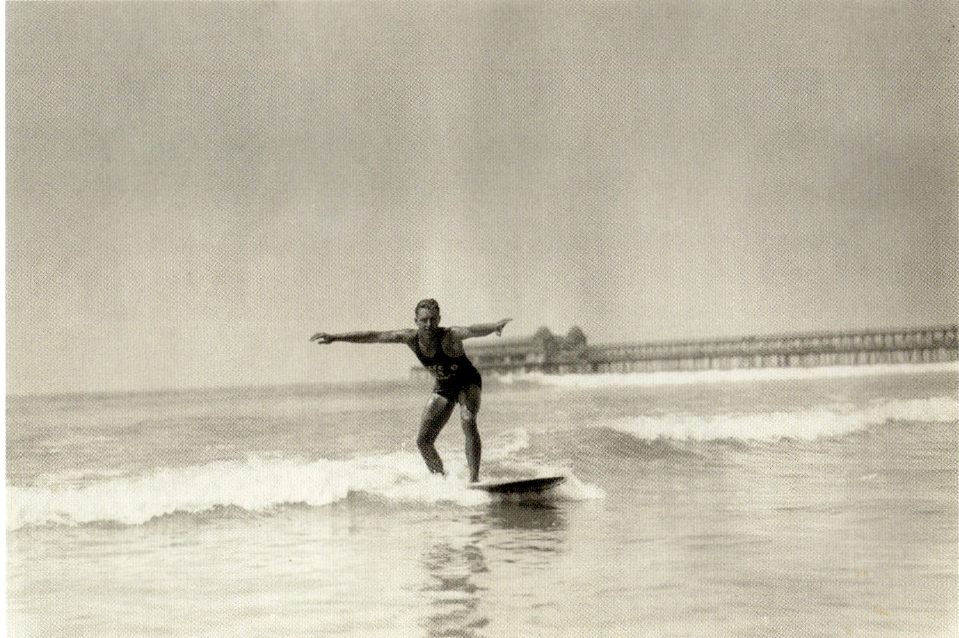

attraction. Here, the water's edge became "the domain of the insouciant, pleasure-seeking amphibian," as historian Thomas A.P. van Leeuwen put it—the archetypal model of modern recreation as a happy, sexualized return to a primitive existence.[49] Even Marilyn Monroe could not escape the primal lure of the sporting life, pumping iron for Philippe Halsman's lens in a pair of Levis and a skimpy terry-cloth bra (see p. 151). Others preferred to pose poolside—epitomes of Van Leeuwen's "aquatic ape," the region's water-borne pleasure-hunters (see p. 148).[50]

Outdoor swimming pools were another lust-inspiring Los Angeles innovation, created as ostentatious leisure spaces for the rich and famous.[51] In 1920, actors Mary Pickford and Douglas Fairbanks were the first to add a pool to their sprawling Beverly Hills mansion. Measuring 100 ft (30 m) long and 50 ft (15 m) wide, it was shaped like a banana, with sand on one side and lush lawn on the other.[52] Outdoor pools soon became vaunted symbols of Southern California's enchanted lifestyle, celebrated in photographs by Julius Shulman (see p. 29), Anthony Friedkin, and many others. Greater Los Angeles has the largest concentration of private swimming pools in the world[53]—a fact that was not lost on British artist David Hockney when he first came to the city in 1970:

> I came [to Los Angeles] because I thought it would be very sexy. . . . And as I flew over San Bernardino and looked down—and saw the swimming pools and the houses and everything and the sun, I was more thrilled than I've ever been arriving at any other city, including New York. . . . California in my mind was a sunny land of movie studios and beautiful semi-naked people. . . . It was only when I went to live in Los Angeles . . . that I realized that my picture was quite close to life.[54]

Inspired by the plethora of Los Angeles fitness magazines, such as Bernard McFadden's *Physical Culture* and Robert Mizer's infamous *Physique Pictorial* (see p. 163), Hockney expressed his erotic attraction to the city in photographs of swimmers submerged in glittering pool waters, showcasing both gay desire and domesticity.[55]

Other artists summoned Southern California's carnal imagery too, if only slyly to subvert it. Robert Heinecken's witty installation *Lingerie for a Feminist Sun Tan #5* from 1973 radically challenges views of both the female body and feminist politics. Jerry McMillan's delightful photo-sculpture *Five Boxes* of 1965–67 (see pp. 22–23) arrays nude bodies as a softly undulating panorama, bringing home the point that in Los Angeles, sexually charged physicality is never far from the land. In fact, the city itself has been envisioned as a body seductively sprawled out and ready for the taking. "Play with that fancy," writer David Thomson would later exhort his readers, as he imagined Mulholland Drive as a drowsy, sex-craved Marilyn Monroe:

> Her toes twitch at the Hollywood freeway. . . . From the knob of her ankle you can look down on the Hollywood bowl. . . . As the legs

become thighs, Mulholland enters its richest stretch, full of designer security systems for houses hiding from the road. . . . At the most precious, privileged part of the body, where the thighs widen and foliage starts, you can find the secret mansion of Warren Beatty, high on its own escarpment, guarded by trees and Bauhaus bars.[56]

Here, in the land's erogenous zone, where the "night goes MTV in black fur and diamond lights," Los Angeles's lustful corporeality reaches its final climax. Mulholland Drive, this most spectacular of all Los Angeles highways, then languidly winds its way down to the Pacific, where it exhausts itself in the "platinum surf [that is] like Marilyn's hair in her last pictures."[57]

Lust denied

"Whatever California was, good or bad, it was charged with human hope," wrote historian Kevin Starr. "It was linked imaginatively with the most compelling of all American myths, the pursuit of happiness."[58] When that promise went unfulfilled, and Los Angeles turned into the most brutal of American "dream dumps," despair and bitterness ensued. As thousands streamed into the city looking for health and good fortune, Edenic descriptions of Los Angeles inevitably clashed with reality. In 1939, novelist John Fante brilliantly evoked the dreary fate that awaited the city's nameless, luckless multitudes:

> You'll eat hamburger year after year and live in dusty, vermin-infested apartments and hotels, but every morning you'll see the mighty sun, the eternal blue of the sky, and the streets will be full of sleek women you will never possess, and the hot semi-tropical nights will reek of romance you'll never have, but you'll be in paradise, boys, in the land of sunshine.[59]

Writer Nathanael West called Los Angeles's anonymous, disenchanted masses "The Cheated"—the original title of his apocalyptic novel of 1939, *The Day of the Locust*: "They realize they've been tricked and burn with resentment. . . . The sun is a joke. Oranges can't titillate their jaded palates. . . . They have slaved and saved for nothing."[60] As boosters and Babbitts extolled the city's halcyon future, poverty, unemployment, and worker unrest presented darker realities. The deadly bombing of the *Los Angeles Times* offices in 1910 (see p. 188) offers a glimpse into the city's violent labor history, beset by low wages, bitter strikes, and a savage insistence on anti-union policies (see p. 192). Racial antagonism, immortalized by such events as the Sleepy Lagoon case of 1942, the Zoot Suit "riots" of the following year, the forced relocation of thousands of Japanese Americans during the Second World War, and the Watts uprising of 1965, revealed troubling currents beneath the city's self-assured claims of harmony and patriotism. Such environmental disasters as the collapse of the St. Francis Dam in 1928 (fig. 11), the devastating Long Beach earthquake of 1933 (see p. 189), perennial wildfires, droughts, and floods further undermined the Elysian dream. Even so, many of the most influential photographers of the day depicted little or nothing of this dark metropolitan underbelly, supporting instead the city's vision of itself as the place where industrial production fed the good life and *vice versa*.

For the city's foremost debunkers—Louis Adamic, Carey McWilliams, Morrow Mayo, H.L. Mencken, and, later, Mike Davis—the real Los Angeles was unlike anything its boosters had promised. In their writing, the city emerged as the great "Hellhole of the West"—a bleak, hallucinatory terrain teetering on the brink of disaster.[61] Playing on the city's corporeal metaphors, Mayo wrote: "Here is an artificial city which has been pumped up under forced drought, inflated like a balloon, stuffed with rural humanity like a goose with corn, . . . endeavoring to eat up this too rapid avalanche of anthropoids, the sunshine metropolis heaves and strains, sweats and becomes pop-eyed, like a young boa constrictor trying to swallow a goat."[62] For Louis Adamic, the City of Angels was simply "a *bad* place—full of old, dying people, who were born old of tired pioneer parents, victims of America—full of curious wild and poisonous growth . . . a jungle."[63] In Adamic's eyes, Los Angeles's distended body slowly choked on its ever-increasing multitudes, many of whom never made it in the land of sunshine. These are the unfortunate, deracinated masses of West's fiction: the immigrants, bit players, health nuts, and beauty queens who bought into pubescent fantasies nurtured by boosters and Hollywood and came up short. For them, Los Angeles was the end of the road, a place where hope and possibility, desire and allure, dramatically turned and devoured one another.

From the very beginning, Los Angeles had been a city of newcomers, a place of fresh starts, last hopes, and second chances. Among the millions of settlers who came to Los Angeles during the real estate booms of the 1880s, 1920s, and post-Second World War years—from the East, the South, the Midwest, and everywhere in between—were, of course, health-seekers lured west by relentless advertising, cheap train fares, and the promise of miraculous cures. "Health is a big thing in Los Angeles," wrote Adamic, the inveterate critic of Los Angeles life in the 1920s:

> Most of the people come here to be sun-kissed and made well, and so healing is one of the big industries in town. Besides thousands of more or less regular doctors, there are in Los Angeles no end of chiropractors, osteopaths, 'drugless physicians,' faith-healers . . . psychoanalysts, hypnotists, mesmerists, the glow-of-life-mystics, astro-therapists, miracle men and women—in short, quacks and charlatans of all descriptions. . . . In Los Angeles health is the leading topic of conversation.[64]

Los Angeles was soon home to a disproportionately high number of invalids, suffering from asthma, rheumatism, tuberculosis (TB), and myriad other diseases. They were housed and cared for in specially built clinics, such as Monrovia's renowned Pottenger Sanatorium, which

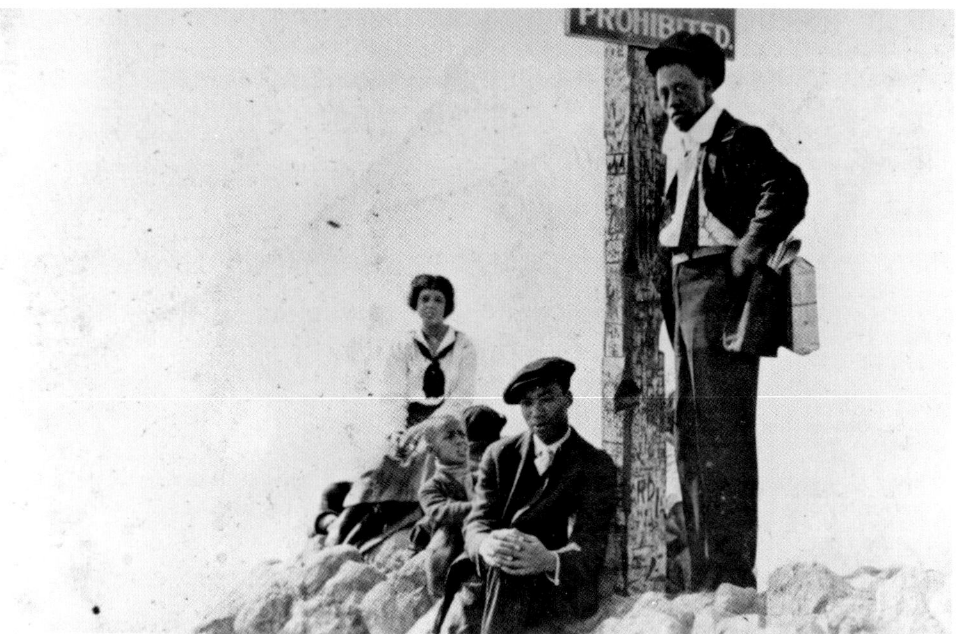

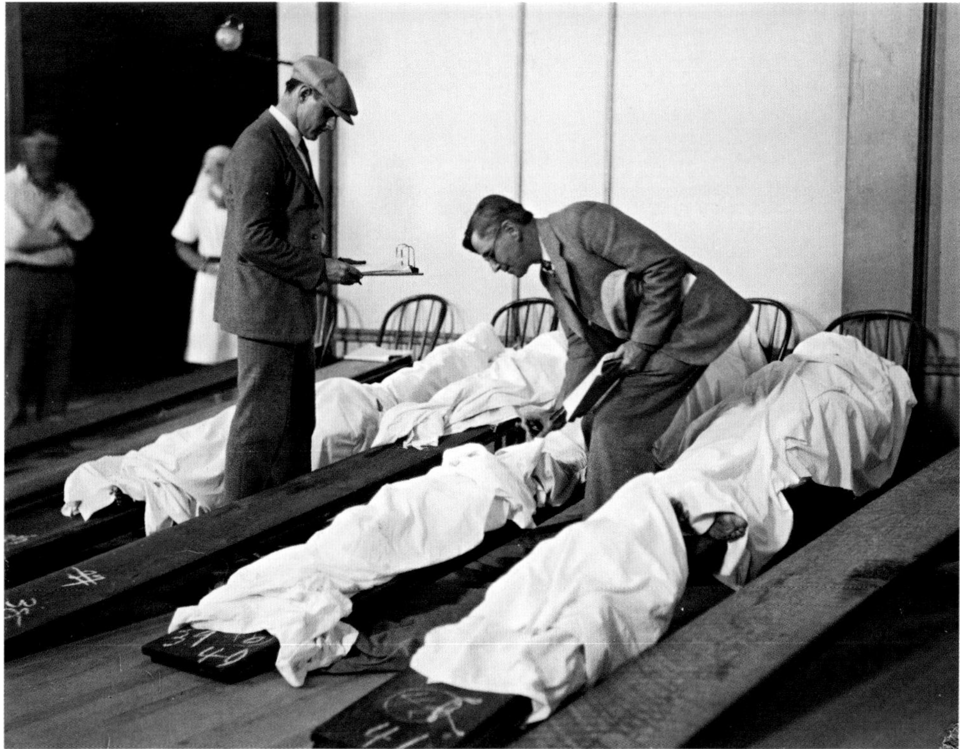

treated consumptives with an optimistic mixture of sunshine, exercise, and fresh air.[65] Initially, civic leaders welcomed the sick and infirm, many of them wealthy and eager to invest in local business and real estate.[66] But, as historian Emily Abel has concluded, official sentiment soon turned hostile:

> The flip side of exalting good health was denigrating those who did *not* get well. Once recovery became the only permissible public outcome, sufferers increasingly met suspicion. . . . Those with advanced disease drew particularly fierce condemnation because they represented everything boosters had promised migrants they could avoid—failure, subjection to fate, deterioration, and premature death.[67]

Sufferers of TB met with particular resentment, especially if they were poor. Mexicans, the largest ethnic minority in Los Angeles since the mid-1920s, were most affected. Their high rate of infection, due to poor housing and sanitary conditions in the *barrios*, was frequently construed as racial inferiority.[68] In the 1930s, authorities "solved" the problem by either deporting or repatriating tubercular Mexicans, effectively excluding them from the vaunted culture they promoted to white Anglo-Saxons.

Minorities in general fared poorly in the Southland, hampered by prejudice and virulent racial bigotry. By the 1870s, some four thousand Chinese lived in Los Angeles, working on the fringes of society, as C.C. Pierce's rare photograph of 1898, *Chinese Field Hands*, vividly shows (see p. 135).[69] A.C. Vroman's *Men at Mission San Fernando* of the 1890s (see p. 130), Pierce's *Harvesting Grain on Van Nuys Lankershim Ranch* (see p. 131) of around 1905, and his undated picture *Making Adobe Brick at Casa Verdugo* confirm that Mexicans rarely did better. "It must be recognized," one city official declared in 1924, "that the Mexican whom we find in Los Angeles is, as a class, of relatively low mentality; he is probably best fitted for work demanding ability of an inferior grade."[70] Accordingly, Mexican labor was predominantly menial, even while boosters extolled the city's halcyon Spanish past.[71]

African Americans arrived in the city as early as the late 1700s. Racial covenants and segregation laws soon drew near-impermeable residential boundaries, prohibiting blacks from living west of Slauson Avenue and restricting minority access to both the beach and public pools. During the 1920s, when an exultant white body culture first peaked in Los Angeles and beach communities flourished, the only place African Americans could set foot on the sand were, briefly, Bruce's Beach in the South Bay and the "Inkwell," a stretch of beach 200 ft (61 m) long between Ocean Park and Pico boulevards in Santa Monica (fig. 10).[72] In an undesirable area far from the glittering amusement district of the Pier, the Inkwell was a haven for black beach-goers. It was here that the first black surfer, Nick Gabaldon, mastered the art of wave-riding, awing his all-black audience.[73] Racial segregation on Los Angeles's beaches officially ended in 1927, and generally disappeared within a decade. However, when the Hollywood

Negro Ballet rehearsed on the sprawling white sands of Laguna Beach in 1953, they inevitably evoked a disquieting past. In an exhilarating picture by an unknown photographer, the troupe, led by principal dancer Graham Johnson, triumphantly executes a *grand jeté*, one of the most spectacular movements of classical ballet (fig. 12).[74]

"Los Angeles has always been a city of dreams, of flesh, and bone," artist-historian Ken Gonzalez-Day has observed, suggesting that racial bodies have been among the region's most problematic and contested terrains.[75] Such images as Max Yavno's *Street Talk* and *Two Women* of 1946 (see pp. 166, 167) and Garry Winogrand's iconic *Los Angeles* of 1964 (see pp. 200–201) clearly betray their subjects' outsider status, both in dress and in the stereotypes that drive their depiction. Yavno's photographs capture Mexican youngsters in zoot suits, an exaggerated fashion that had provoked a bloody confrontation with authorities just three years earlier. These are *pachucos*, urban rebels who flaunt their alienation from mainstream society through provocative clothing and a distinctive dialect called *caló*. According to Mexican novelist Octavio Paz, the *pachuco* wears his marginality like an ulcer on his body—"a wound that is also grotesque, capricious, barbaric adornment. A wound that laughs at itself and decks itself out for the hunt."[76] The *pachuco* is the prey of society, relishing his outrageous appearance as a sign of his "otherness"—a sentiment clearly expressed in Yavno's pictures. Taken eighteen years later, Garry Winogrand's image of a Latino man in his open convertible reinforces deep racial stereotypes, raising more troubling questions. The man's bandaged nose and furtive glance at his female companion present him as potentially dangerous, suggesting he is less a good-natured joyrider than a menace to white society.

Such biased representations, rampant in the media even today, provided ample fodder for later image-makers. Harry Gamboa, Jr.'s photographic series *Chicano Male Unbonded* (see pp. 202–203) deliberately plays on such racial interpretations, defying viewers' expectations and uncovering their deeply rooted prejudices. In Gamboa's work, and in the powerful documentary imagery of Gusmano Cesaretti (see pp. 204, 205), bodies are markers of social identities that articulate a person's relationship to the dominant culture. Los Angeles photographer Willie Middlebrook uses his own body to convey profound and often painful messages. His multi-media installation *In His "Own" Image* (see p. 197), created after the bloody riots in Los Angeles in 1992, is a physiognomic record of his response to the fateful events. Like a martyr in the original sense of the word, he "bears witness" to the wounds he has suffered, allowing the viewer to participate, at least temporarily, in his experience of "blackness." The body as signifier of psychic pain is also the theme of Catherine Opie's self-portrait of 1993 (fig. 13), an image rich in symbolism and autobiographical detail. Posed against a lush, dark-green fabric, the artist displays a child-like drawing of lesbian domesticity stippled into her back. Her reddened skin oozes rivulets of blood, revealing that the wounds are real and recent, like a ritual cutting.

Fig. 12
Unknown
*Members of the Hollywood
Negro Ballet in a Publicity
Photograph for Ebony
Magazine*, November 1953

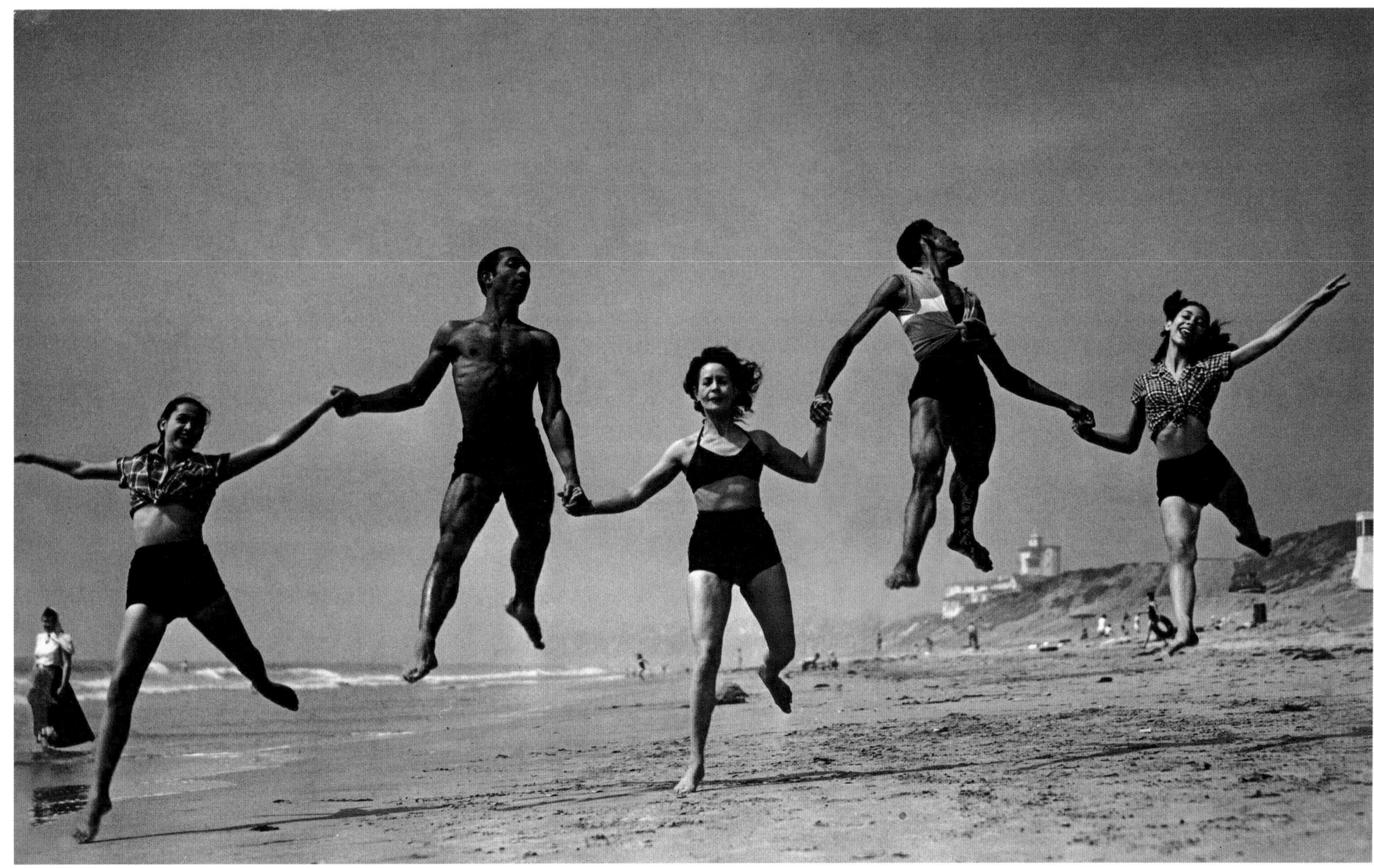

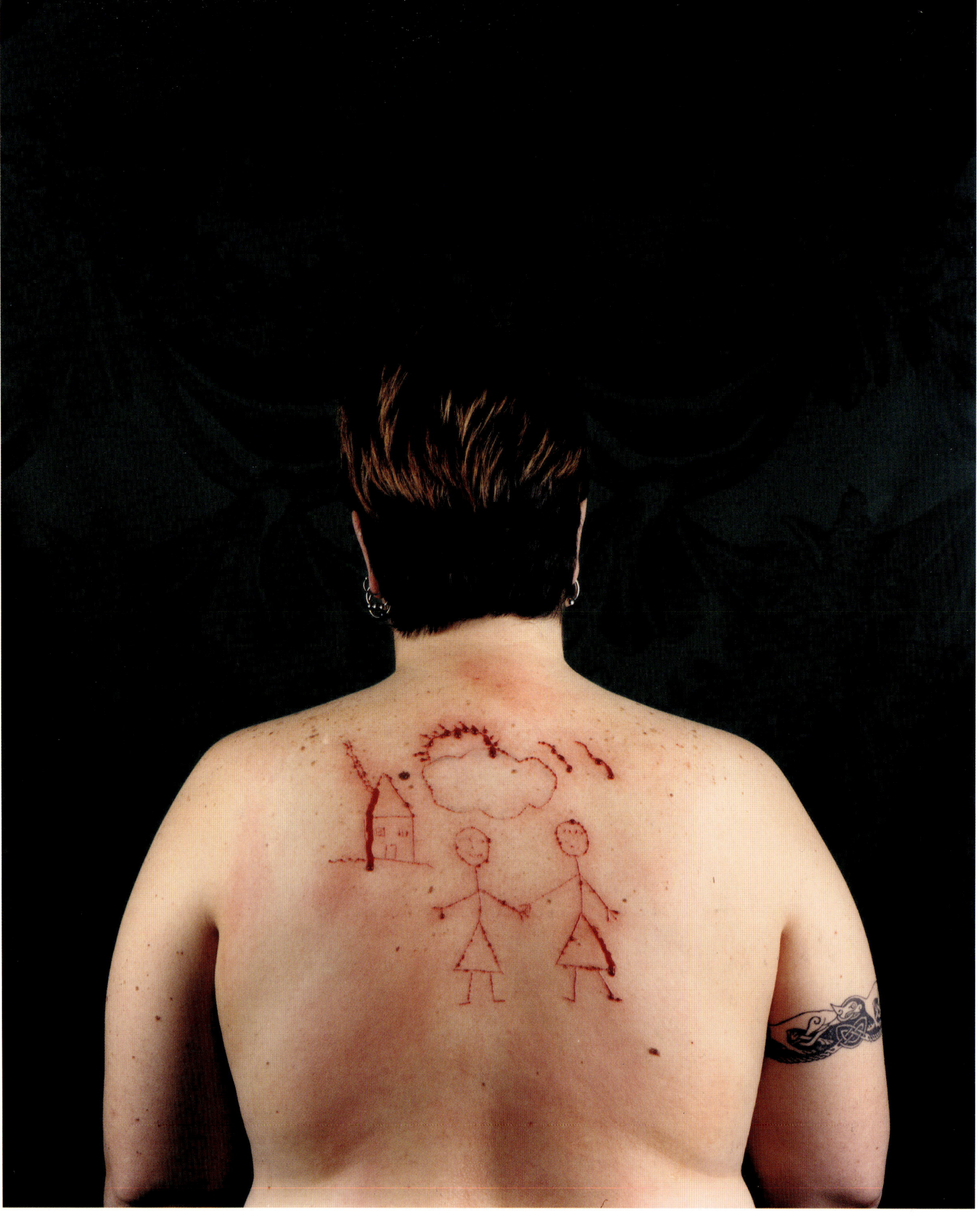

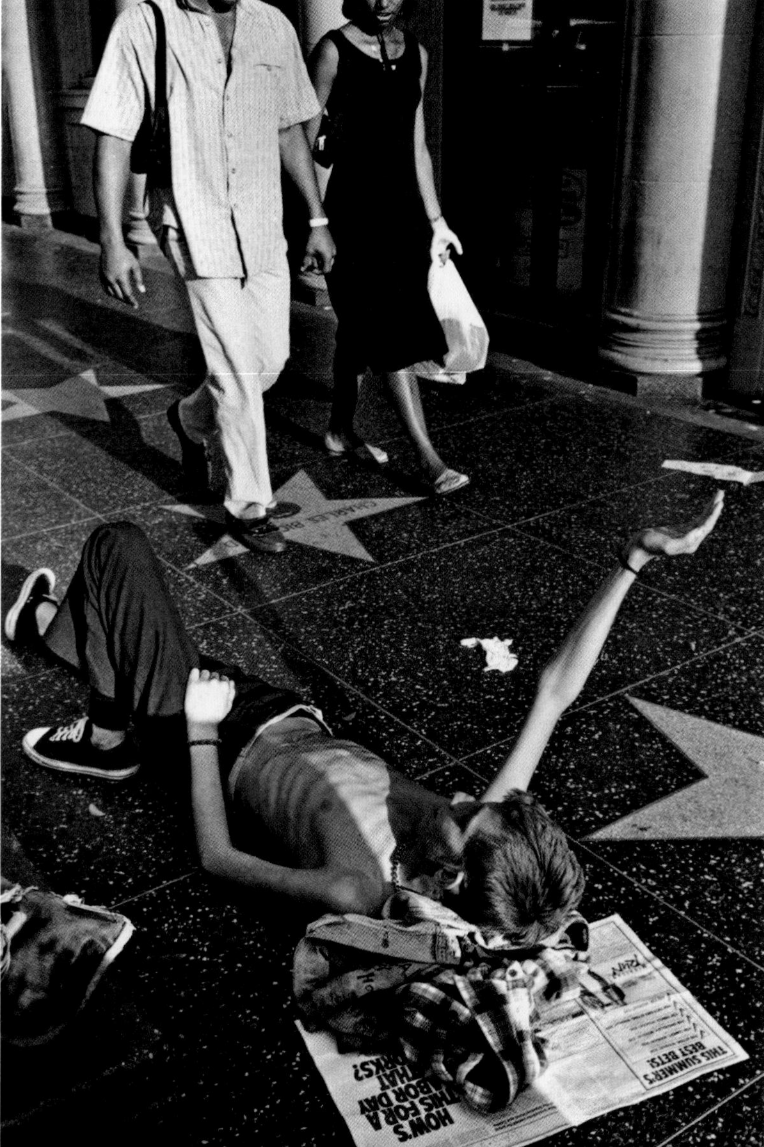

Fig. 14
Jim Goldberg
Dave Panhandling, Hollywood,
1988

Wounds of another kind are evident in photographs of homelessness in Los Angeles, with bodies ravaged by neglect, abuse, malnutrition, and mental illness. Mary Ellen Mark's heart-wrenching photograph of the Damm family from 1987 (see p. 105), published in *Life* magazine the same year, shows them in their car outside a North Hollywood shelter for the homeless.[77] The embrace of the parents and the girl's tender gesture toward her little brother only add to the utter bleakness of the scene. In Jim Goldberg's photograph of 1989 of a homeless teen peddling his wares on Hollywood Boulevard, the dream and hopelessness of Los Angeles come agonizingly face to face (fig. 14).[78] Part of a multi-year documentation of America's street kids, the image recalls an earlier picture by Garry Winogrand of a wheelchair-bound veteran on Hollywood's Walk of Fame (see p. 122). Here, the unfulfilled promise of Los Angeles collides with the quintessential evocation of Hollywood glamour, dramatically undercutting images of what Los Angeles was supposed to be. German artist Karin Apollonia Müller created *Power Lines* in 1997 (see p. 90), its title suggesting imperial politics as both cause and foundation of homelessness in America. Only at second glance does one discover the body in this dreary industrial wilderness, sprawled in the middle of nowhere, partially covered by an orange tarpaulin. In Anthony Hernandez's series *Landscapes for the Homeless* from 1990 (see p. 93), the destitute body has disappeared altogether. It is as if the landscape has swallowed the man, leaving only his jacket, covered with pollen and lint, to account for his erstwhile presence.

"LA is the loneliest and most brutal of American cities," Jack Kerouac wrote from Los Angeles in 1947. "The beatest characters swarmed on the sidewalks—all of it under those soft California stars that are lost in the brown halo of the huge desert encampment LA really is."[79] The continuous influx of down-and-out migrants and desperados of every variety ensured that corruption, organized crime, and crackpot schemes thrived. Lust, greed, vengeance, and, ultimately, death are themes that rivet Los Angeles's audiences, fed on sensational Hollywood scandals and unsolved murder mysteries, such as the infamous Black Dahlia and Winnie Judd murder cases. "They worship death here," Raymond Chandler once said about Los Angeles—and when death finally comes, it is a powerful equalizer, respecting neither class nor race, age, or gender.[80]

Photographer Leigh Wiener often photographed Tinseltown's rich and famous, but covering the death of thirty-six-year-old Marilyn Monroe was perhaps his most challenging assignment.[81] After a long day of chasing news on the star's untimely demise, he located her body at the Los Angeles County Morgue. With three bottles of whiskey as a bribe, he persuaded the guards to let him take pictures. Locked away in a Hollywood vault, only a few of these photographs have ever been seen in public. One of them shows a sobering and shockingly ordinary scene: a foot with a toe tag inside a stainless-steel cooler (see p. 198). Death, of course, is the ultimate denier of pleasure and lust, and nowhere did this become more apparent than at Marilyn's funeral, when the most

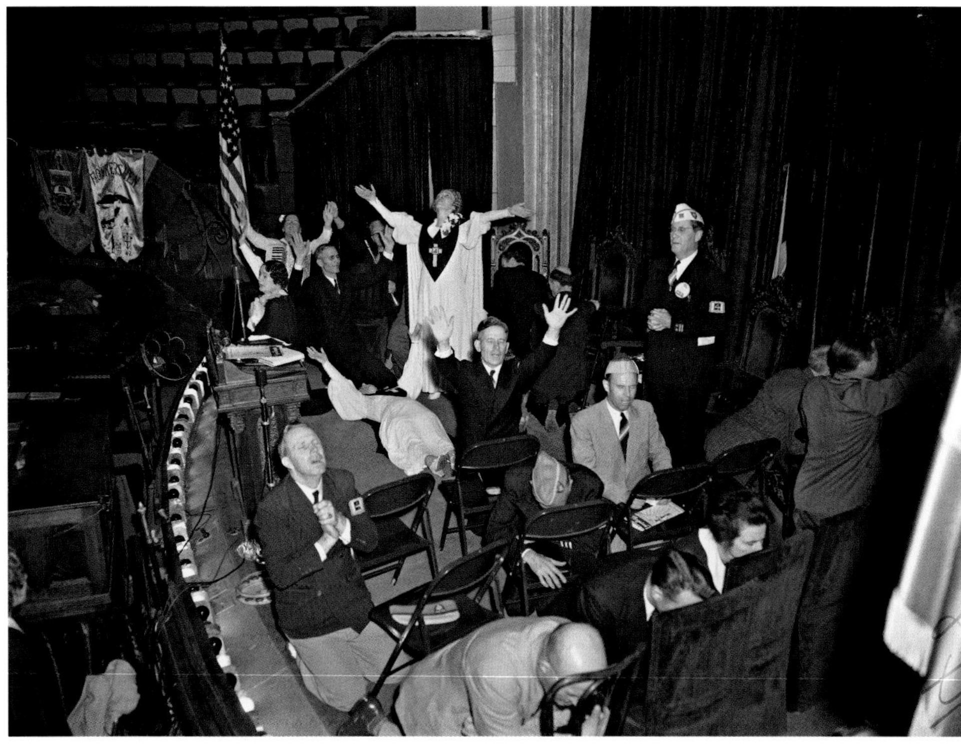

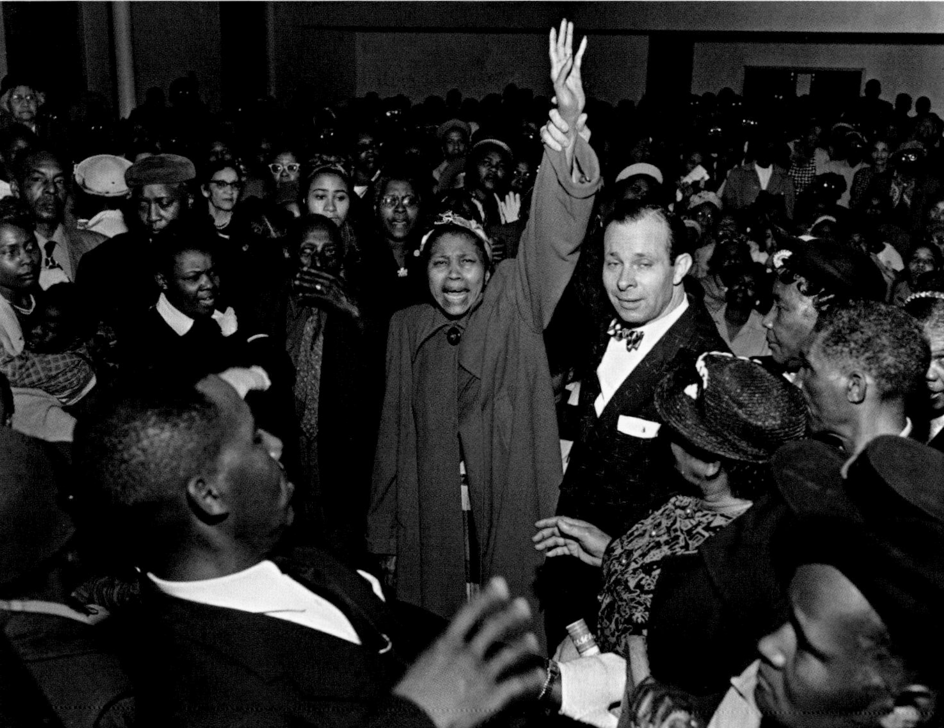

scintillating of all Hollywood stars was laid to rest by her adoring fans at a small cemetery in Westwood Village. It was the end of a dream, not only for the magnetic young actor but also for the multitudes who had vicariously lived out their fantasies through her.

Lust transcended

Just across the hills from Westwood, on a once-arid hillside in Glendale, sits the spectacular necropolis of Forest Lawn.[82] With its faux-European castles, fairy-tale chapels, Italianate marble statues, and sprawling parkland setting, it is a celebrity among cemeteries. Here, in themed sections named Slumberland, Vale of Memory, and Whispering Pines, Los Angeles's quest for youth goes eternal, reconfiguring death as not an end but a blissful foreshadowing of pleasures yet to come.[83] Aldous Huxley's satirical fantasy *After Many a Summer Dies the Swan* of 1939 and Evelyn Waugh's hilarious burlesque *The Loved One* from 1948 skewered Los Angeles's death industry for its gaudy fixations. To Huxley, the park's "exuberantly nubile" sculptures represented the victory of "the well-fed body, forever youthful, immortally athletic, indefatigably sexy," promising those they memorialize "everlasting tennis, eternal golf, and swimming."[84] Waugh's brilliant essay "Death in Hollywood," published in *Life* magazine in 1947, is an equally blistering indictment, mercilessly dissecting local customs of preserving and displaying the deceased. "Embalming is so widely practiced in California," wrote Waugh, "that many believe it to be a legal obligation." He continued:

> At Forest Lawn the bodies lie in state, sometimes on sofas, sometimes in open coffins, in apartments finished like those of a luxurious hotel and named Slumber Rooms. Here the bereaved see them for the last time, fresh from the final beauty parlor, looking rather smaller than life and much more dandified. . . . In Forest Lawn . . . the body does not decay; it lives on, more chic in death than ever, in its indestructible Class A steel-and-concrete shelf; the soul goes straight from the Slumber Room to Paradise, where it enjoys an endless infancy.[85]

For writer David Reid, the cult of sex and beauty in Los Angeles has always had "more than a hint of the whited sepulcher" to it.[86] Conversely, one might argue that death in Los Angeles can be surprisingly lustful, denying as it does the crushing finality and ordinariness of life's end. Los Angeles, like Forest Lawn, promises immediate, ever-lasting happiness to all who come to its vaunted shores. "You can rot there without feeling it," novelist John Rechy acidly observed, suggesting that in Los Angeles even death, in all its ugly inevitability, might offer one last shot at the good life.[87]

Nestled amid the numerous celebrities buried at Forest Lawn is Aimee Semple McPherson, Southern California's most illustrious and charismatic evangelist.[88] Young, beautiful, and fervent in her Christian beliefs, she arrived in Los Angeles in 1918 after brief stints as a tent revivalist and a missionary to China. She ministered to the city's immigrant masses at Angelus Temple, a sprawling house of worship built for her in 1923 in picturesque Echo Park. There, she entertained her large and devoted following with flamboyant religious spectacles and miraculous healings (fig. 15). In May of 1926, McPherson suddenly "vanished," only to resurface five weeks later amid claims of abduction and foul play. In reality, she had run off with her married lover, nursing a drug addiction and a severe mood disorder. After she faced a brief trial for obstruction of justice, her empire eventually crumbled. In 1944, she died despondent at an Oakland hotel, only fifty-four years old.

At the height of the scandal swirling around McPherson's trial, critic H.L. Mencken came to Los Angeles to cover the event for the *Baltimore Evening Sun*. No friend of either Southern California or Christian revivalists, Mencken delivered a scathing indictment of both the celebrity preacher and the town in which she had built her "evangelical bull ring."[89] Mencken asked:

What brought this commonplace and transparent mountebank to her present high estate, with thousands crowding her tabernacle daily and money flowing in upon her from whole regiments of eager dupes? . . . For the plain reason that there were more morons collected in Los Angeles than in any other place on earth—because it was a pasture foreordained for evangelists, and she was the first comer to give it anything low enough for its taste and comprehension.[90]

For Mencken, Los Angeles "swarmed with swamis, spiritualists, Christian scientists, crystal-gazers and the allied necromancers," ready to pull the gullible masses into their metaphysical orbit. Others, too, observed in the Southland "a spiritual quickening, an enlarged will to believe" that sprang from the unfulfilled desires of its uprooted migrant masses.[91] That yearning made Los Angeles prime territory for people seeking and selling transcendence—a place of "superior spiritual vibrations," "of shouting churches, marabouts, *brujas*, dervishes, and desert prophets," that eventually engendered perhaps the largest proliferation of faiths in the world.[92] It is here that the famous neon sign "Jesus Saves" beckons darkly in the night, inspiring multitudes to seek salvation. Photographer Michael Light captured the historic sign in 1995 in a magnificent aerial image of downtown Los Angeles, rendering it a silent beacon of hope amid the sprawling urban jungle (see p. 224). Other photographers attest to Los Angeles's penchant for religious expression bordering on the bizarre and extreme. In Harry Adams's *Evangelist at Shrine Auditorium* from the 1940s (fig. 16), a minister incites his flock to writhe and whoop in what was then the city's largest theater and entertainment complex. Farnsworth Crowder, ever the acerbic critic, noted that "in the South of California has gathered the largest and most miscellaneous assortment of Messiahs, Sorcerers, Saints, and Seers known to the history of aberrations."[93] Even science took a turn for the metaphysical here, when one of the country's leading physicists,

Robert A. Millikan of the California Institute of Technology, extolled some startling connections between Jesus and particle theory.[94] For historian Mike Davis, science and religion became the strangest of bedfellows in Los Angeles, fusing Luciferian Magic, psychoanalysis, quantum mechanics, and science fiction with the illicit excitements of sexual necromancy.[95]

Not all aspirants to spiritual transcendence in Los Angeles, however, sought it in esoteric teachings. Many simply went to the beach, dedicating themselves to the primal lure of physical pleasure as the source of all moral and spiritual good. "Los Angeles is a middle-aged obese woman from somewhere else in the Middle West, lying naked in the sun," novelist Myron Brining wrote in what may well be the most delicious evocation of California hedonism.[96] "As she sips from a glass of buttermilk and bites off chunks of hamburger sandwich, she reads Tagore to the music of Carrie Jacobs Bond." Here, enraptured by the warm sand, cool breezes, and sparkling surf of Southern California, life is but a heartbeat away from enlightenment. For Reyner Banham, that is what life in Los Angeles is all about:

The cultivation and cult of the physical man (or woman) is obviously a deeply ingrained trait in the psychology of Southern California. Sun, sand, and surf are held to be ultimate and transcendental values, beyond mere physical goods. . . . The culture of the beach is in many ways a rejection of the values of consumer society, a place where a man needs to own only what he stands up in—usually a pair of frayed shorts and sunglasses.[97]

"Give me a beach, something to eat, and a couple of broads, and I can get along without material things," a Santa Monica bus driver supposedly said to Banham, echoing a widespread sentiment that in Los Angeles, spiritual fulfillment is inextricably tied to the pleasures of physical well-being.[98] But true transcendence, as an existence above and apart from the world, is equally possible in Los Angeles, if not easily attained. Anthony Friedkin's photograph *Surfboard with Setting Sun* from 1980 (see pp. 222–23) evokes the singular, ethereal beauty of a surfboard drifting toward the distant horizon. The surfer's body in this picture can only be imagined, eternally one with the board and the gentle undulations of the ocean. "When I'm in the water," Friedkin said, "I feel like I'm connecting to something so mighty and so primordial it's beyond description. All the mysteries of life and death, light and darkness, space and time, are to be found there."[99] As John Humble's *From Lifeguard Station 26 #15* reiterates, humanity in Los Angeles is drawn to the liminal spaces along the water's edge, gazing out into space as if in a trance (see p. 207). In Humble's picture, people seem to melt into the misty evening sky, suffused by the golden haze of the setting sun. In *6:30 a.m. #106 10/28/03*, by Robert Weingarten, sky and sea merge to form a single radiant color plane (see p. 229). Here, bodies have disappeared, subsumed by waves of cosmic light washing across the early morning Southland.

As their pictures make clear, people in Los Angeles are uniquely attuned to the rhythms of the land and the solar cycle, eagerly yielding themselves to the siren call of their surroundings. Their ultimate quest for transcendence is perhaps nowhere more apparent than in Ken Ohara's timed exposures of ordinary Angelenos (see pp. 226, 227). In one-hour sittings with the shutter open, they become soft impressions of light and dark against a static background. The blurred contours of their heads and bodies take on a radiant new power that bespeaks both the incandescence and the melancholy of life in Los Angeles.

NOTES

1   Eve Babitz, "Bodies and Souls," in *Sex, Death and God in L.A.*, ed. David Reid, Berkeley (University of California Press) 1992, p. 108.

2   Gaston Bachelard, *The Psychoanalysis of Fire*, London (Quartet Books) 1987, quoted in Mike Featherstone *et al.*, *The Body: Social Process and Cultural Theory*, London (Sage) 1991, p. 4.

3   A "huge desert encampment," Jack Kerouac, quoted in Reid, *Sex, Death and God in L.A.*, p. xxxvi; a "city of dreadful joy," Aldous Huxley, "Los Angeles. A Rhapsody" [1926], in *Writing Los Angeles: A Literary Anthology*, ed. David L. Ulin, New York (Library of America) 2002, p. 59; Mike Davis, *City of Quartz: Excavating the Future in Los Angeles*, London and New York (Verso Press) 1990.

4   Ralph Hancock, *Fabulous Boulevard*, New York (Funk & Wagnalls Company) 1949, p. 149.

5   Huxley, "Los Angeles. A Rhapsody," in Ulin, *Writing Los Angeles*, p. 60.

6   Jennifer A. Watts, "Photography in the Land of Sunshine," *Southern California Quarterly*, 87, Winter 2005–06, pp. 349–76.

7   For my discussion of the origins of Los Angeles's physical culture, I am greatly indebted to Heather Addison's comprehensive study *Hollywood and the Rise of Physical Culture*, New York and London (Routledge) 2003. For general overviews of American consumer and physical culture, see Hillel Schwartz, *Never Satisfied: A Cultural History of Diets, Fantasies and Fat*, New York (Macmillan) 1986; Roberta Pollack Seid, *Never Too Thin: Why Women Are at War With Their Bodies*, New York (Prentice Hall) 1989; and Mike Featherstone, "The Body in Consumer Culture," in Featherstone *et al.*, *The Body*, pp. 170–96.

8   David Thomson, "Beneath Mulholland," in *Beneath Mulholland: Thoughts on Hollywood and Its Ghosts*, New York (Vintage Books) 1997, p. 15.

9   *Ibid.*

10 *Ibid.*, p. 18.

11 *Ibid.*

12 Davis, *City of Quartz*, p. 30.

13 Thomson, "Beneath Mulholland," p. 17.

14 Quoted in Leonard Pitt and Dale Pitt, *Los Angeles A–Z: An Encyclopedia of the City and County*, Berkeley (University of California Press) 1997, p. 340.

15 Larry Sultan in conversation with Terri Whitlock, San Francisco Museum of Modern Art, Resource Library, available

online at sfmoma.org, accessed October 2007.

16 Reyner Banham, "Ecology III: The Plains of Id," in *Los Angeles: The Architecture of Four Ecologies* [1971], Berkeley (University of California Press) 1999, p. 143.

17 Larry Sultan, *The Valley*, Göttingen (Steidl) 2004, pp. 7, 8.

18 *Ibid.*, p. 8.

19 Sultan in conversation with Whitlock.

20 Huxley, "Los Angeles. A Rhapsody," in Ulin, *Writing Los Angeles*, p. 61.

21 Nathan Silver, quoted in Pitt and Pitt, *Los Angeles A–Z*, p. 145.

22 Carey McWilliams, *Southern California Country: An Island on the Land*, New York (Duell, Sloan & Pearce) 1946; see also Clark Davis, "From Oasis to Metropolis: Southern California and the Changing Context of American Leisure," *Pacific Historical Review*, 61, August 1992, pp. 357–86.

23 Kevin Starr, *Inventing the Dream: California Through the Progressive Era*, New York (Oxford University Press) 1985, pp. 54–55.

24 Davis, *City of Quartz*, pp. 24, 25.

25 *Ibid.*, p. 26.

26 Watts, "Photography in the Land of Sunshine," pp. 349–76.

27 *Ibid.*, p. 375.

28 *Ibid.*, p. 353.

29 Davis, *City of Quartz*, p. 27; see also David M. Fine, *Imagining Los Angeles: A City in Fiction*, Albuquerque (University of New Mexico Press) 2000, pp. 40–45.

30 *Pictorialism in California: Photographs 1900–1940*, exhib. cat. by Michael G. Wilson and Dennis Reed, Los Angeles, The J. Paul Getty Museum; San Marino, Calif., The Henry E. Huntington Library and Art Gallery, 1994.

31 Quoted in Kirse Granat May, *Golden State, Golden Youth: The California Image in Popular Culture*, Chapel Hill and London (The University of North Carolina Press) 2002, p. 24.

32 *Ibid.*

33 Morrow Mayo, *Los Angeles*, New York (Knopf) 1933, p. 319, quoted in Davis, *City of Quartz*, p. 17.

34 See Addison, *Hollywood*, pp. 10–31.

35 Featherstone, "The Body in Consumer Culture," in Featherstone *et al.*, *The Body*, p. 177.

36 Farnsworth Crowder, "Where Life is Better—For What?" *Westways*, November 1936, p. 24.

37 Quoted in Heather Addison, "'Must the Players Keep Young?': Early Hollywood's Cult of Youth," *Cinema Journal*, 45, Summer 2006, p. 16.

38 *Ibid.*

39 Dorothy Manners, "The Flesh and the Blood Racket," *Motion Picture Magazine*, April 1929, p. 34.

40 For a history of Hollywood photography, see David Fahey and Linda Rich, *Masters of Starlight: Photographers in Hollywood*, New York (Ballantine Books) 1987; see also Dana Polan, "California Through the Lens of Hollywood," in *Reading California: Art, Image, and Identity, 1900–2000*, ed. Stephanie Barron *et al.*, Berkeley and Los Angeles (University of California Press and Los Angeles County Museum of Art) 2000, pp. 129–50.

41 Don Waldie, quoted in Lawrence Weschler, "L.A. Glows," in Ulin, *Writing Los Angeles*, p. 675.

42 Herb Ritts in an interview with François Quintin, conducted before the Herb Ritts exhibition at the Fondation Cartier pour l'art Contemporain, Paris, December 11, 1999–March 12, 2000. Available online at herbritts.com/about/interview, accessed October 2007.

43 "Most of the jazz photography before me showed sweaty musicians with shiny faces in dark, smoky little bars. . . . That was jazz to most people. But being on the West Coast, I wanted to bring out the fact that musicians here were living in such a health-conscious environment. So I purposely put them on the beach or in the mountains or on the road in their convertibles." William Claxton, quoted in *The Jazz Cadence of American Culture*, ed. Robert G. O'Meally, New York (Columbia University Press) 1998, p. 179; see also williamclaxton.com, accessed October 2007.

44 *Ibid.*

45 Crowder, "Where Life is Better," p. 24; emphasis added.

46 Reyner Banham would later coin his term "surfurbia" to describe the Southland's beach communities. Banham, "Ecology III," p. 19.

47 Kevin Starr, *The Dream Endures: California Enters the 1940s*, New York and Oxford (Oxford University Press) 1997, p. 10.

48 Marla Matzer Rose, *Muscle Beach: Where the Best Bodies in the World Started a Fitness Revolution*, Los Angeles (LA Weekly Books) 2001, p. 16.

49 Thomas A.P. van Leeuwen, *The Springboard into the Pond: An Intimate History of the Swimming Pool*, Cambridge, Mass. (MIT Press) 1999, p. 159.

50 Van Leeuwen, *The Springboard into the Pond*, p. 155.

51 Jeff Wiltse, *Contested Waters: A Social History of Swimming Pools in America*, Chapel Hill (University of North Carolina Press) 2007, p. 102.

52 Van Leeuwen, *The Springboard into the Pond*, p. 159.

53 *Ibid.*, p. 225.

54 David Hockney, quoted in Cécile Whiting, *Pop L.A.: Art and the City in the 1960s*, Berkeley (University of California Press) 2006, pp. 114, 117.

55 Wayne E. Stanley, *The Complete Reprint of Physique Pictorial*, Cologne (Taschen) 1997.

56 Thomson, "Beneath Mullholland," p. 15.

57 *Ibid.*, p. 17.

58 Kevin Starr, *Americans and the California Dream, 1860–1915*, cit. in Fine, *Imagining Los Angeles*, p. 231.

59 John Fante, *Ask The Dust* [1930], quoted in Fine, *Imagining Los Angeles*, p. 179.

60 Nathanael West, *The Day of the Locust* [1939], quoted in Fine, *Imagining Los Angeles*, p. 158.

61 Davis, *City of Quartz*, pp. 30–38.

62 Mayo, *Los Angeles*, p. 327, quoted in Davis, *City of Quartz*, p. 45.

63 Louis Adamic, quoted in Davis, *City of Quartz*, p. 36.

64 Louis Adamic, *Laughing in the Jungle* [1932], quoted in Ulin, *Writing Los Angeles*, p. 53.

65 Pitt and Pitt, *Los Angeles A–Z*, pp. 194–95; see also Emily Abel, *Suffering in the Land of Sunshine: A Los Angeles Illness Narrative*, New Brunswick, NJ (Rutgers University Press) 2006, p. xiv.

66 Pitt and Pitt, *Los Angeles A–Z*, p. 195.

67 Abel, *Suffering*, p. xvi.

68 Emily K. Abel, "From Exclusion to Expulsion: Mexicans and Tuberculosis Control in Los Angeles, 1914–1940," *Bulletin of the History of Medicine*, 77, 2003, pp. 823–49.

69 Pitt and Pitt, *Los Angeles A–Z*, p. 90.

70 S.H. Bowman, "A Brief Study of Arrests of Mexicans" [1924], quoted in William Deverell, *Whitewashed Adobe: The Rise of Los Angeles and the Remaking of Its Mexican Past*, Berkeley (University of California Press) 2004, p. 37.

71 Deverell, *Whitewashed Adobe*, p. 49ff.

72 Ronald Davidson, "Before 'Surfurbia': The Development of the South Bay Beach Cities Through the 1930s," *Yearbook of the Association of Pacific Coast Geographers*, 66, 2004, pp. 80–94.

73 Cecilia Rasmussen, "L.A. Then and Now," *Los Angeles Times*, July 3, 2005, p. B2.

74 "Beach Ballet," *Ebony*, 9, November 1953, pp. 128–31, 135.

75 See kengonzalesday.com/projects/hangtrees/walkingtour.htm, accessed October 2007.

76 Octavio Paz, *The Labyrinth of Solitude: Life and Thought in Mexico* [1961], quoted in Ulin, *Writing Los Angeles*, p. 366.

77 Mary Ellen Mark, *Exposure: Mary Ellen Mark, The Iconic Photographs*, New York (Phaidon Press) 2005, pp. 280–81.

78 Jim Goldberg and Philip Brookman, *Raised by Wolves*, Zurich (Scalo Publishers) 1995.

79 Jack Kerouac, quoted in Reid, *Sex, Death and God in L.A.*, p. xxxvi.

80 Raymond Chandler, quoted in Lynelle George, "City of Specters," in Reid, *Sex, Death and God in L.A.*, p. 153.

81 Leigh Wiener, *Marilyn: A Hollywood Farewell: The Death and Funeral of Marilyn Monroe*, New York (Seventy Four Ten) 1990.

82 David Charles Sloane, "Selling Eternity in 1920s Los Angeles," in *Metropolis in the Making: Los Angeles in the 1920s*, ed. Tom Sitton and William Deverell, Berkeley (University of California Press) 2001, pp. 341–60.

83 Hubert L. Eaton, "The Builder's Creed," repr. in Barbara Rubin *et al.*, *L.A. in Installments: Forest Lawn*, Santa Monica, Calif. (Westside Publications) 1979, p. 24.

84 Aldous Huxley, quoted in Fine, *Imagining Los Angeles*, p. 166.

85 Evelyn Waugh, "Death in Hollywood," *Life*, September 29, 1947, repr. in Ulin, *Writing Los Angeles*, pp. 363–64.

86 Reid, *Sex, Death and God in L.A.*, p. xxxvii.

87 John Rechy, *City of Night* [1963], quoted in Davis, *City of Quartz*, p. 36.

88 Pitt and Pitt, *Los Angeles A–Z*, p. 320.

89 H.L. Mencken, quoted in Fine, *Imagining Los Angeles*, p. 56.

90 H.L. Mencken, "Sister Aimée," in Ulin, *Writing Los Angeles*, p. 65.

91 David Reid, "The Possessed," in Reid, *Sex, Death and God in L.A.*, p. 181.

92 *Ibid.*, p. 77.

93 Farnsworth Crowder, "Los Angeles: The Heaven of the Bunk-Shooters" [n.d.], quoted in Davis, *City of Quartz*, p. 55.

94 Davis, *City of Quartz*, p. 55.

95 *Ibid.*, p. 59.

96 Myron Brining, *The Flutter of an Eyelid*, 1933; cit. in Fine, *Imagining Los Angeles*, p. 53.

97 Banham, "Ecology III," p. 20.

98 *Ibid.*

99 Quoted in *Timekeeper*, exhib. cat., intro. by Julian Cox, Los Angeles, Stephen Cohen Gallery, 2003, p. viii.

DWELL

There are an indefinite number of beginnings and endings on the grid, but you are always somewhere.
D.J. Waldie, writer

Greater Los Angeles is not so much an accidental "city without a center" as a planned grid of interconnected suburban hubs. "The map of L.A. is never complete," a journalist wrote in 1923, as urban sprawl voraciously overtook orange groves and beanfields. Within the region's vast labyrinth of parcels, lots, and city blocks, the single-family home reigns supreme. Los Angeles homes come in every conceivable style, from bungalow to Mission Revival to Tudor, reflecting the diverse and eclectic origins and desires of the city's innumerable newcomers.

From the turn of the twentieth century onward, regional architects designed houses predicated on leisurely indoor–outdoor living that became national trendsetters for middle-class tastes and dwellings. Photographers later reveled in the cheap stucco façades of endless tract houses, the strip malls, and the ubiquitous "dingbat apartments" that helped define the city's modern incarnation.

As nineteenth-century images in this section vividly recall, race and class have long determined how and where one lives in Los Angeles. Restrictive housing covenants pushed racial minorities into segregated neighborhoods well into the 1940s. As photographs of Depression-era shanties and homelessness reveal, the destitute have often made do outdoors or in the flimsiest of shelters, not by choice but because temperate weather allows it. Perhaps the idea of Los Angeles as a city of shattered dreams is nowhere more poignantly revealed than in Mary Ellen Mark's photograph of the Damm family seeking shelter in that other most potent of Los Angeles symbols—their car.

Timothy Street-Porter
Flintstones Set at Vasquez Rocks, 1994

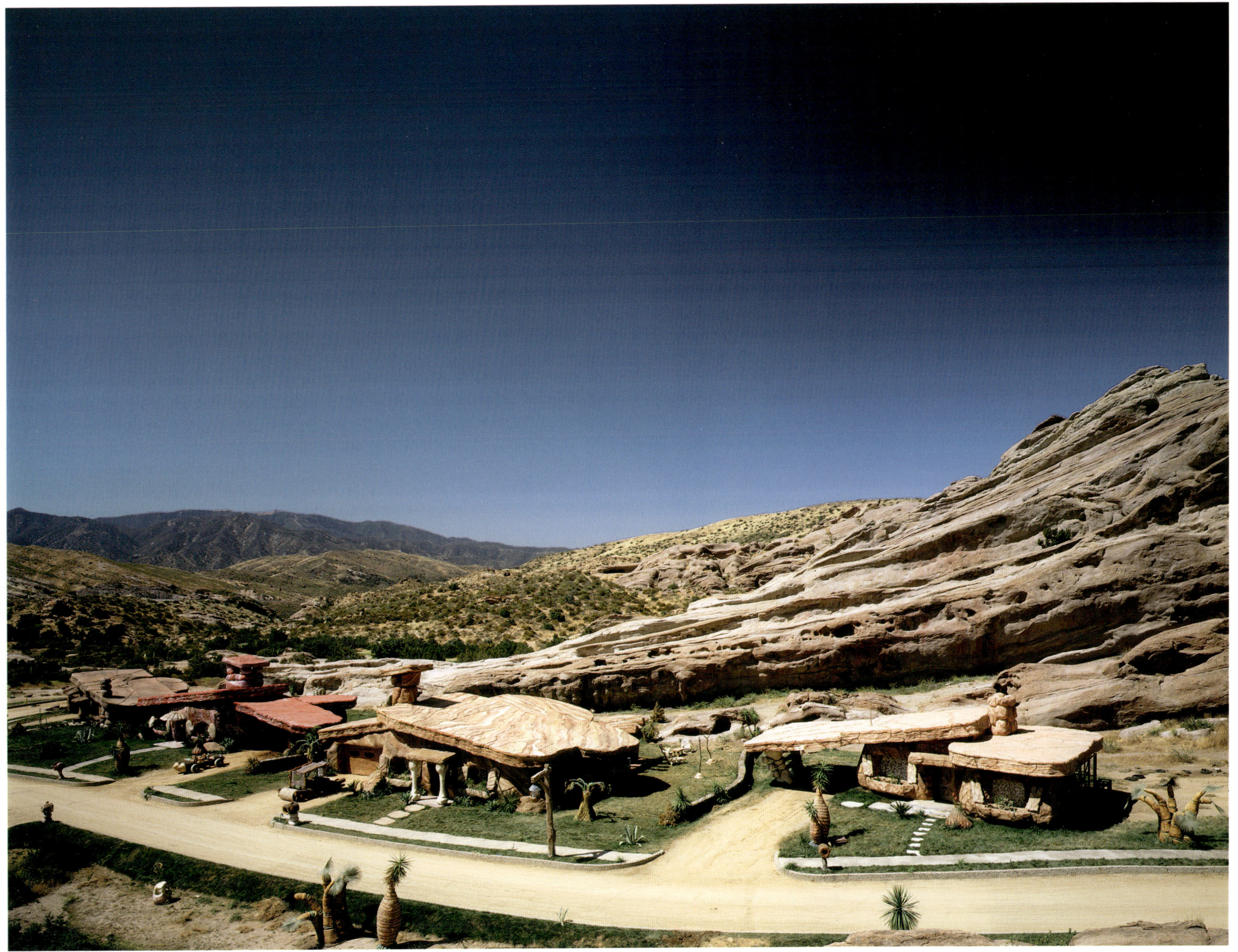

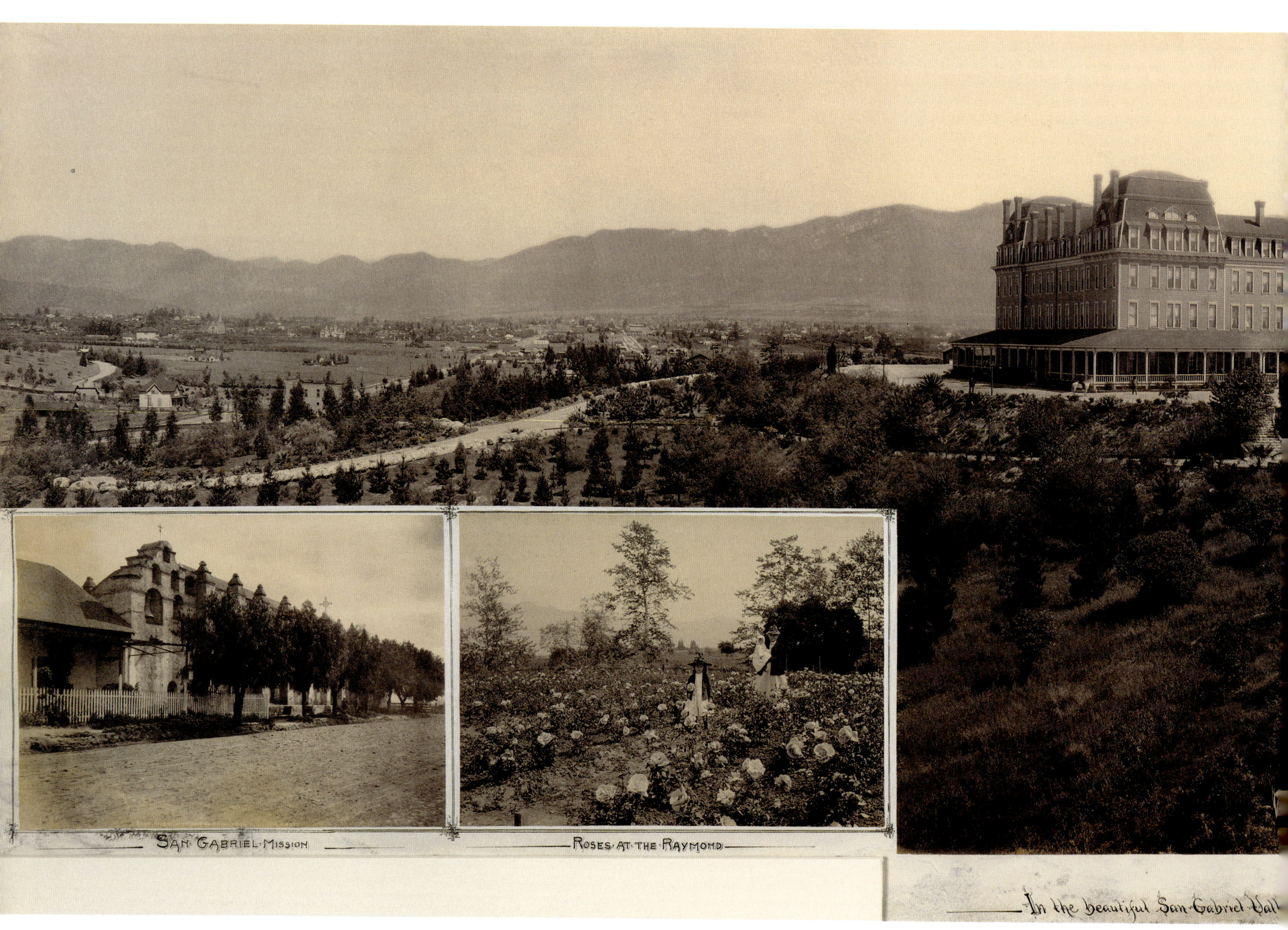

William Henry Jackson
*The Raymond [Hotel], East
Pasadena, California, c. 1889*

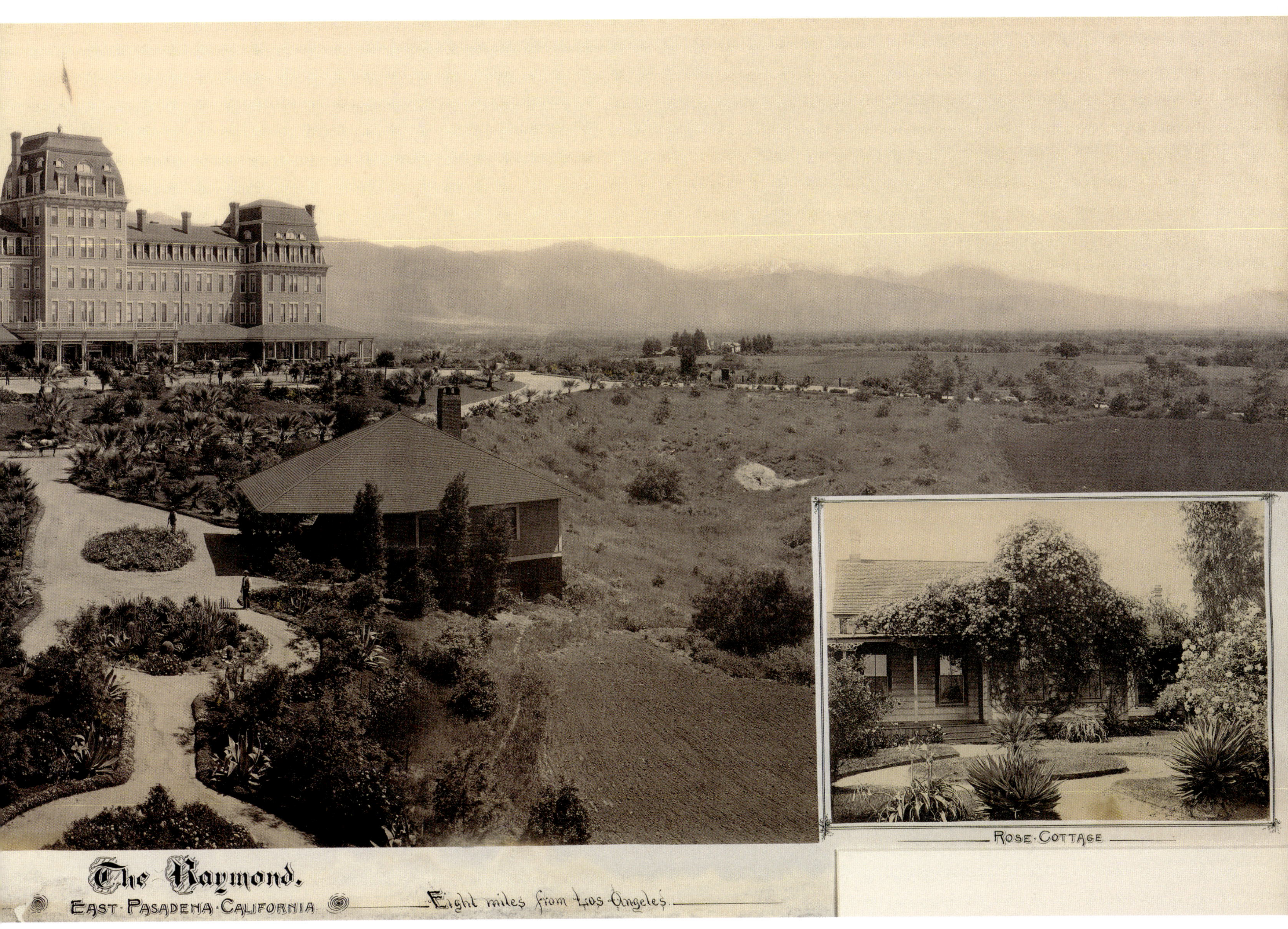

The Raymond.
EAST·PASADENA·CALIFORNIA
Eight miles from Los Angeles
Rose·Cottage

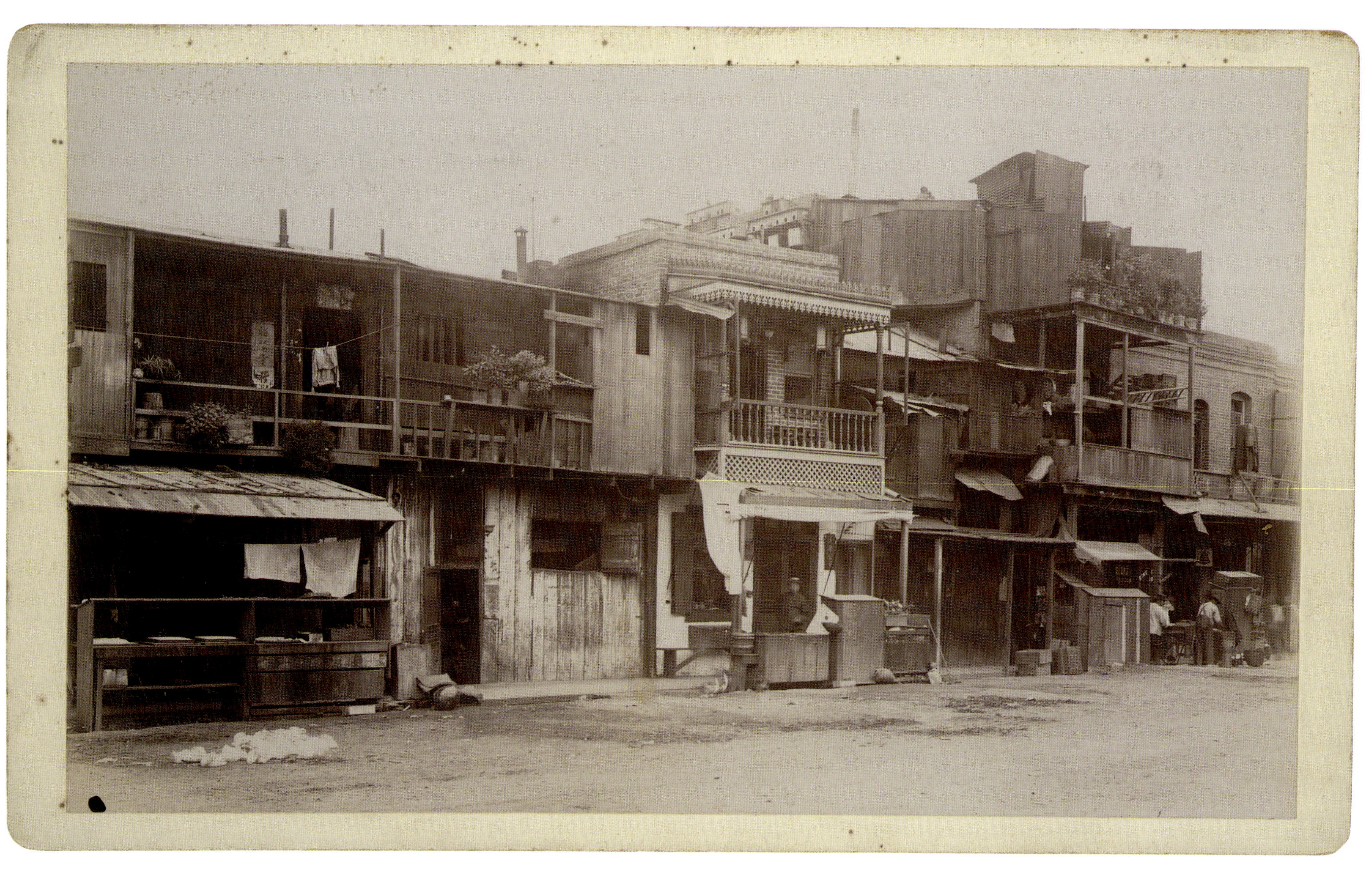

W.H. Fletcher
Old Chinatown, Los Angeles,
1888

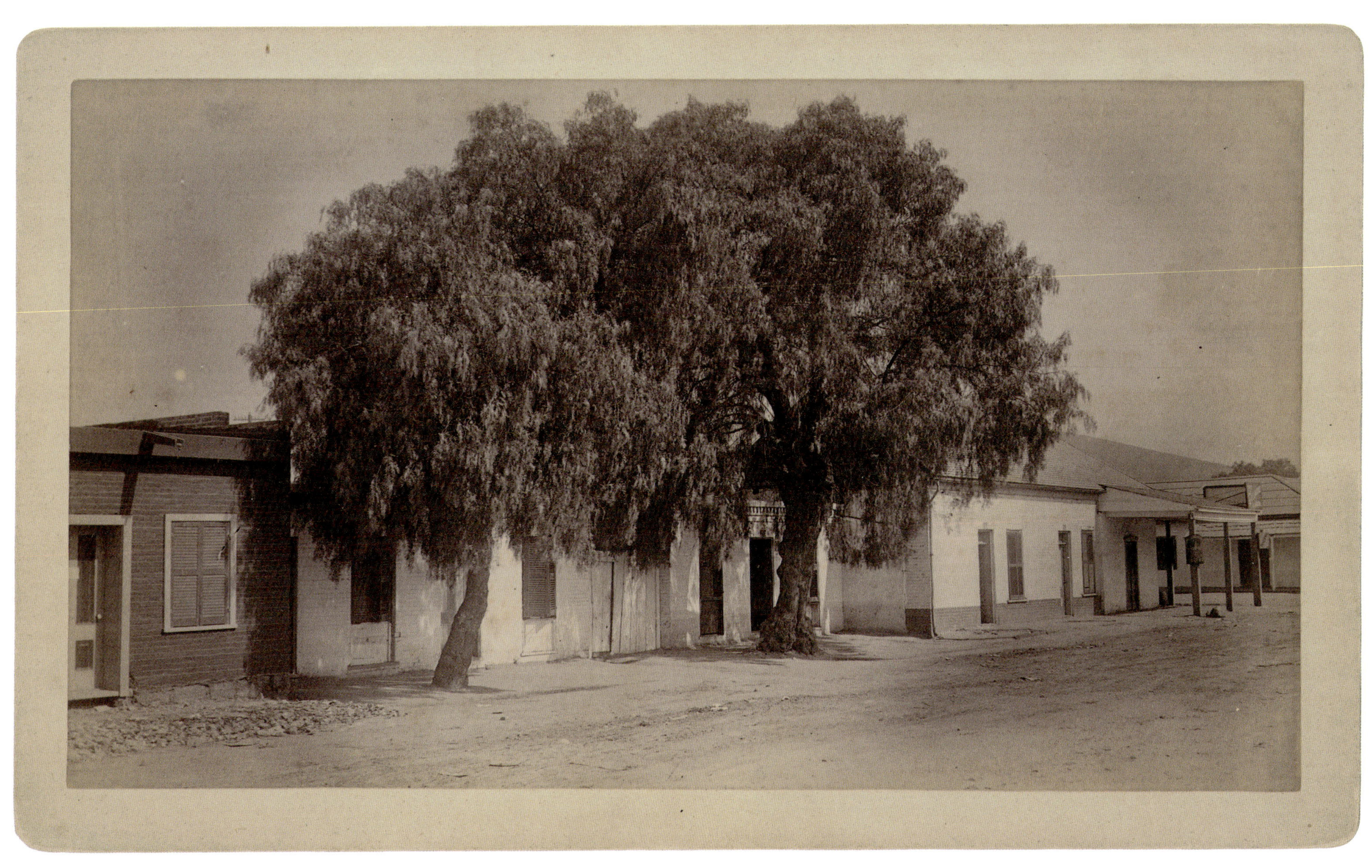

W.H. Fletcher
Sonoratown, Los Angeles,
c. 1885

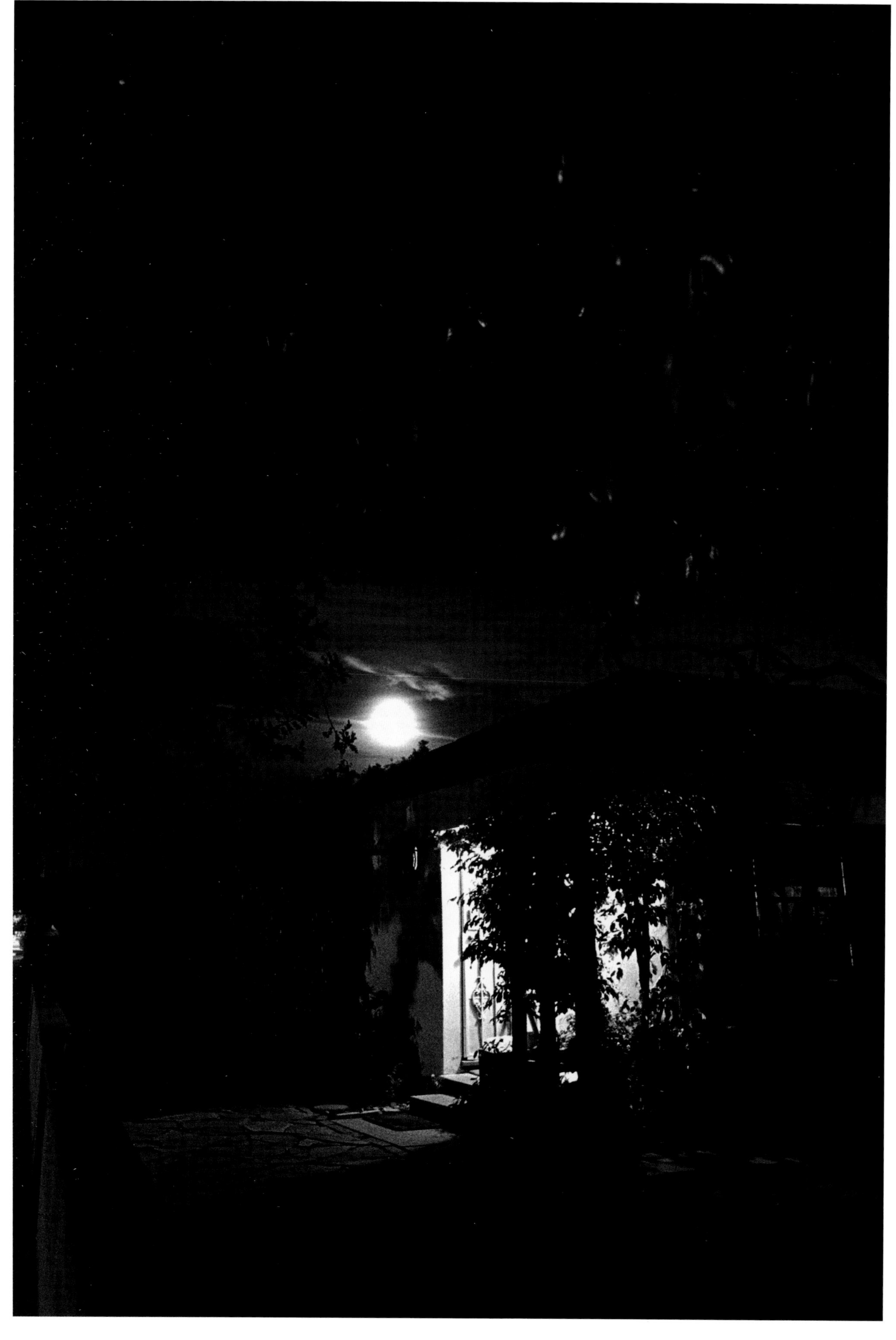

Henry Wessel
Night Walk Series, No. 47,
1998

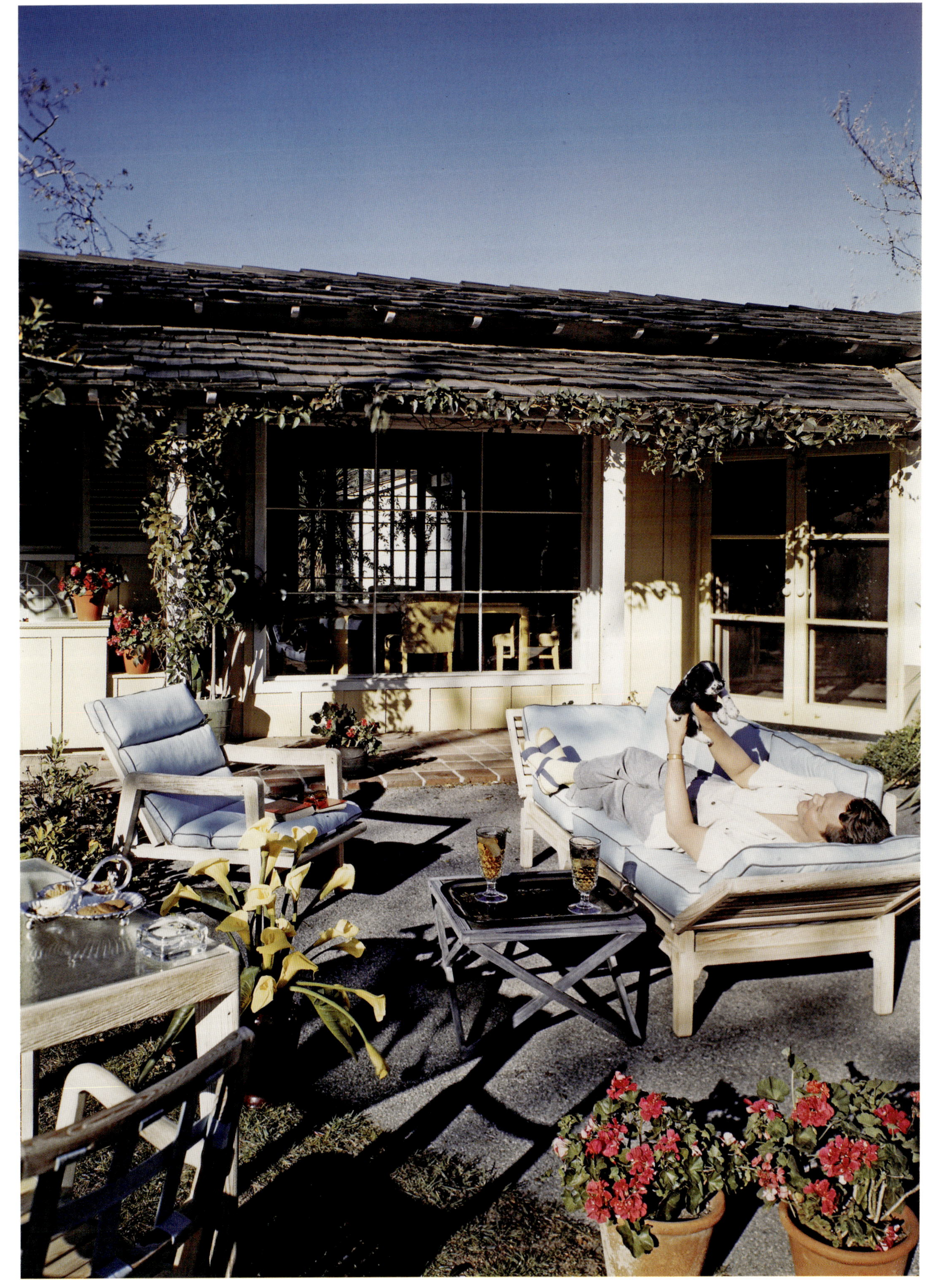

Maynard L. Parker
House Beautiful Pace Setter House Designed by Cliff May, Riviera Ranch Subdivision, Los Angeles, 1946

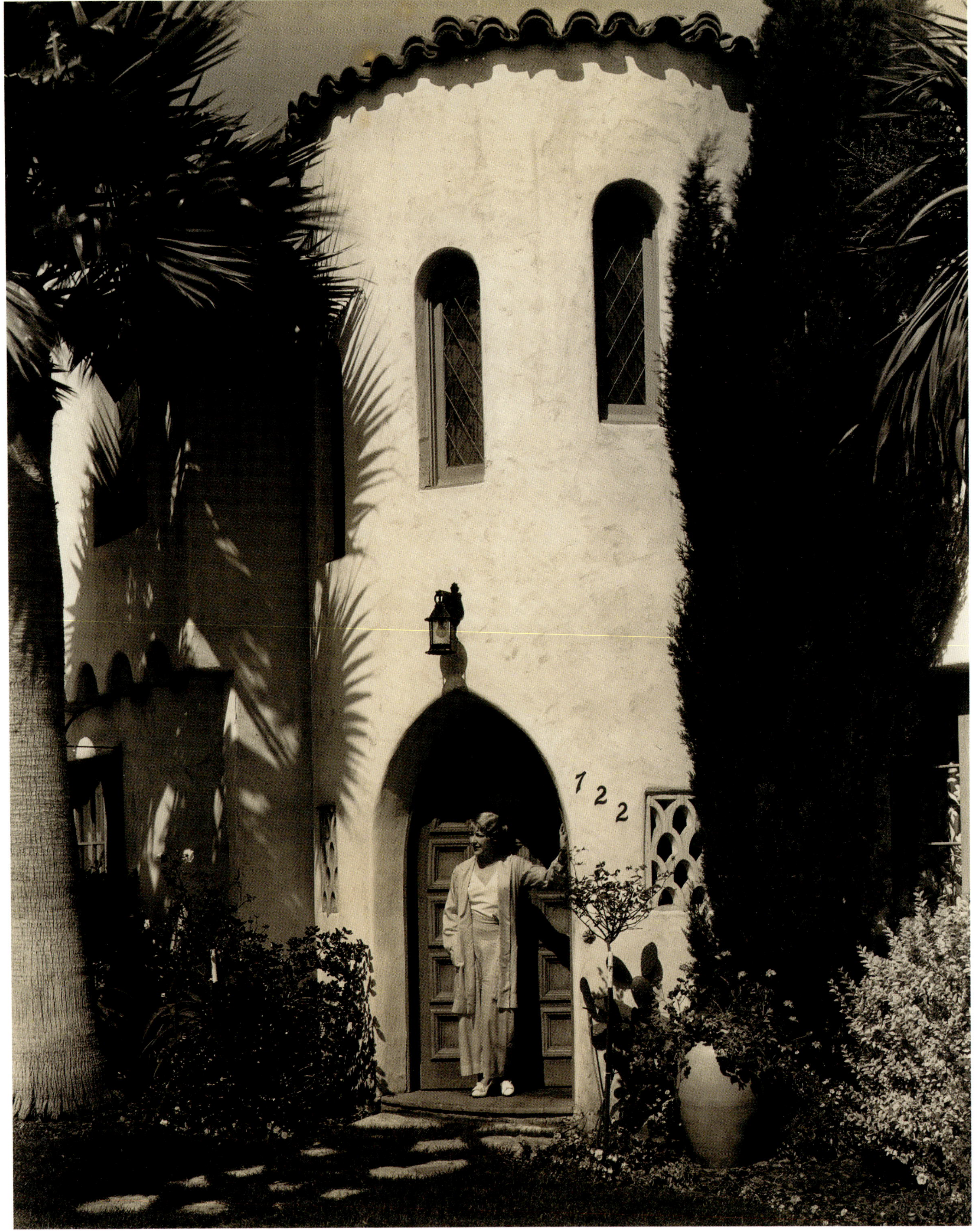

Unknown
*Aileen Pringle in the Doorway
at 722 Adelaide Place,
Santa Monica, c. 1925*

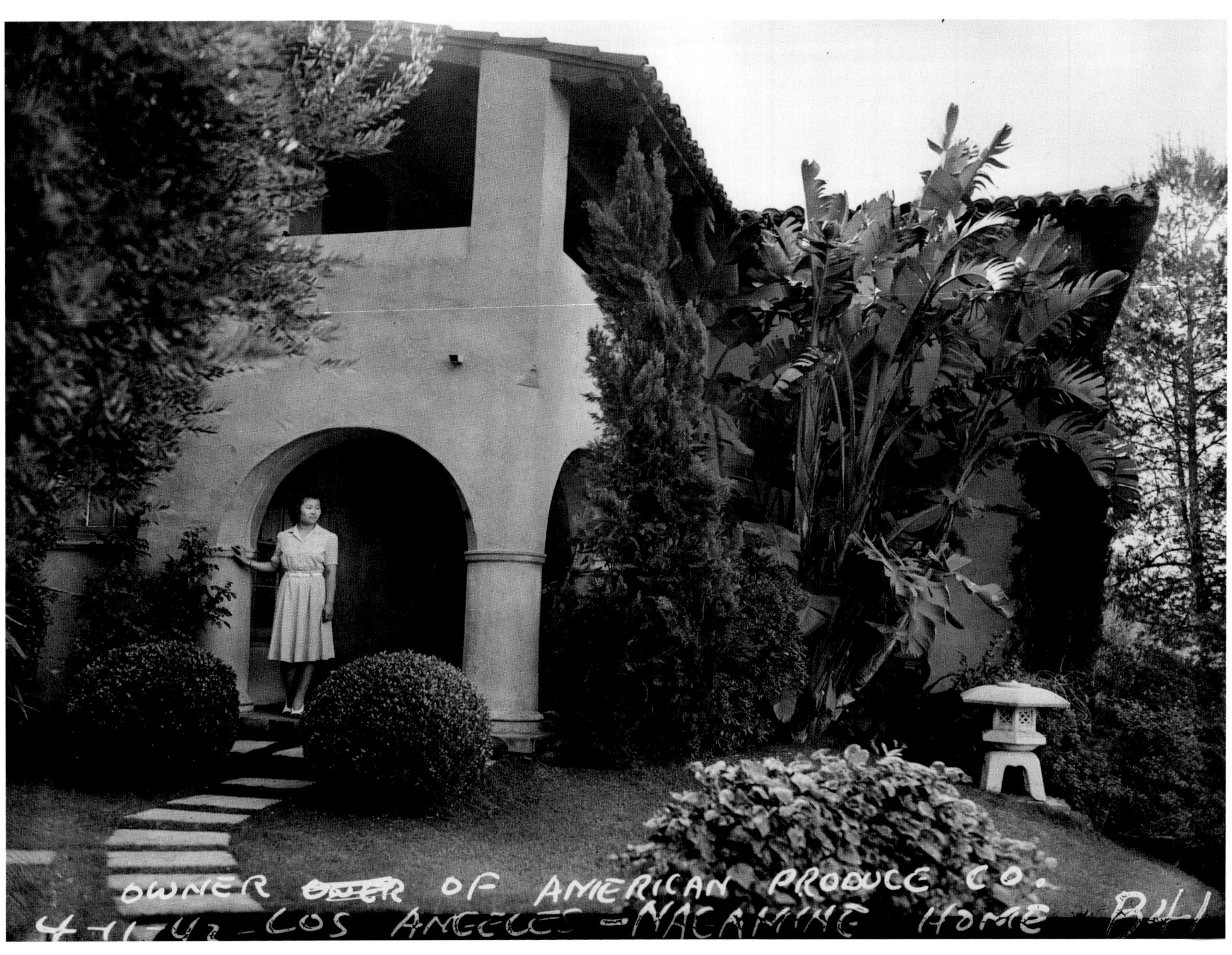

Clem Albers
The Nagamine residence prior to evacuation of people of Japanese ancestry from this area, Los Angeles, California, April 11, 1942

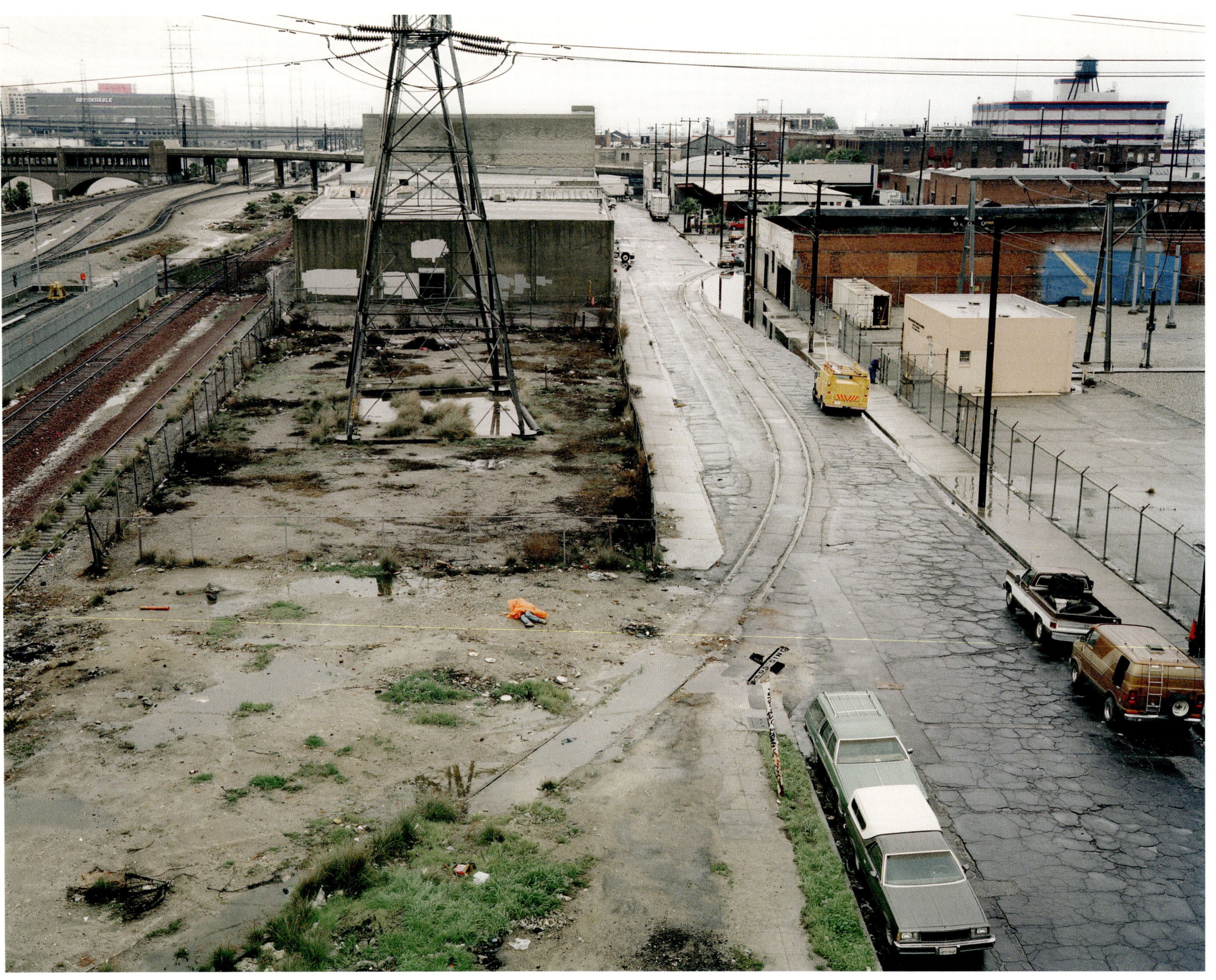

Karin Apollonia Müller
Power Lines, 1997

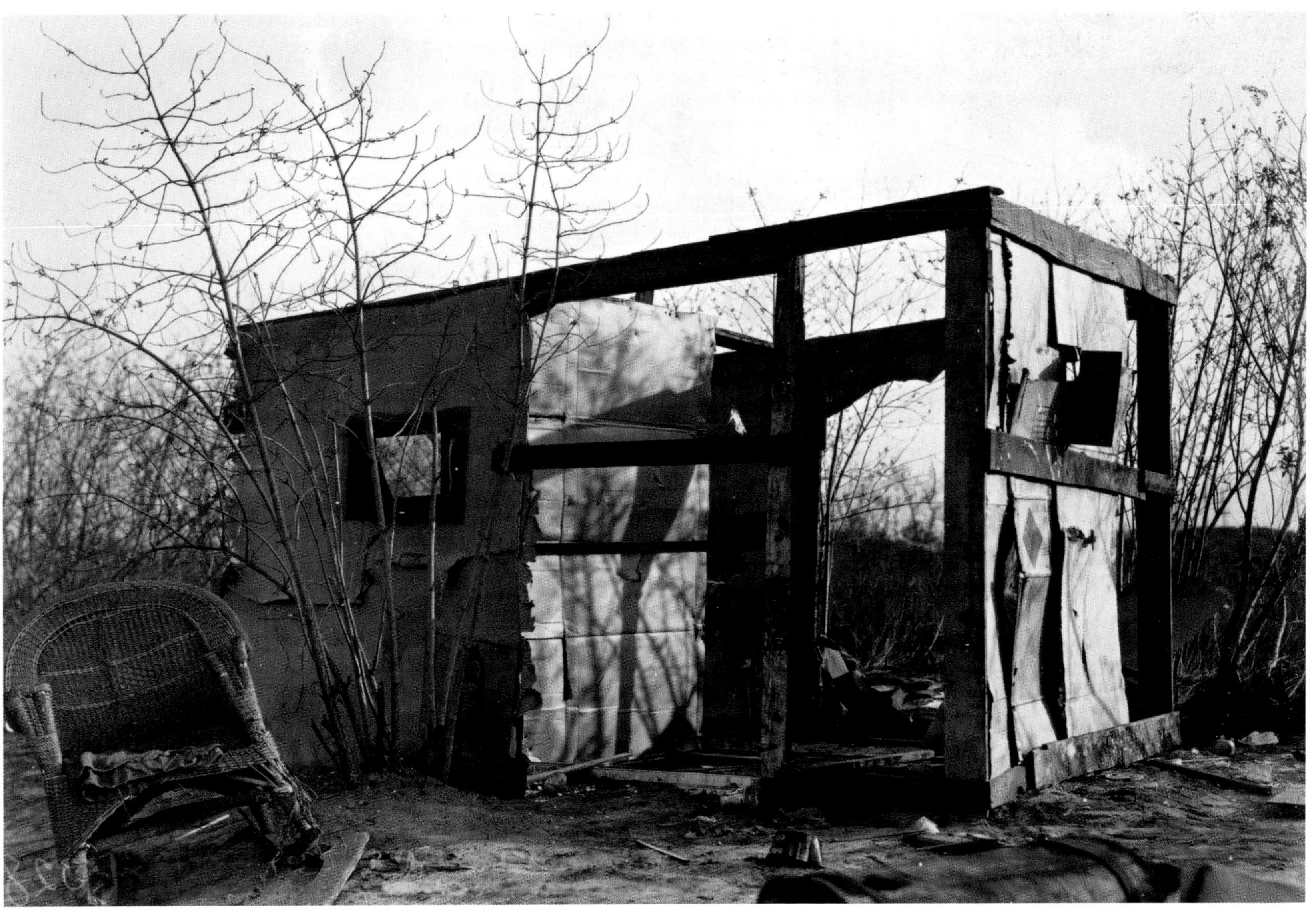

**Los Angeles County
Health Department**
Glendale, December 7, 1931

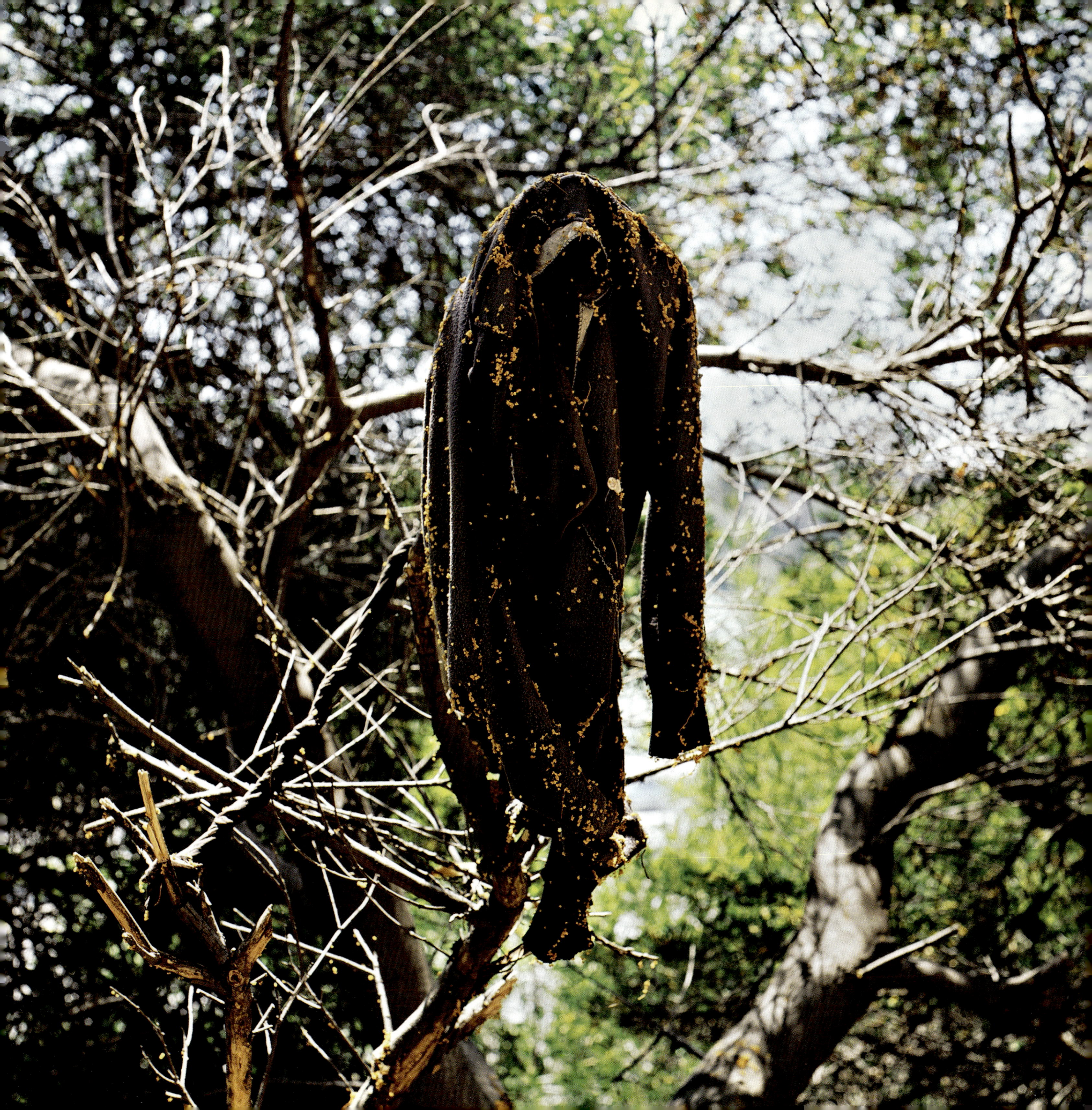

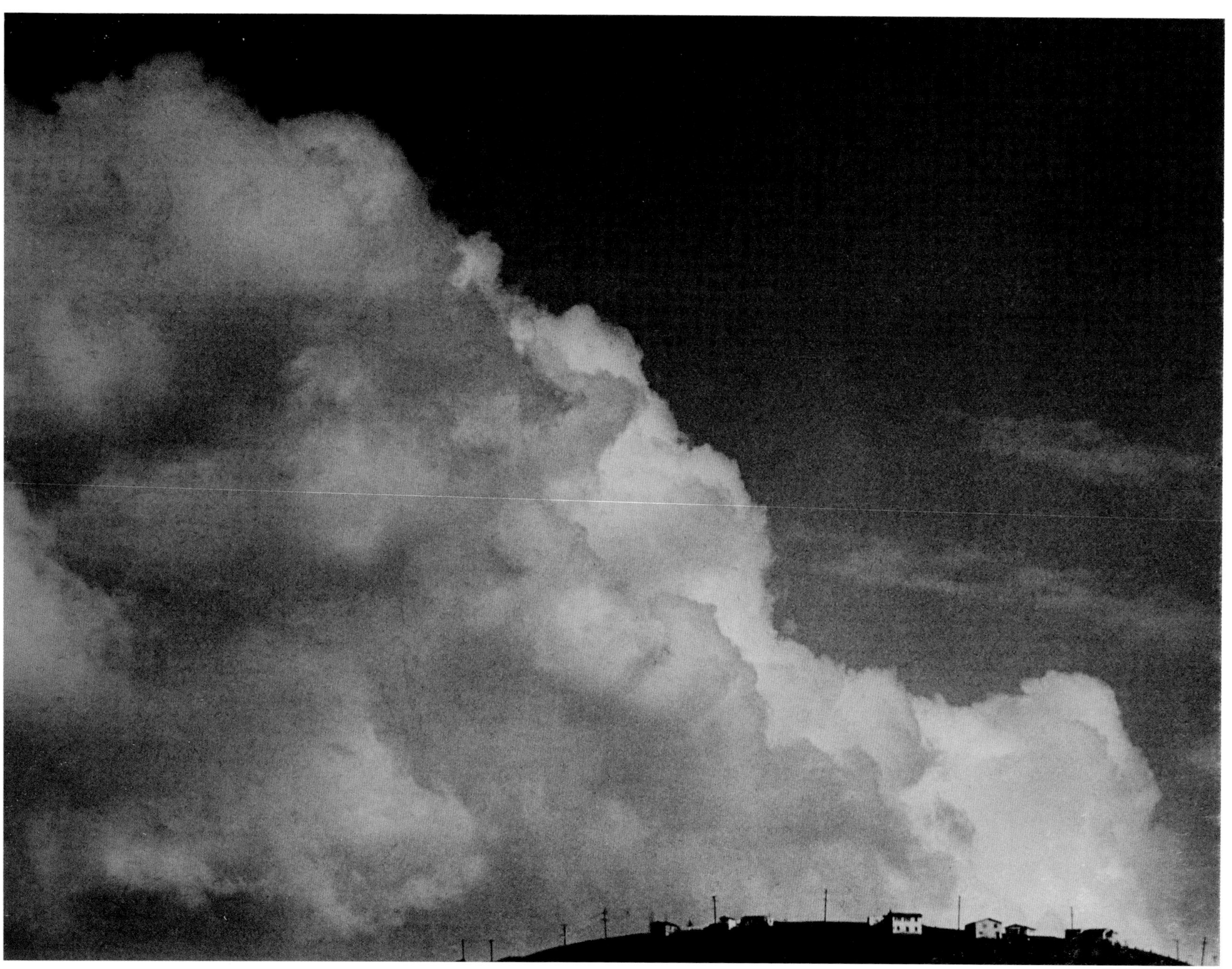

Will Connell
L.A. Subdivision, 1939

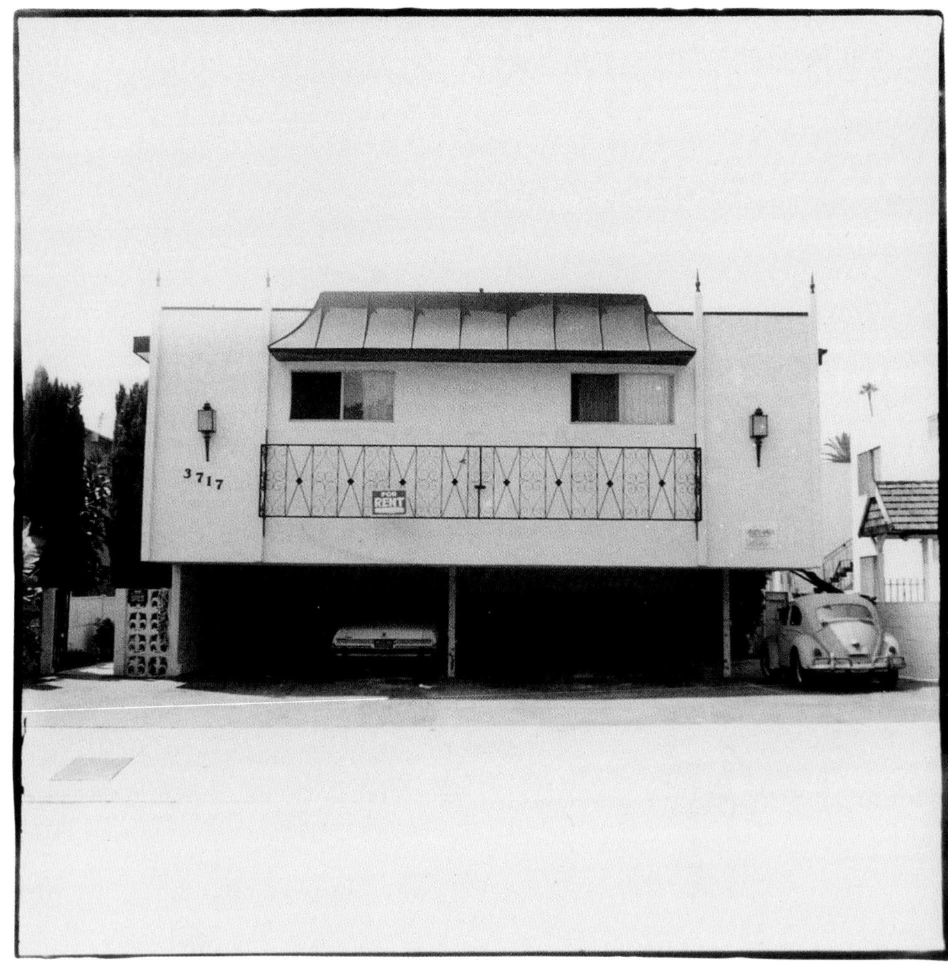

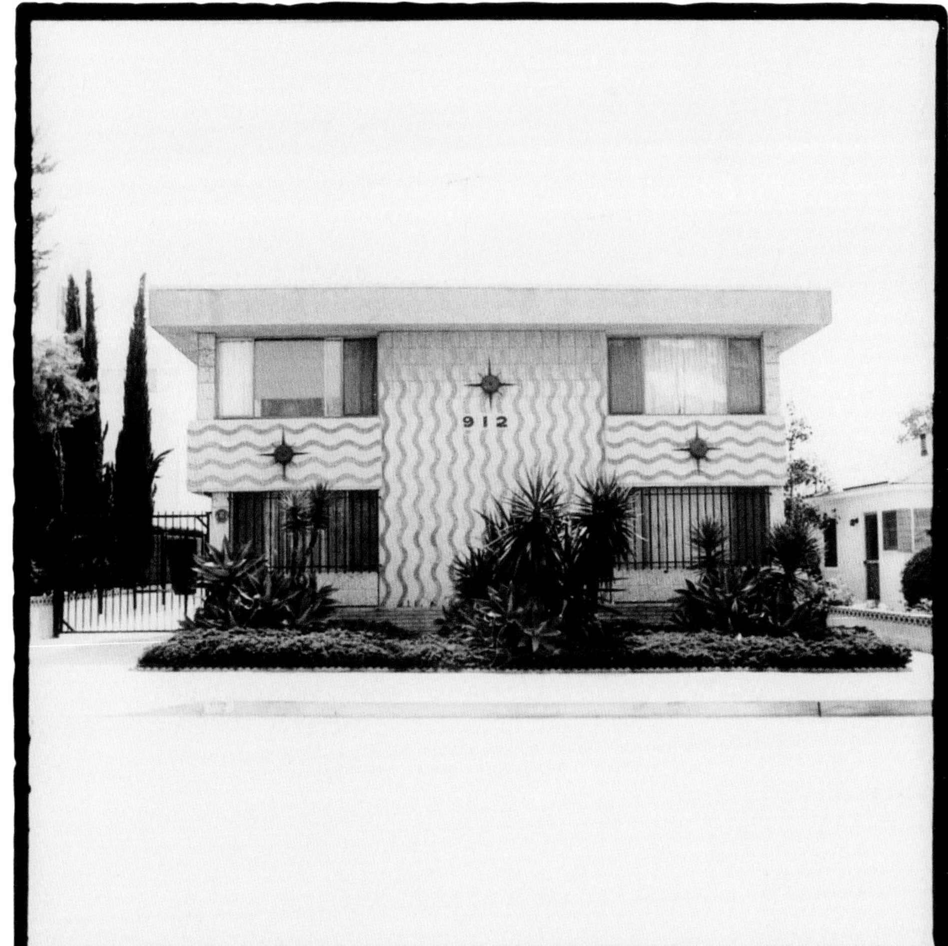

Top and bottom
Judy Fiskin
Untitled, c. 1983

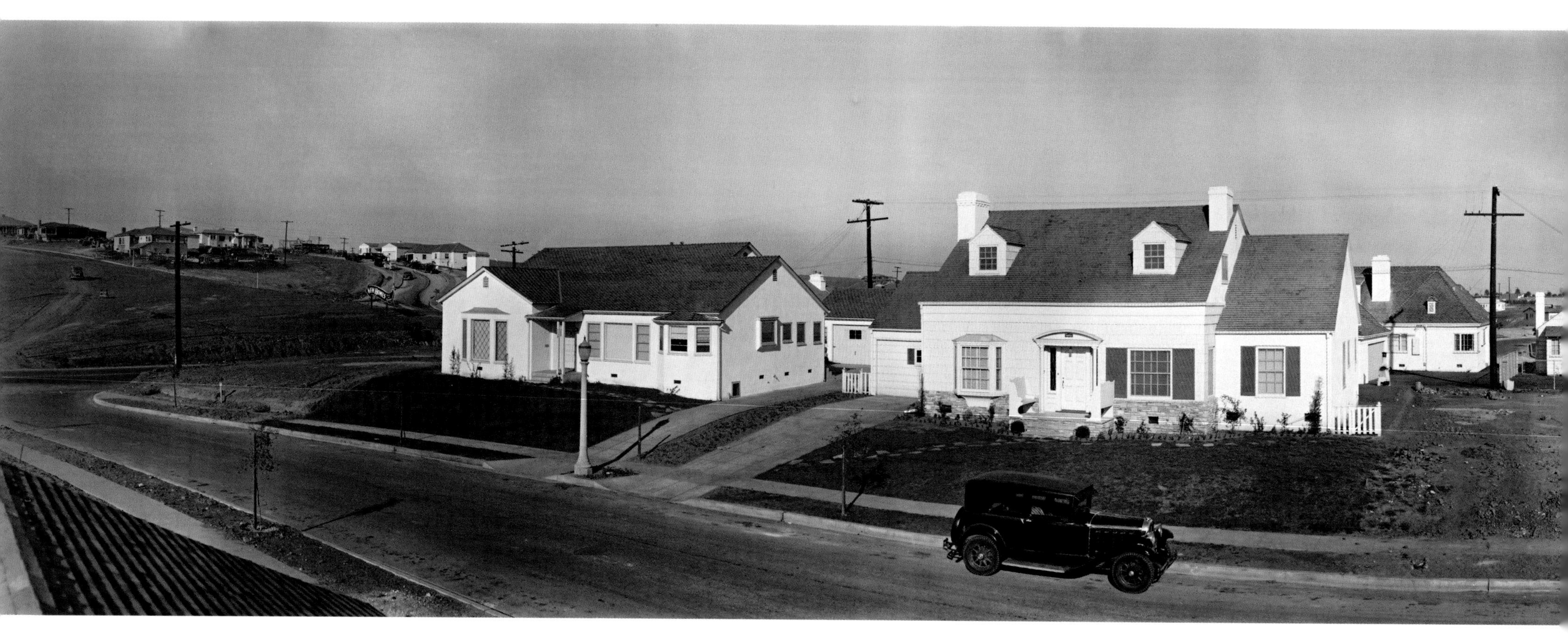

Unknown
Marlow-Burns Subdivision,
Windsor Hills, Los Angeles,
December 1938

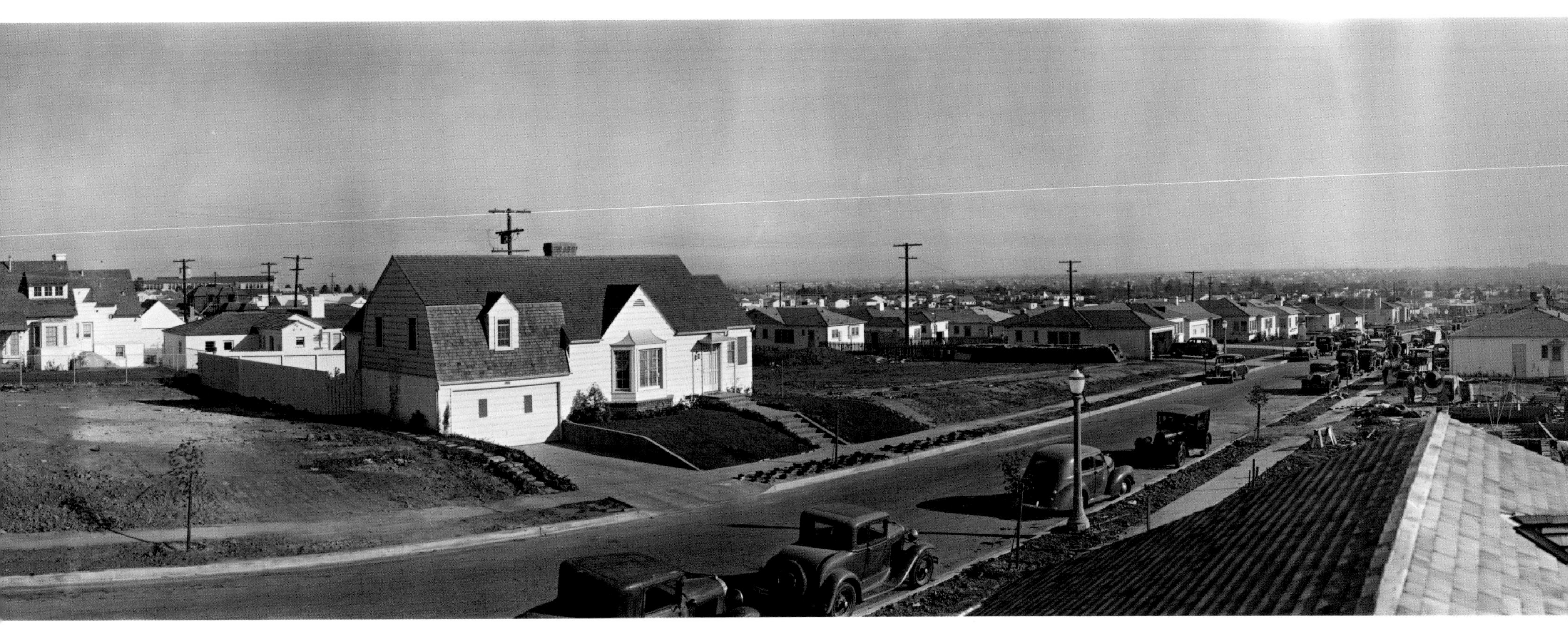

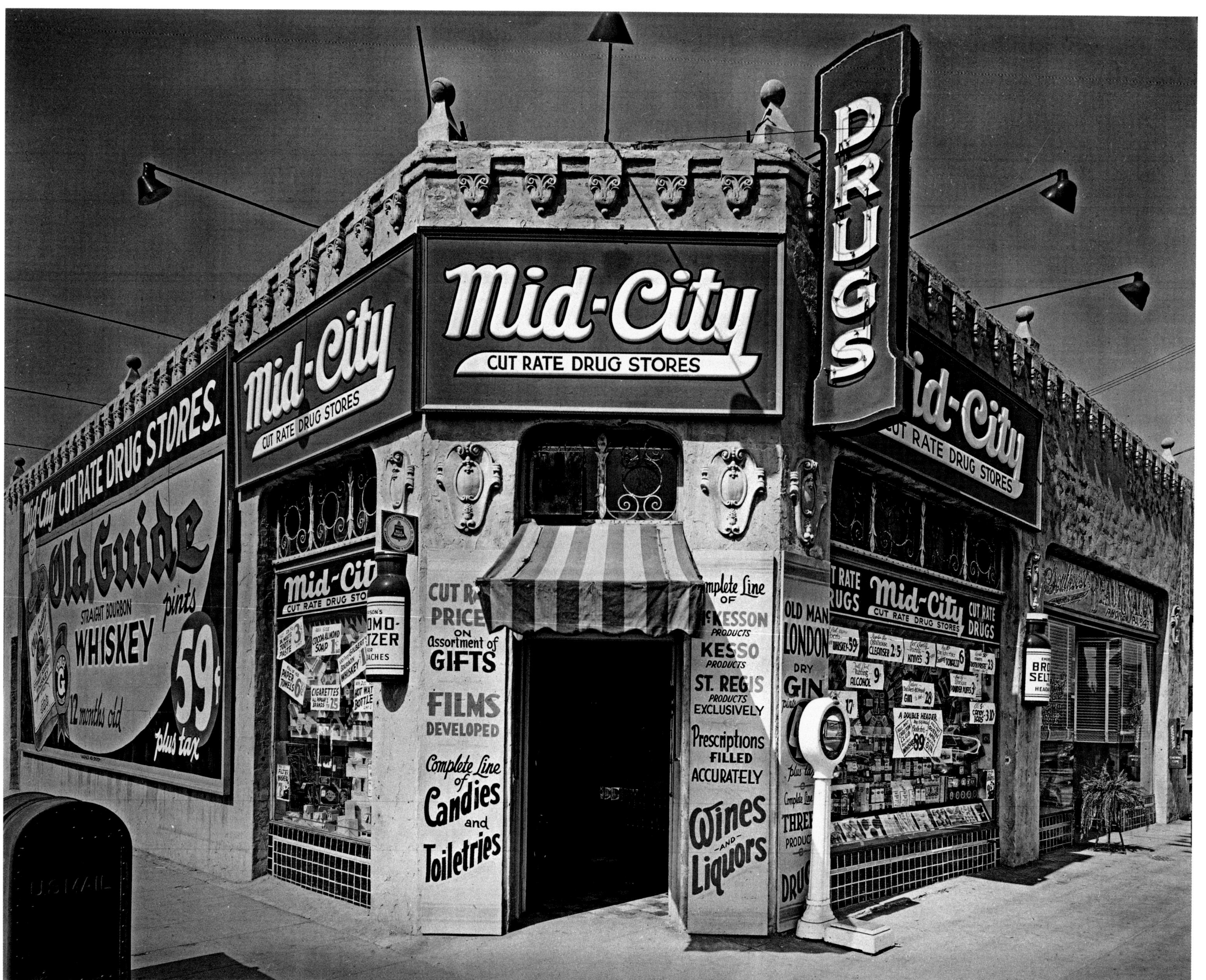

DRUGS
Mid-City
CUT RATE DRUG STORES
Mid-City
CUT RATE DRUG STORES
Mid-City
CUT RATE DRUG STORES
Mid-City
CUT RATE DRUG STORES
MID-CITY CUT RATE DRUG STORES
Old Guide
STRAIGHT BOURBON
WHISKEY
pints
59¢
plus tax
12 months old
CUT RATE PRICE ON Assortment of GIFTS
FILMS DEVELOPED
Complete Line of Candies and Toiletries
Complete Line OF McKESSON PRODUCTS
KESSO PRODUCTS
ST. REGIS PRODUCTS EXCLUSIVELY
Prescriptions FILLED ACCURATELY
Wines AND Liquors
DRUGS
OLD MAN LONDON DRY GIN
CUT RATE DRUGS
CUT RATE DRUGS
U.S. MAIL

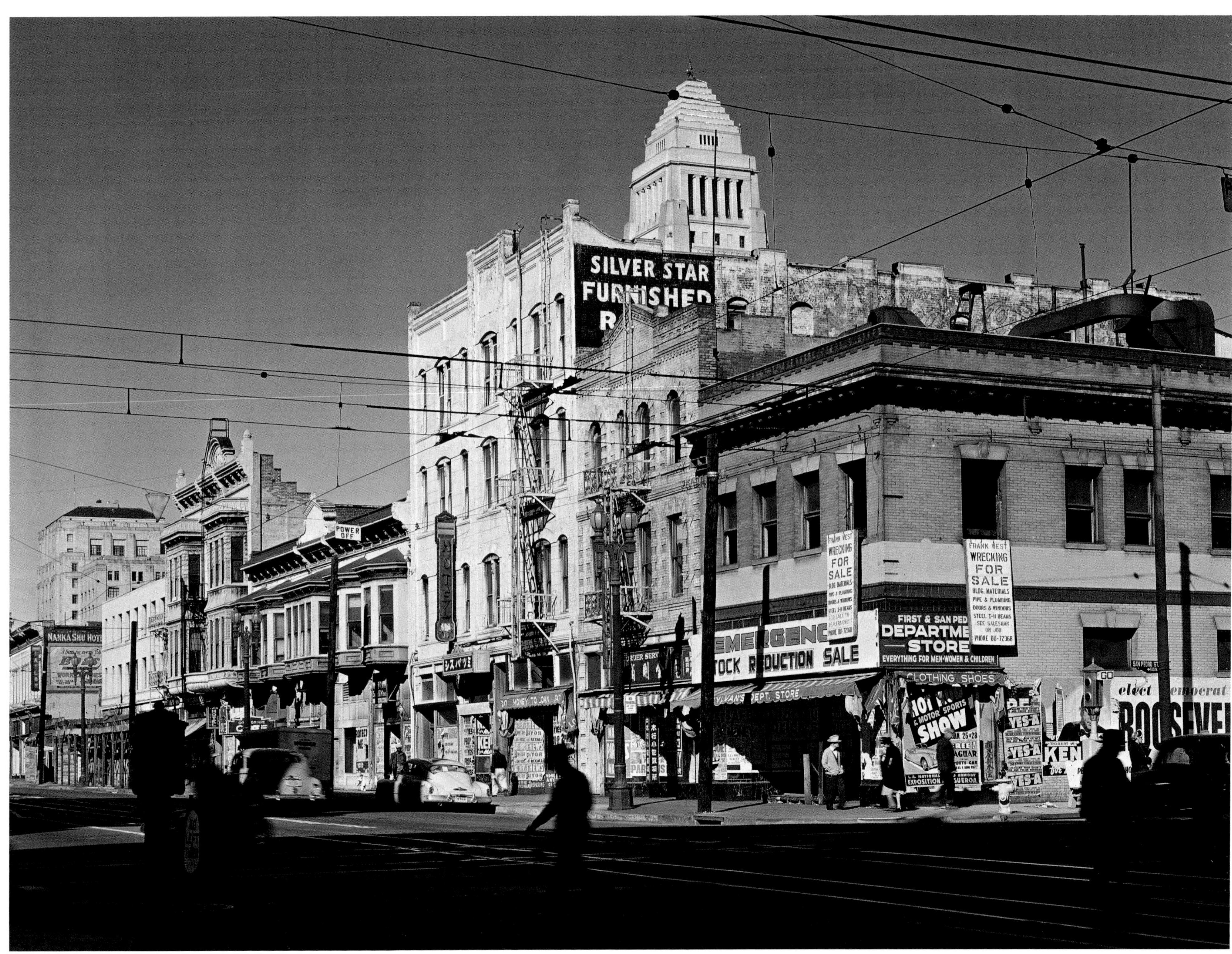

Leonard Nadel
*First Street Before
Demolition, c.* 1952

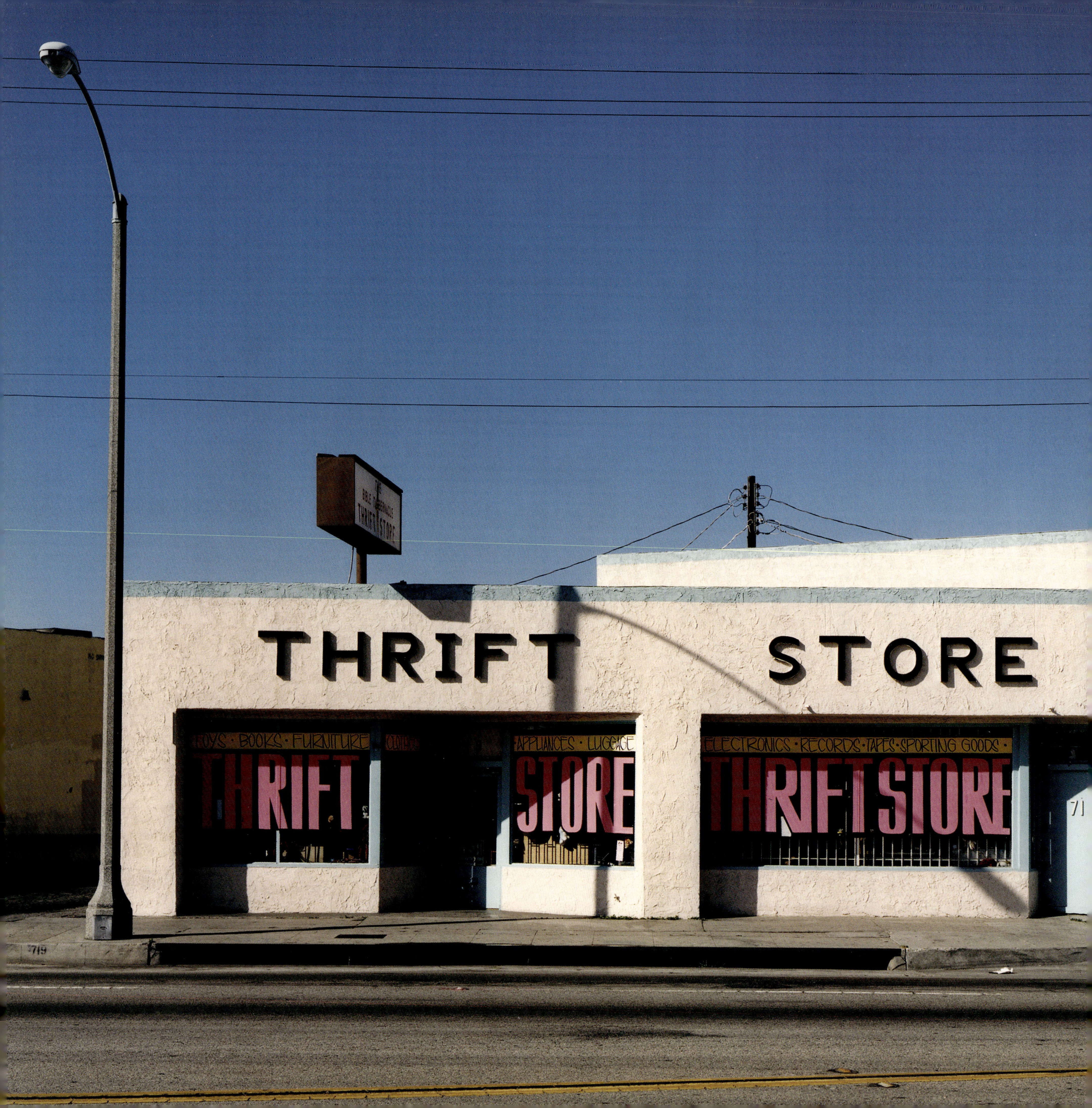

THRIFT
STORE
TOYS · BOOKS · FURNITURE · CLOTHES
·APPLIANCES · LUGGAGE
·ELECTRONICS · RECORDS · TAPES · SPORTING GOODS ·
THRIFT
STORE
THRIFT STORE
719

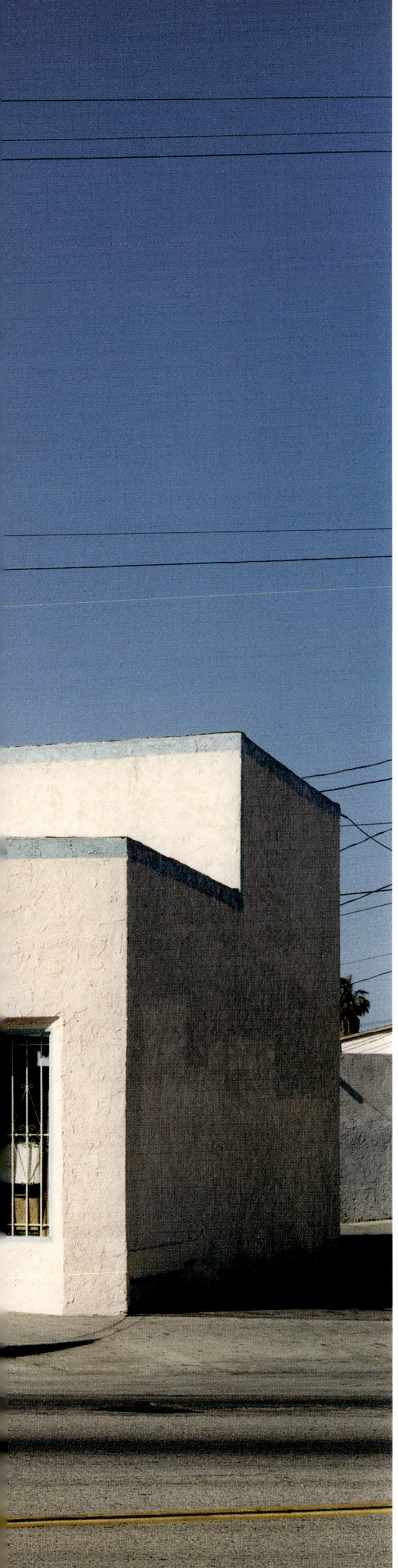

John Humble
*719 Lincoln Boulevard, Venice,
May 13, 1995*, 1995

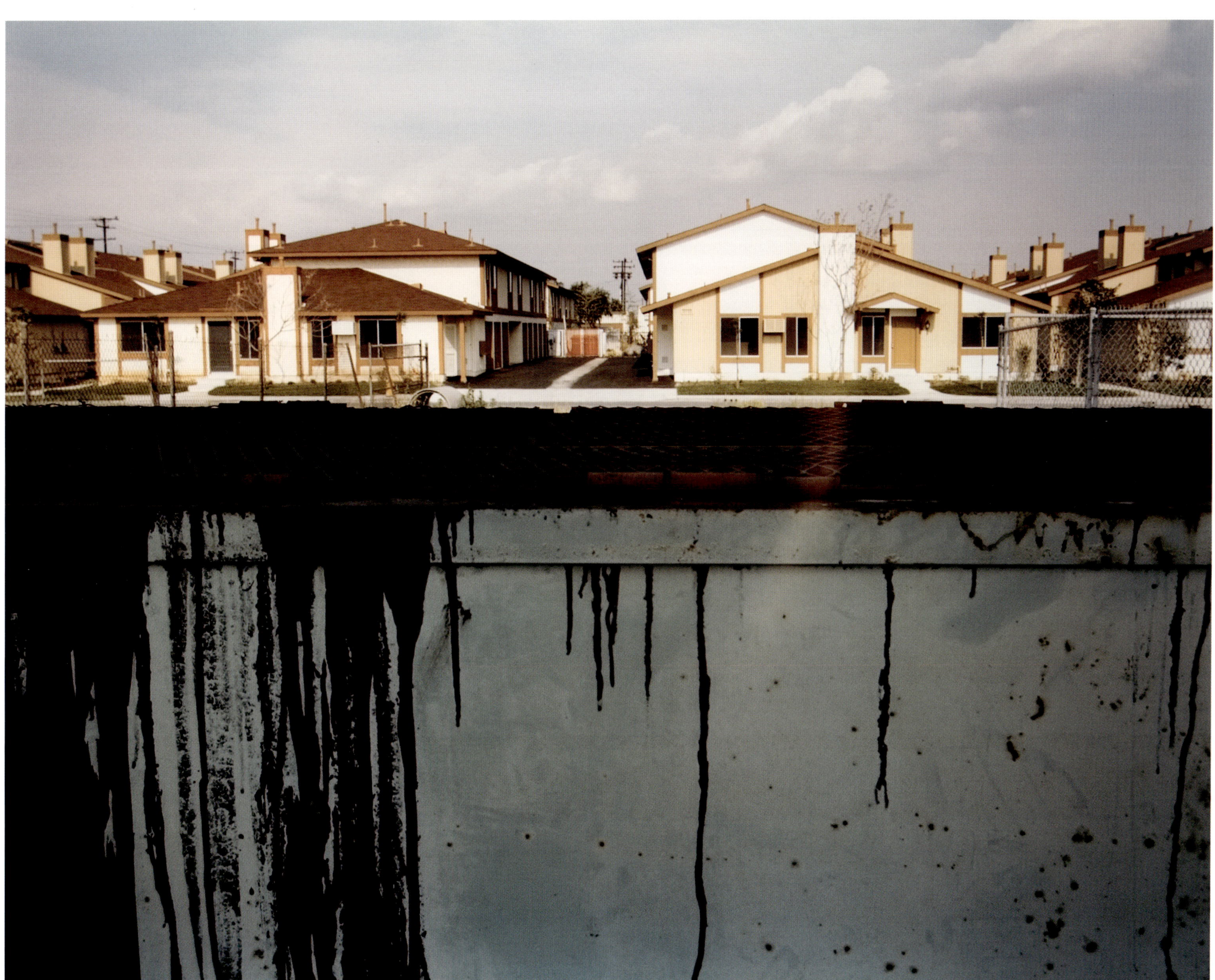

Leland Rice
*Tar Covered Vat and
Condominiums*, 1980

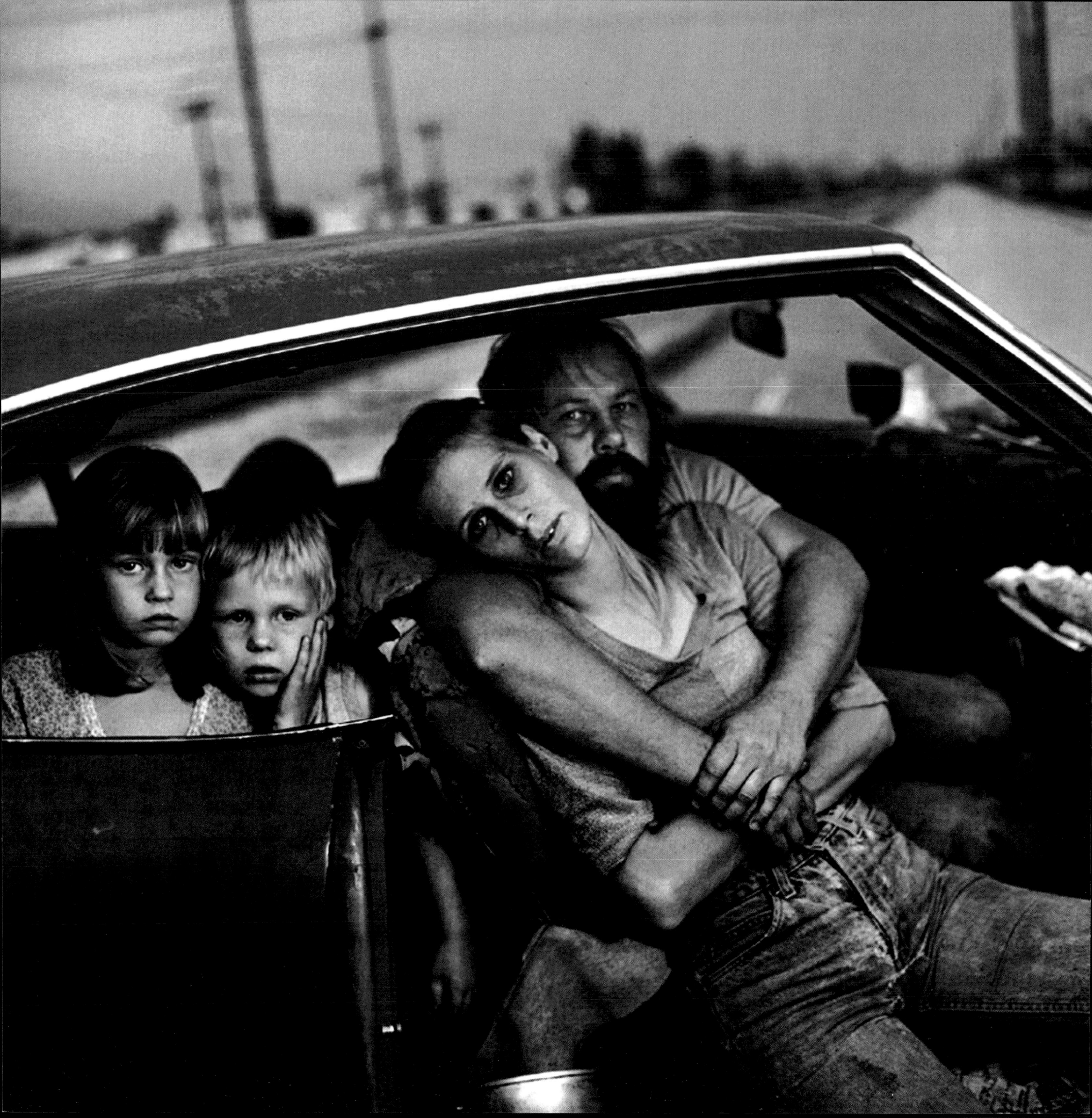

MOVE

The vehicle becomes now a capsule,
its dashboard the brain, the surrounding
landscape unfolding like a televised screen.
Jean Baudrillard, writer

No city on earth is so inextricably linked with the automobile and all its pleasures and perils as Los Angeles. Complex networks of freeways and boulevards crisscross the still fast-growing region, extending into every corner of Southern California. Next to beaches and balmy climes, the freeways are one of the region's prime signifiers, linking suburbs and outlying foothills with vast areas in between.

In the late nineteenth century, railroad barons built many of Los Angeles's initial trolley and traction lines, in part to connect their far-flung real estate and business interests. A sprawling overlay of high-speed roads eventually replaced these rail lines in a takeover that was born not of corporate conspiracy but of a populist desire for freedom and mobility. Images by C.C. Pierce, "Dick" Whittington Studio and others make plain the far simpler truth: Angelenos love to drive.

The city's dominant automobile culture gave rise to the trite maxim "no one walks in Los Angeles." However, the meandering footpaths and trails of the early city, alluringly captured in a photograph by Charles Puck, are often hidden in plain sight, displaced in the mind's eye by images of lone walkers amid clipped suburban lawns. John Divola and Garry Winogrand's street photography captures pedestrians in a paved world of traffic signs and streaming sunlight. Meanwhile, the stationary waiting of Anthony Hernandez's discontented subjects makes the rushing motion around them seem all the more inevitable.

Yet, it is the automobile and all its by-products that visually define Los Angeles. Such artists as Ed Ruscha and Robbert Flick have exploited visions of and from the car to great pictorial effect, merging the canonical symbols of Los Angeles with those of high art.

Michael Light
*Highways 5, 12, 60, and 101
Looking West, L.A. River
and Downtown Beyond*,
February 12, 2004

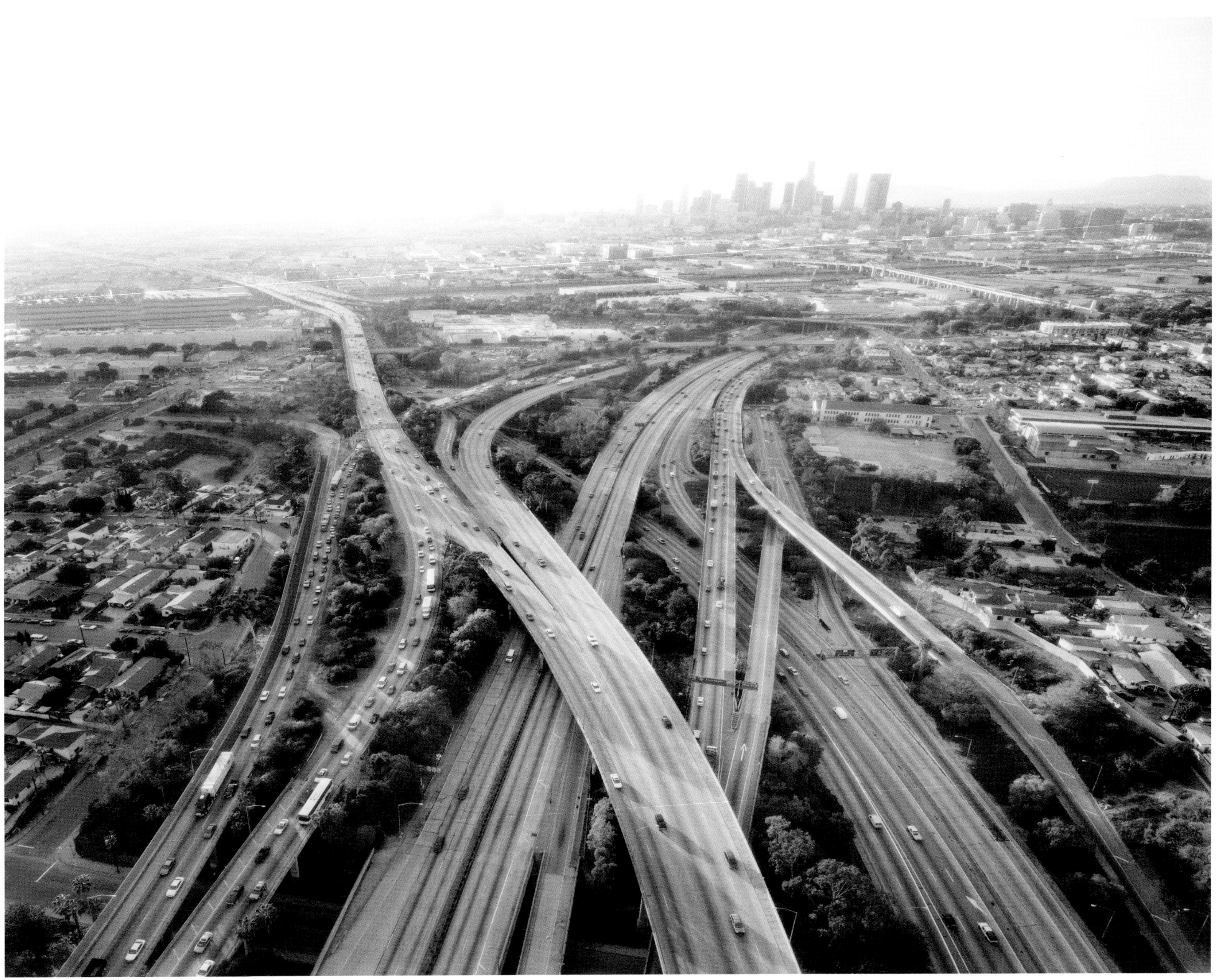

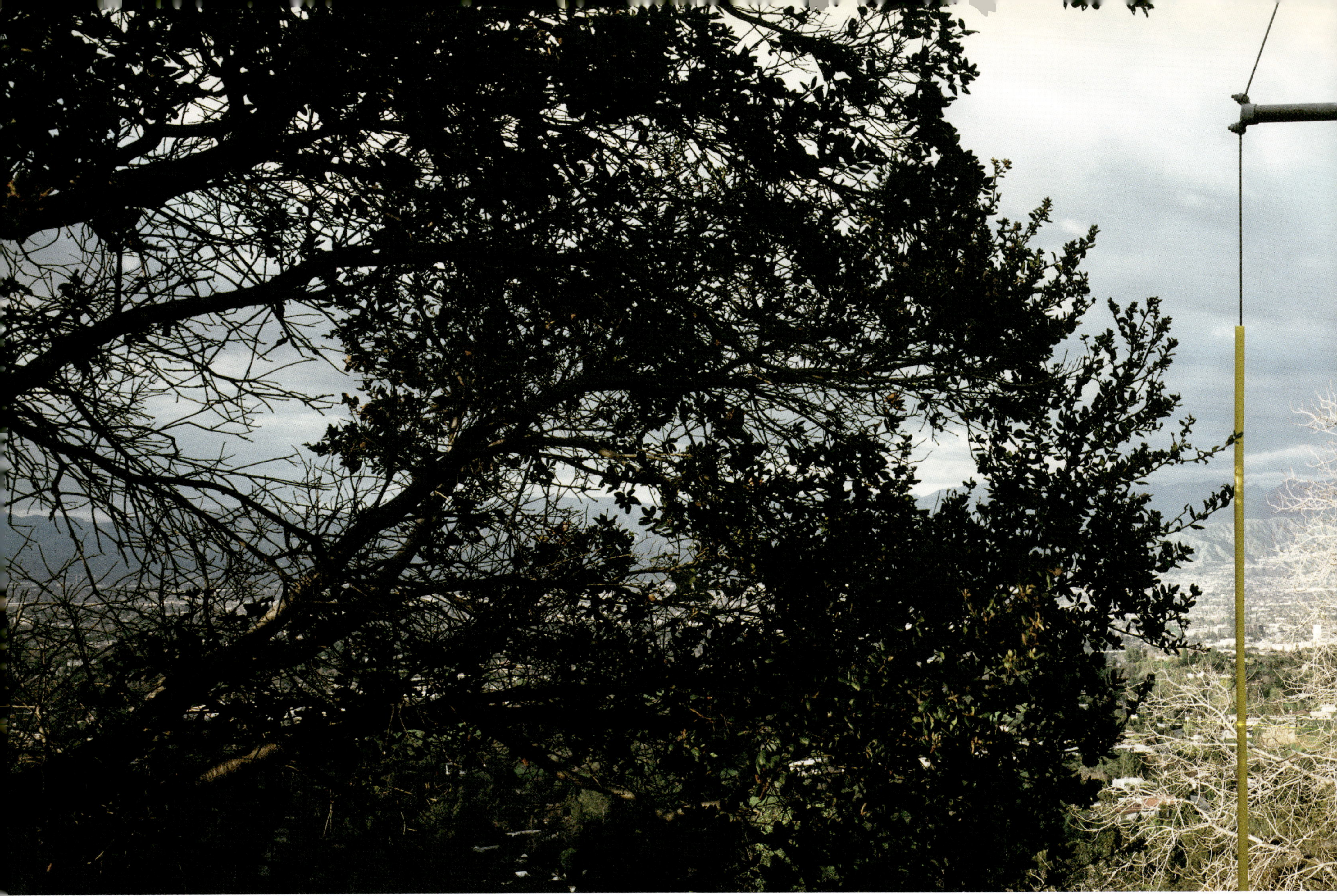

Karen Halverson
*Mulholland Near Skyline Drive,
Los Angeles,* 1993

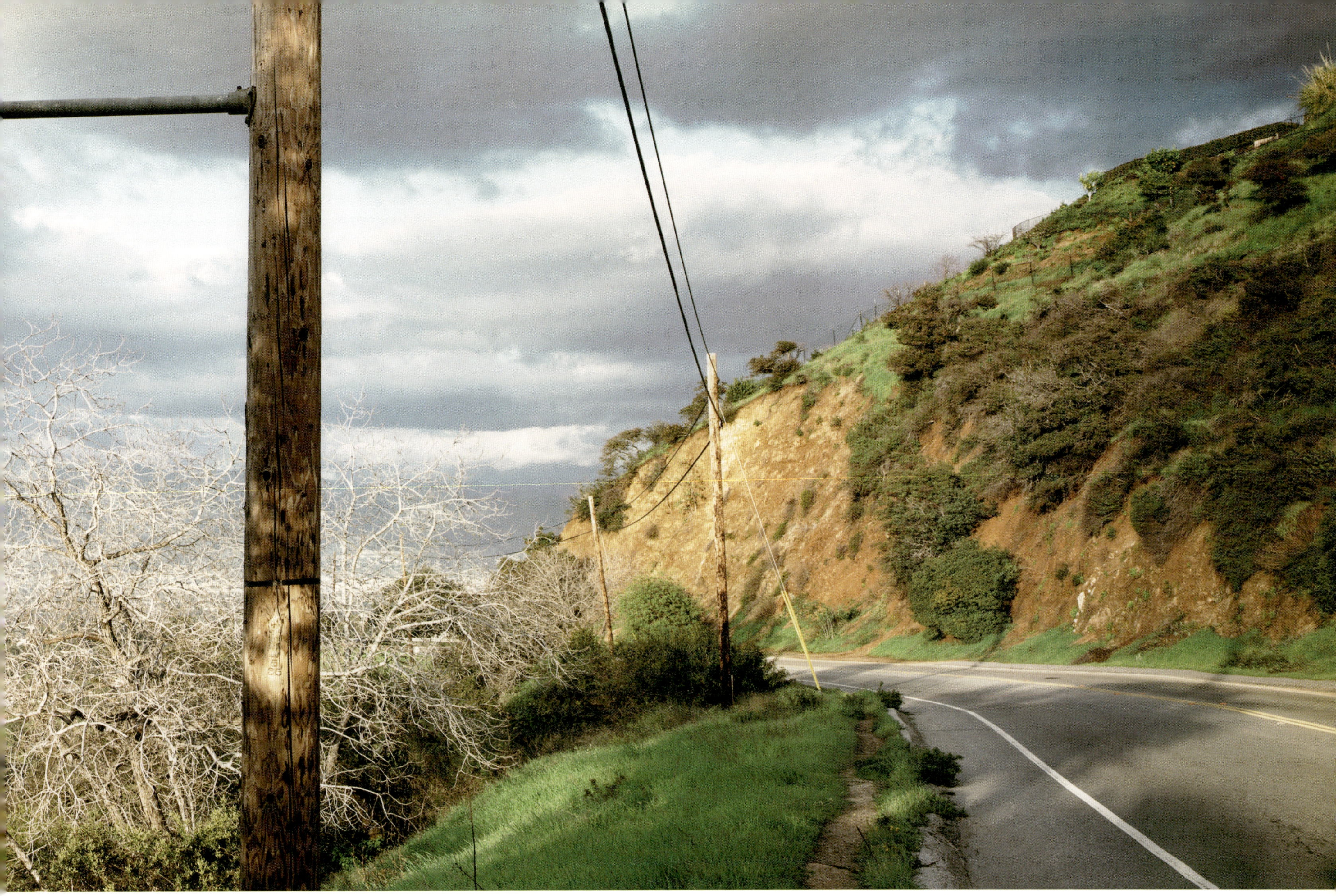

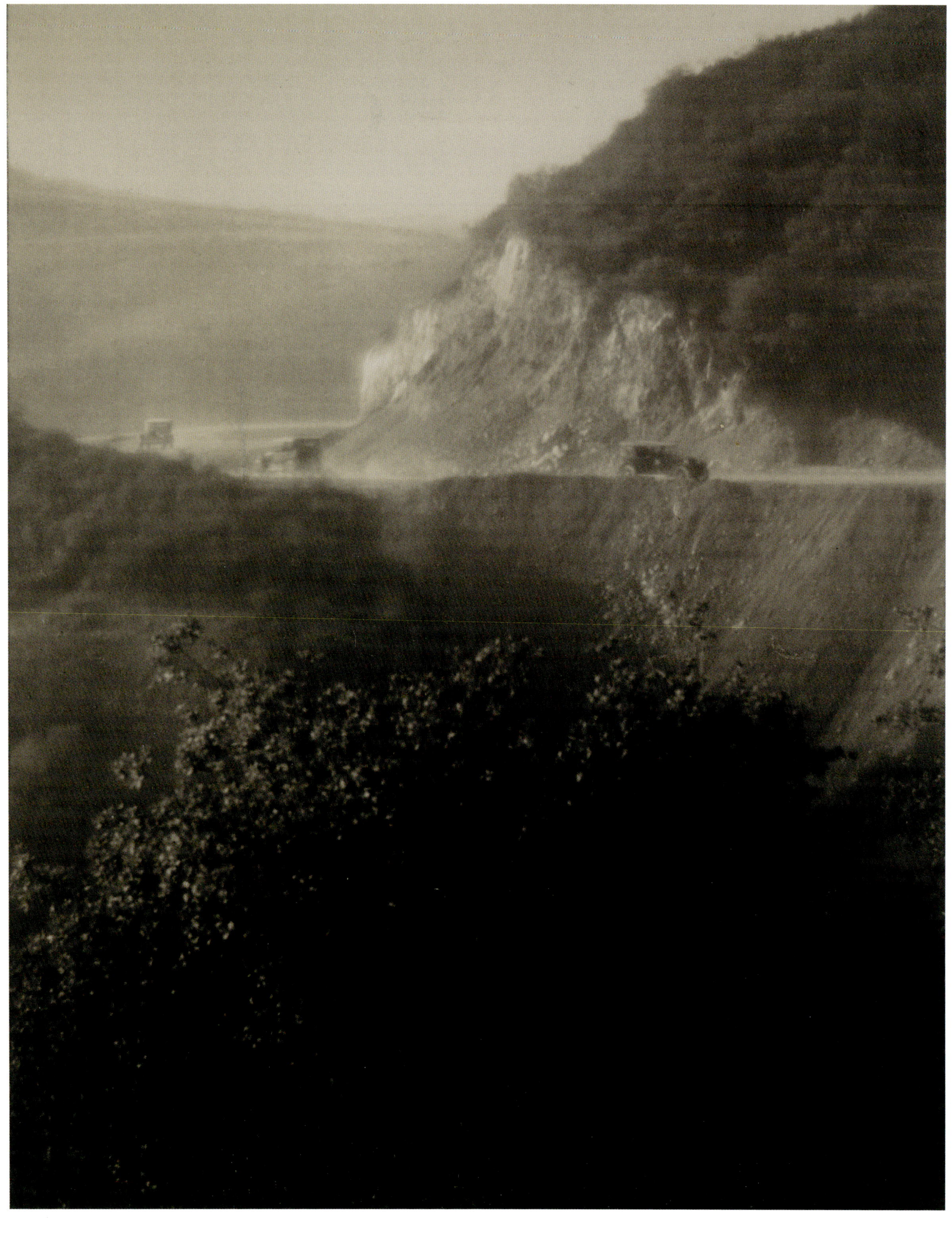

Ernest M. Pratt
Mulholland Highway, 1925

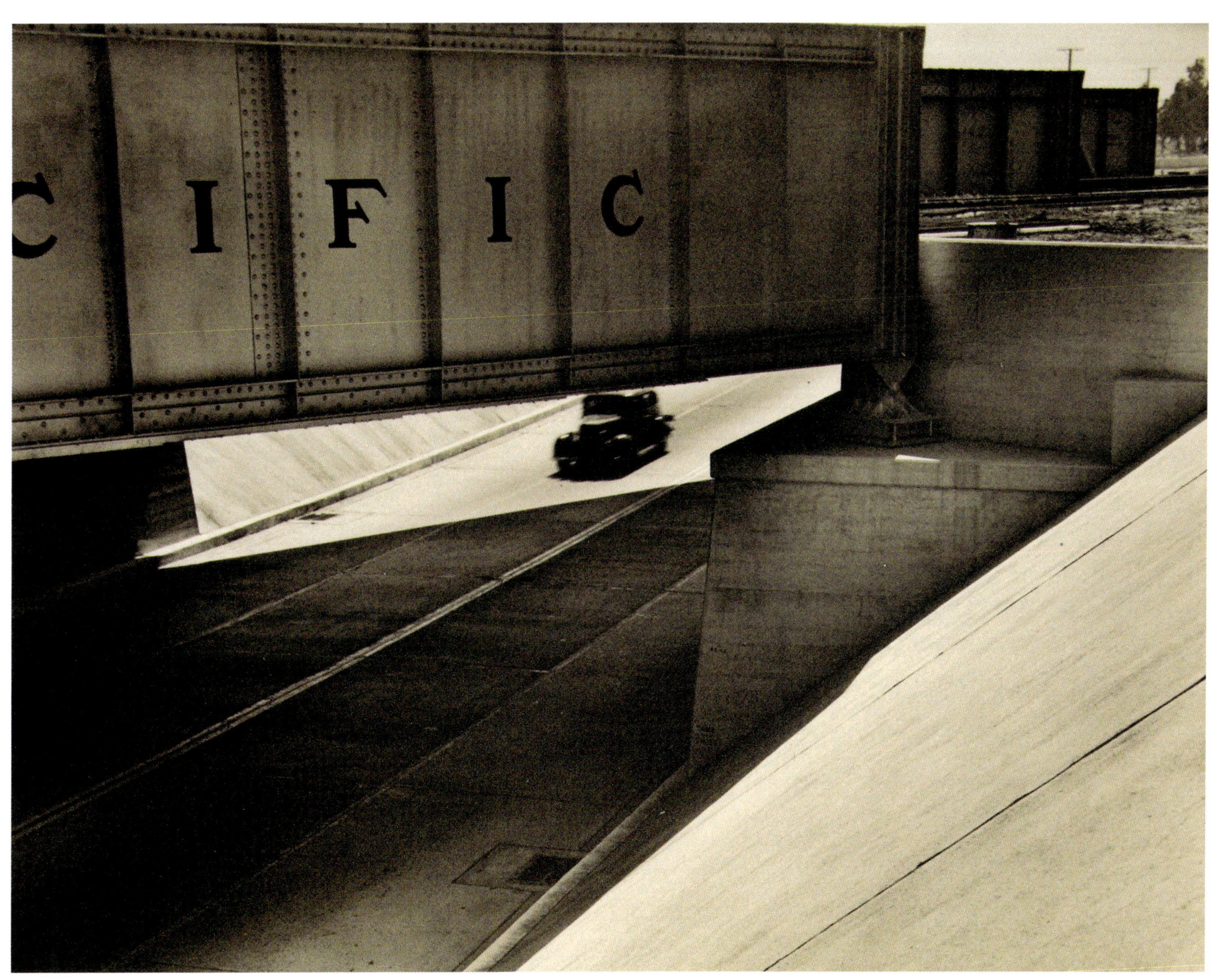

Will Connell
Underpass, 1937

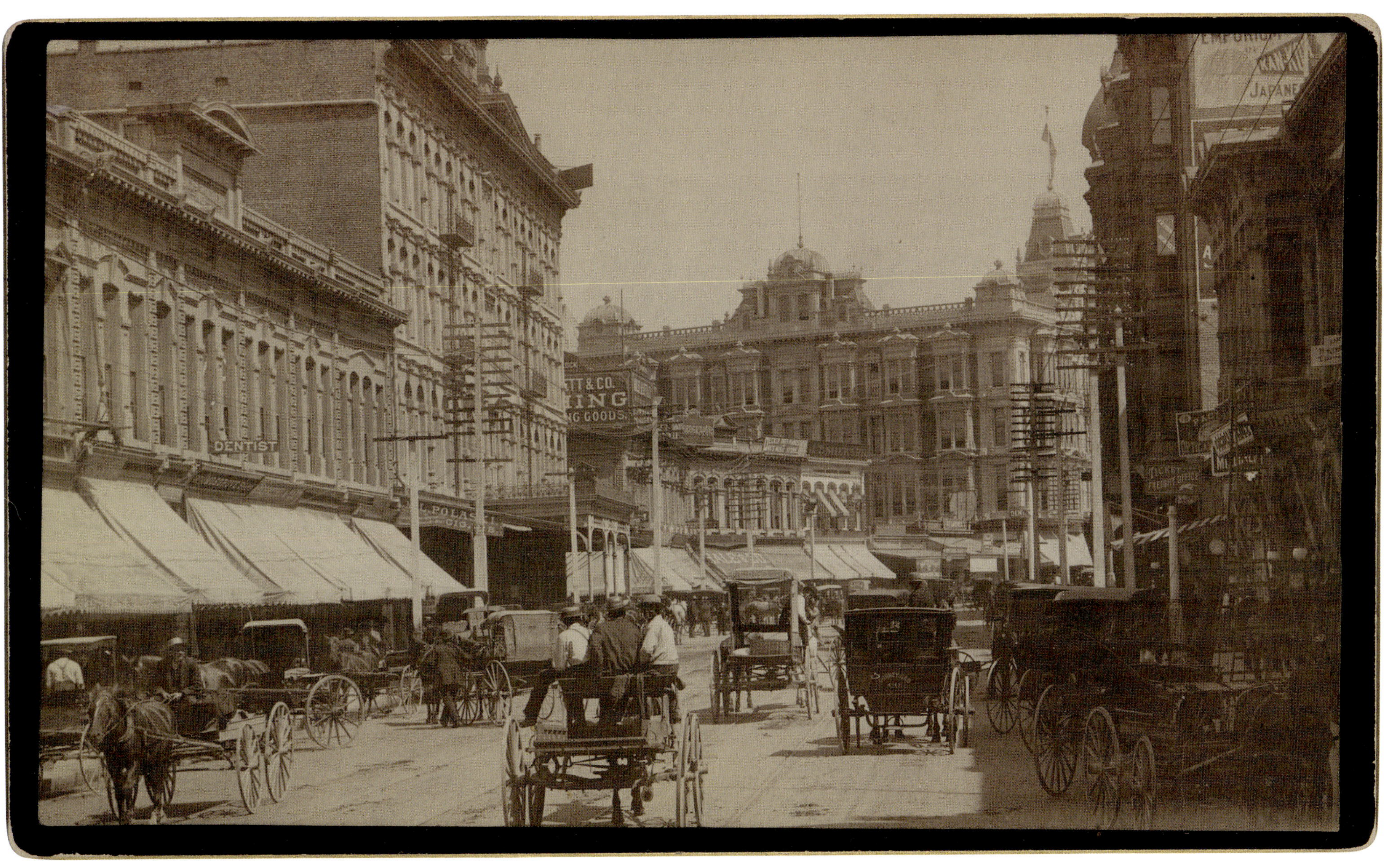

Herve Friend
Los Angeles, c. 1890

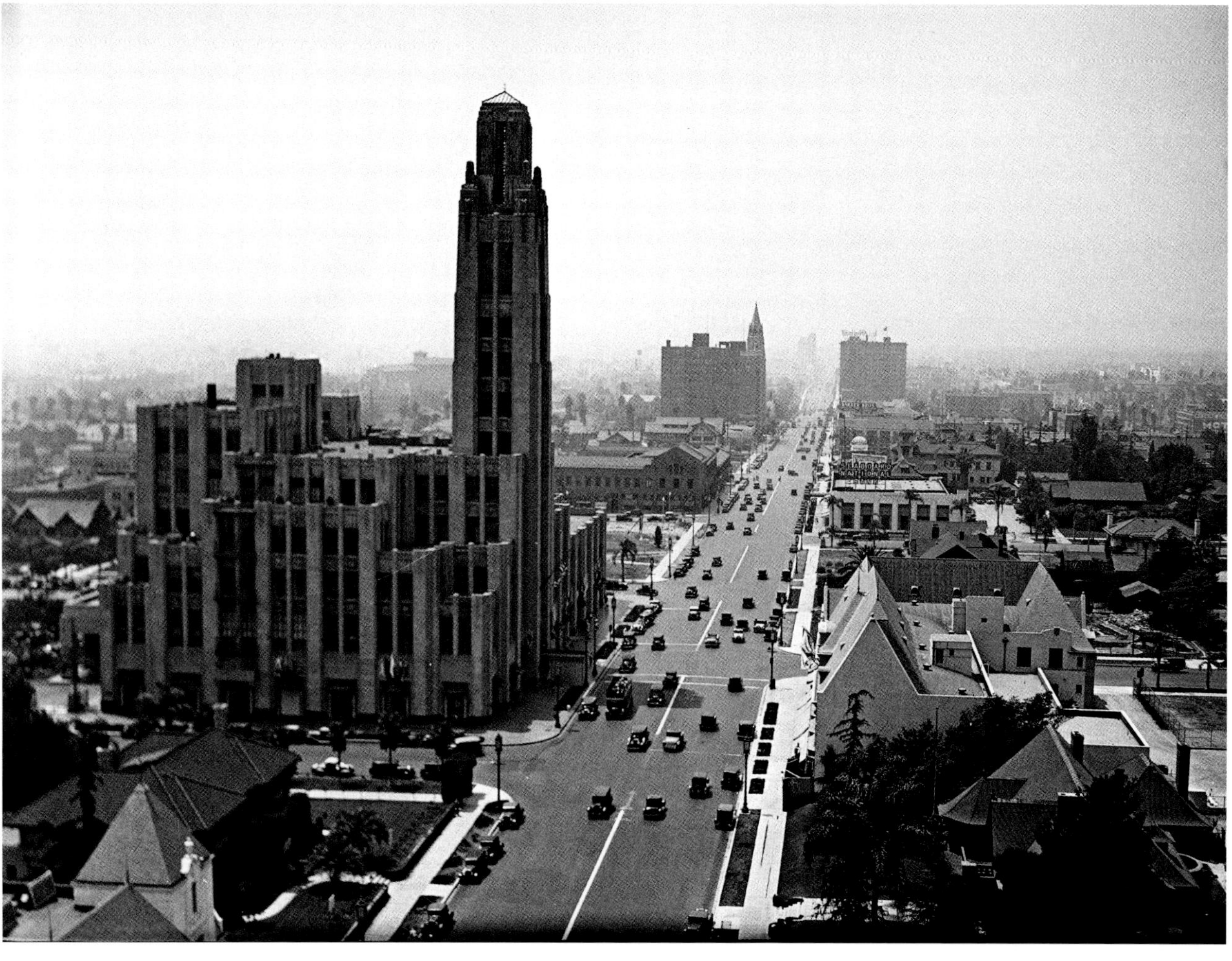

Charles Puck
Wilshire Boulevard Looking West with Bullock's Wilshire on Left, n.d.

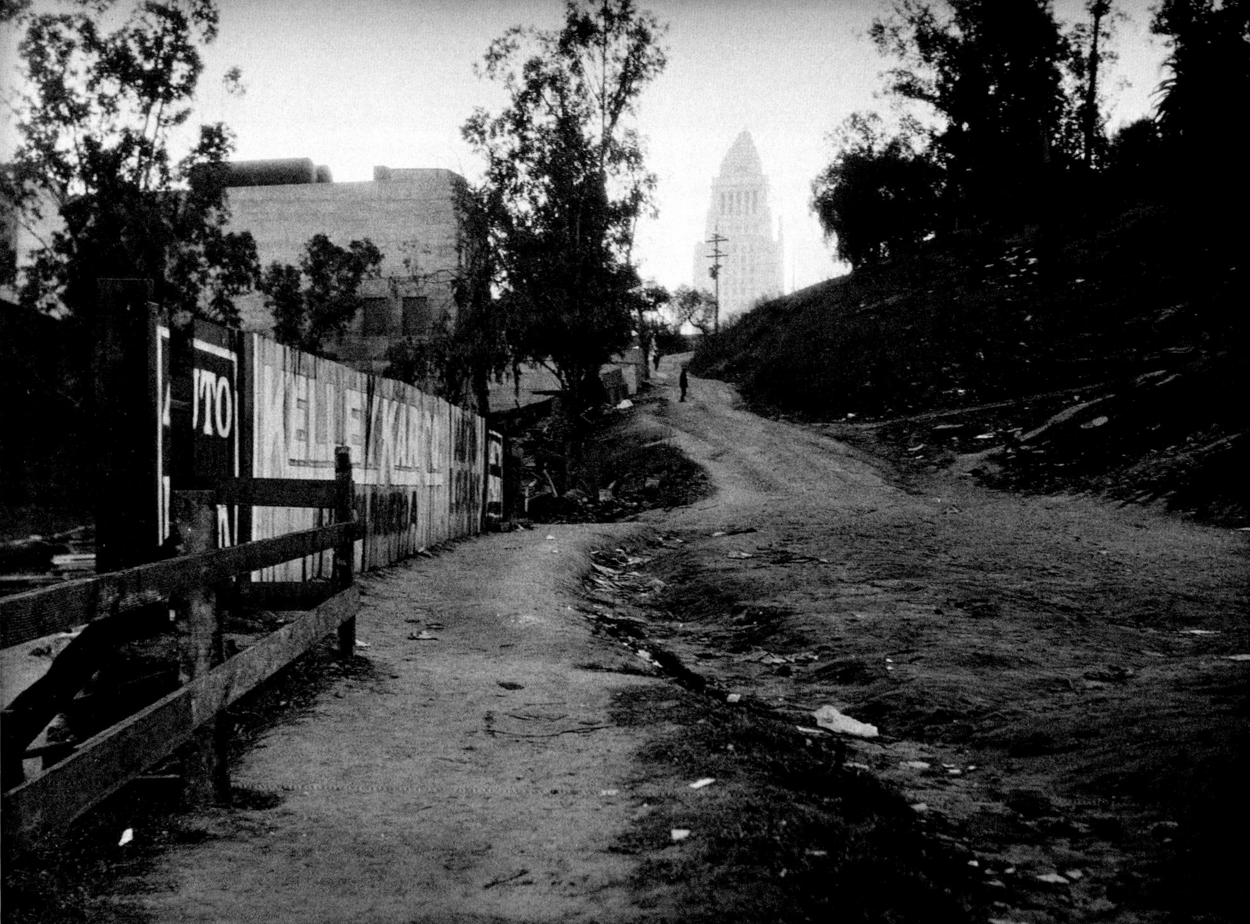

Charles Puck
Buena Vista Street with City Hall in the Distance, Los Angeles, n.d.

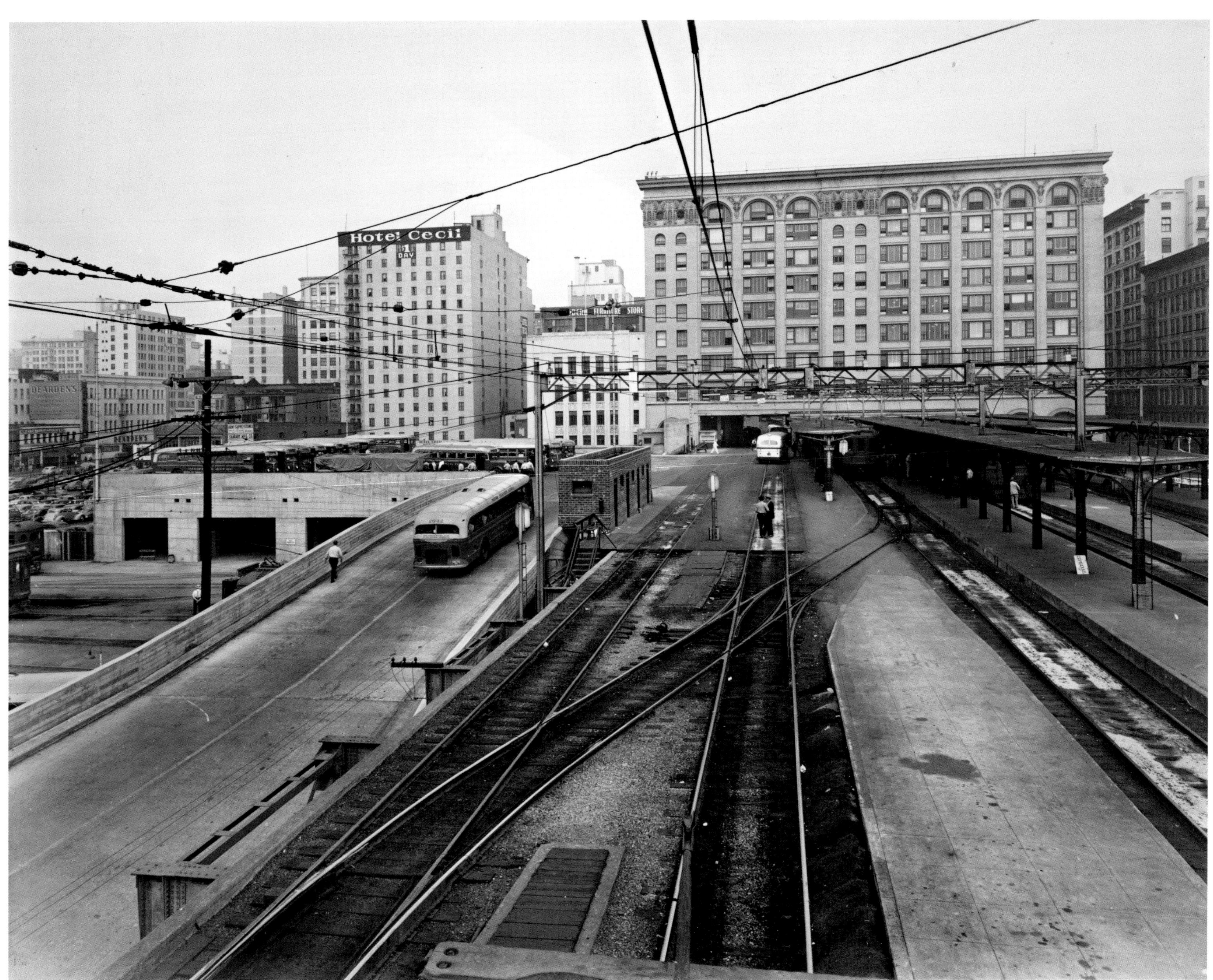

Pacific Electric Railway Company
Main Street Station, Los Angeles, 1944

115

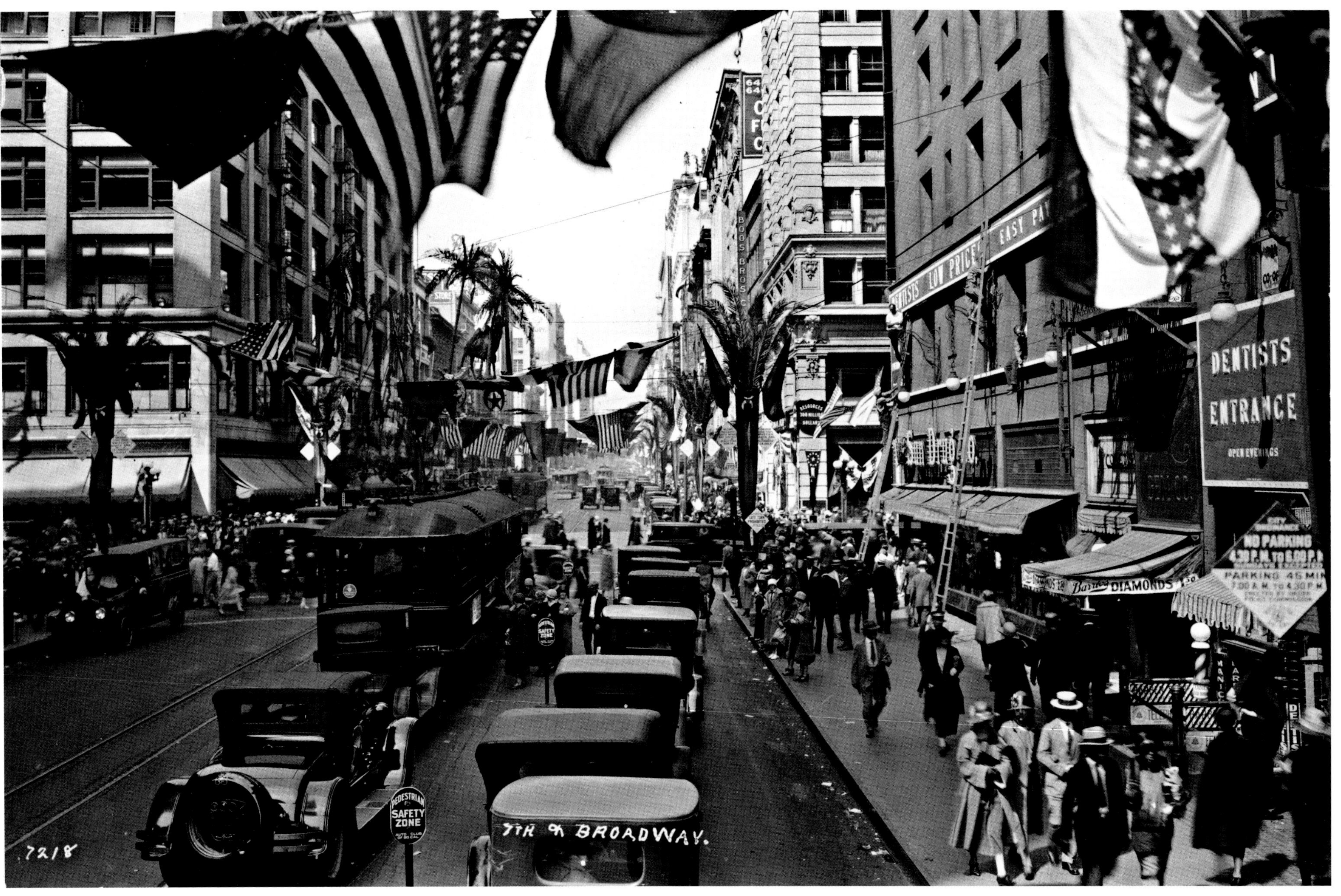

C.C. Pierce
Seventh and Broadway
Looking North, 1925

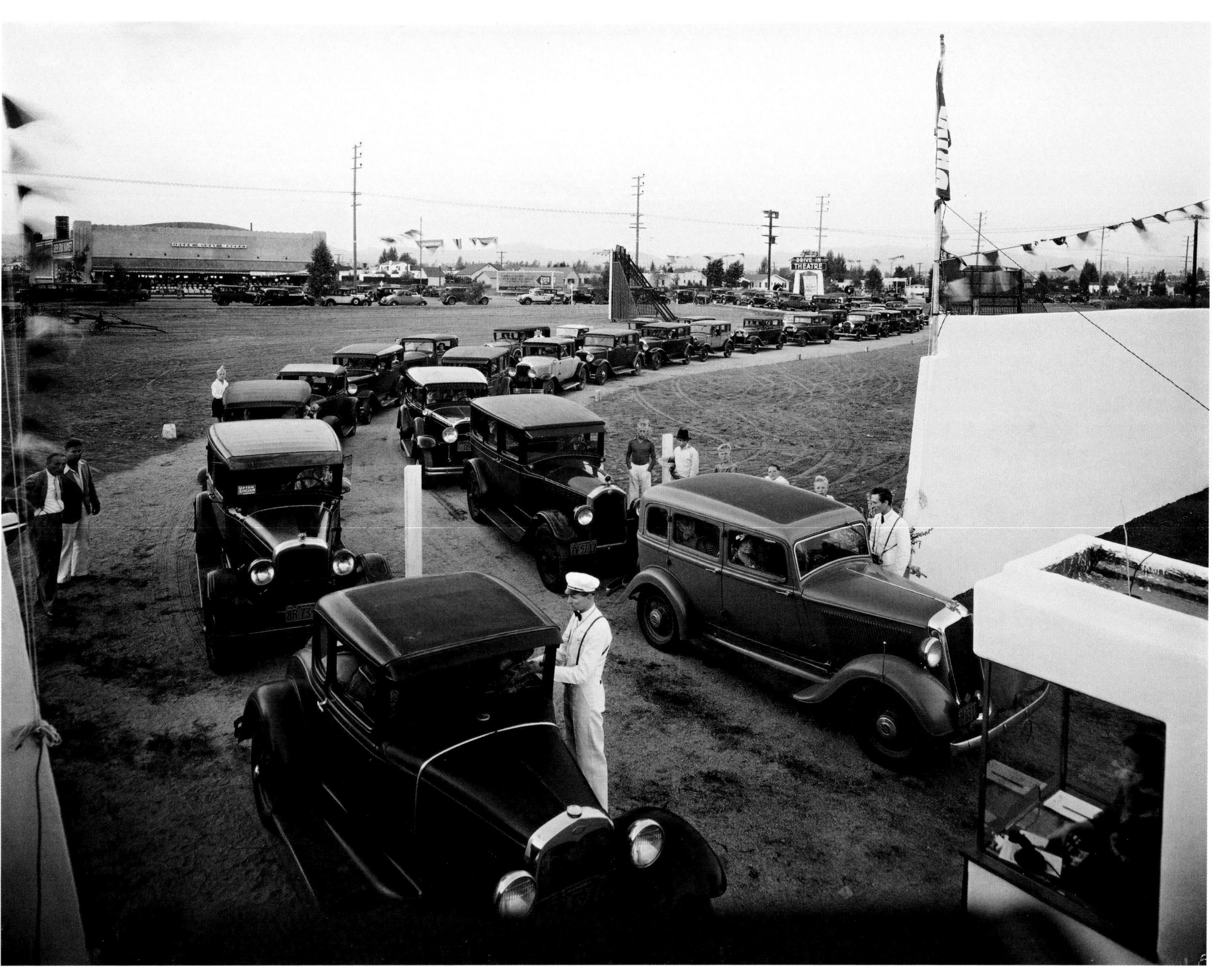

"Dick" Whittington Studio
L.A.'s First Drive-In Theater,
10860 West Pico Blvd, 1934

117

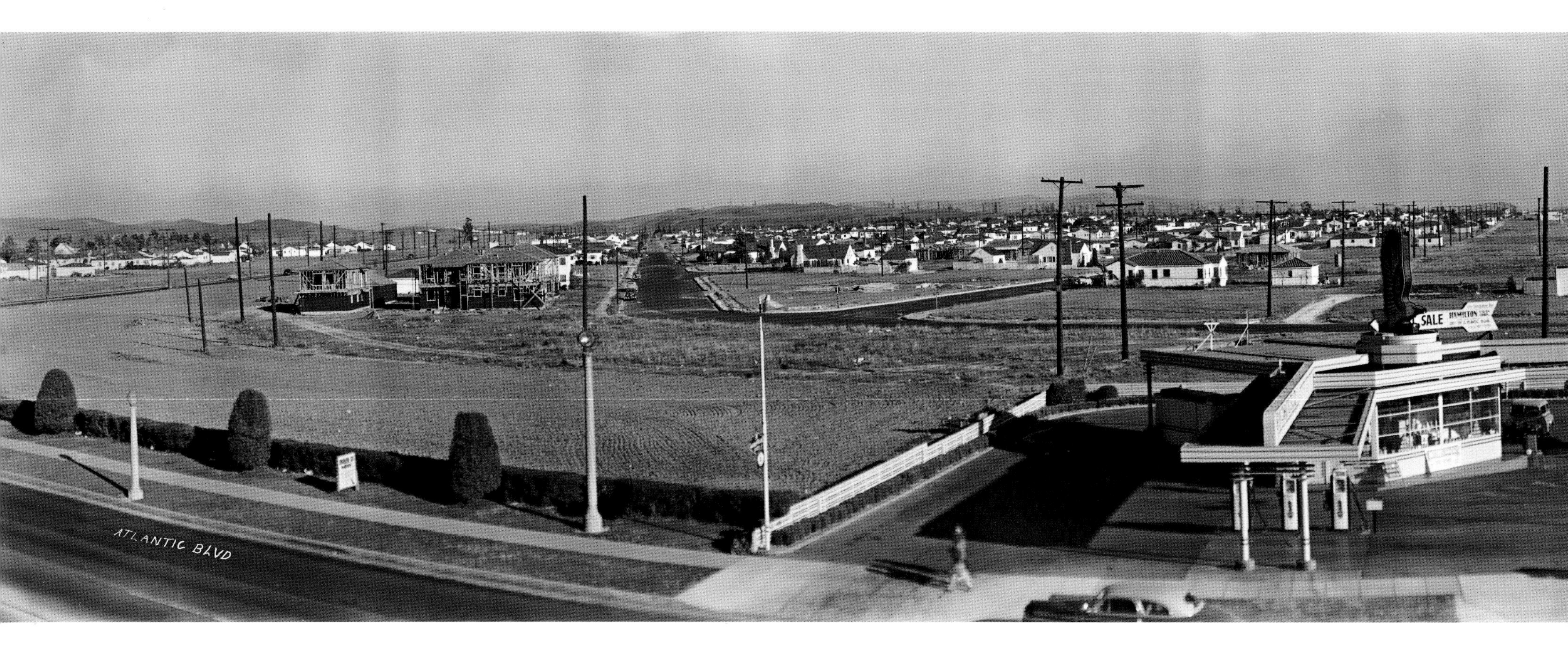

Petit's Studio
*Atlantic and Beverly
Boulevards Looking South
and East*, January 29, 1946

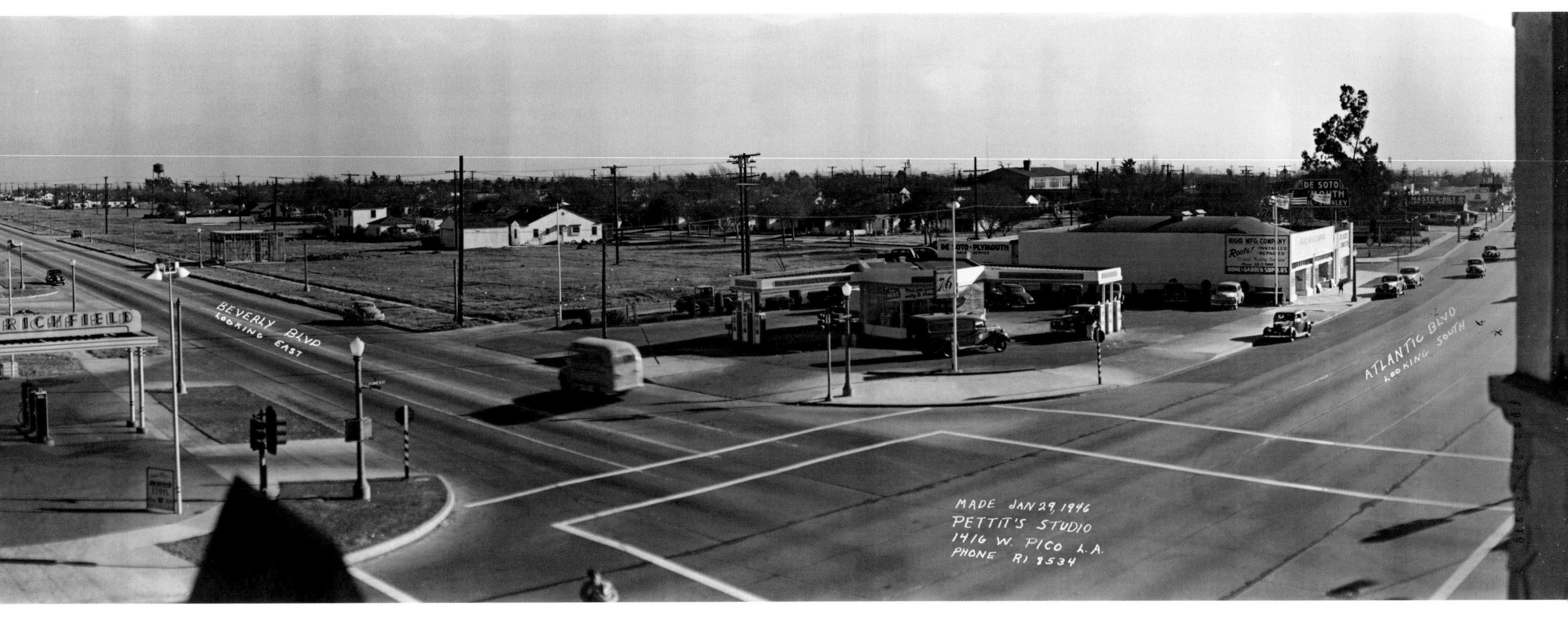
RICHFIELD
BEVERLY BLVD
LOOKING EAST
ATLANTIC BLVD
LOOKING SOUTH
DE SOTO - PLYMOUTH
RIGID MFG. COMPANY
76
DE SOTO
PLYMOUTH
MADE JAN 29, 1946
PETTIT'S STUDIO
1416 W. PICO L.A.
PHONE RI 8534

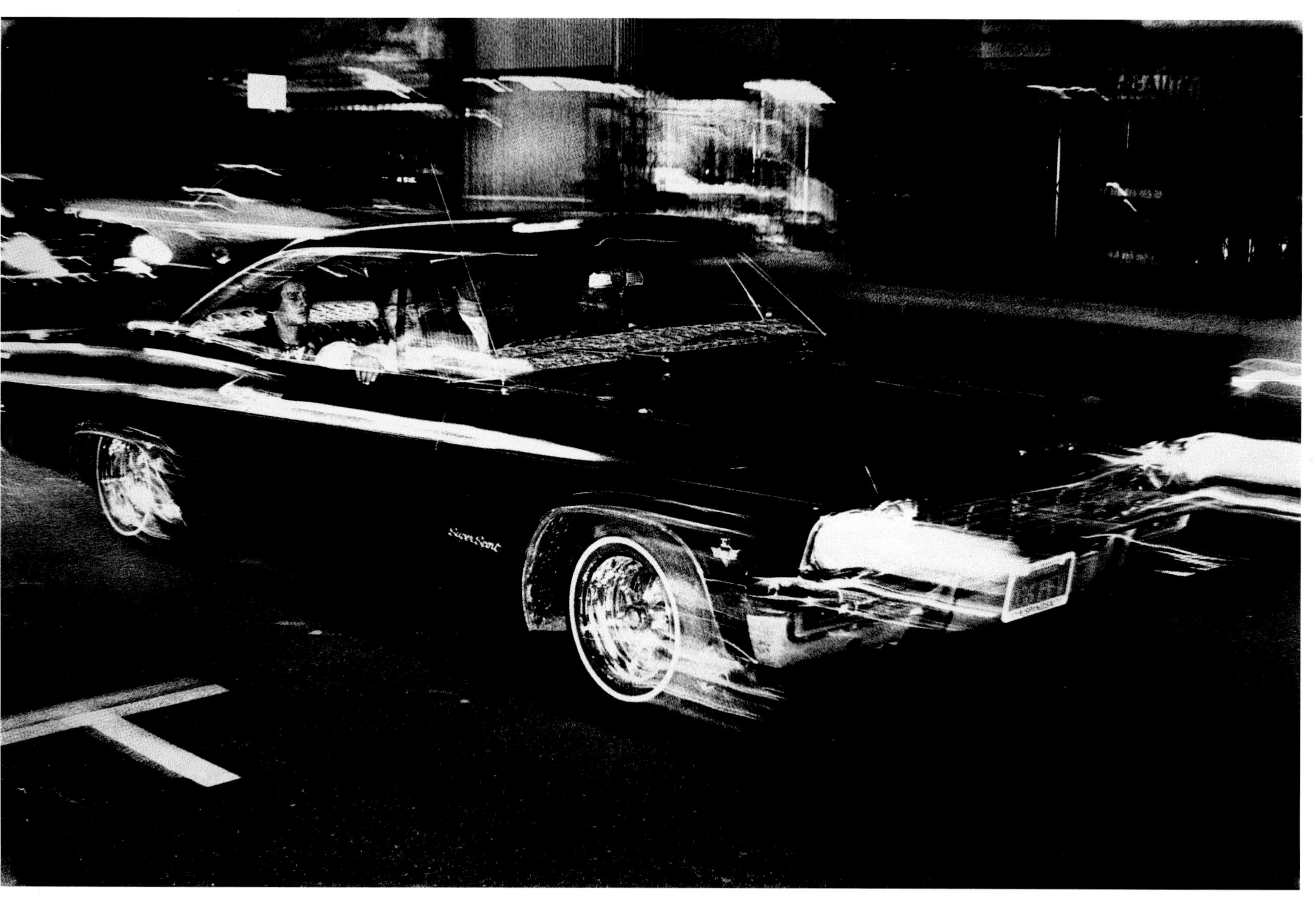

Gusmano Cesaretti
Whittier Boulevard, Night,
1975

Opposite
Edward Ruscha
Shell, Daggett, California,
1962

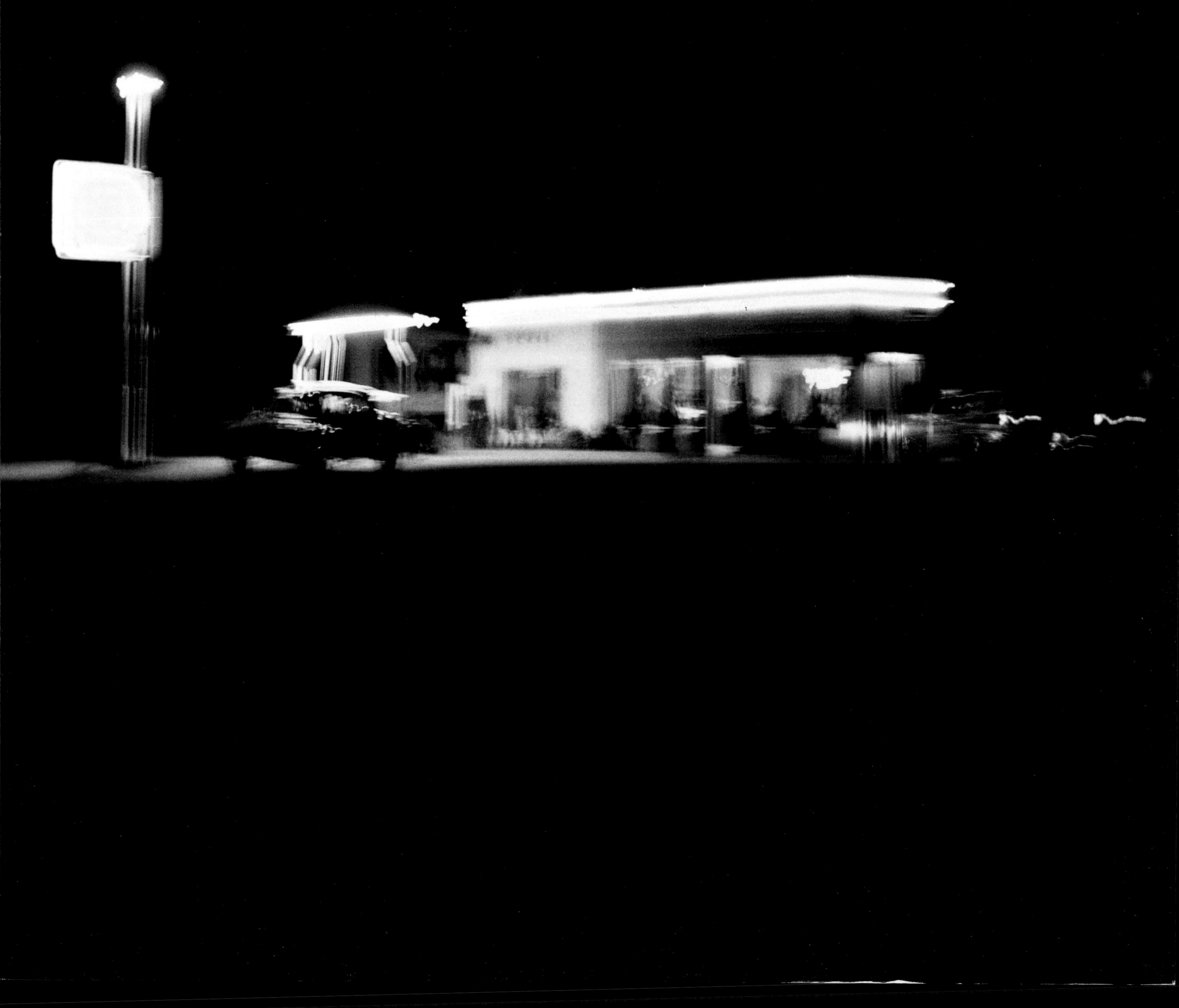

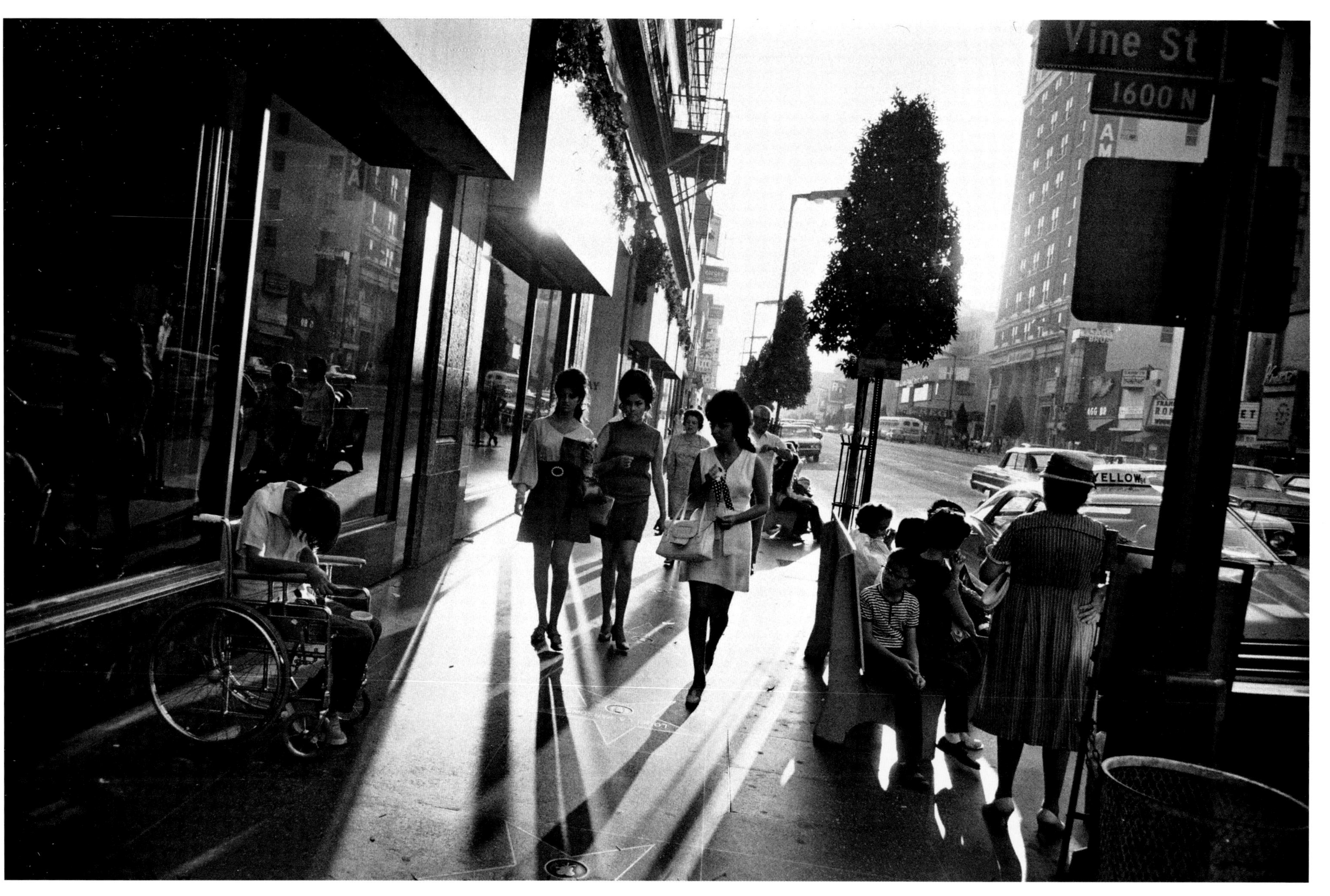

Garry Winogrand
Hollywood and Vine,
Los Angeles, 1969

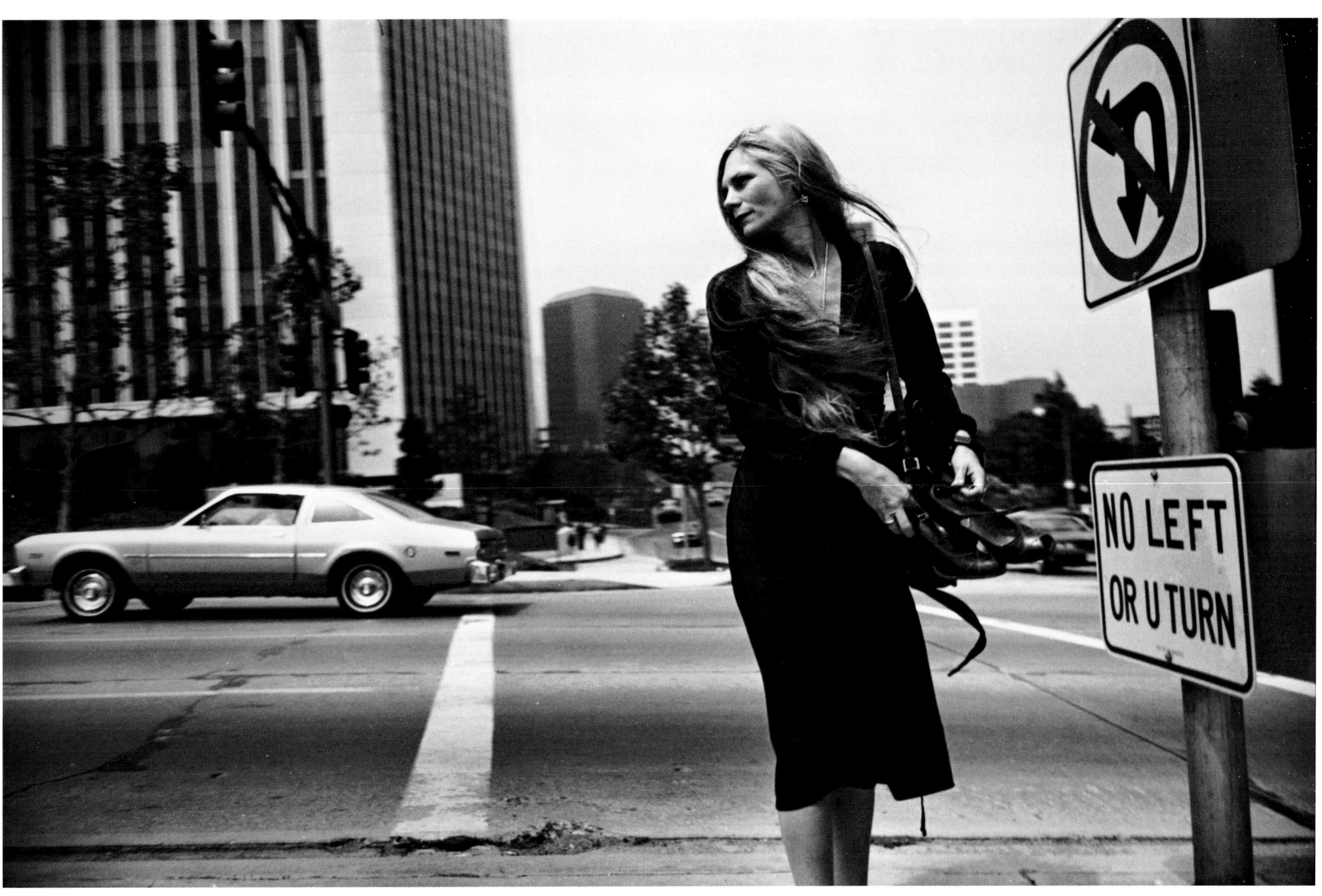

Garry Winogrand
Los Angeles, *c.* 1980–81

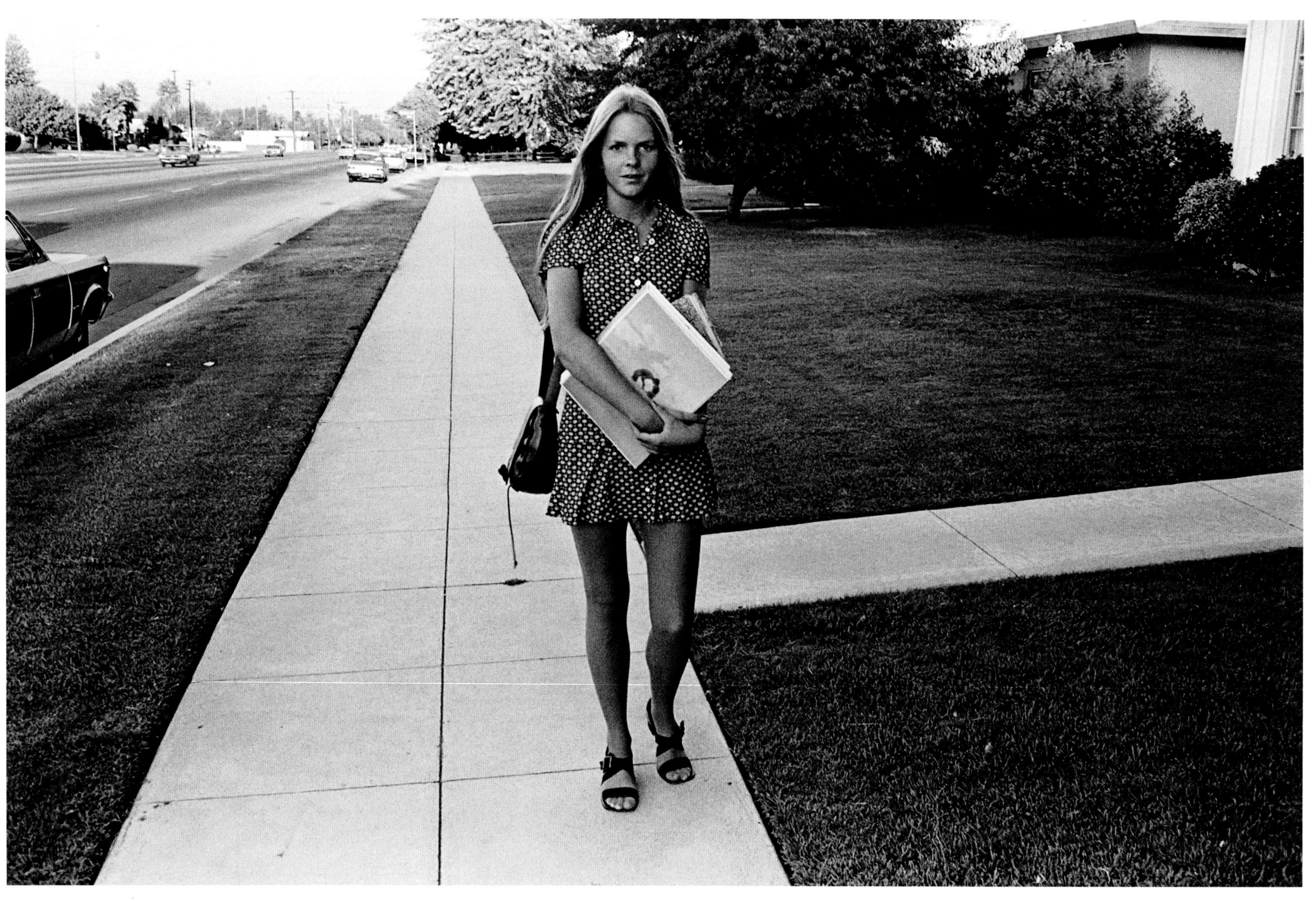

John Divola
*Untitled (Young Woman
on Sidewalk)*, 1971–73

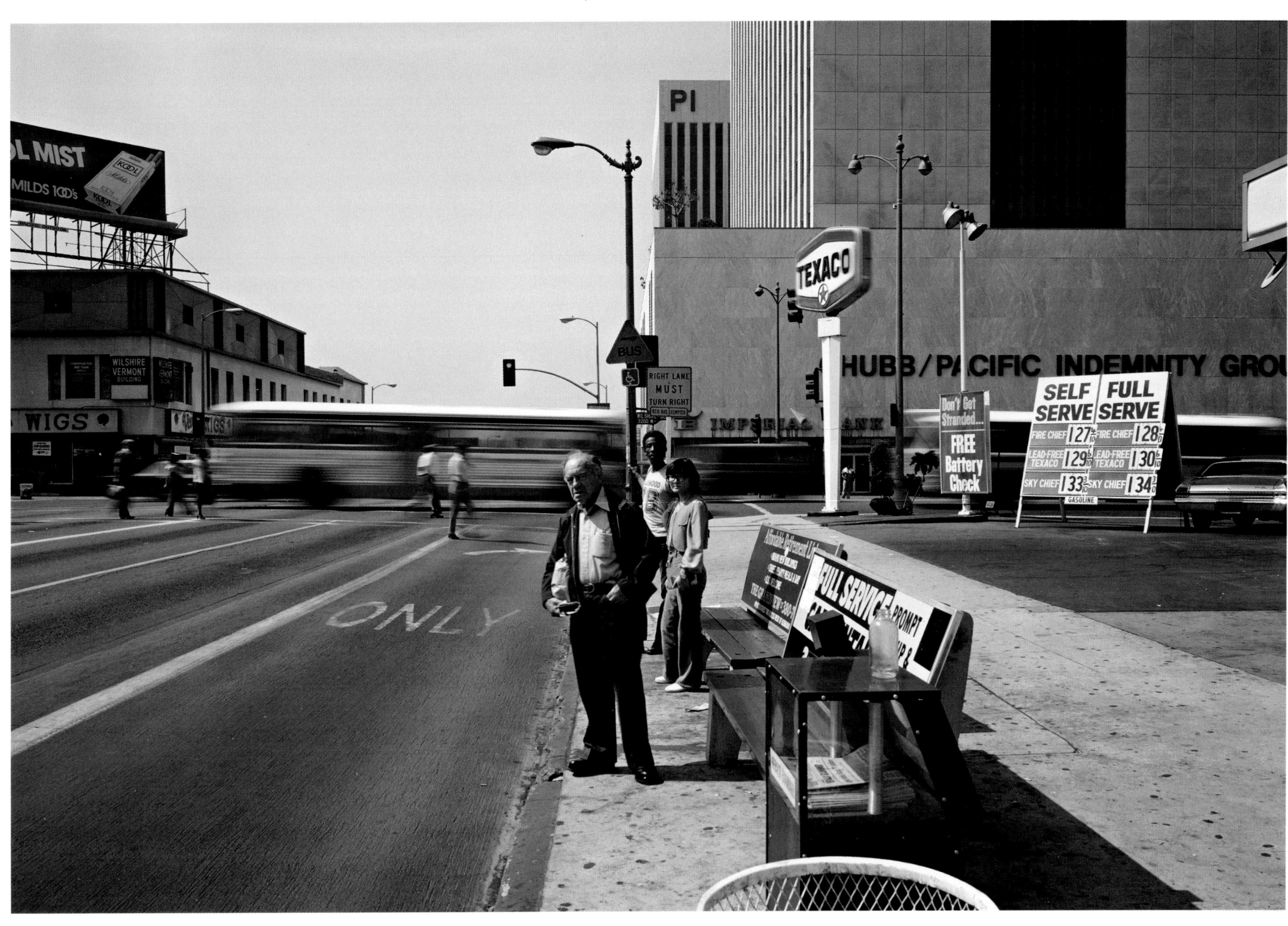

Anthony Hernandez
Vermont and Wilshire
Boulevard #11, 1979

On April 29, 1992, four white police officers on trial for the beating of motorist Rodney King were acquitted. A videotape of King's beating had been extensively televised. The not guilty verdicts became a catalyst for widespread civil unrest.

Riots began with several mob assaults at this intersection. Reginald Denny, a white truck driver, was pulled from his truck and severely beaten as a camera crew broadcast the event live from a news helicopter.

The Los Angeles Riots caused more than fifty deaths and an estimated $1 billion worth of damage.

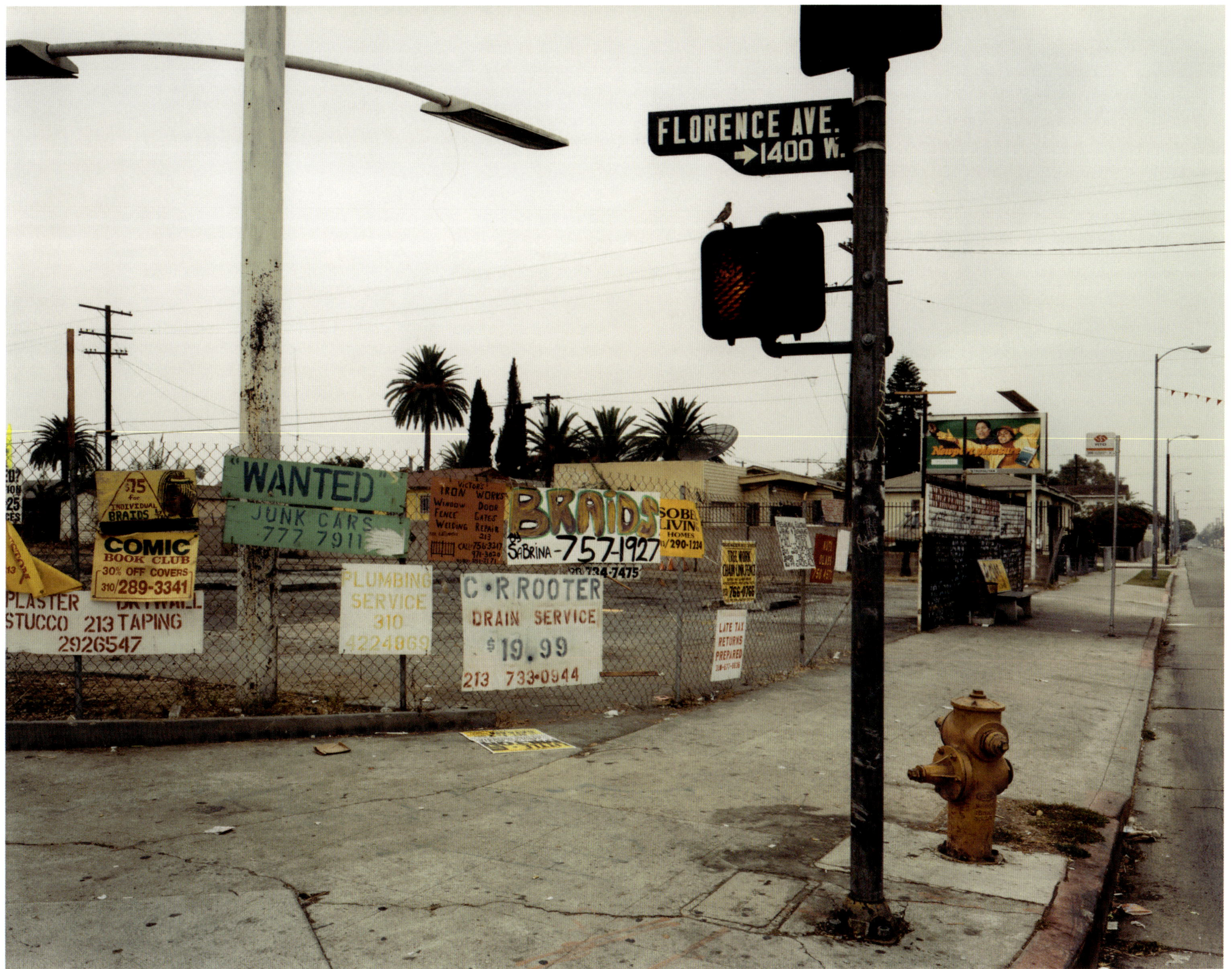

Joel Sternfeld
The northwest corner of Florence and Normandie Avenues, Los Angeles, California, October 1993, 1993
Courtesy of the artist and Luhring Augustine, New York

WORK

Photographs of Los Angeles inevitably speak of a multi-faceted place: a golden city wrenched from its Mexican past, a city of complex ethnic and racial origins, a city proudly emblematic of the American nation's stride into the future. Los Angeles's industries—agriculture, construction, manufacturing, oil refining, shipbuilding, and motion pictures—arose in response to economic opportunities engendered by the region's climate, topography, and burgeoning workforce.

Natural and other assets notwithstanding, Los Angeles has been plagued by episodes of violent labor unrest. As the city grew, few of the city's commercial photographers showed this dark urban underbelly, supporting instead the booster vision of Los Angeles as a place where industrial production and the good life peacefully coexisted. George Hurrell, Louise Dahl-Wolfe, Phil Stern, and Philippe Halsman focused on the glamorous new workforce of Hollywood, depicting its members in both stylized and natural settings. Peter Stackpole revealed the other side of celebrity culture, focusing his lens on the anonymous hopefuls at Central Casting.

In quieter realms of visual expression, Edward Weston and Ansel Adams ventured behind Hollywood's glittering façades to offer a subtle critique of its deceptive realities. The modernist beauty of their images owes much to the vision of commercial image-makers who intuitively grasped the crisp visual language engendered by the era's new, streamlined technologies. Still others captured beautifully the workers pouring into the Southland's industries during and after the Second World War, showing their heroic, everyday struggles.

Edmund Teske
*Newspaper Vendor,
Los Angeles*, 1943

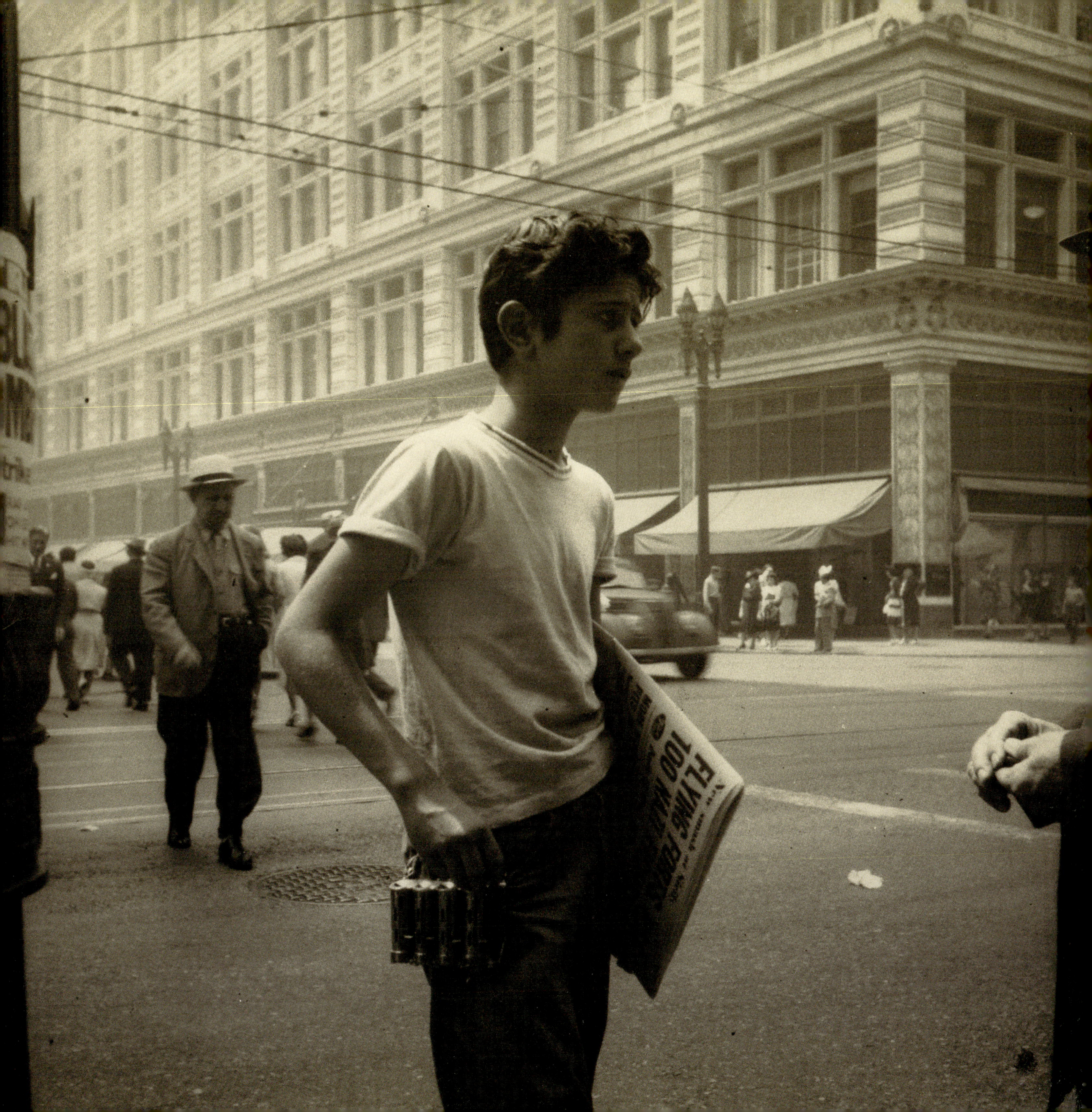
FLYING FORT
100 MILES

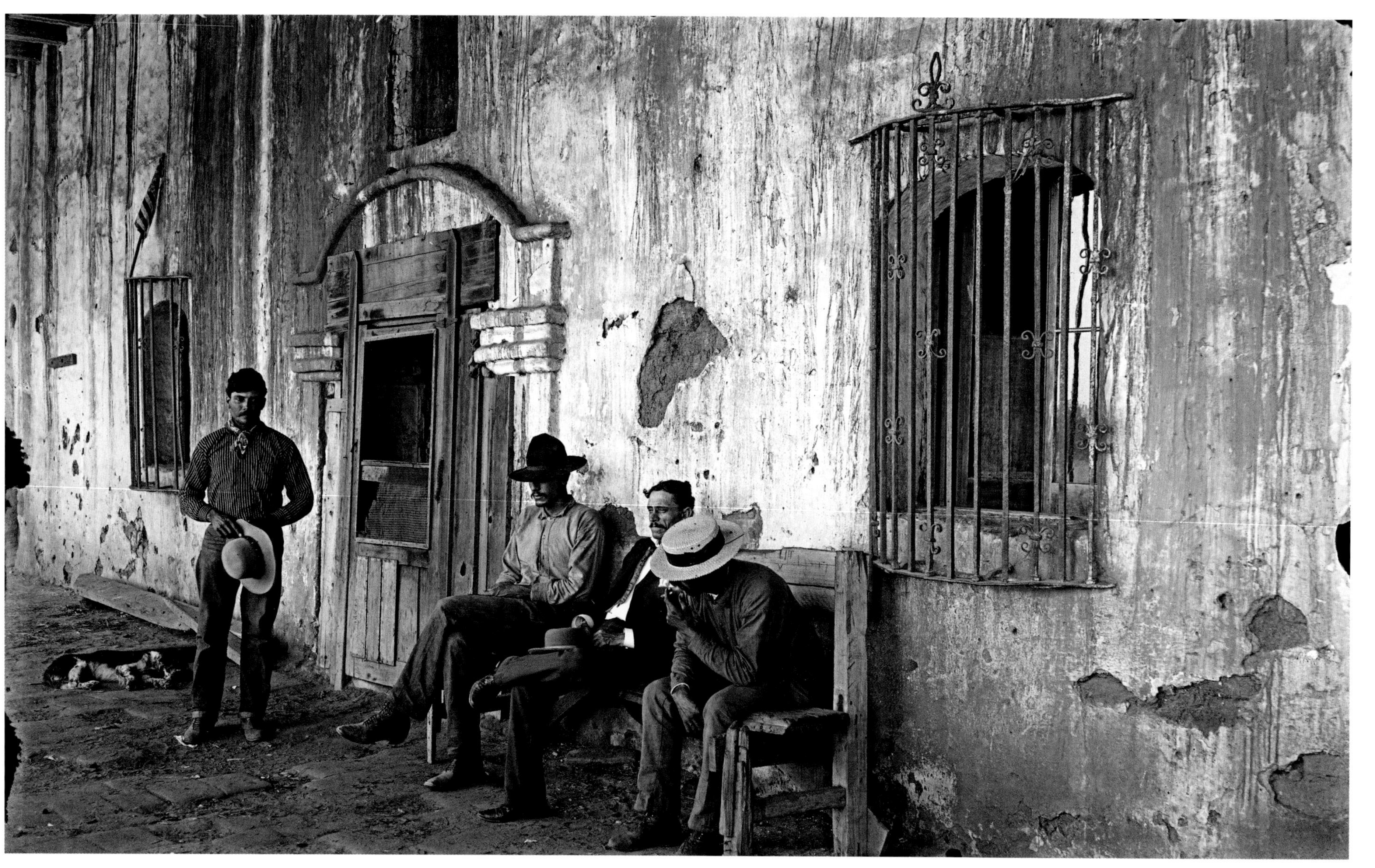

Adam Clark Vroman
Men at Mission San Fernando,
c. 1897

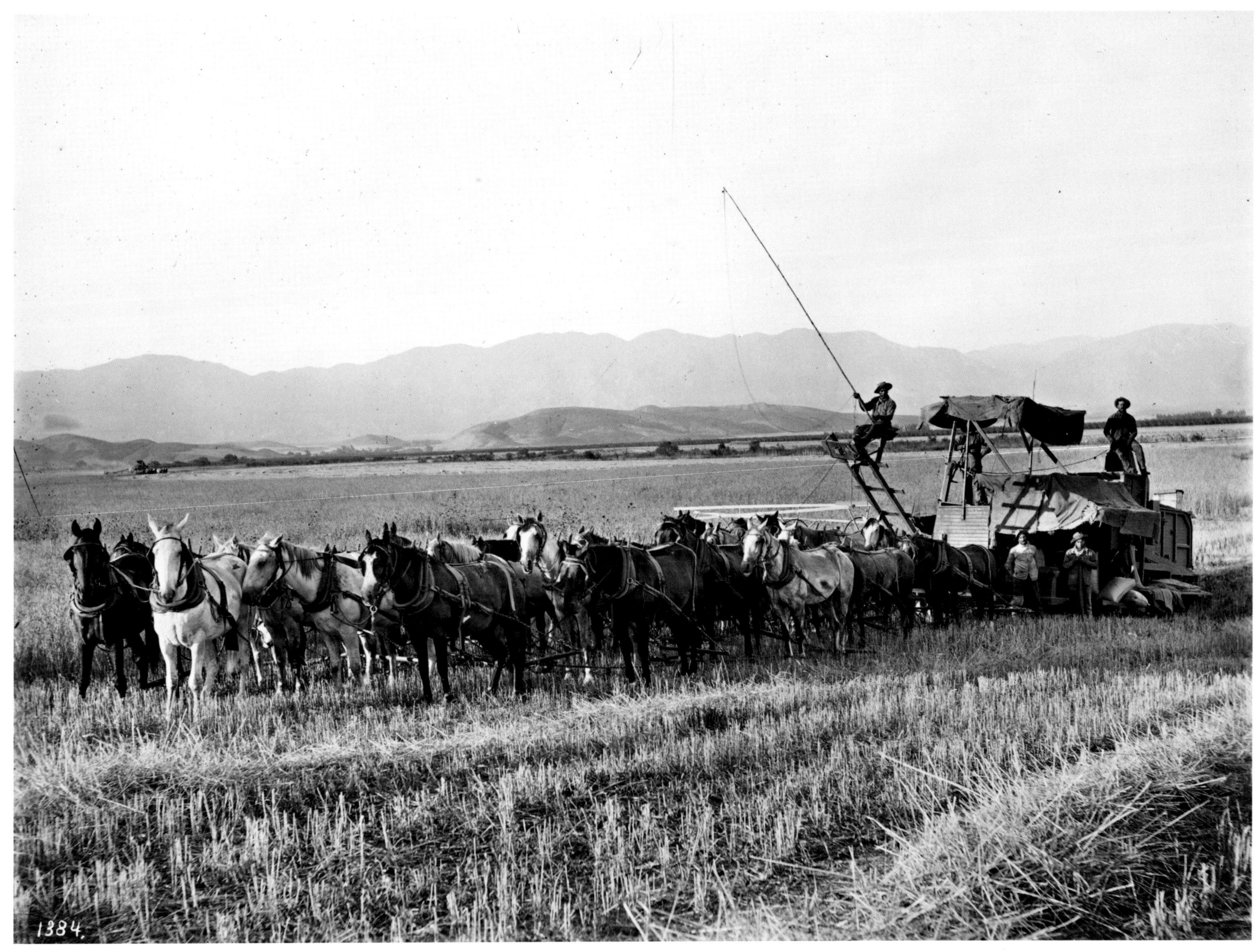

C.C. Pierce
Harvesting Grain on Van Nuys
Lankershim Ranch, c. 1905

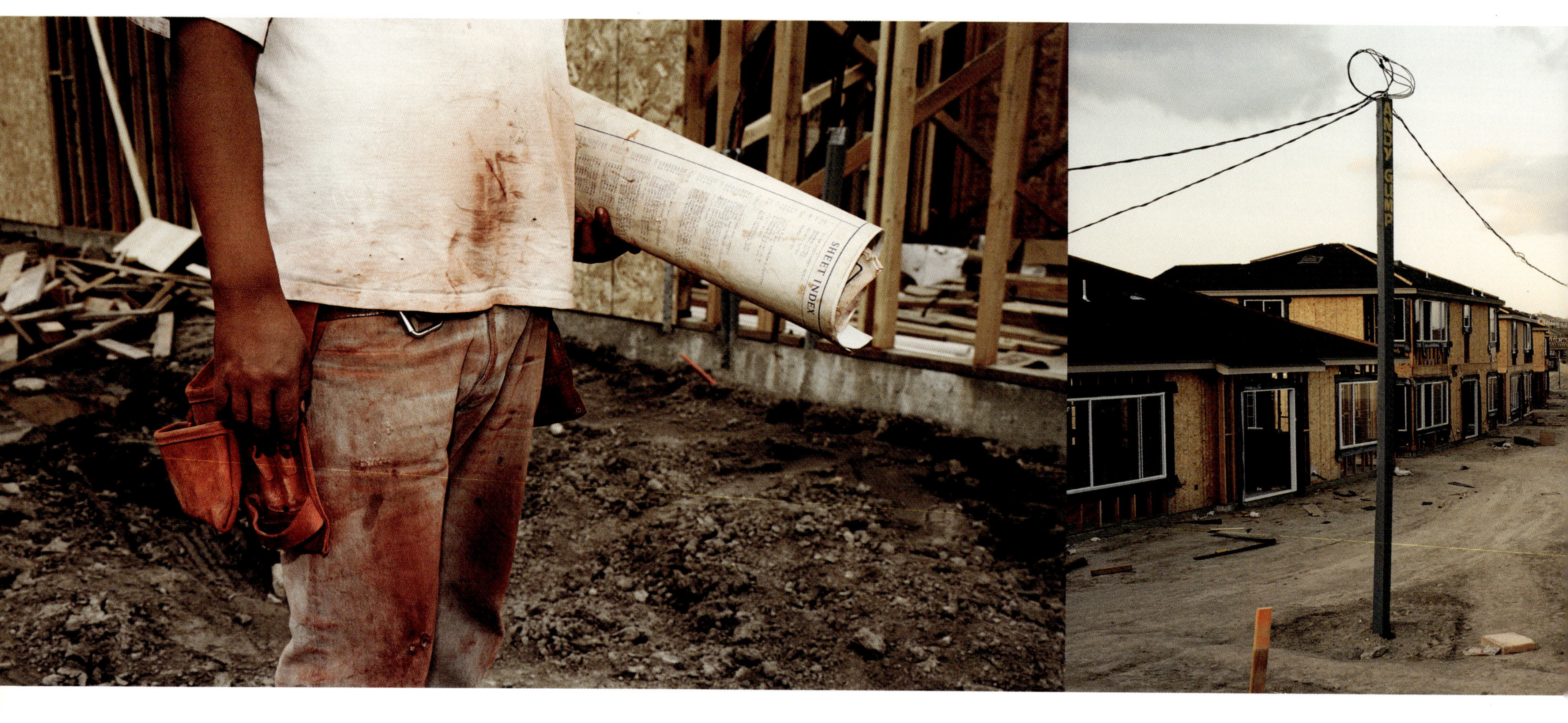

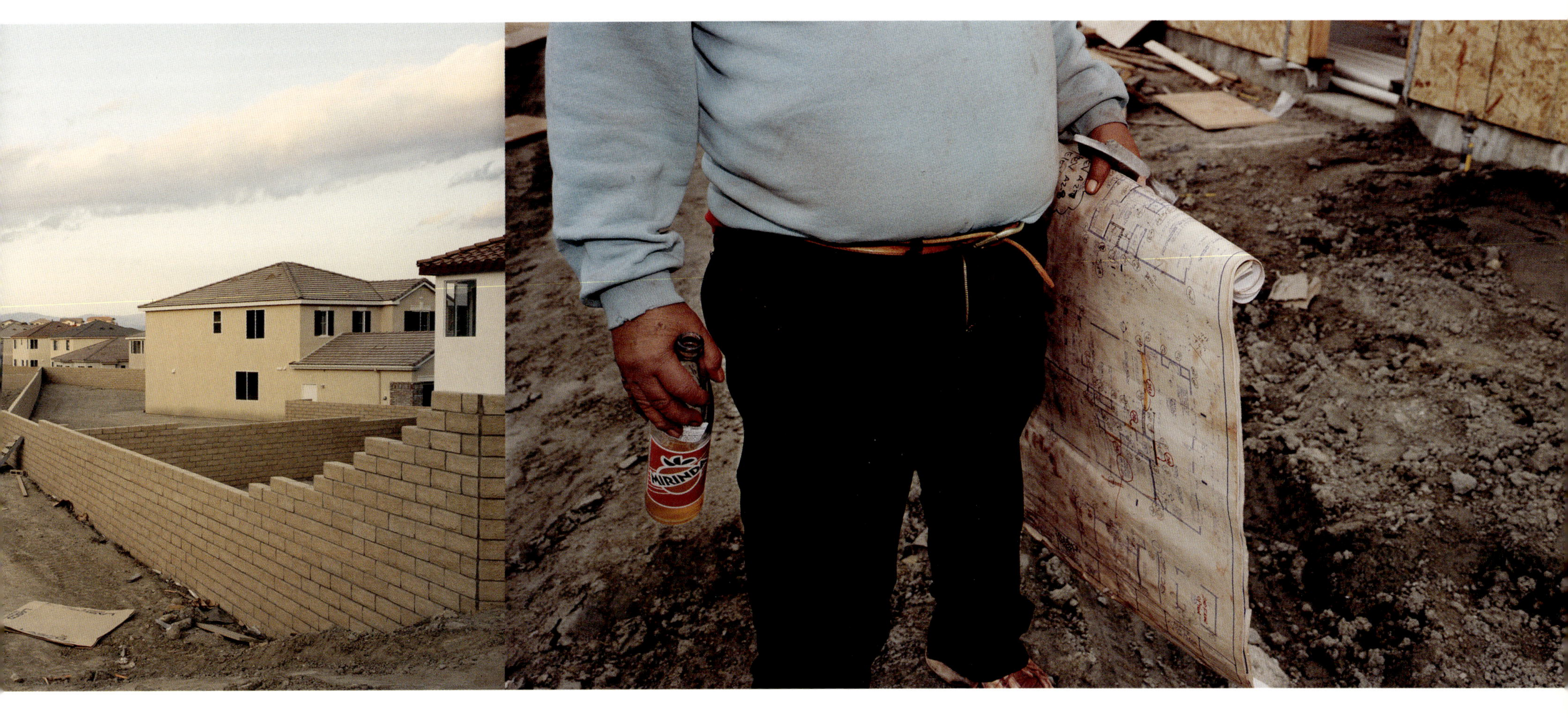

James Baker
Home Sweet Home,
1999–2001

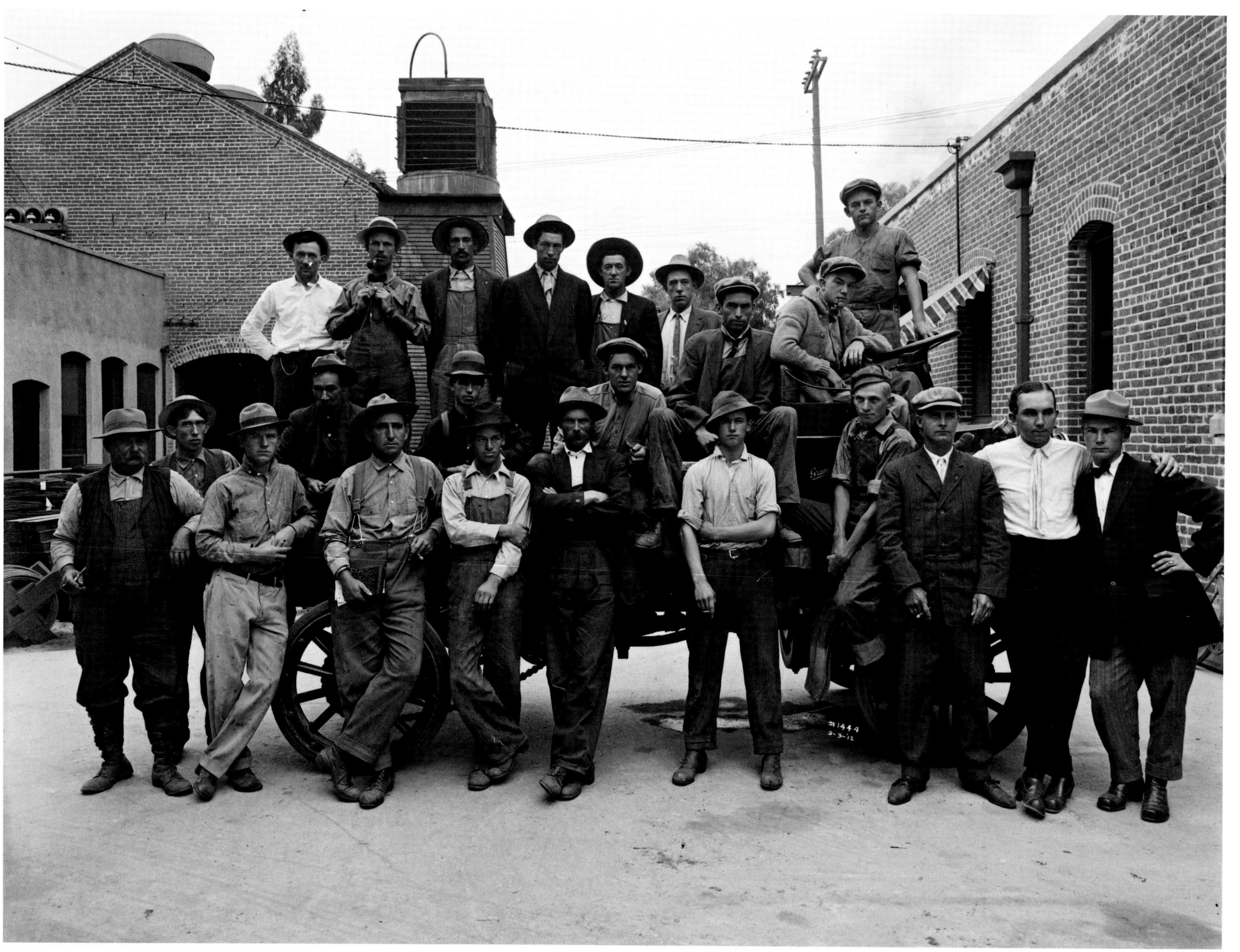

G. Haven Bishop
Group Portrait of the
E[lectric] D[istribution]
S[ystems] Gang in Pomona,
September 3, 1912

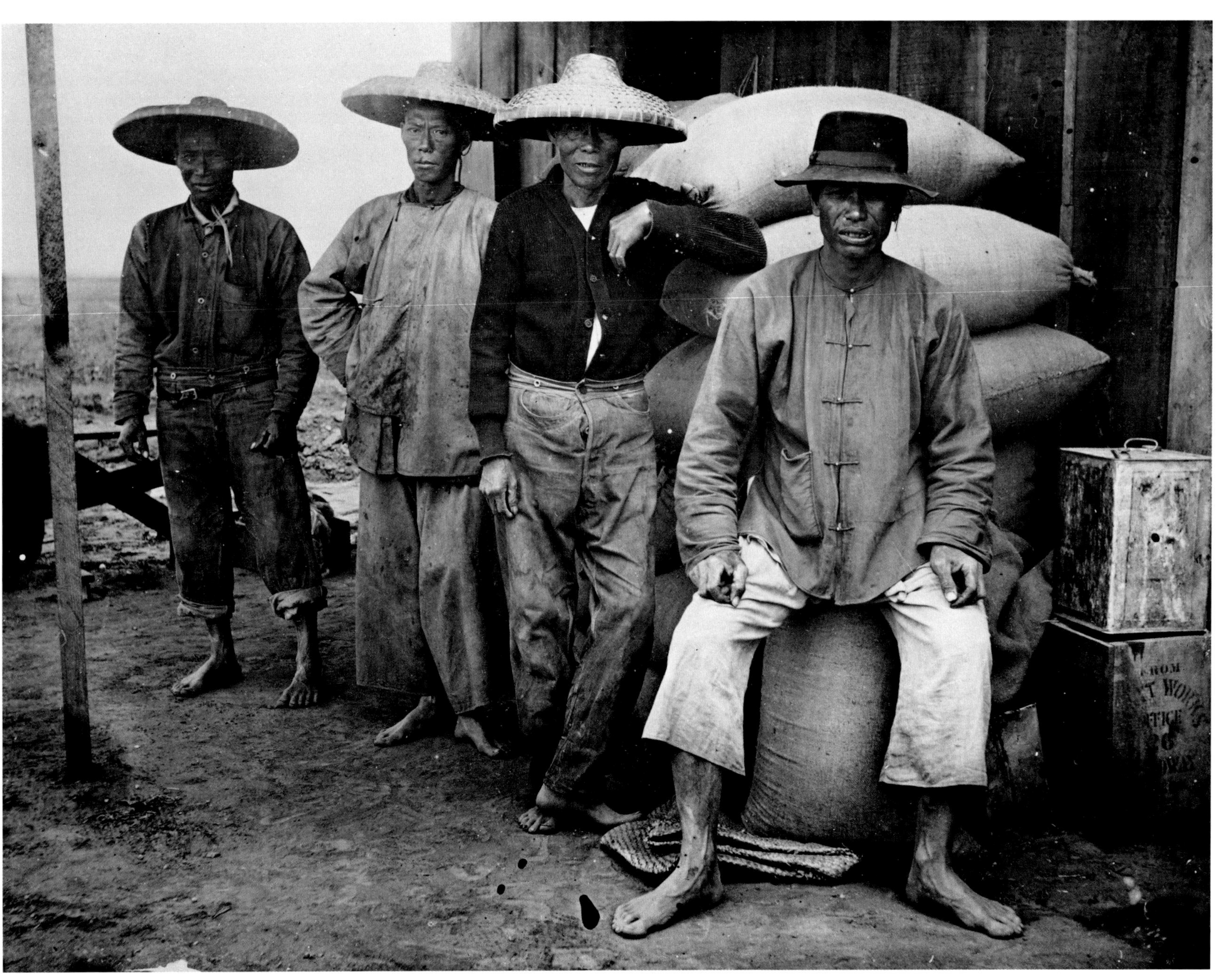

C.C. Pierce
Chinese Field Hands, 1898

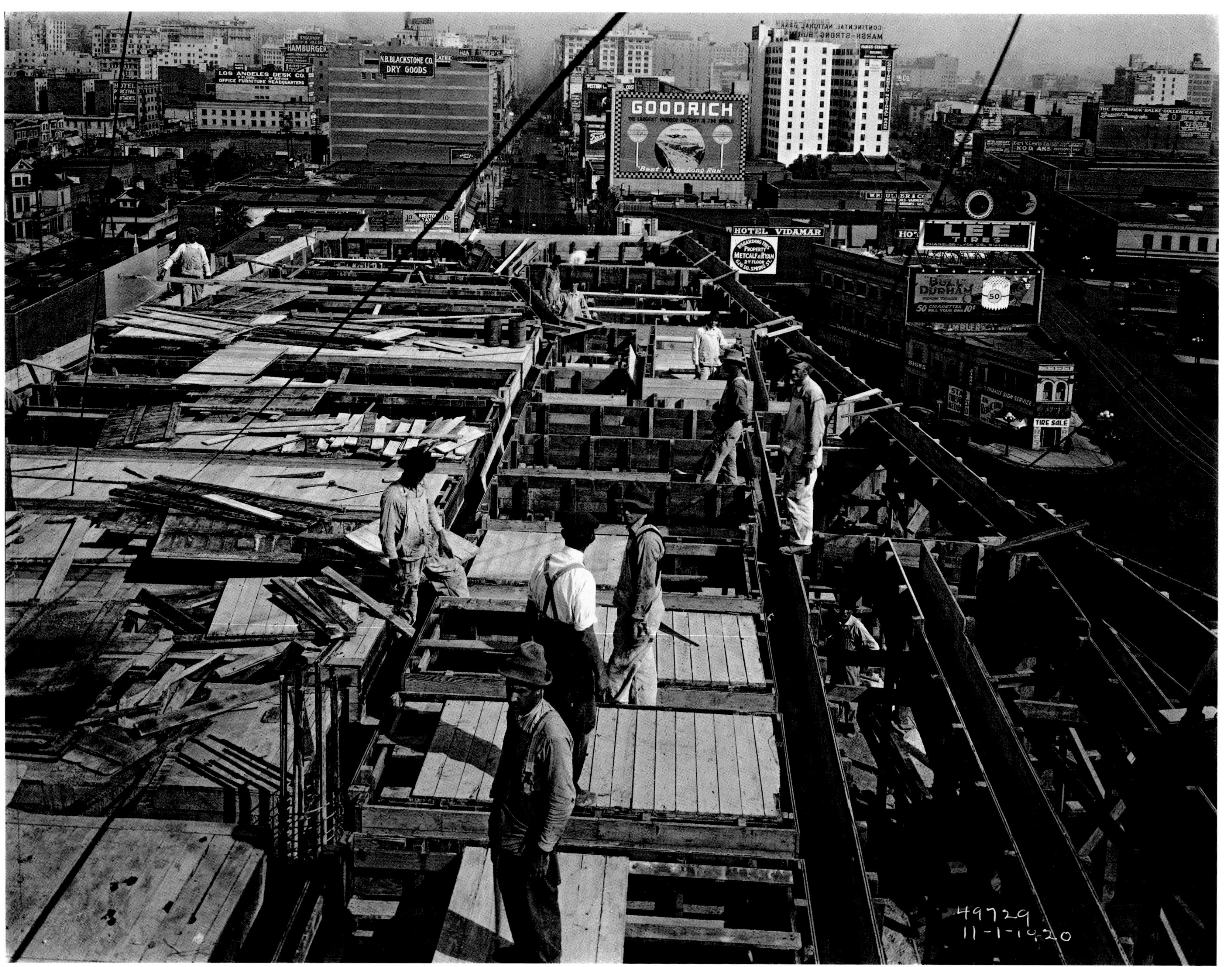

Unknown
*Construction View of Los
Angeles Railway Building, Los
Angeles*, November 1, 1920

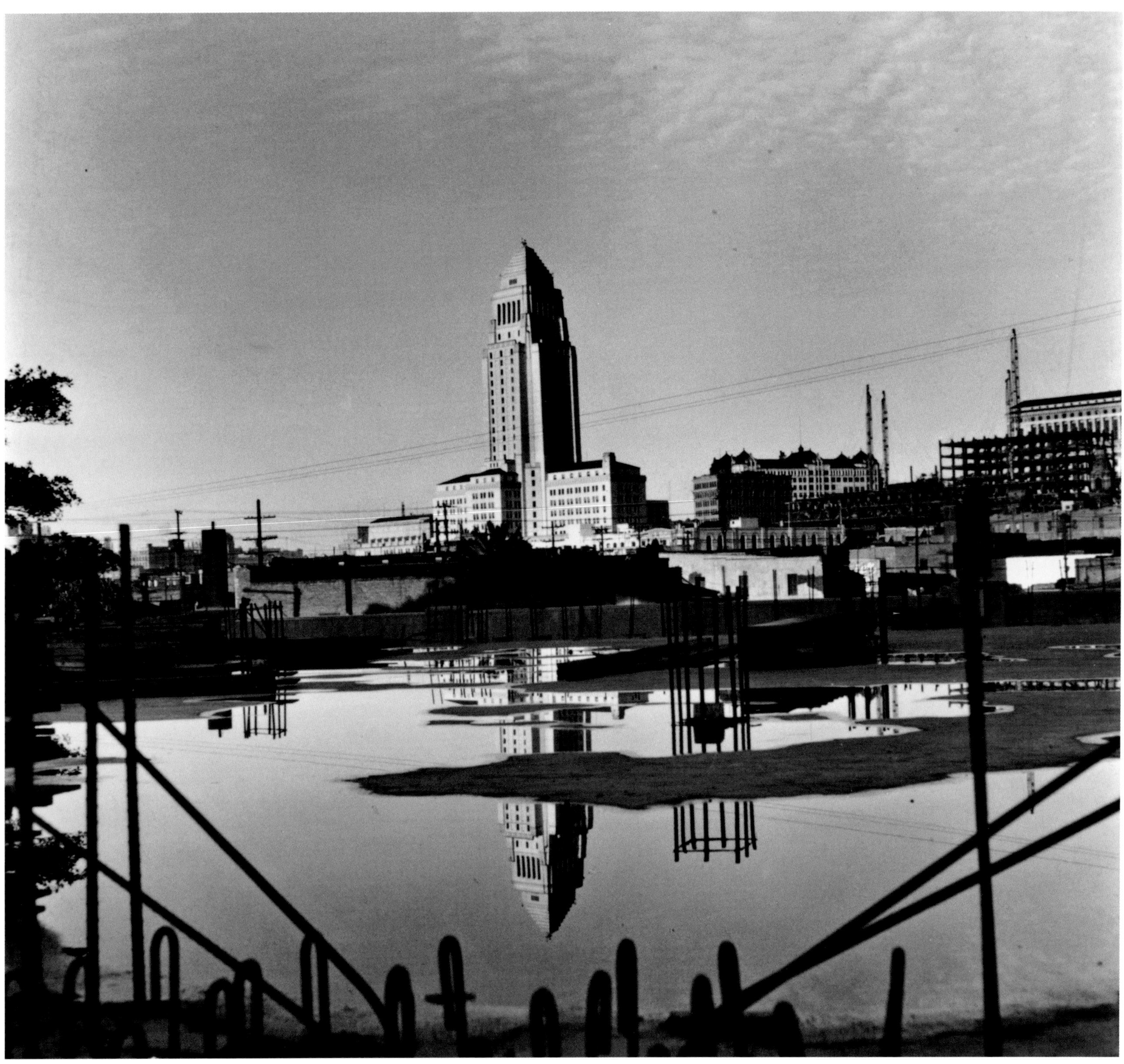

Julius Shulman
City Hall and Construction of
Union Terminal, Los Angeles,
1934

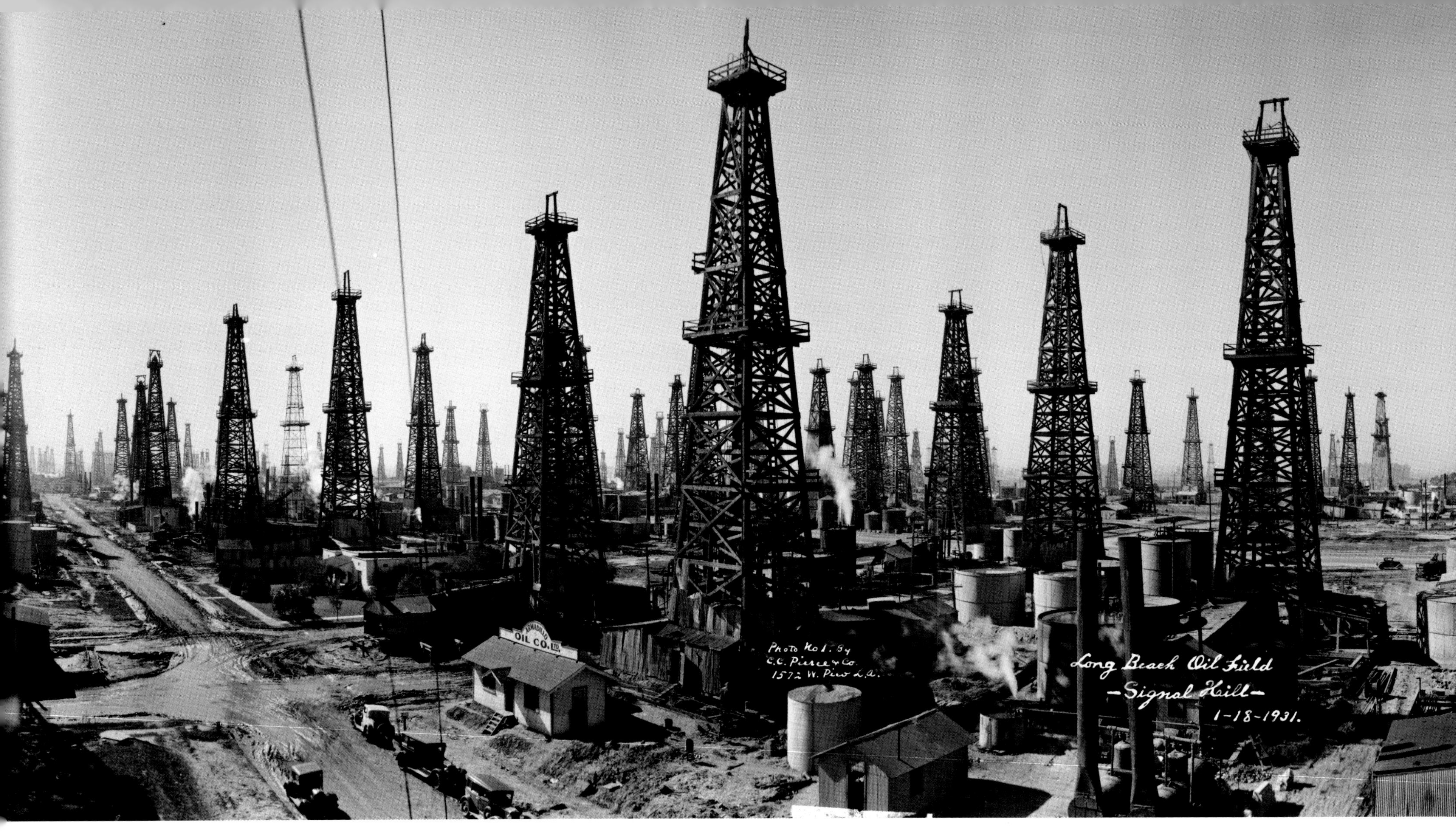

AMARADO
OIL CO. LTD
Photo No. 184
C.C. Pierce & Co.
1572 W. Pico L.A.
Long Beach Oil Field
—Signal Hill—
1-18-1931.

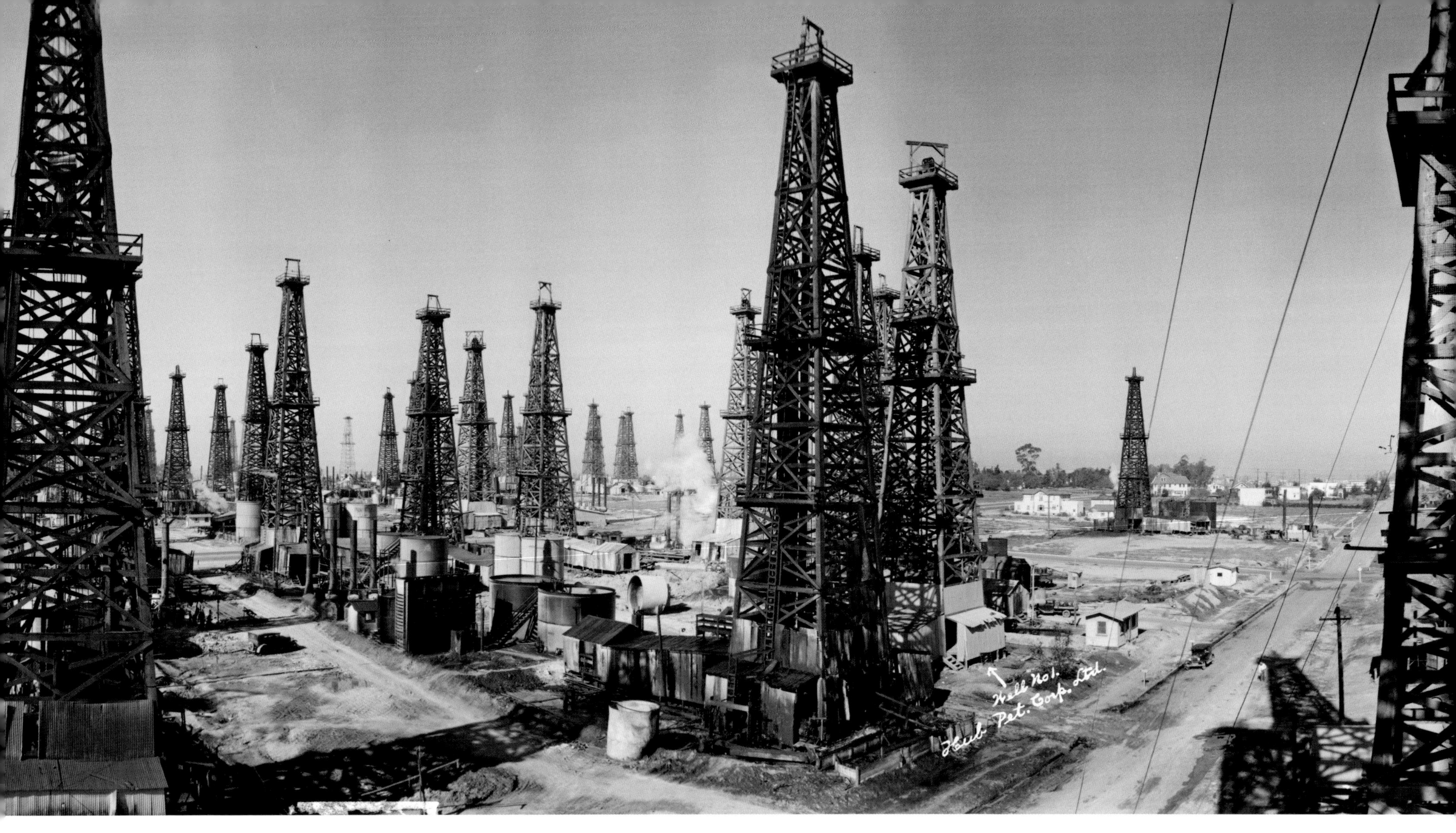

C.C. Pierce
*Long Beach Oil Field, Signal
Hill*, January 18, 1931

139

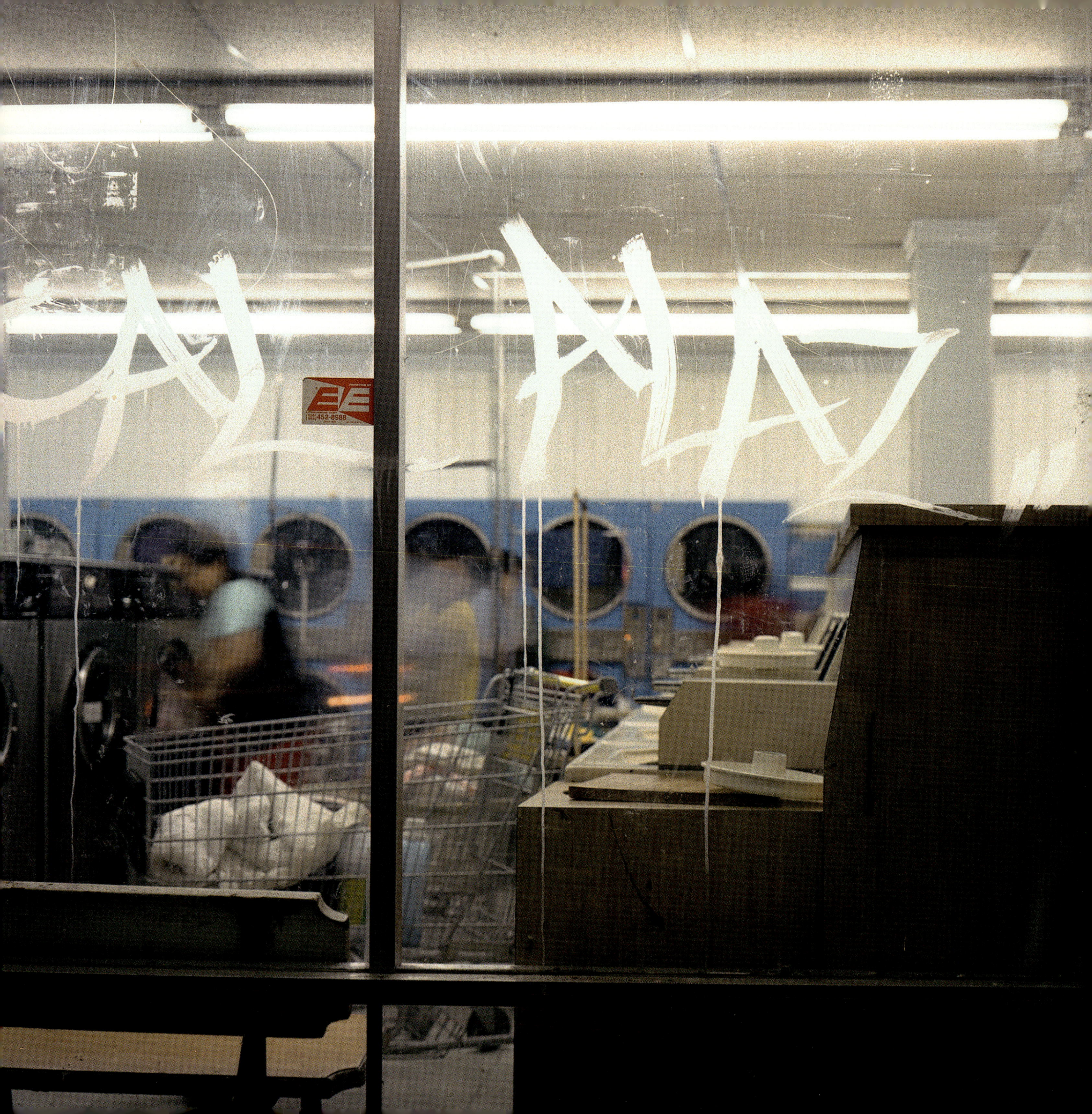
452-8988

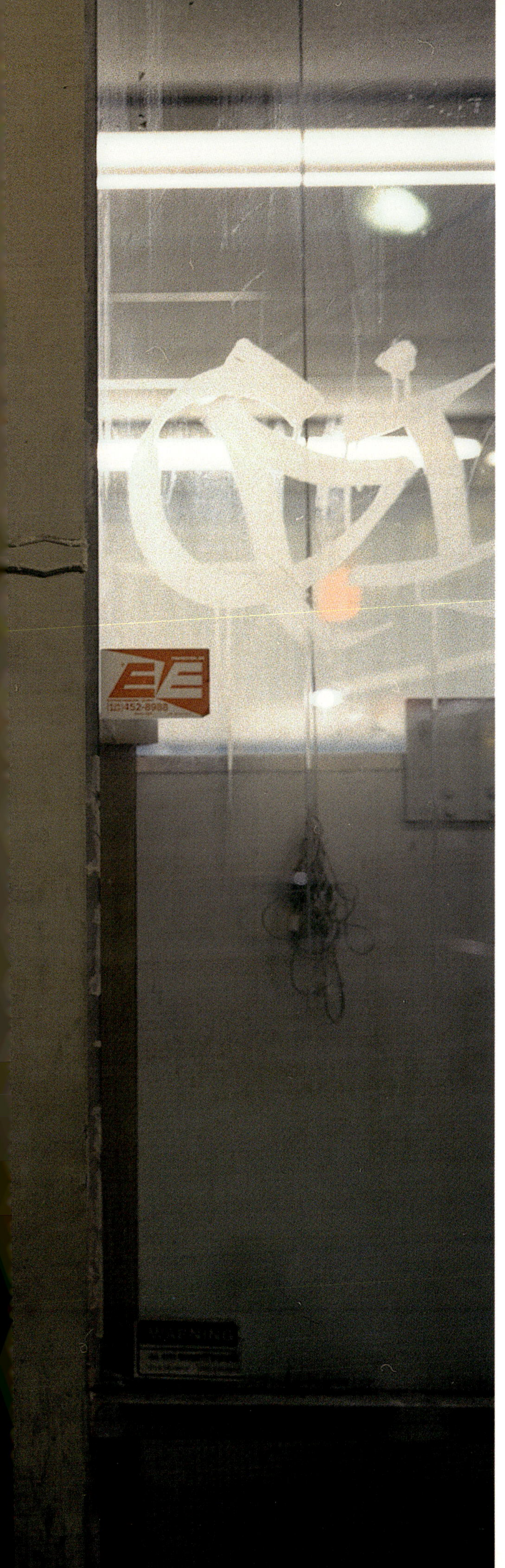

Christina Fernandez
Lavanderia #11, 2003

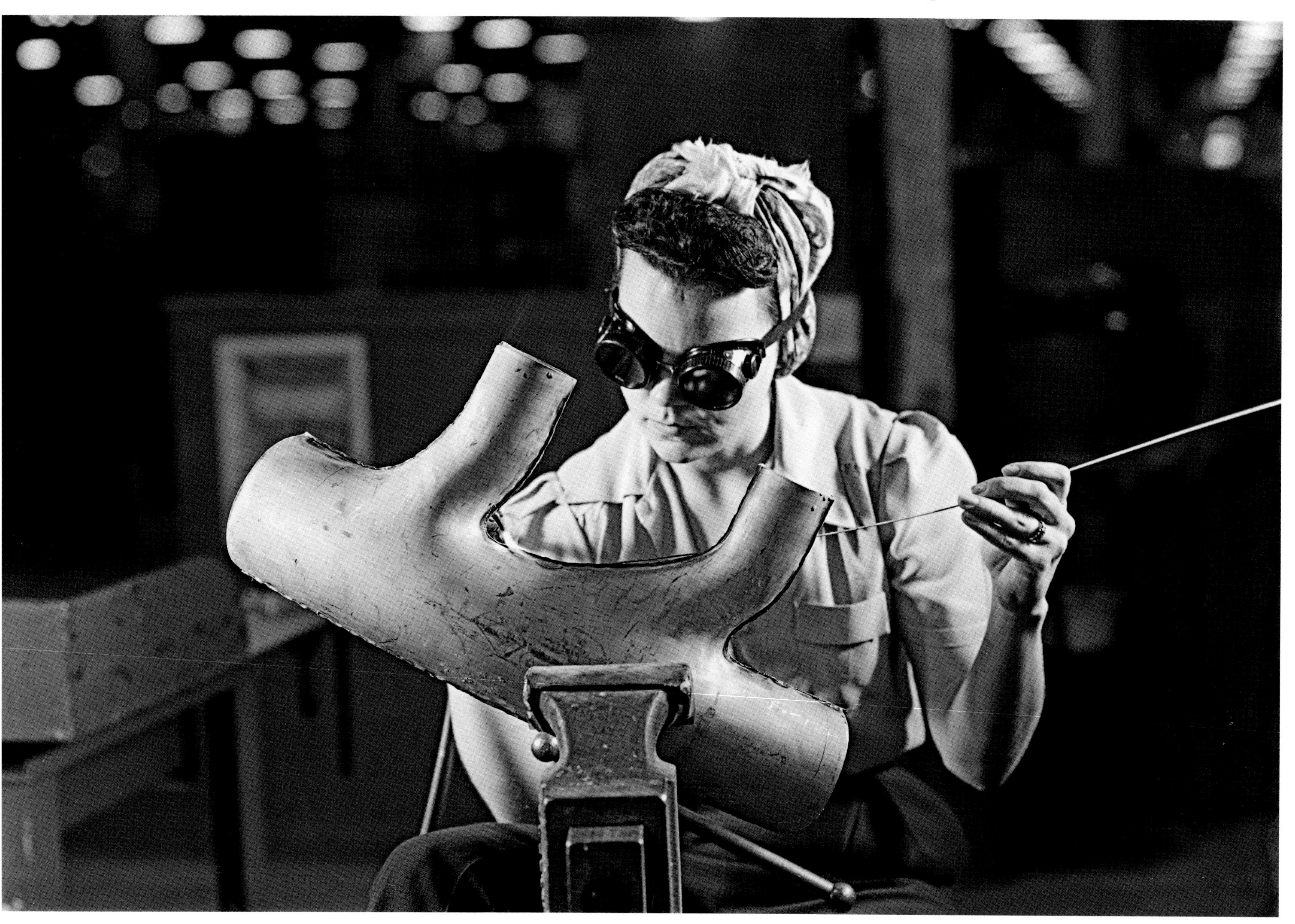

"Dick" Whittington Studio
*Solar Aircraft Plant
Operations*, 1943

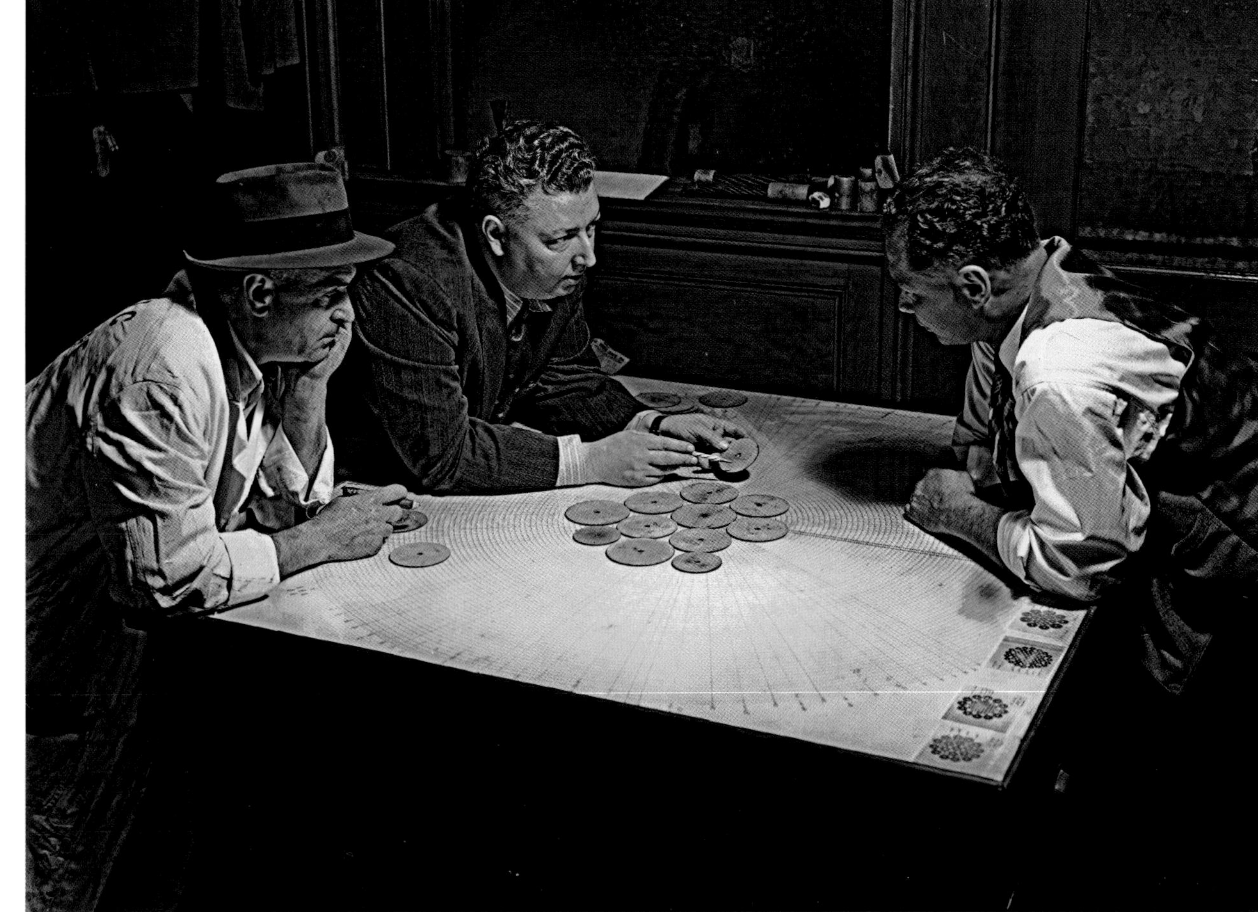

"Dick" Whittington Studio
*Pacific Wire Rope Plant
Interior*, 1940

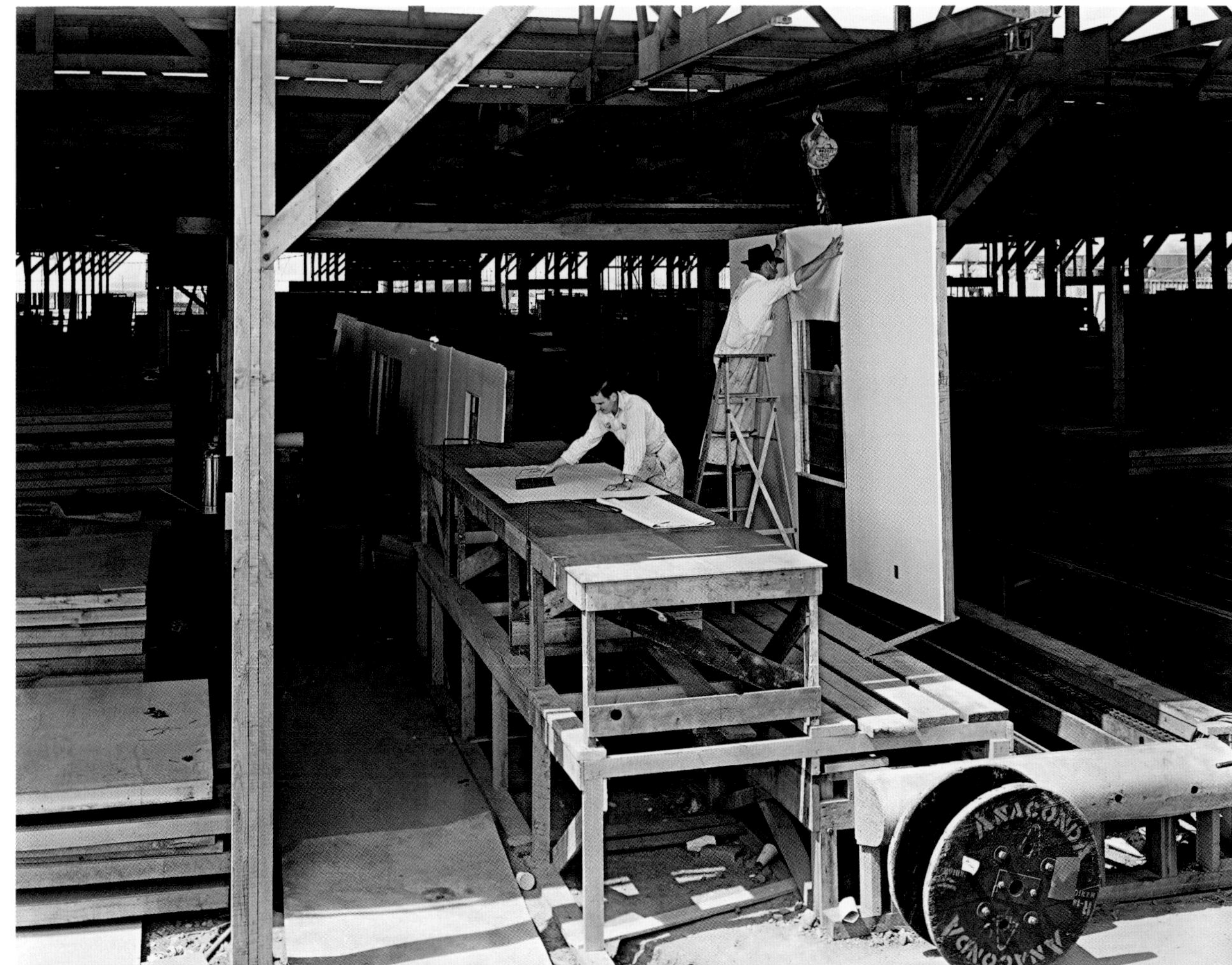

"Dick" Whittington Studio
*Marlow-Burns House
Assembly*, 1946

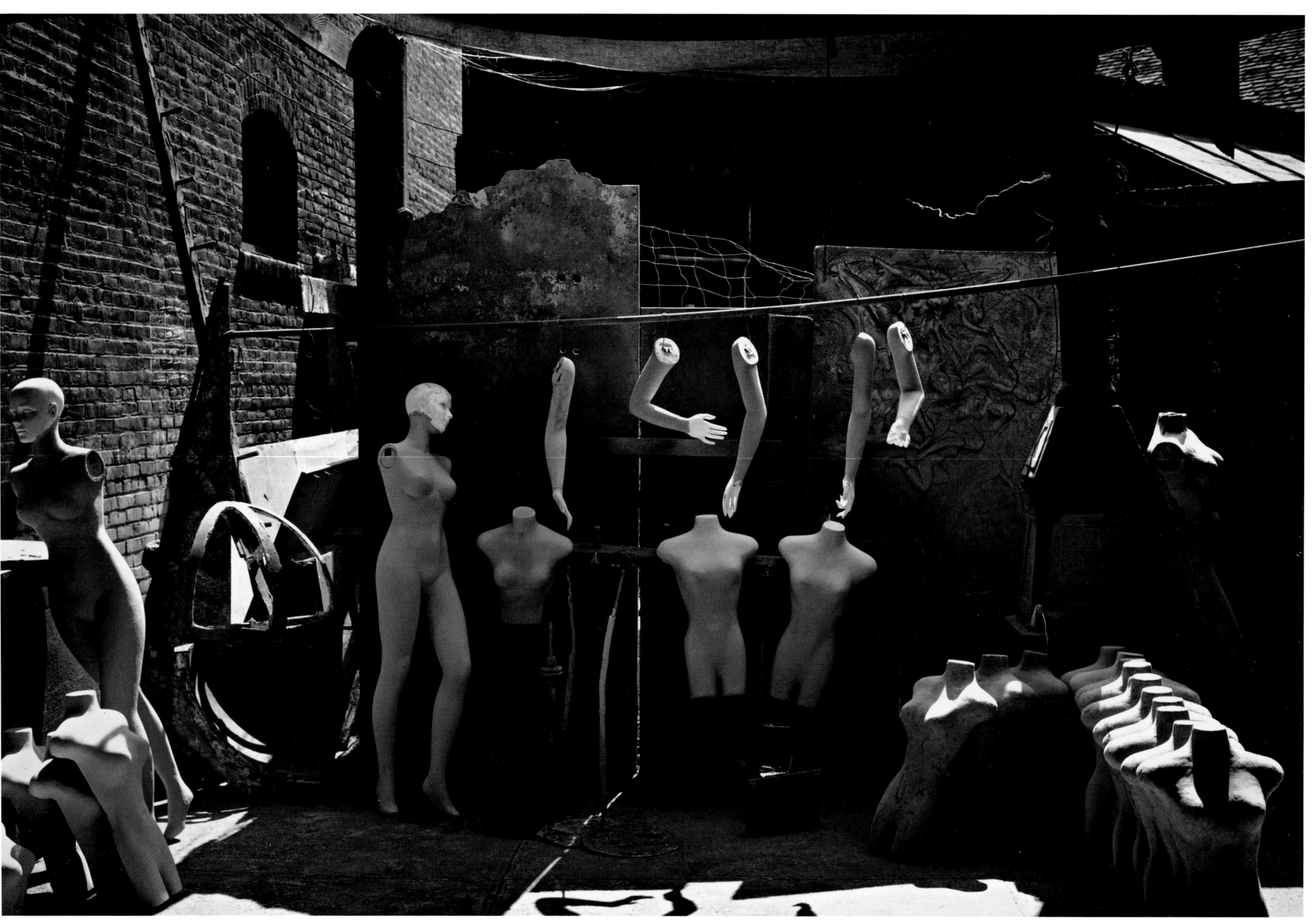

Ansel Adams
Mannequins, Columbia Movie
Lot, Los Angeles, 1942

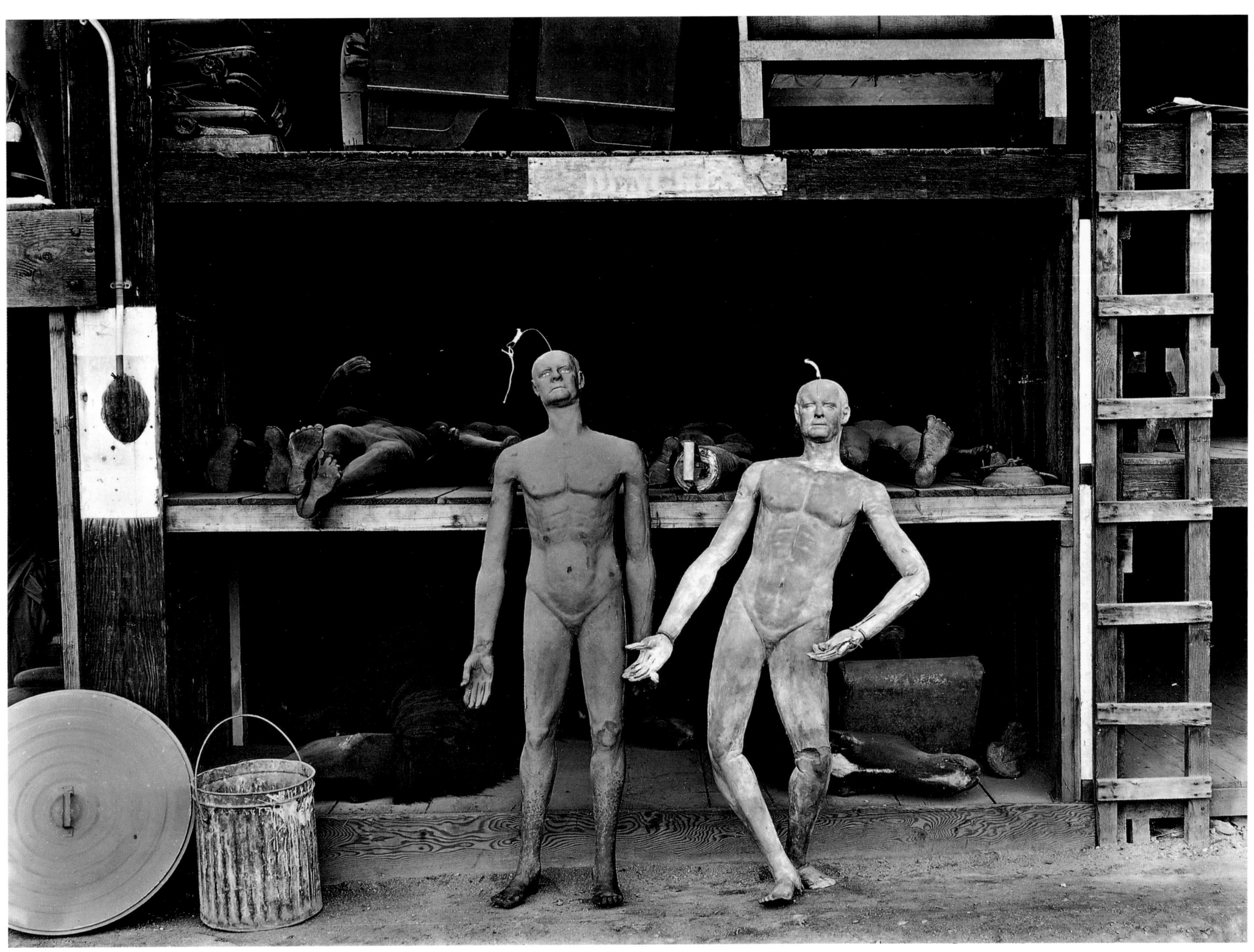

Edward Weston
Rubber Dummies, MGM,
1939

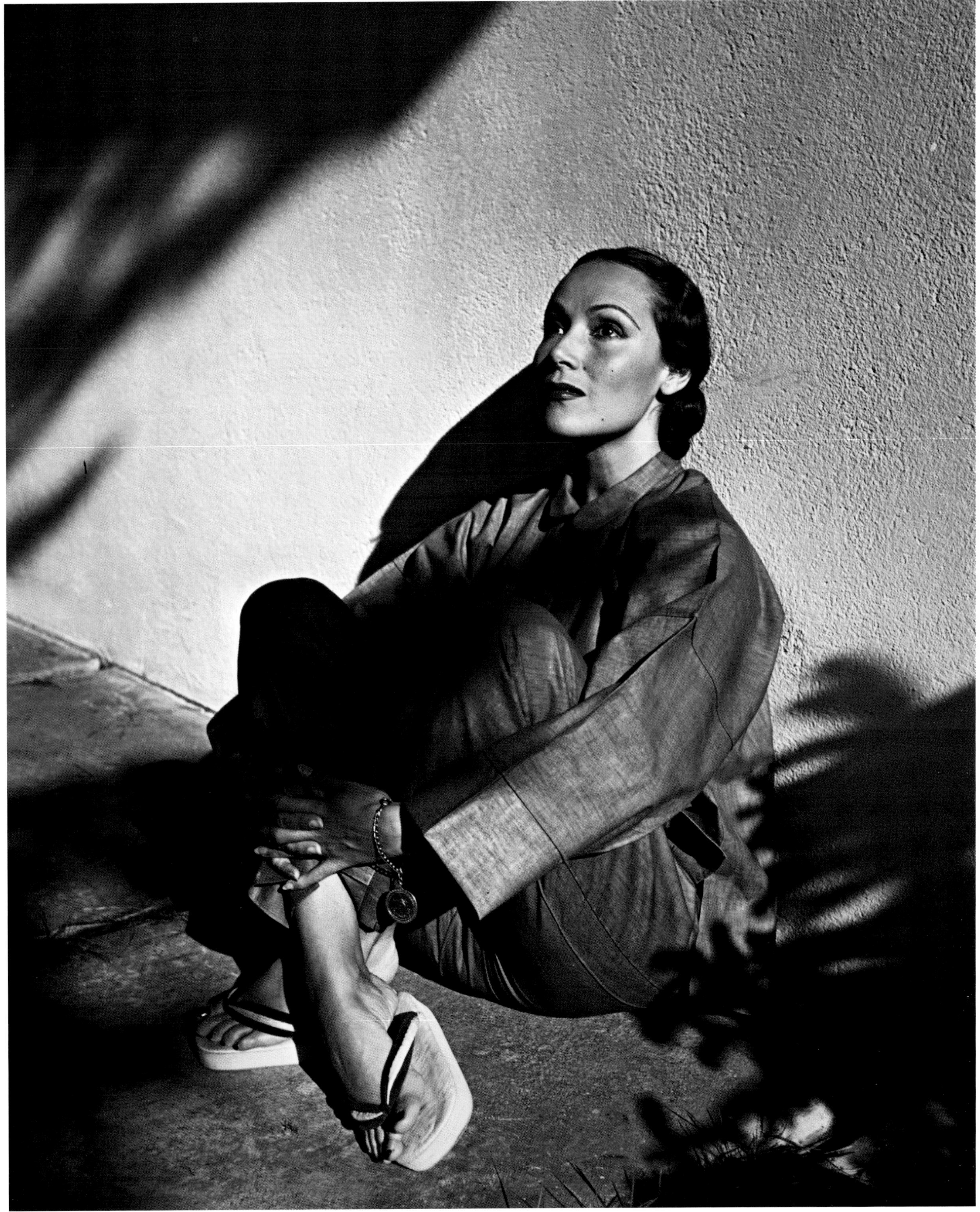

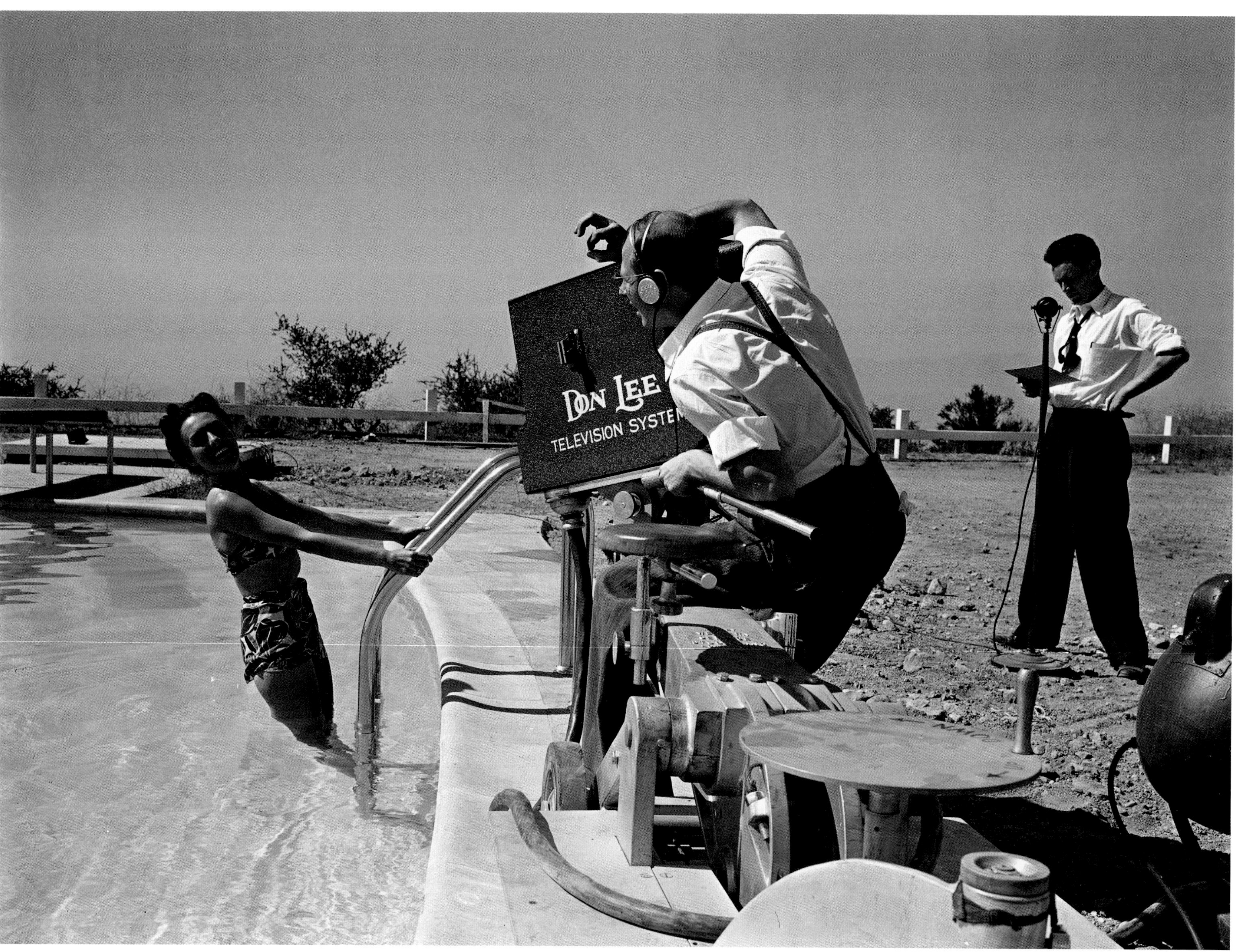

"Dick" Whittington Studio
Don Lee TV Station, 1941

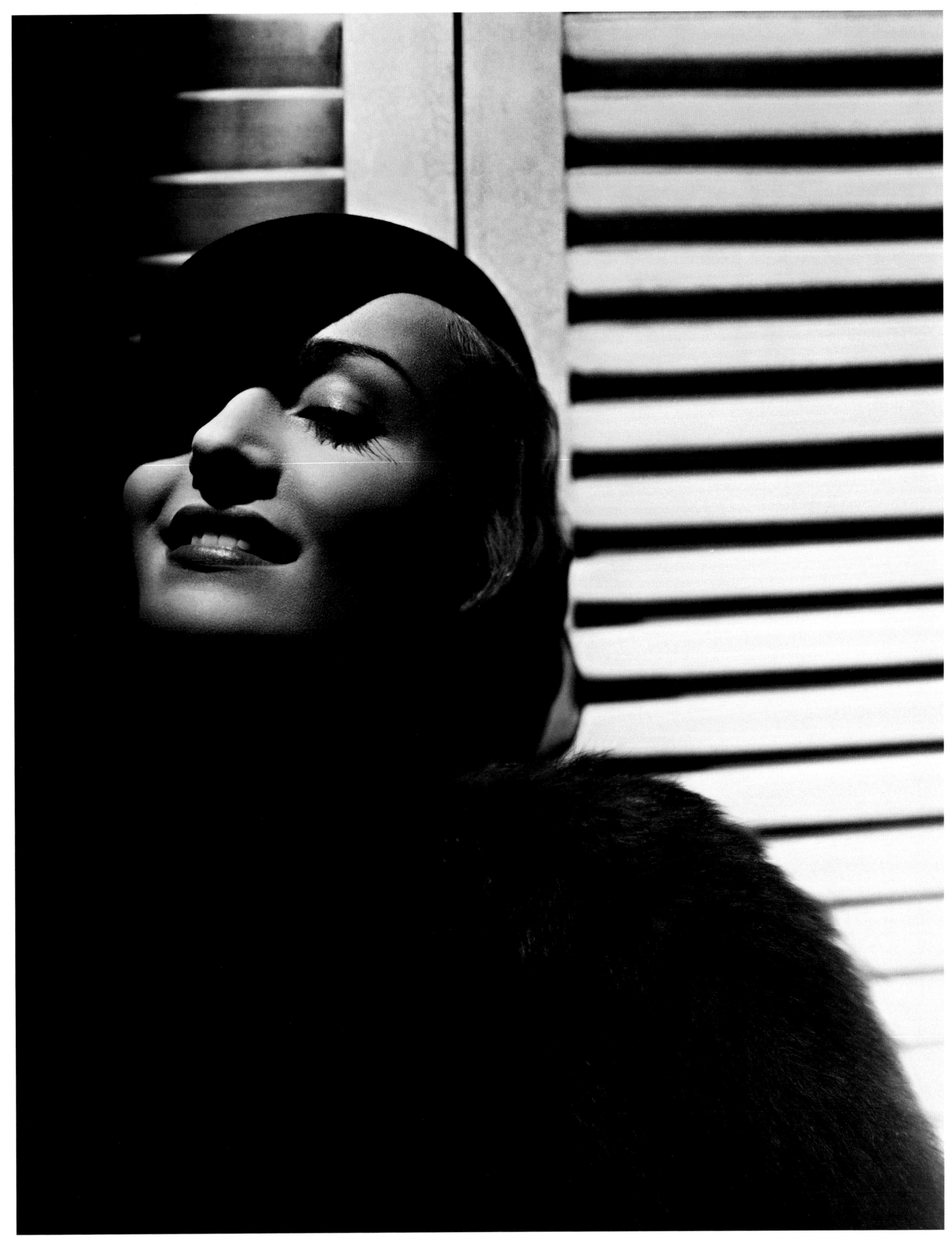

George Hurrell
Carole Lombard, 1937

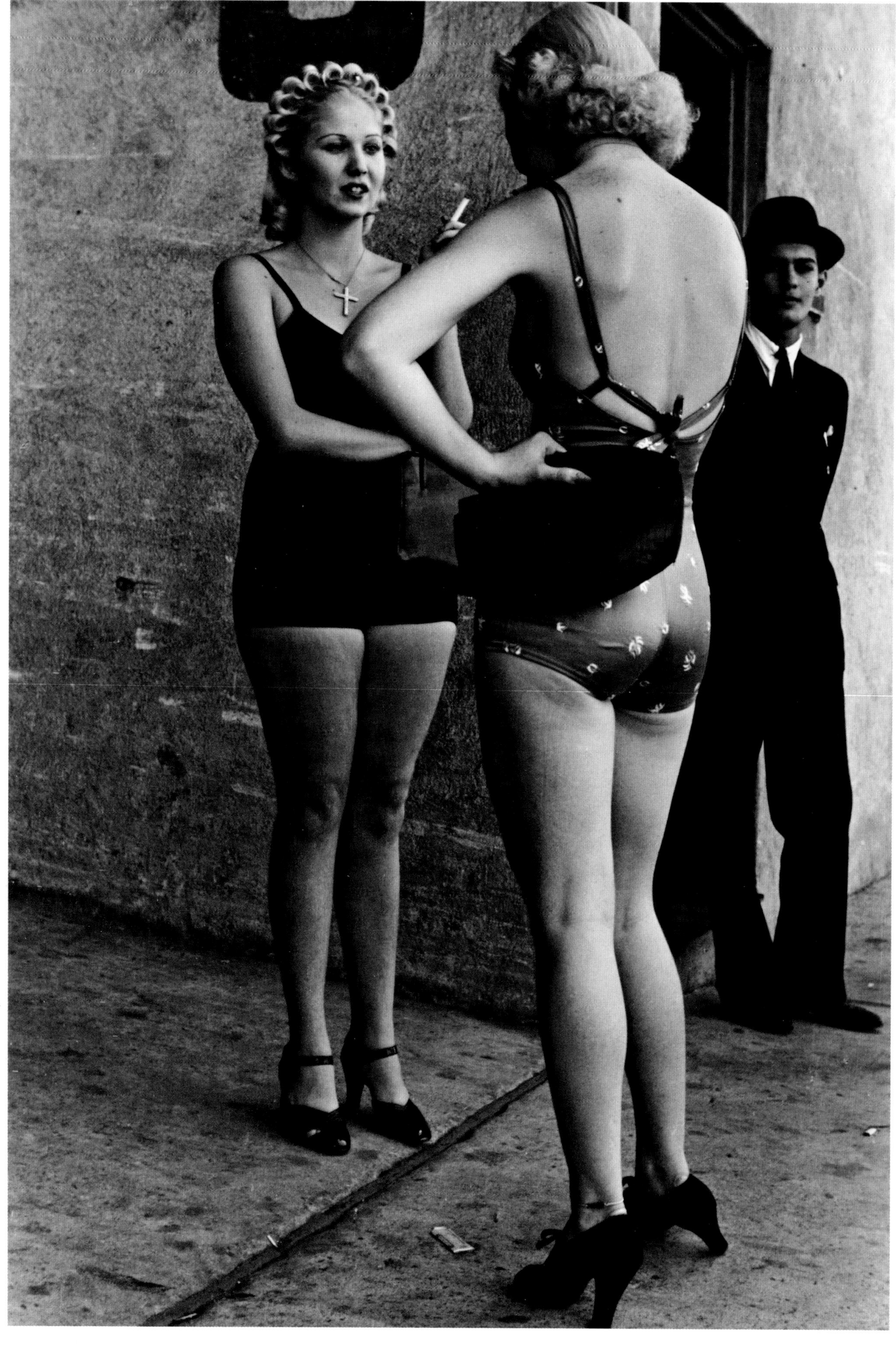

Peter Stackpole
Extra Tryouts, 1938

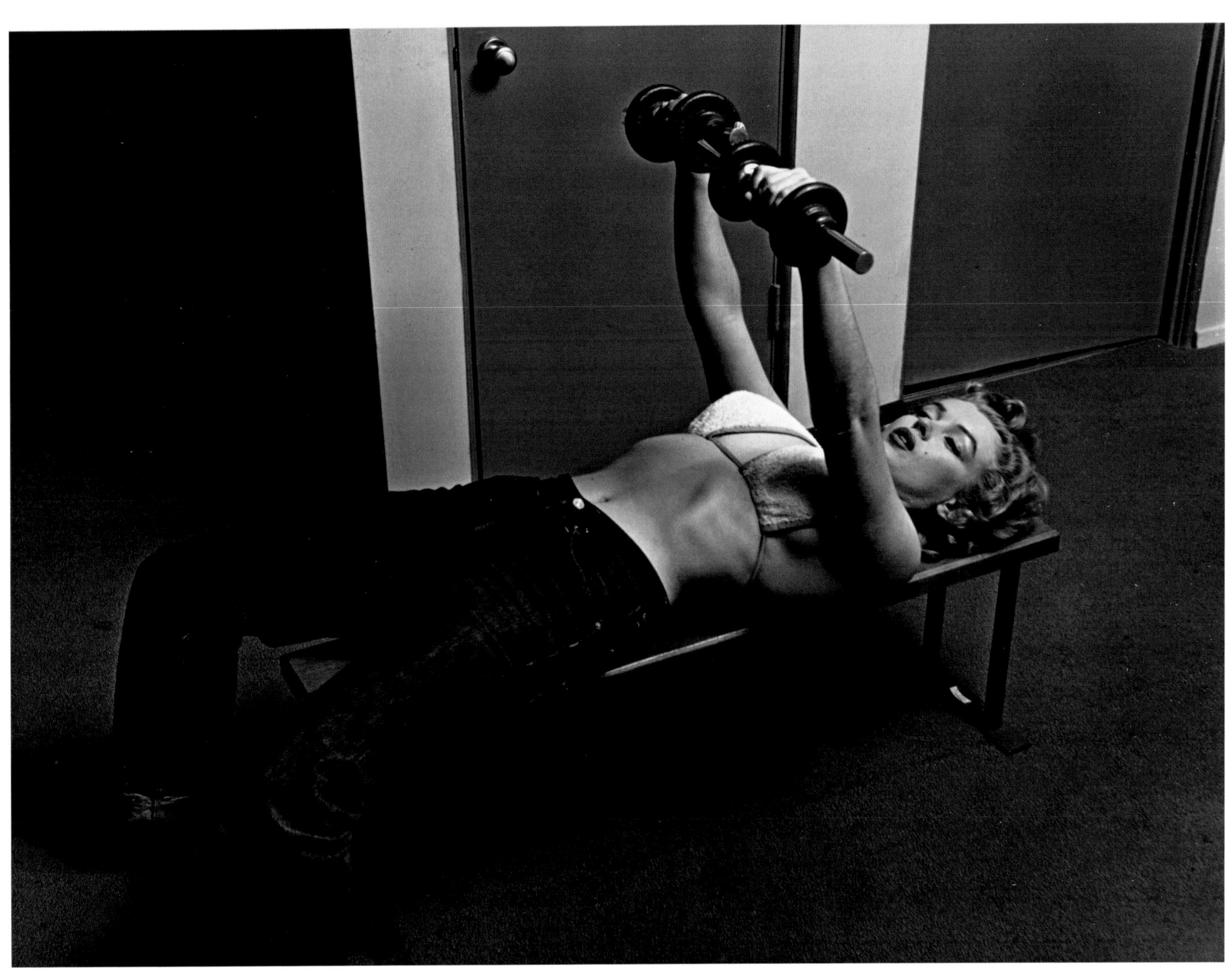

Philippe Halsman
Marilyn with Barbells, 1952

Phil Stern
Sammy Davis Jr., (Front Kick),
1947

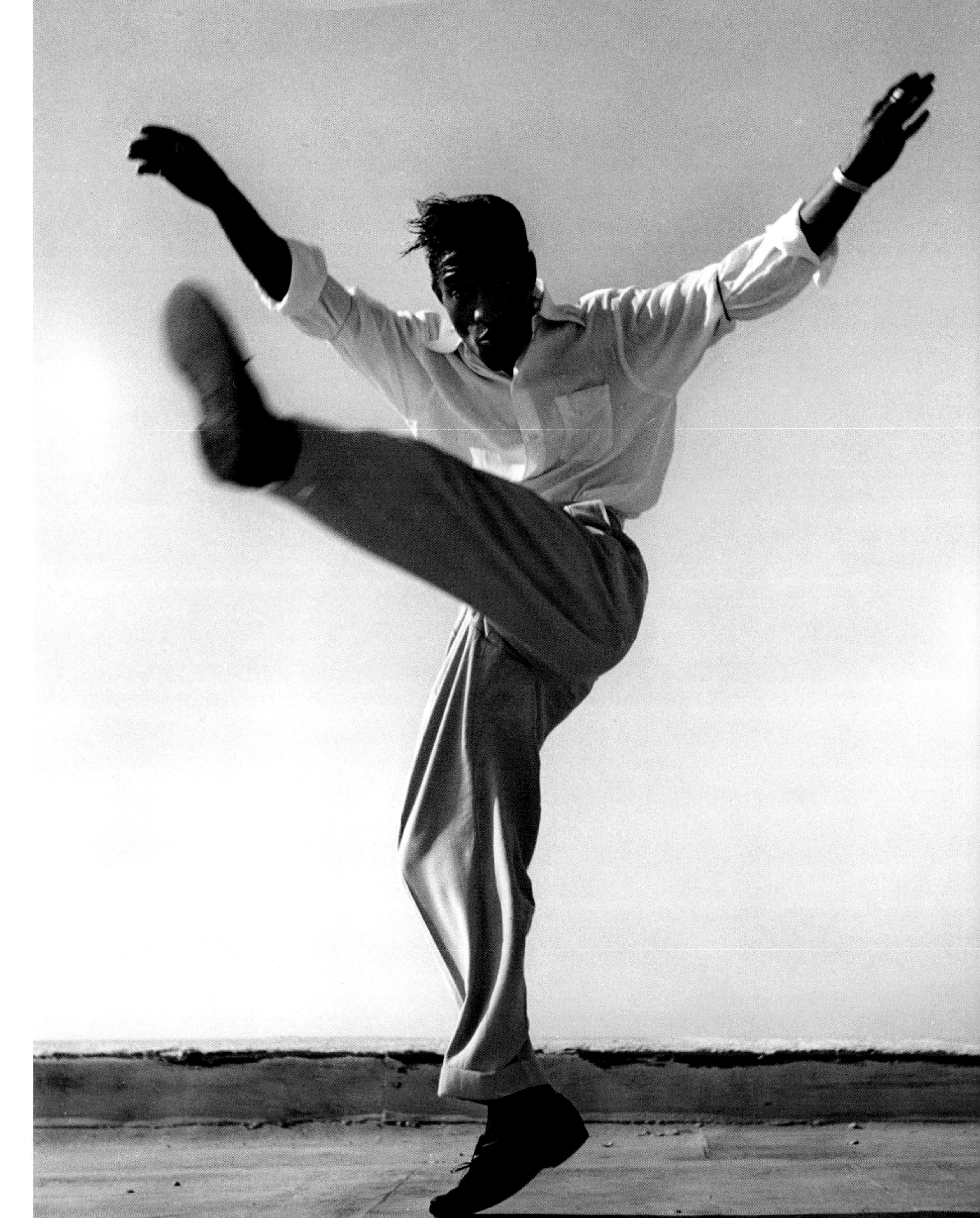

PLAY

Cheap pedicures, perpetual sun, guilt-free careerism, seeing Vincent Price at the 7-Eleven, having a backyard, no cockroaches, true love, and Disneyland. Every day is like Saturday.
Ann Magnuson, performance artist

Health, sunshine, and bronzed bodies had become virtually synonymous with Southern California by the 1920s. That era's economic boom, an aggressive consumer culture, new sexual mores, fashion, and the rise of Hollywood all helped to focus attention on the body as the new site of leisure and consumption. When a Southern California magazine claimed in 1933 that "Californians know the art of living," it stated the obvious—people found a luxurious playground in the balmy, sun-kissed terrain of the region.

Naturally, photographers capitalized on imagery as deliriously happy and fun-loving as Southern California itself, celebrating a culture of year-round athleticism, outdoor lounging, and public display. In 1953, an unknown photographer for *Ebony* magazine showed an African American dance troupe joyfully leaping in the sands of Laguna Beach, subtly alluding to the recent segregation of Southland beaches. Later practitioners, such as Jo Ann Callis, Lyle Ashton Harris, and Catherine Opie, used the city's penchant for playful abandon to subvert established gender roles. Still others took to Los Angeles's glittering, celebrity-infused nightlife to capture scenes of nocturnal carousing, establishing the city as a place infused with both glamour and melancholy solitude.

Where does it all lead? Larry Sultan's provocative images of porn sets in the San Fernando Valley are one destination, where the Los Angeles cult of the body, of fantasy, of lust, and of physical pleasure collides with alternative views and emotions: banality, pain, exploitation, and crushing anonymity.

Leroy Grannis
*Henry Ford, 22nd Street,
Hermosa Beach,
November 3, 1963*, 1963

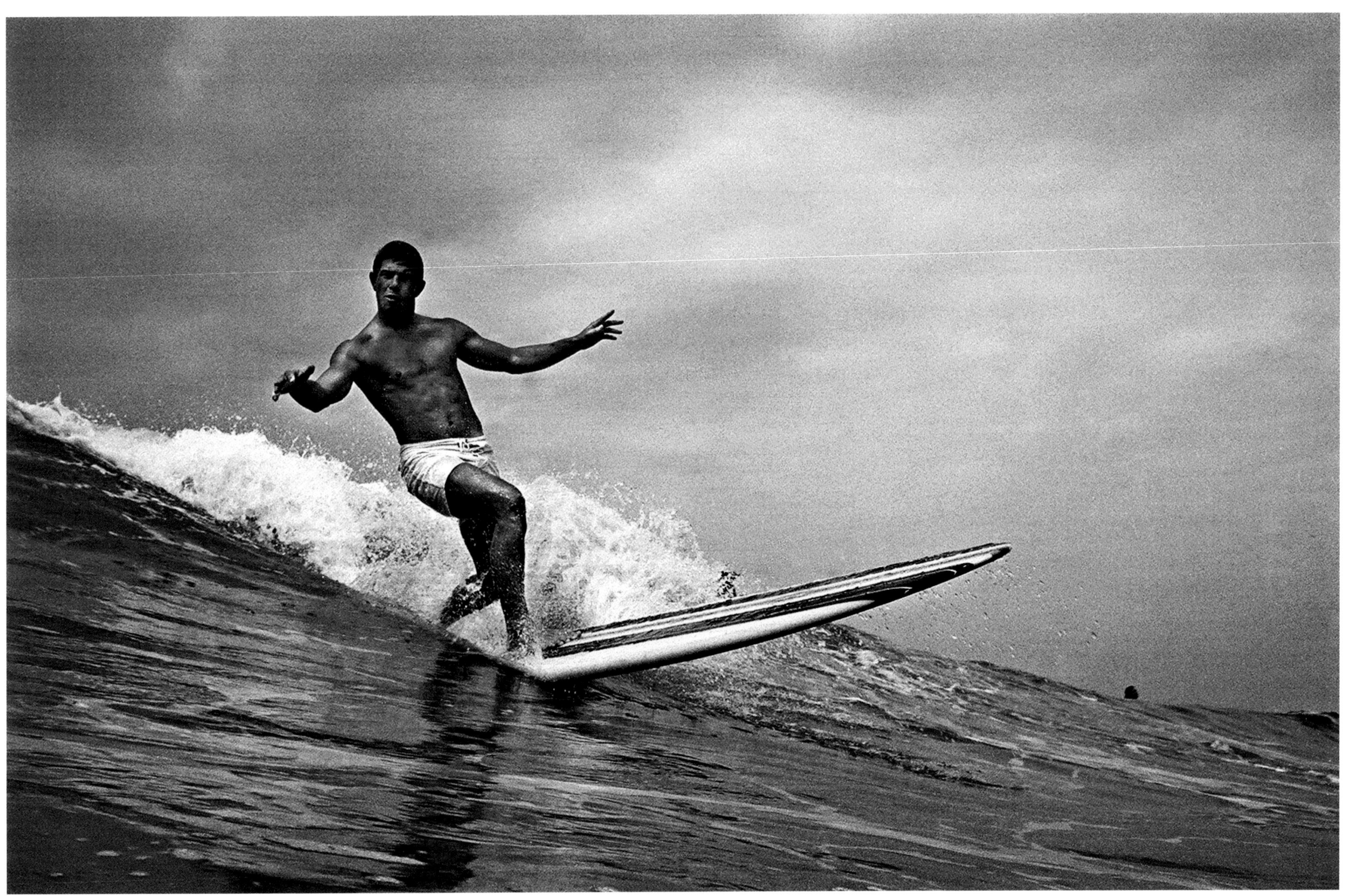

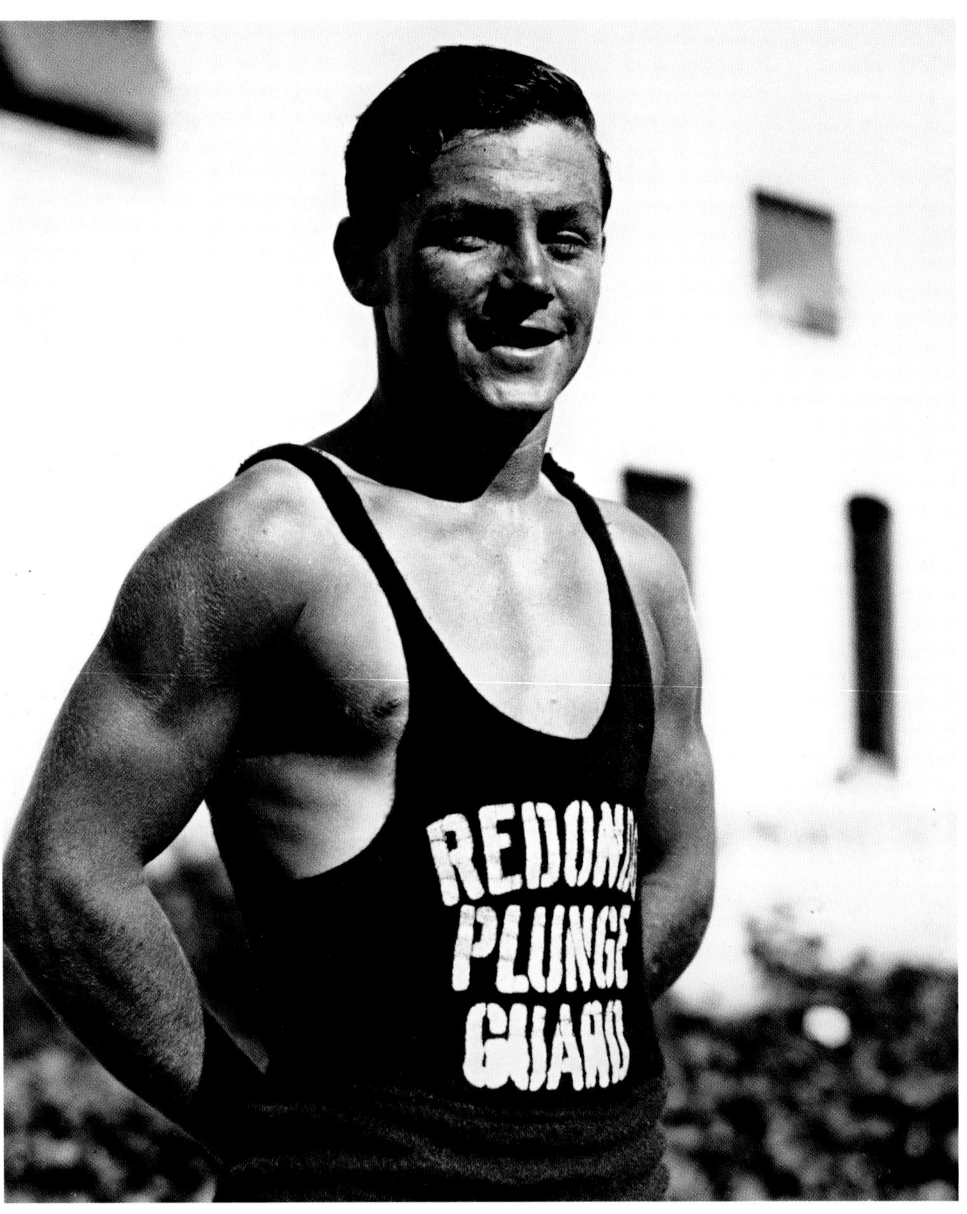

Pacific Electric Railway Company
Redondo Plunge Guard, n.d.

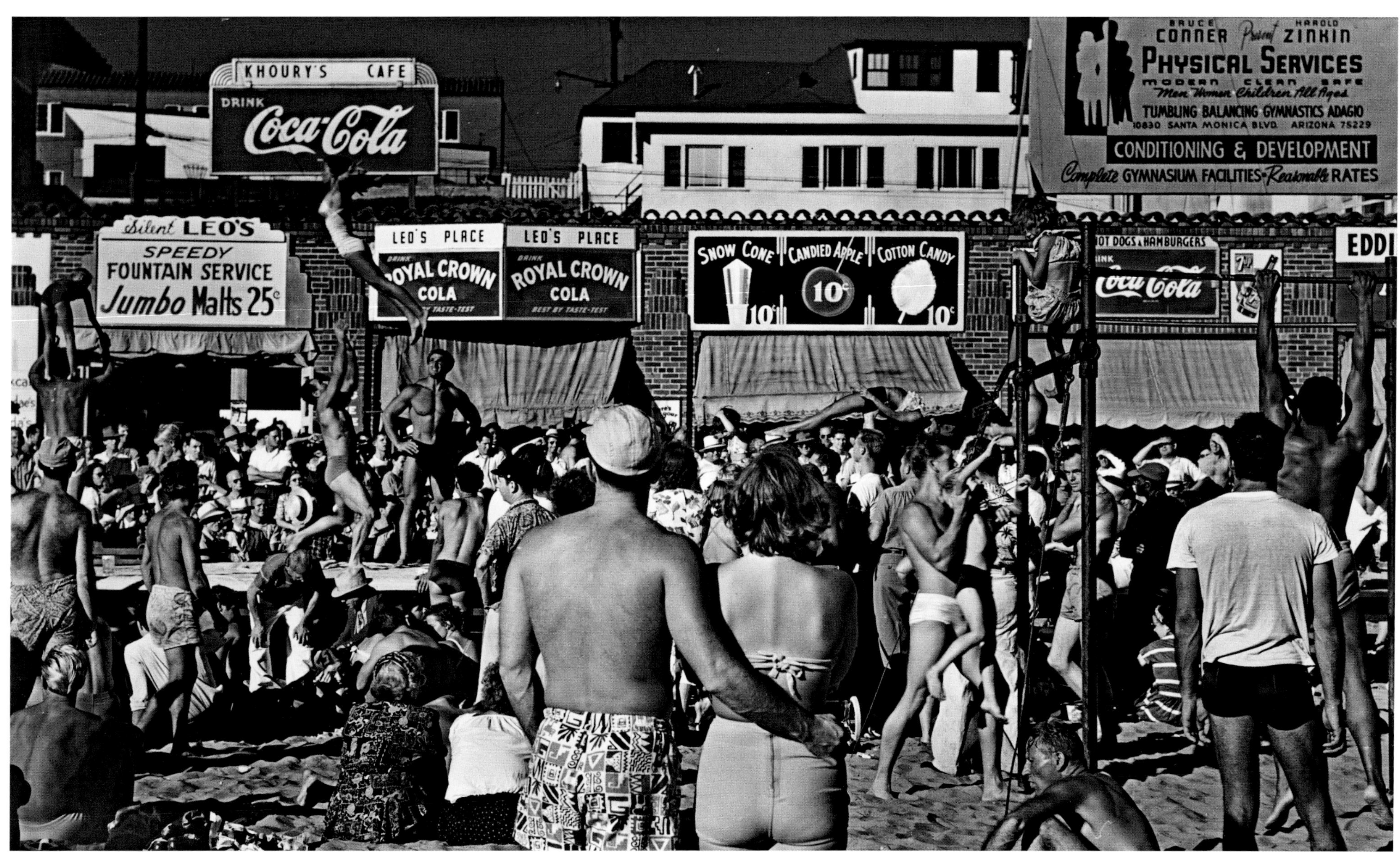

Max Yavno
Muscle Beach, 1949

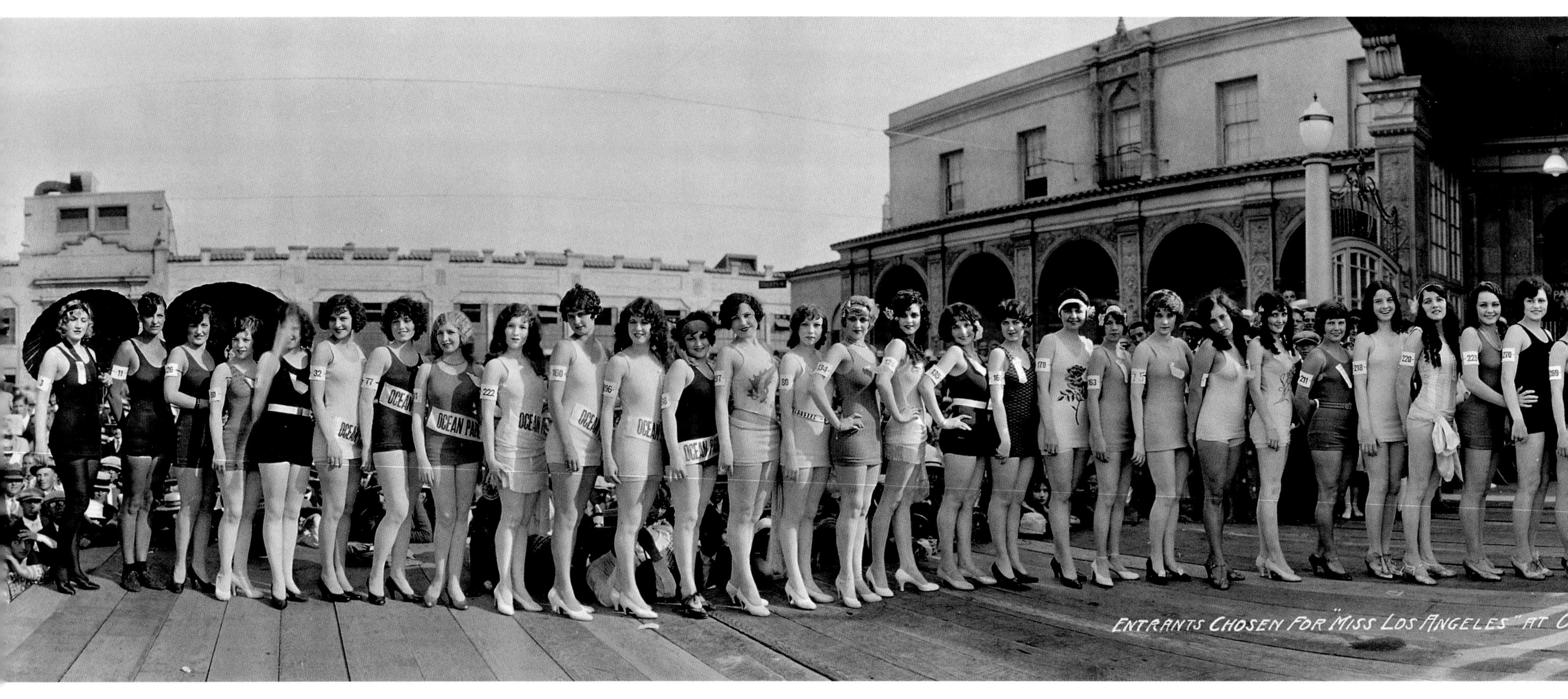

Miles F. Weaver
*Entrants Chosen for "Miss
Los Angeles" at Ocean Park
California Pageant*, 1926

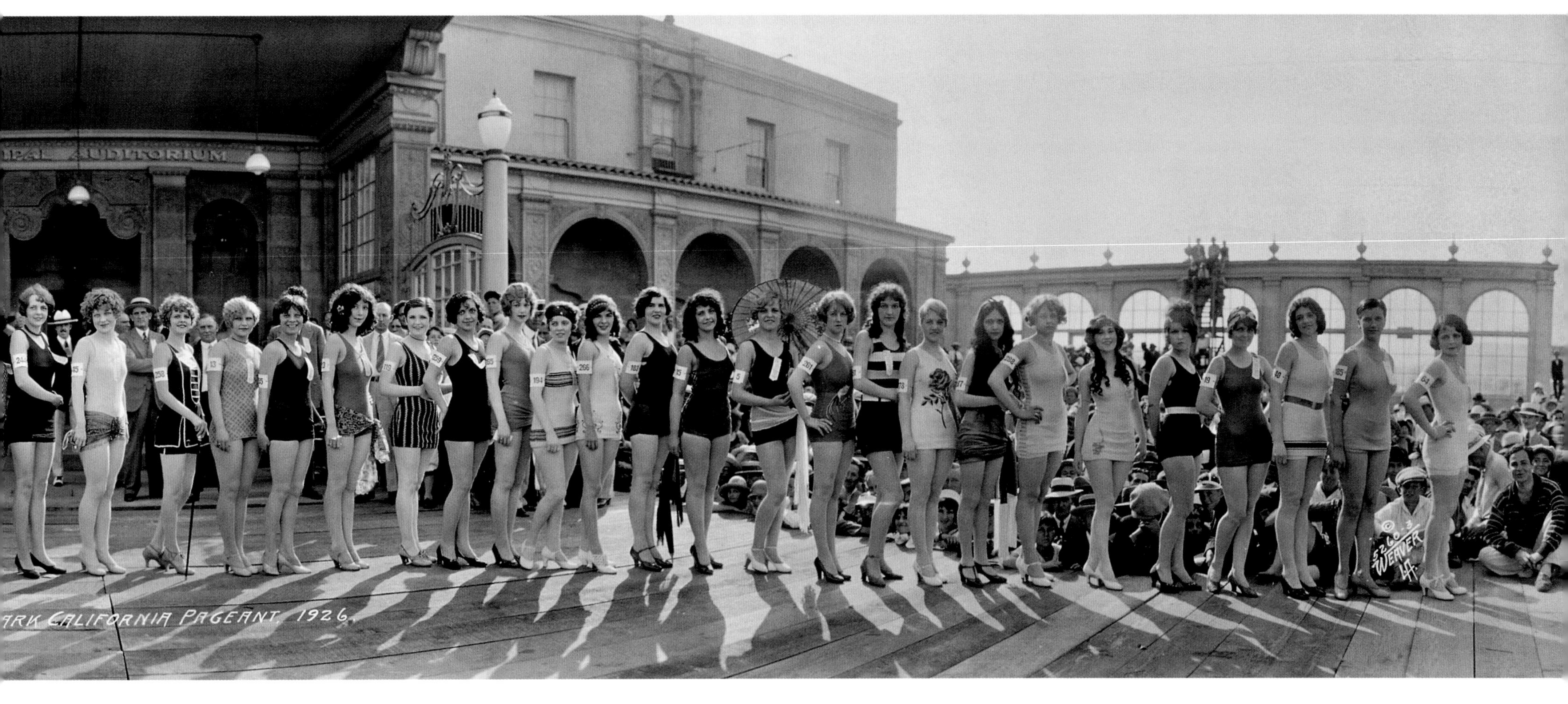
PAL AUDITORIUM
ARK CALIFORNIA PAGEANT. 1926.
WEAVER LA.

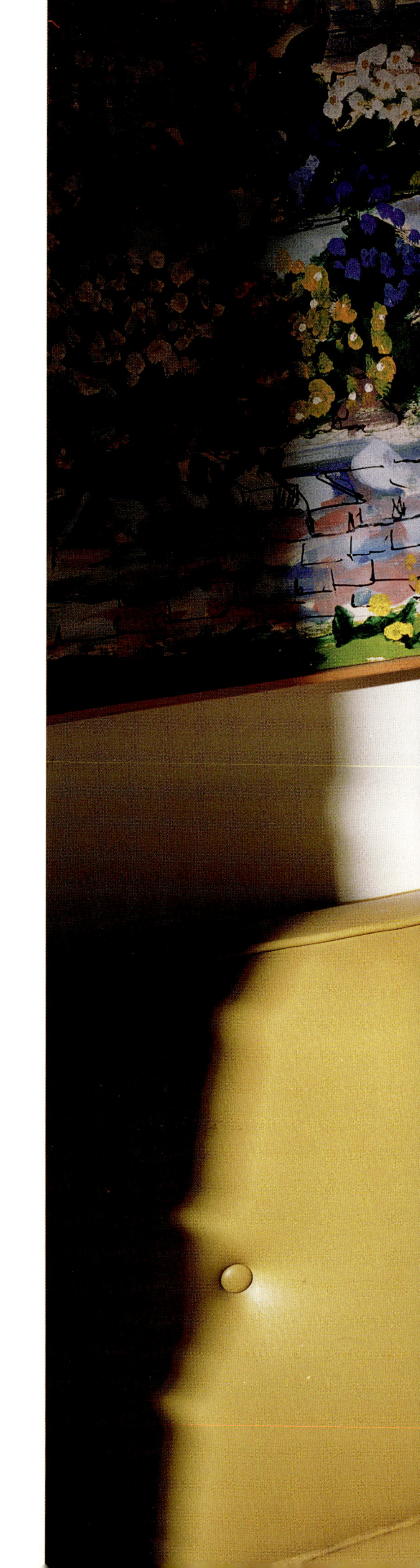

Larry Sultan
Chandler Boulevard, 2000

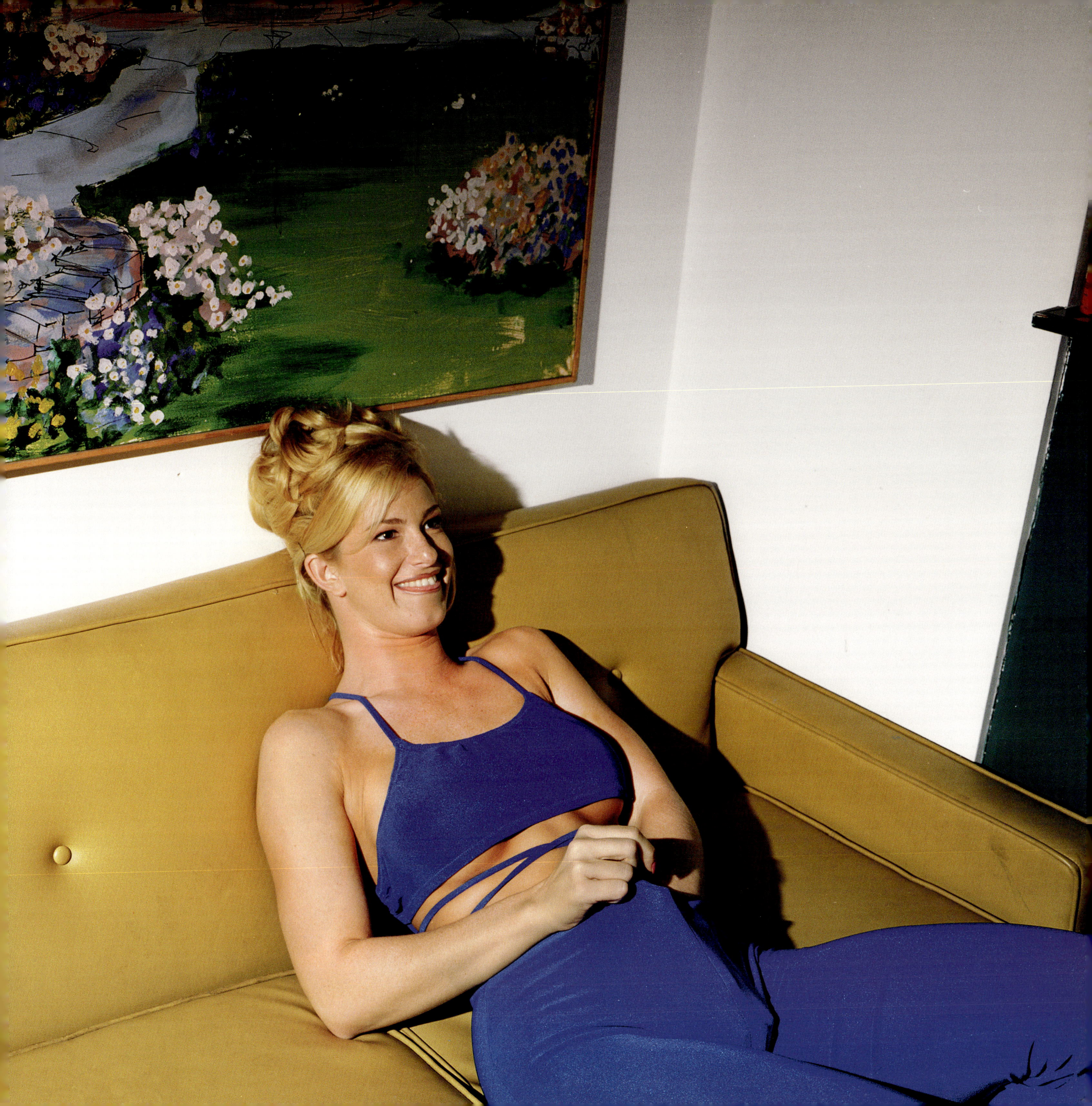

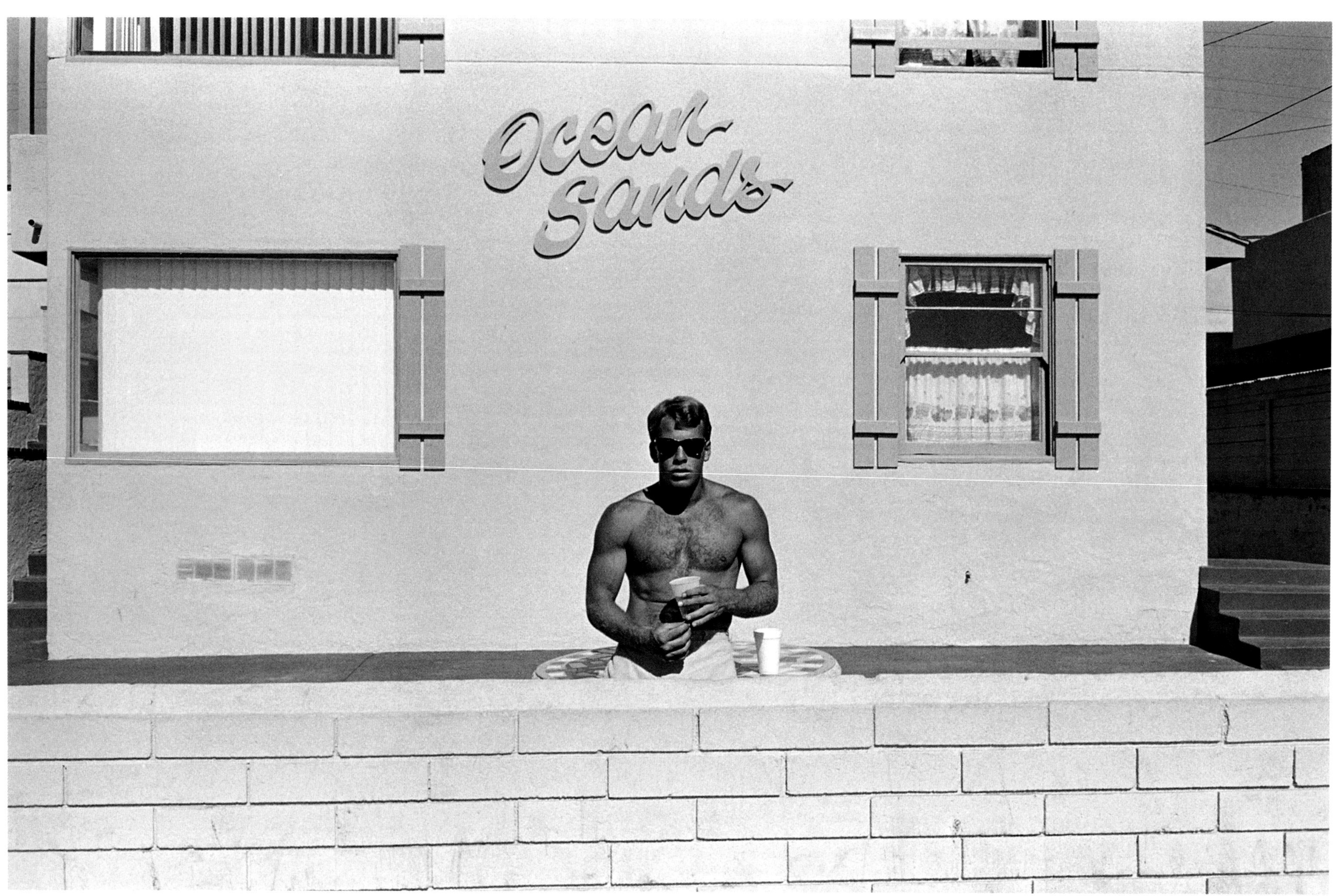

Henry Wessel
Ocean Sands, 1970

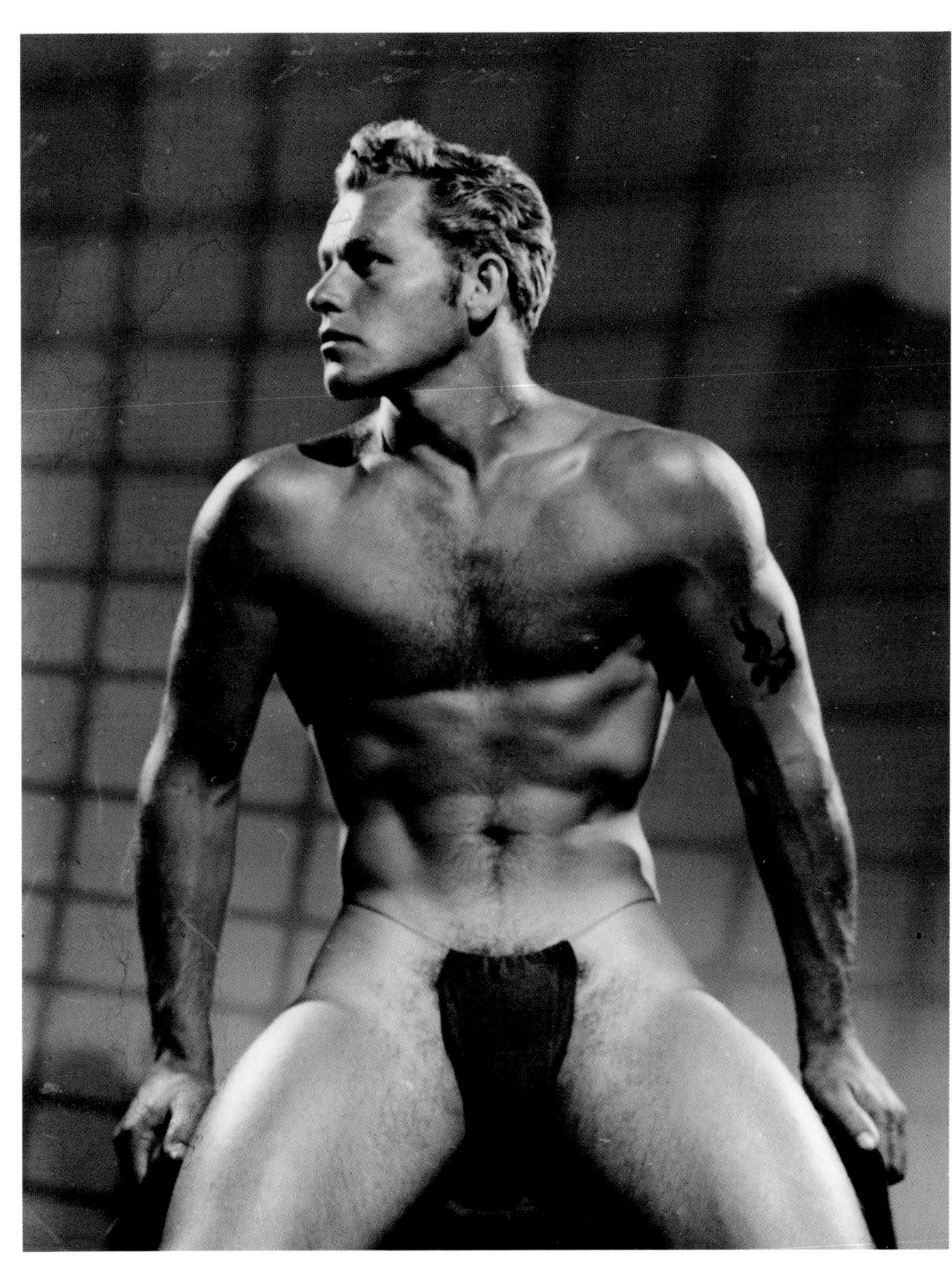

Robert Mizer
Jack Conant, 1949

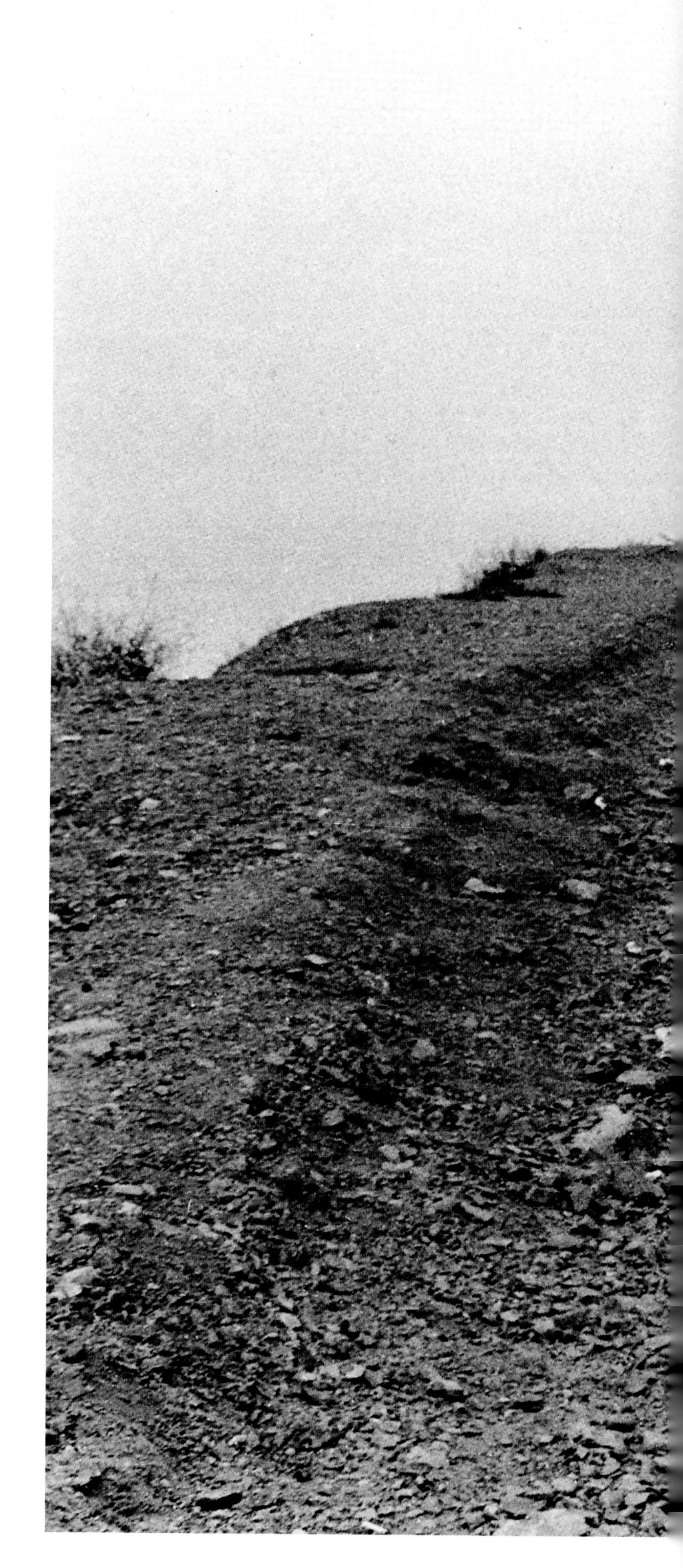

Anthony Friedkin
*Clockwork Malibu/Rick Dano
on the Highway, Malibu,
California*, 1977

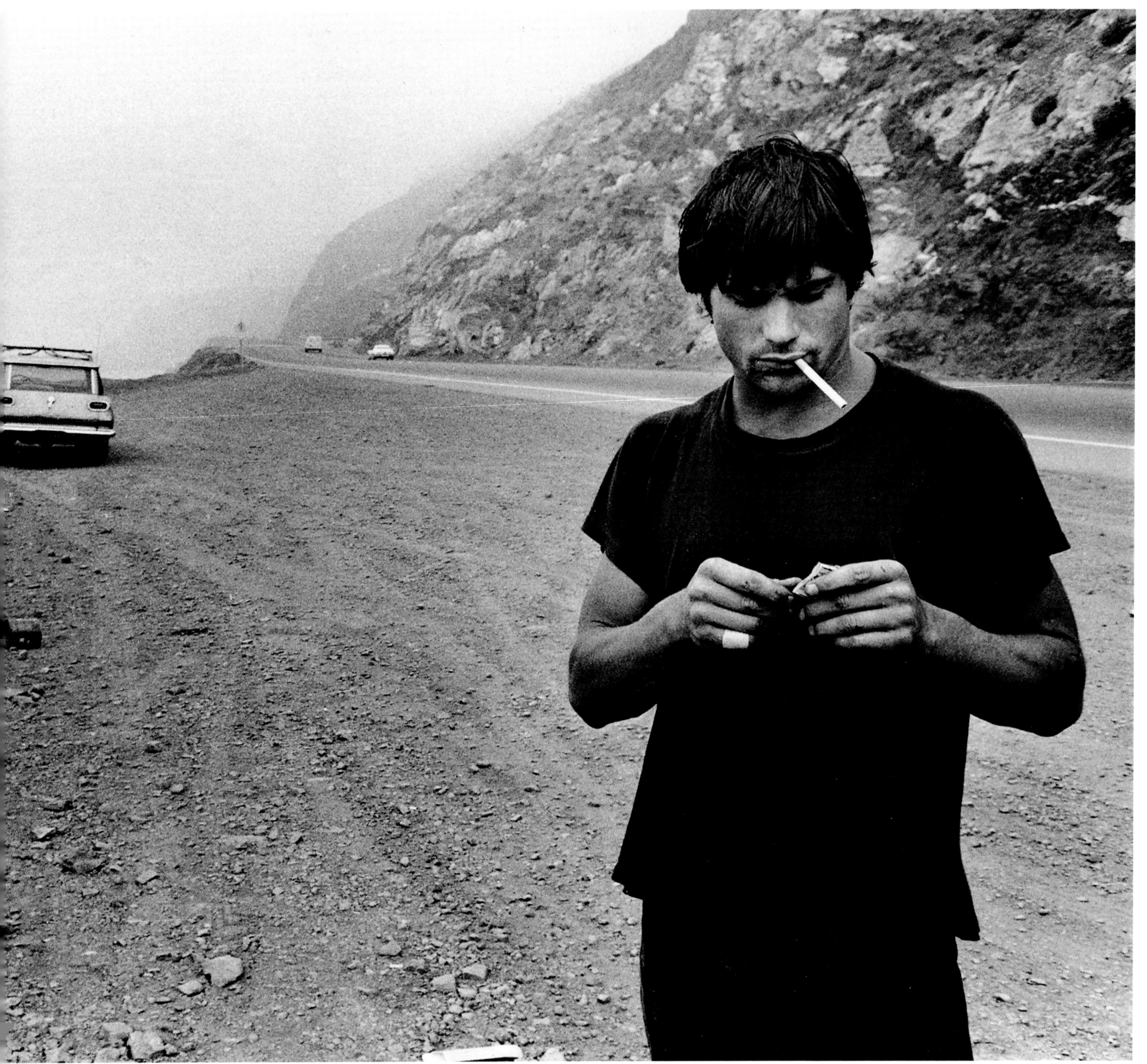

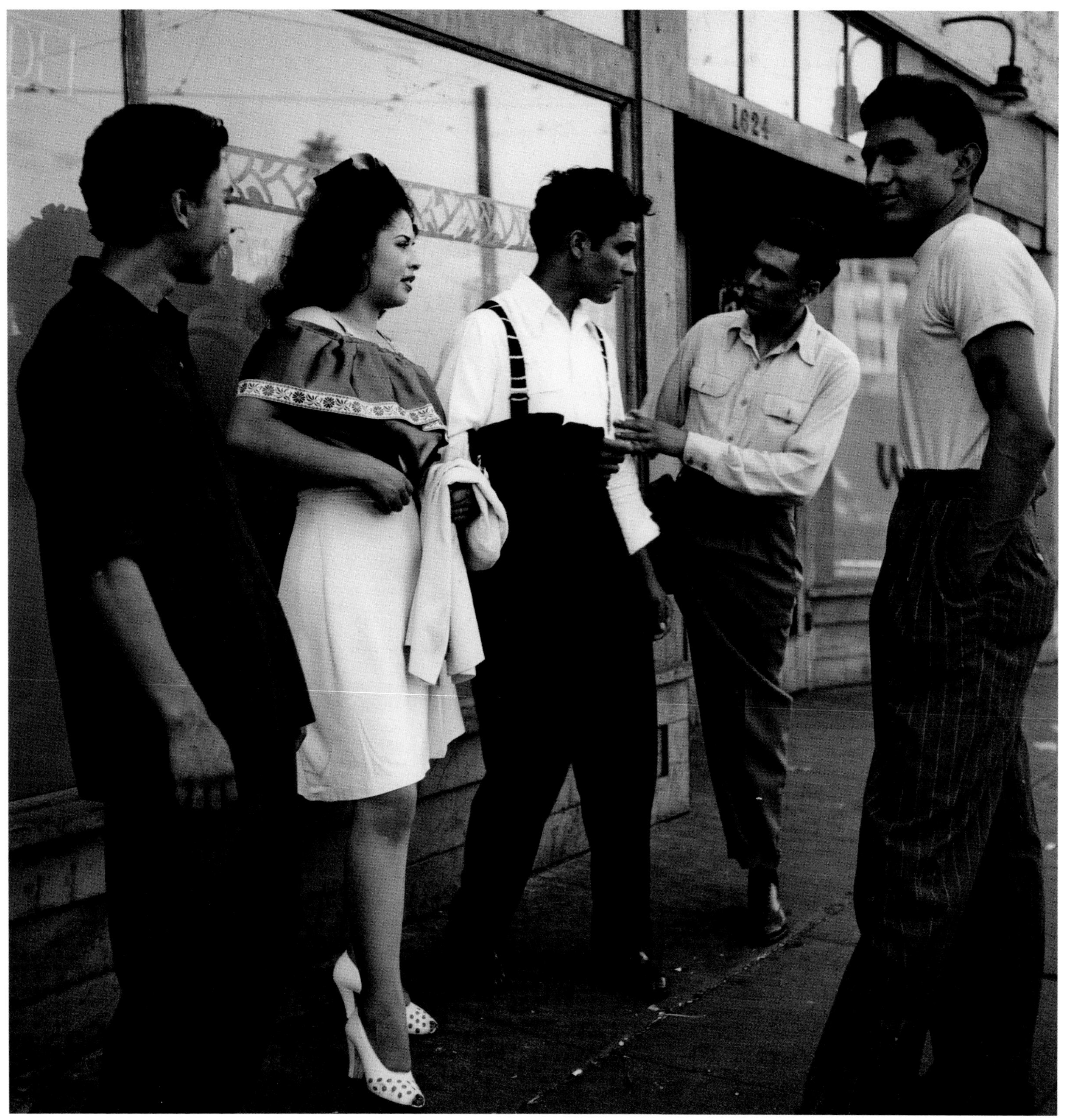

Max Yavno
Street Talk, 1946

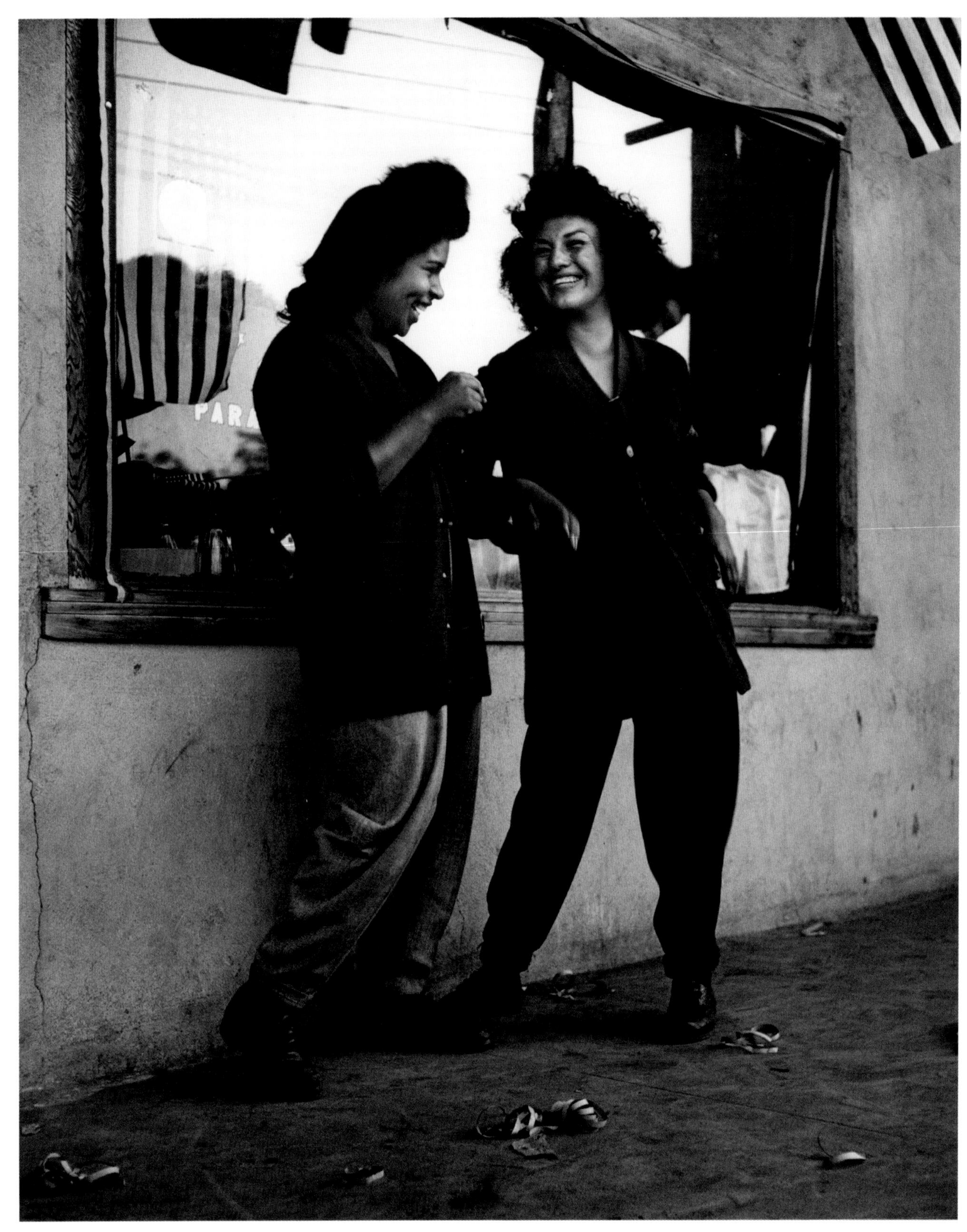

Max Yavno
Two Women, 1946

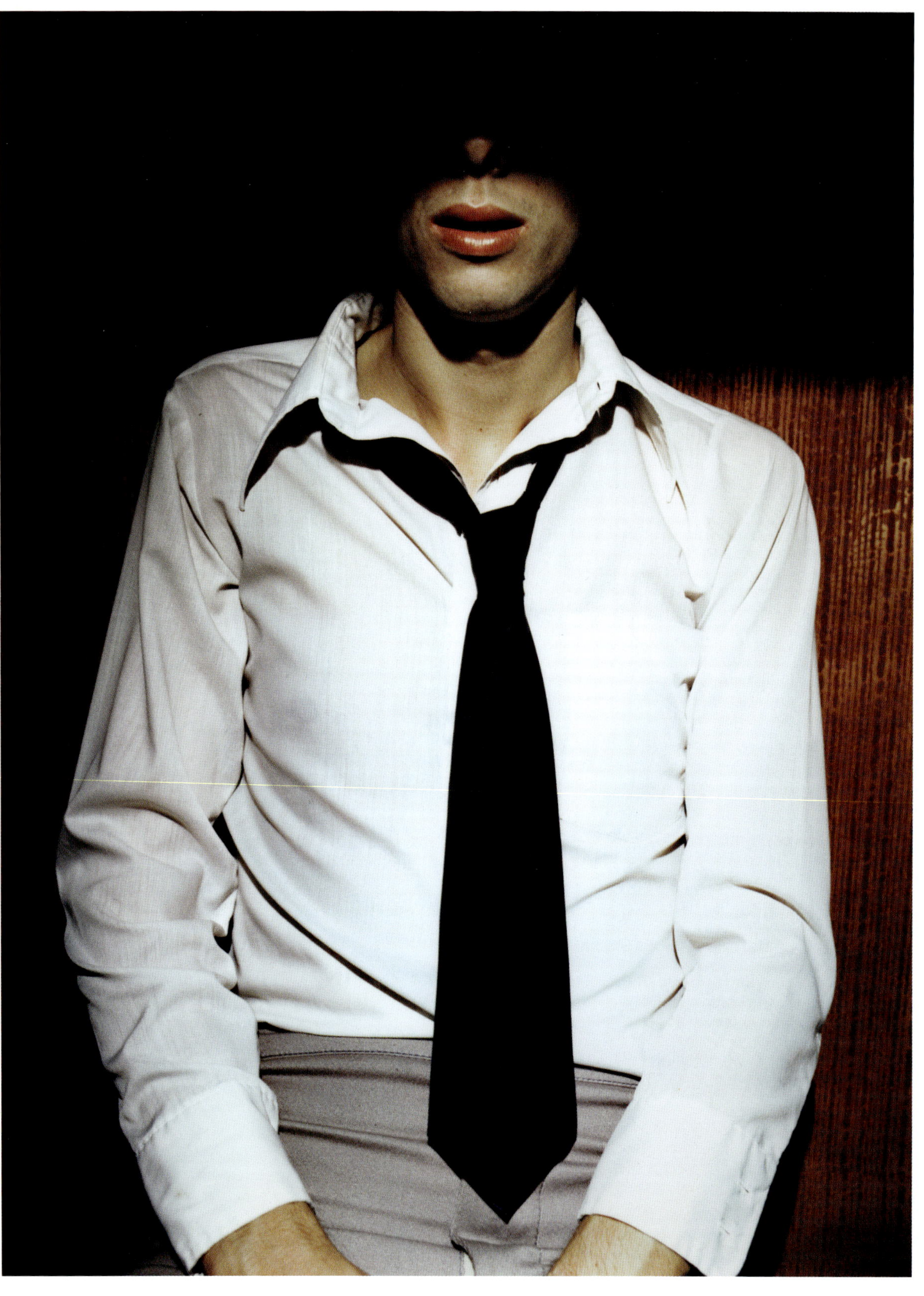

Jo Ann Callis
Man in a Tie, 1977

Opposite
Lyle Ashton Harris
Sisterhood, 1994

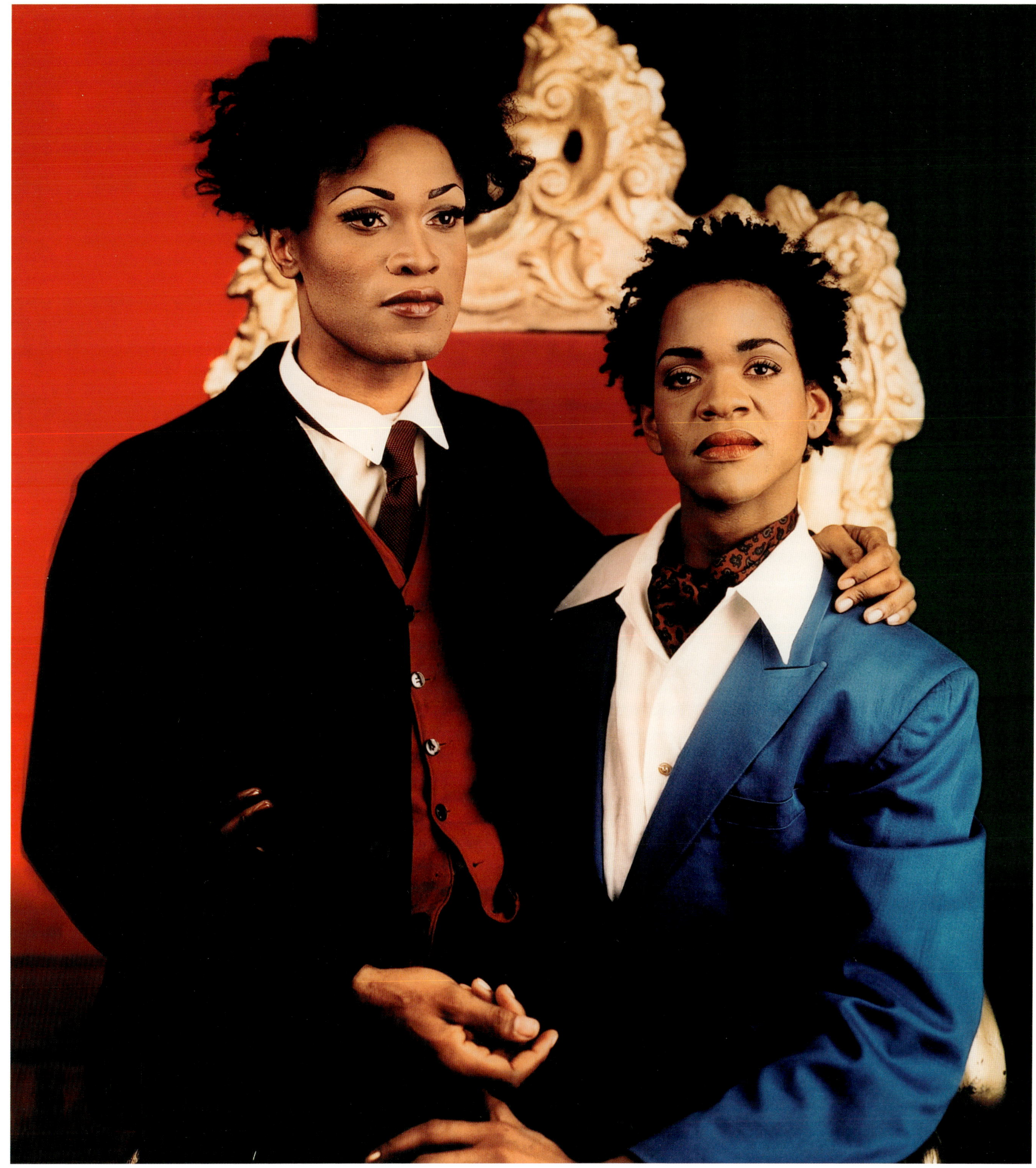

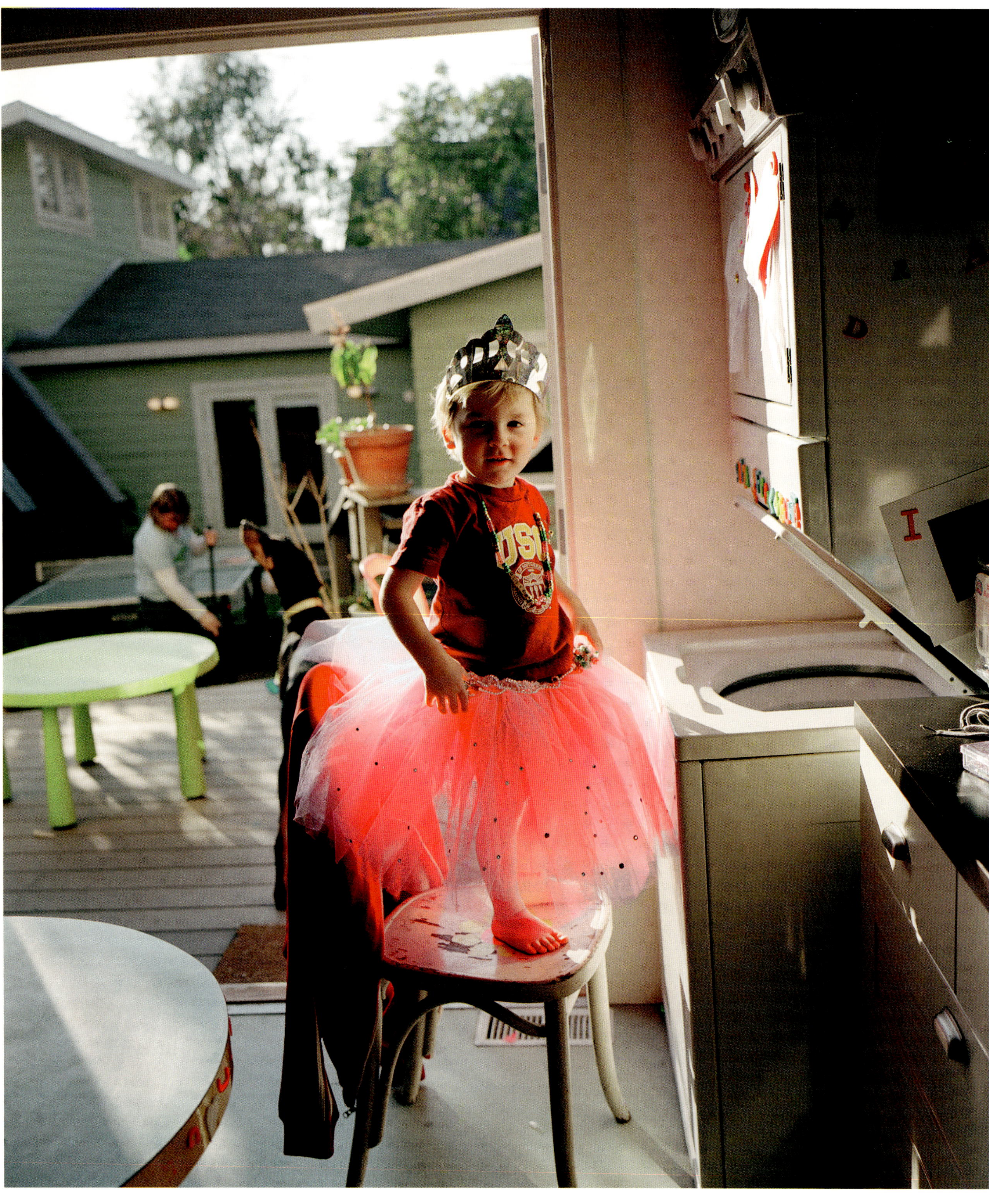

Catherine Opie
Oliver in a Tutu, 2004

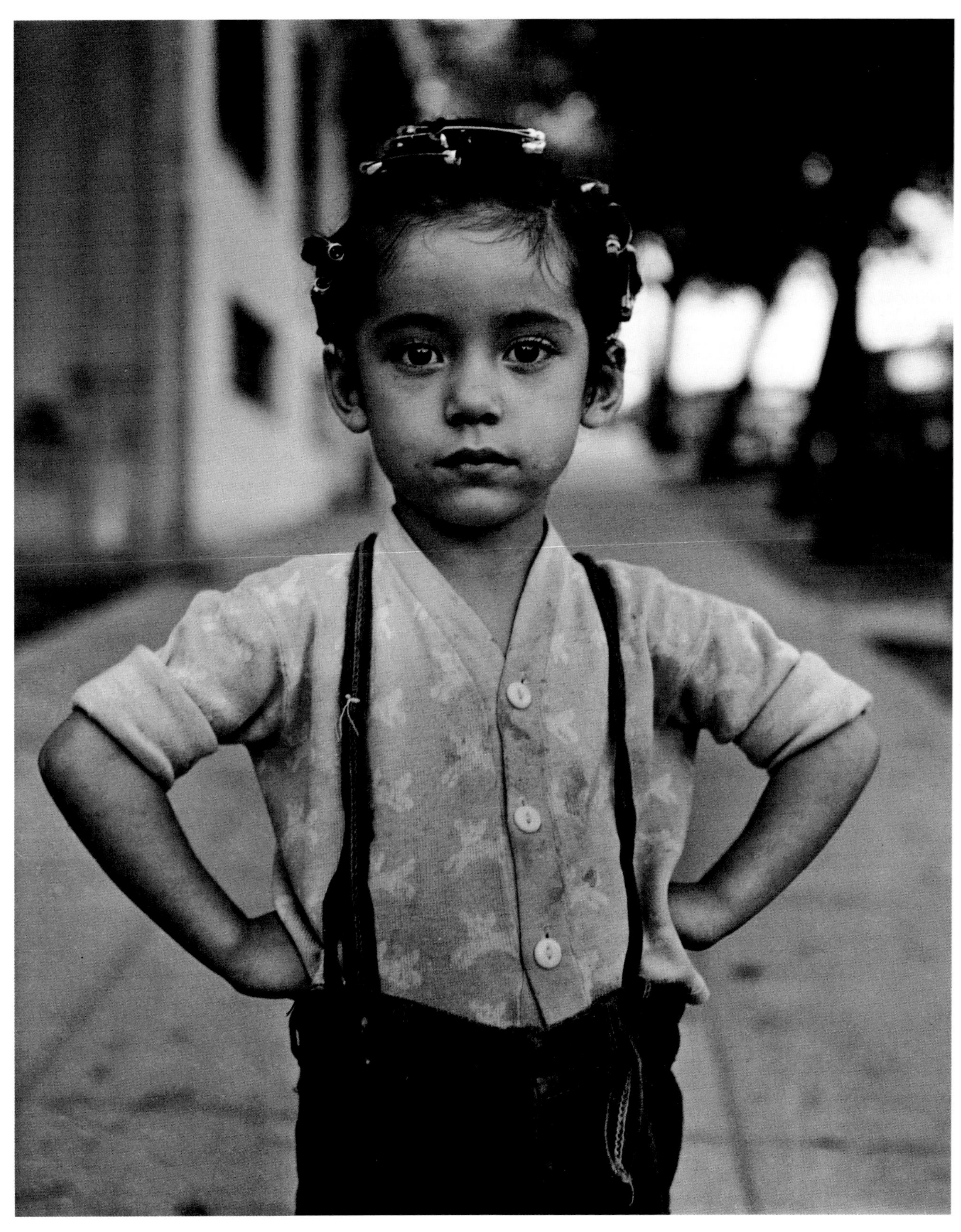

Ida Wyman
Girl with Curlers, Los Angeles,
1949

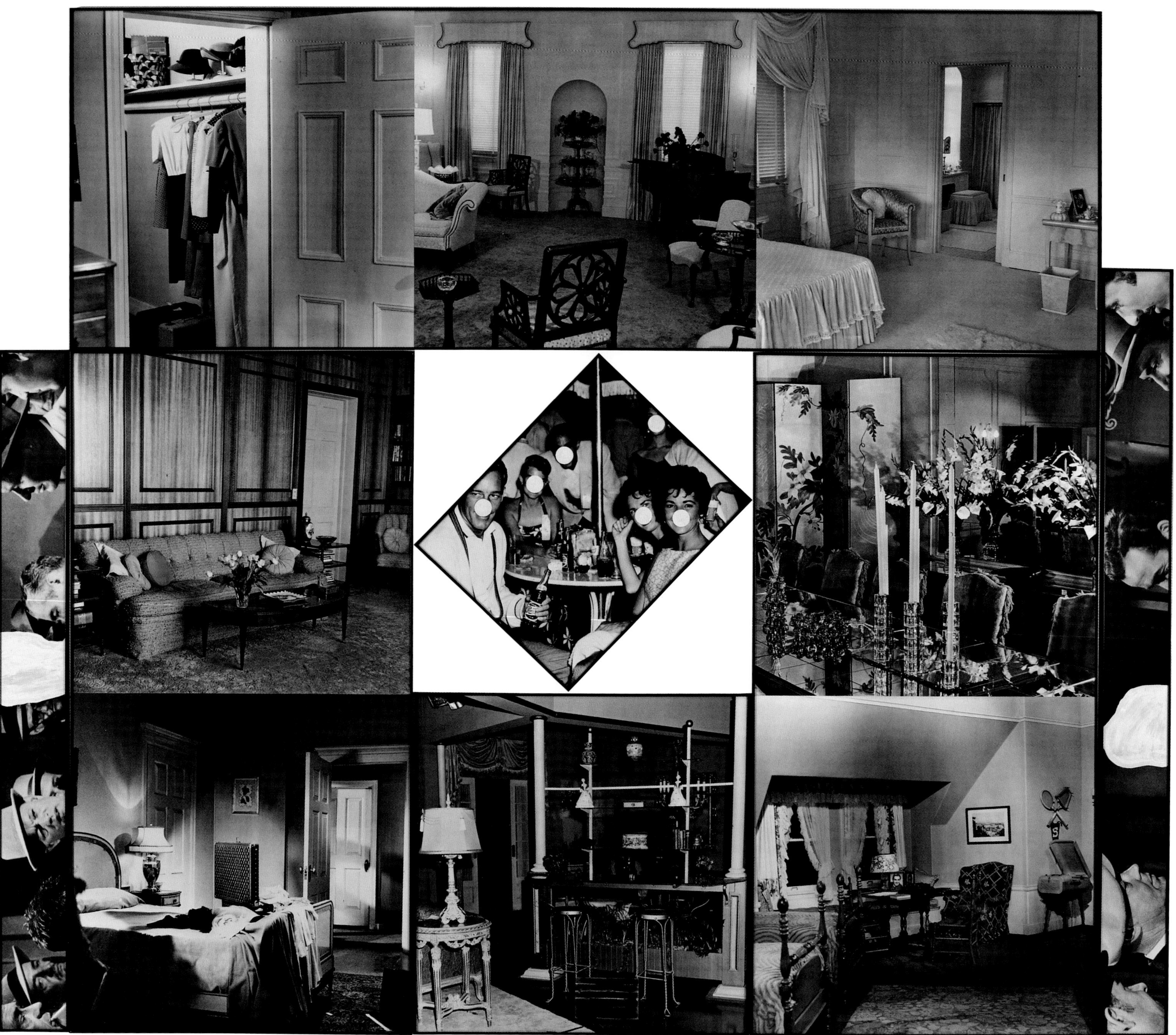

John Baldessari
Some Rooms, 1986

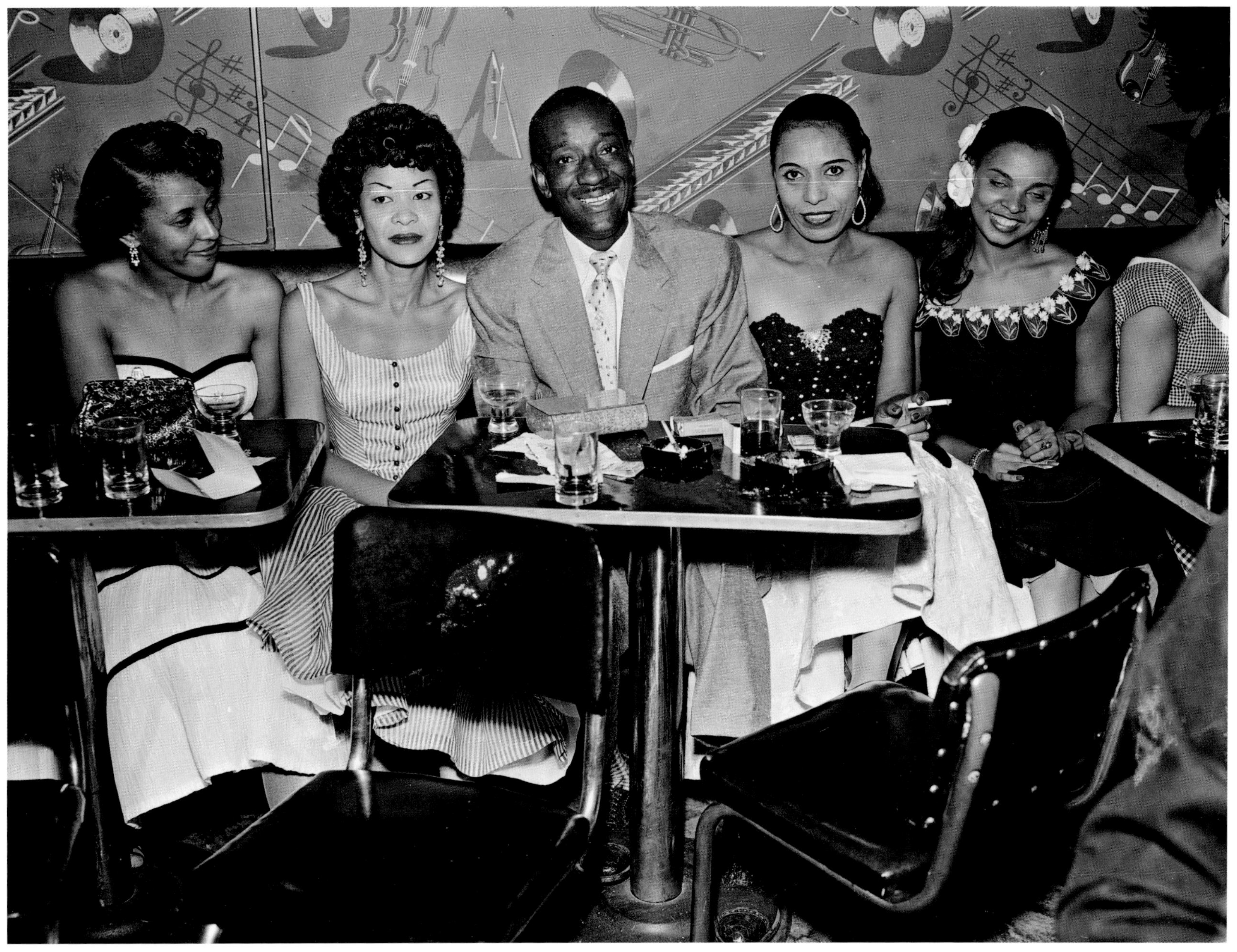

Harry Adams
Black Dot McGee with Friends at Pacific Town Club, Adams and 24th Streets, Los Angeles, 1955

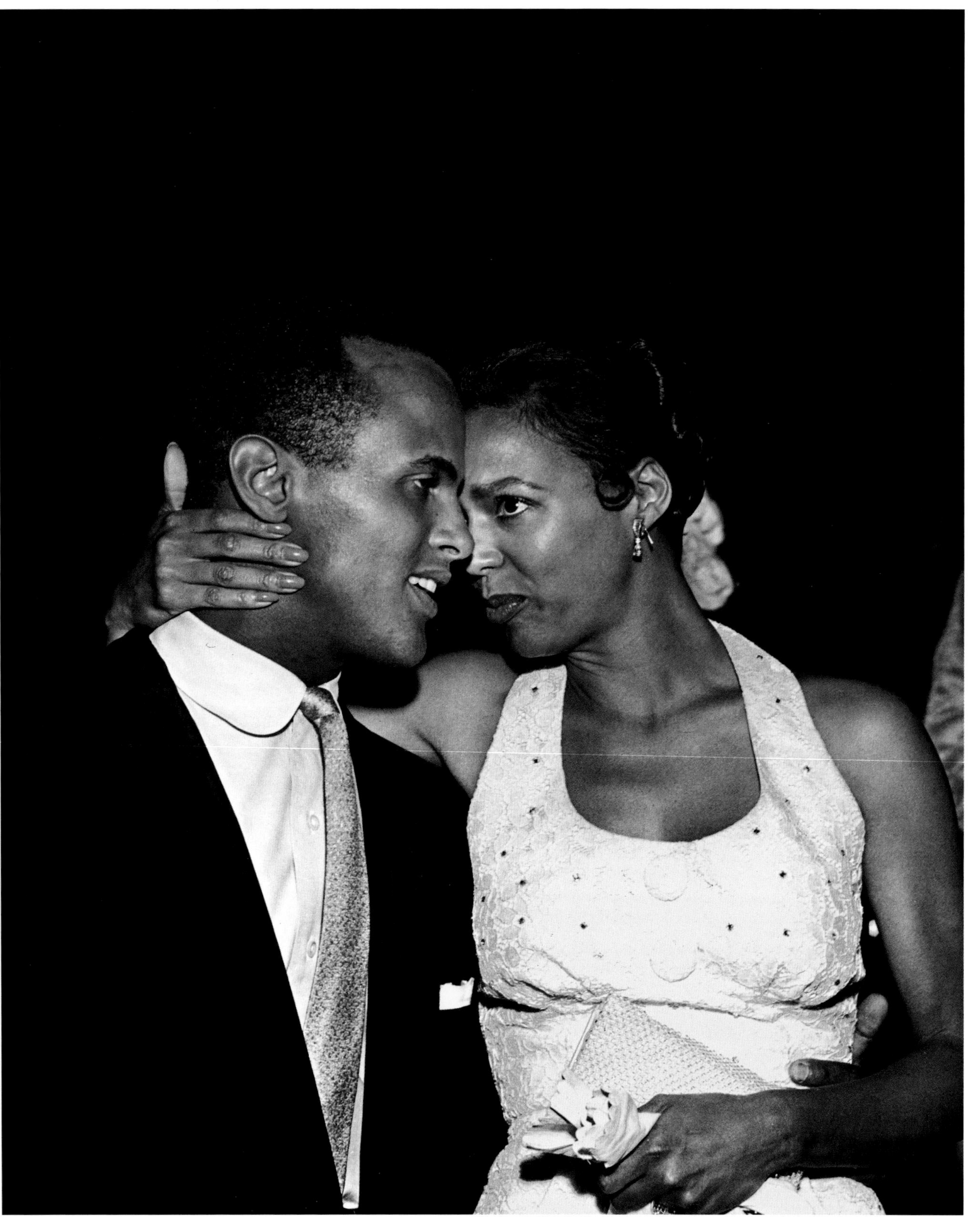

Charles Williams
*Harry Belafonte and Dorothy
Dandridge, c. 1954*

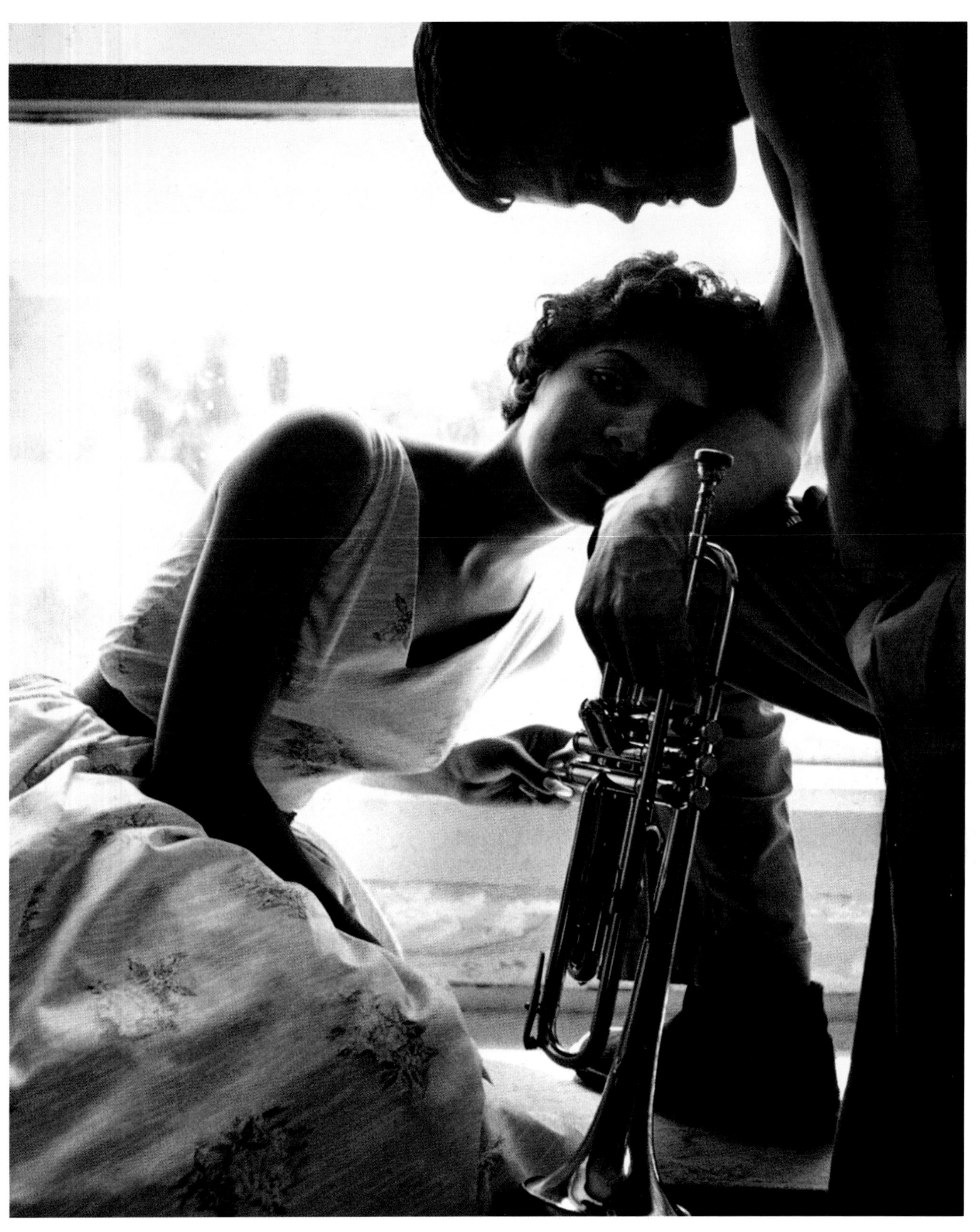

William Claxton
Halima & Chet Baker,
Redondo Beach, 1955

175

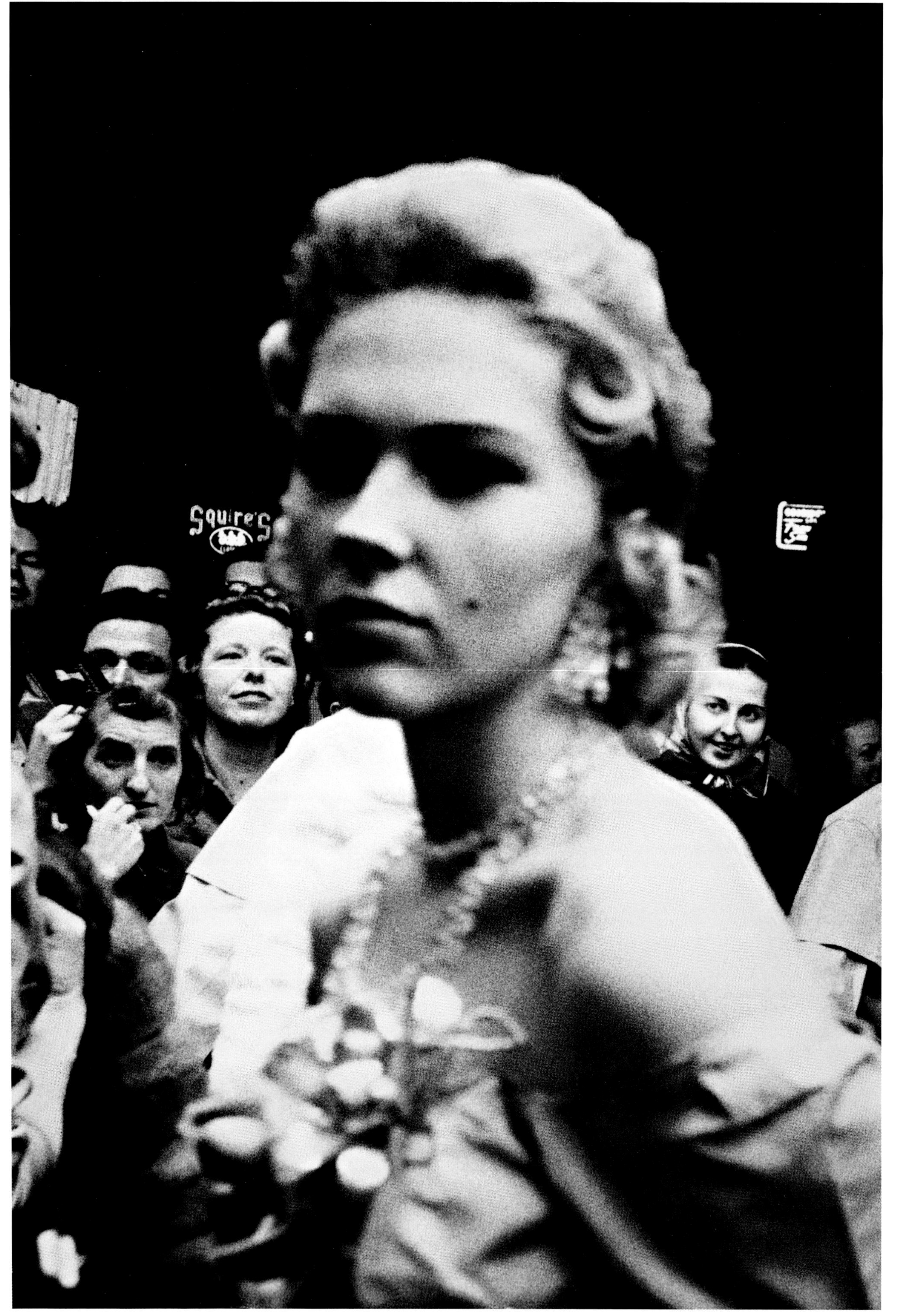

Robert Frank
Movie Premiere, Hollywood,
1955–56

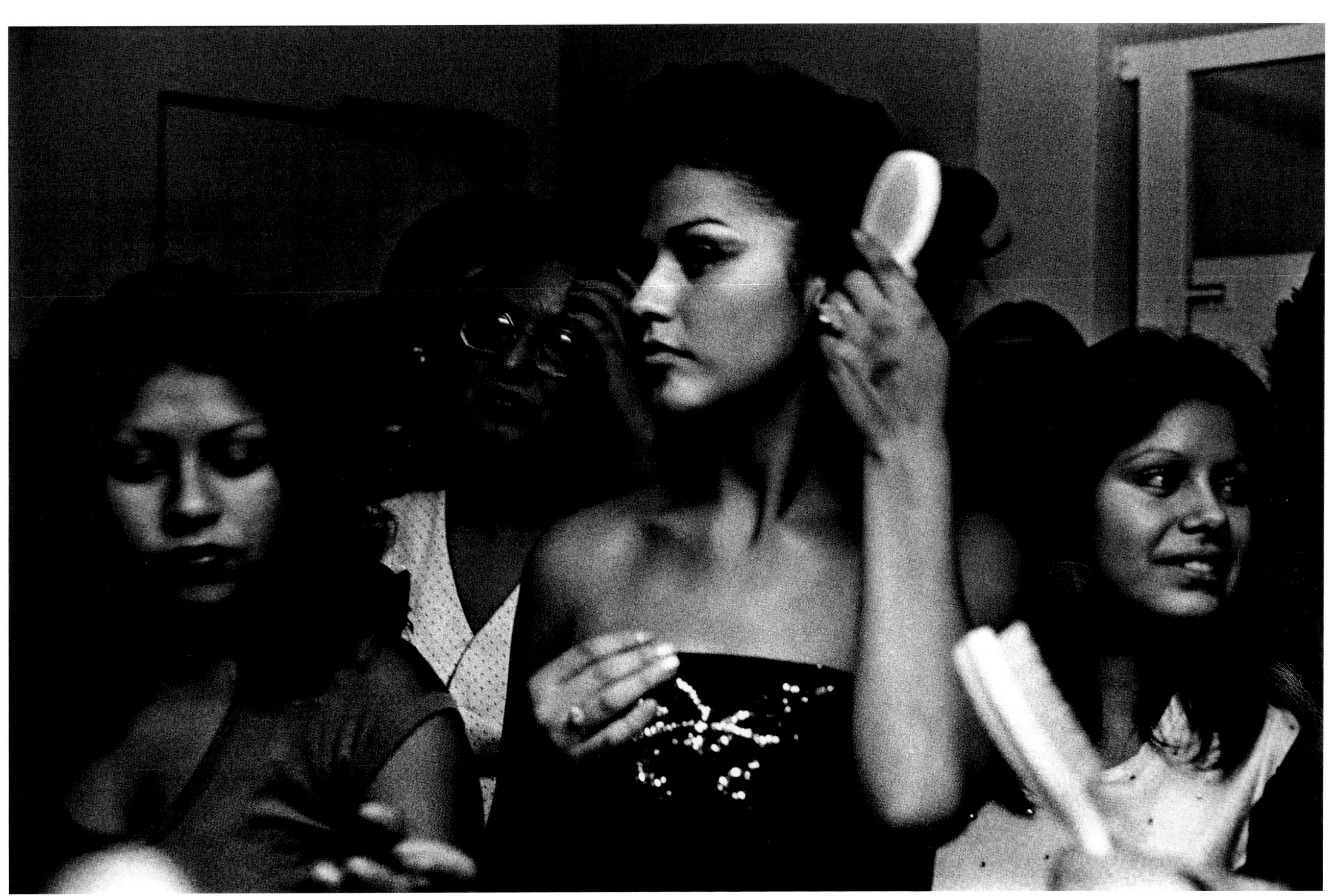

Gusmano Cesaretti
Alexandra Hotel, Klique
Dance, 1976

177

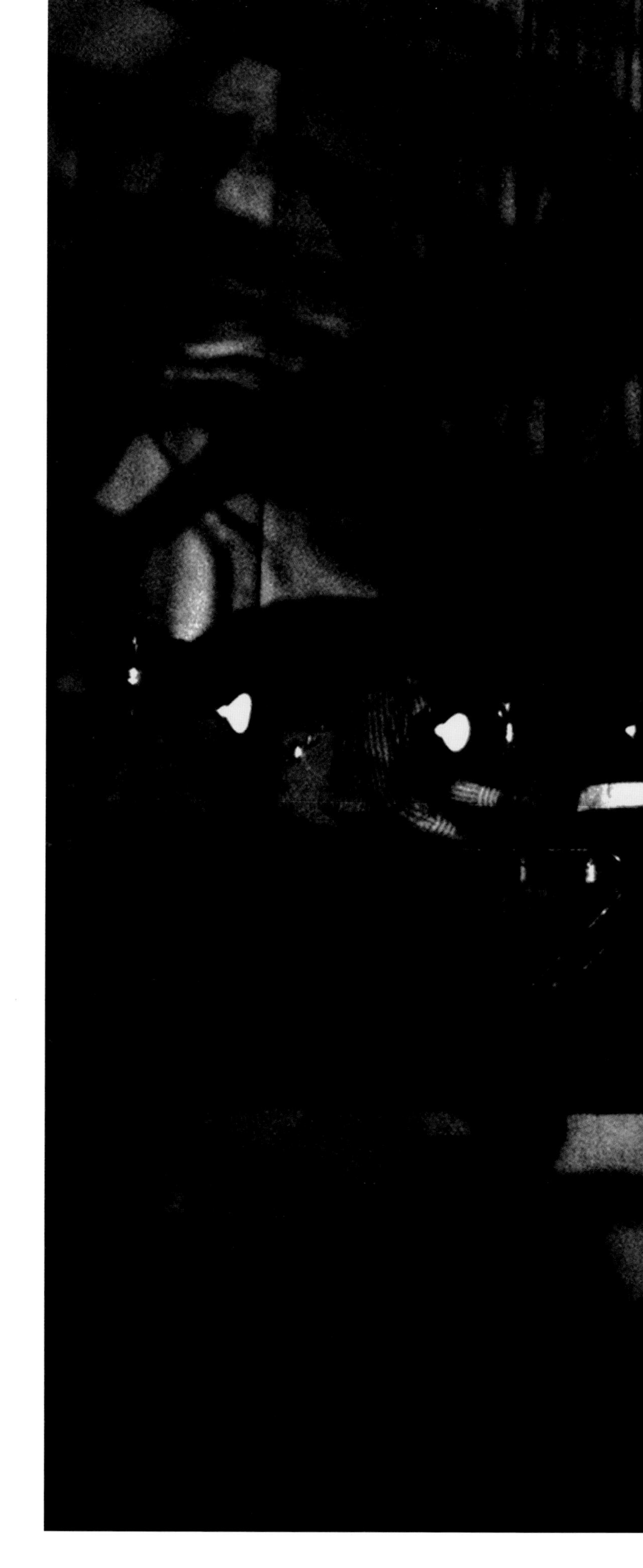

Bobby Klein
*The Doors Performing
on Stage, Los Angeles,
c. 1967*

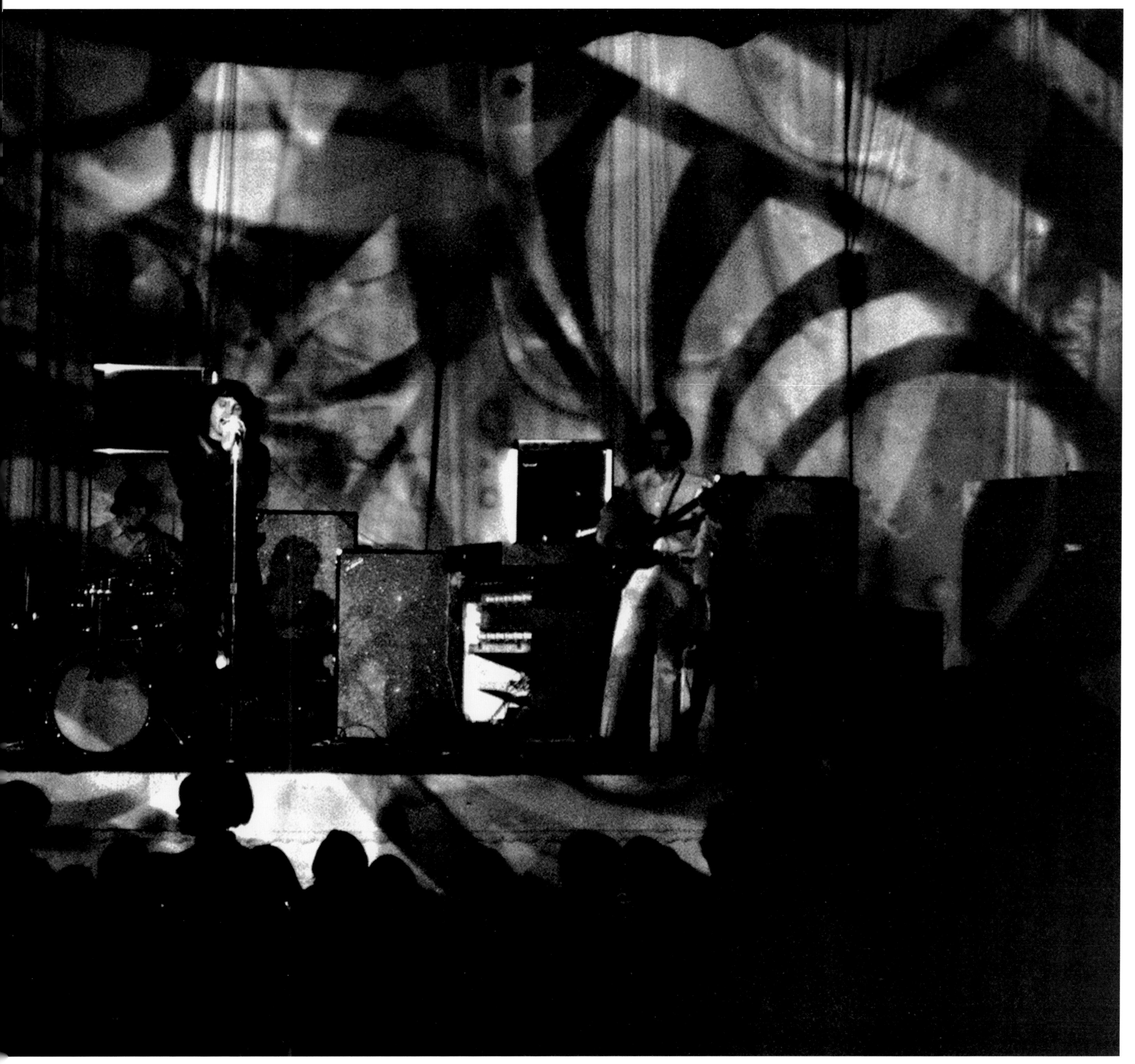

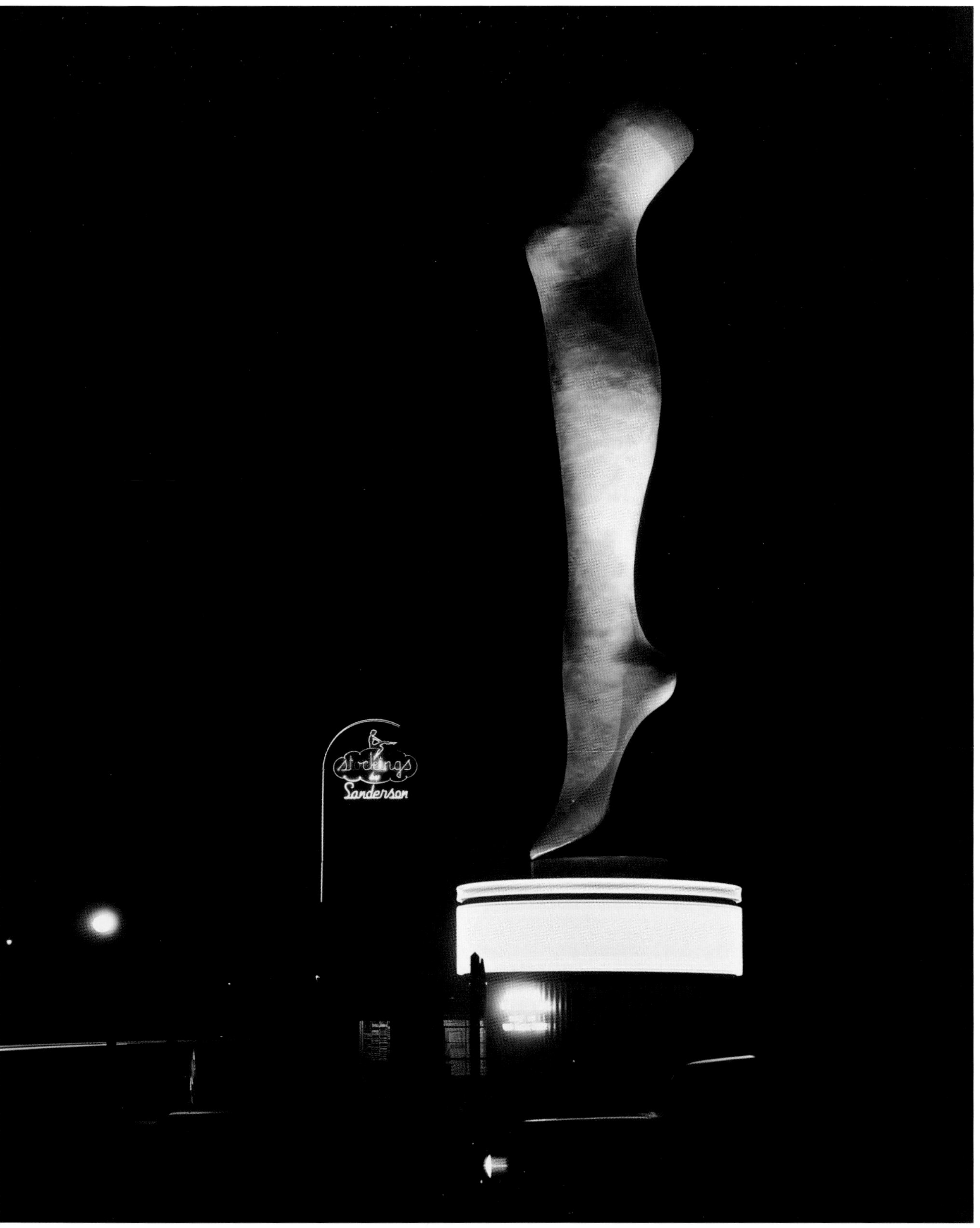

Max Yavno
The Leg, 1949

Opposite
G. Haven Bishop
Street scene at night with illuminated sign advertising the Mission Play at the San Gabriel Mission, Los Angeles, April 12, 1915

Mission Play
EVERY AFTERNOON
Old San Gabriel
Mission
GREENWOOD ADV. CO. (WESTERN)

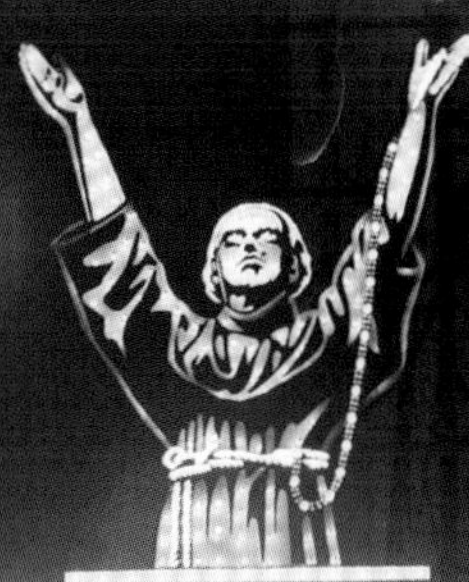

BENJAMIN CLOTHES
ELDEN HOTEL
COHN 2% & BRO.
LOAN OFFICE
JAMES SMITH & CO.
EXCLUSIVE CLOTHIERS
DOCTOR KEDIAN DENTIST
DOCTOR KEDIAN DENTIST
DOCTOR KEDIAN DENTIST
DOCTOR KEDIAN DENTIST
DOCTOR KEDIAN DENTIST
A. Mendelson Tailor

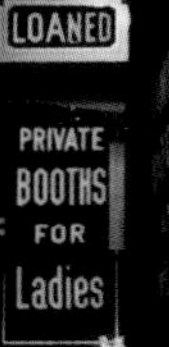

LOANED
PRIVATE BOOTHS FOR Ladies

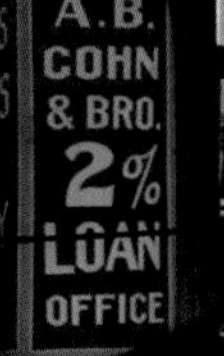

A.B. COHN & BRO. 2% LOAN OFFICE

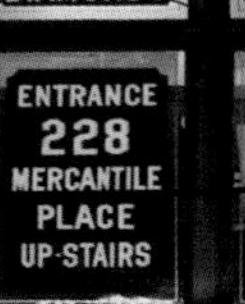

DIAMONDS
ENTRANCE 228 MERCANTILE PLACE UP-STAIRS

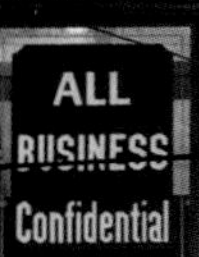

WATCHES
ALL BUSINESS Confidential

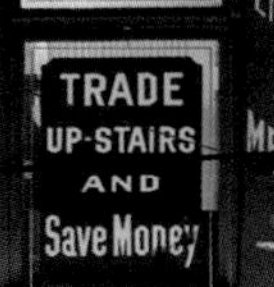

JEWELRY
TRADE UP-STAIRS AND Save Money

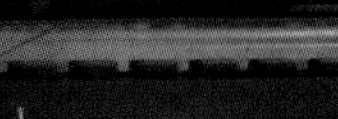

2% ENTRANCE 228 MERCANTILE

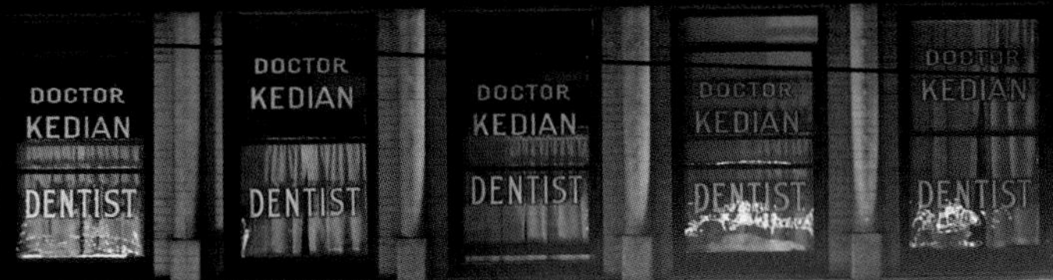

A.C. TAYLOR
JEWELER ~ OPTICIAN
JAMES SMITH Co

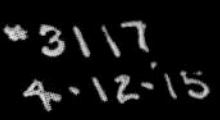

#3117
4-12-15

CLASH

L.A. may seem placid on the surface, but deep down, it is always roiling, always moving, always threatening to become unmoored.
David L. Ulin, writer

Los Angeles as flashpoint of racial violence and natural catastrophe is perhaps the best-known modern vision of the city, an apocalyptic nightmare beamed around the globe in word and image. The earth literally moves in Los Angeles: fire consumes hillsides, houses, and entire neighborhoods; landslides destroy movie star mansions; and earthquakes—the most terrifyingly democratic and unpredictable movement of all—topple buildings and wreak havoc. Los Angeles, or so it seems, is built on a foundation of hopeless optimism ("It can't happen here") and willful amnesia ("It's never happened here").

Southern California's built environment has always existed in precarious relationship to nature. The collapse of the St. Francis Dam in 1928 was one of the most devastating engineering disasters of the twentieth century. Commercial photographers rushed to record other cataclysms, such as the Long Beach earthquake of 1933, the first significant seismic event to hit the upstart metropolis in more than fifty years. Latter-day artists, such as Douglas Hill and Anthony Hernandez, have chosen to offer comment on the environmental degradation born of reckless urbanization. The near-mythical Los Angeles River appears in their images as a wasteland of graffiti and garbage.

The region's bitterly antagonistic relationship between labor and capital erupted violently in 1910 when labor saboteurs blew up the headquarters of the open shop *Los Angeles Times*. Decades of economic inequity and de facto segregation created a tinderbox of racial frustrations that exploded not once but twice: in Watts in 1965, and in South Central Los Angeles in 1992.

This is the dark side of Los Angeles. This is Raymond Chandler's noir city, in which boyfriends beat their movie star look-alike girlfriends, and Marilyn Monroe ends up dead in the city morgue, her toe sticking out of a cold, stainless-steel vault.

Anthony Hernandez
Everything #5, 2003-04

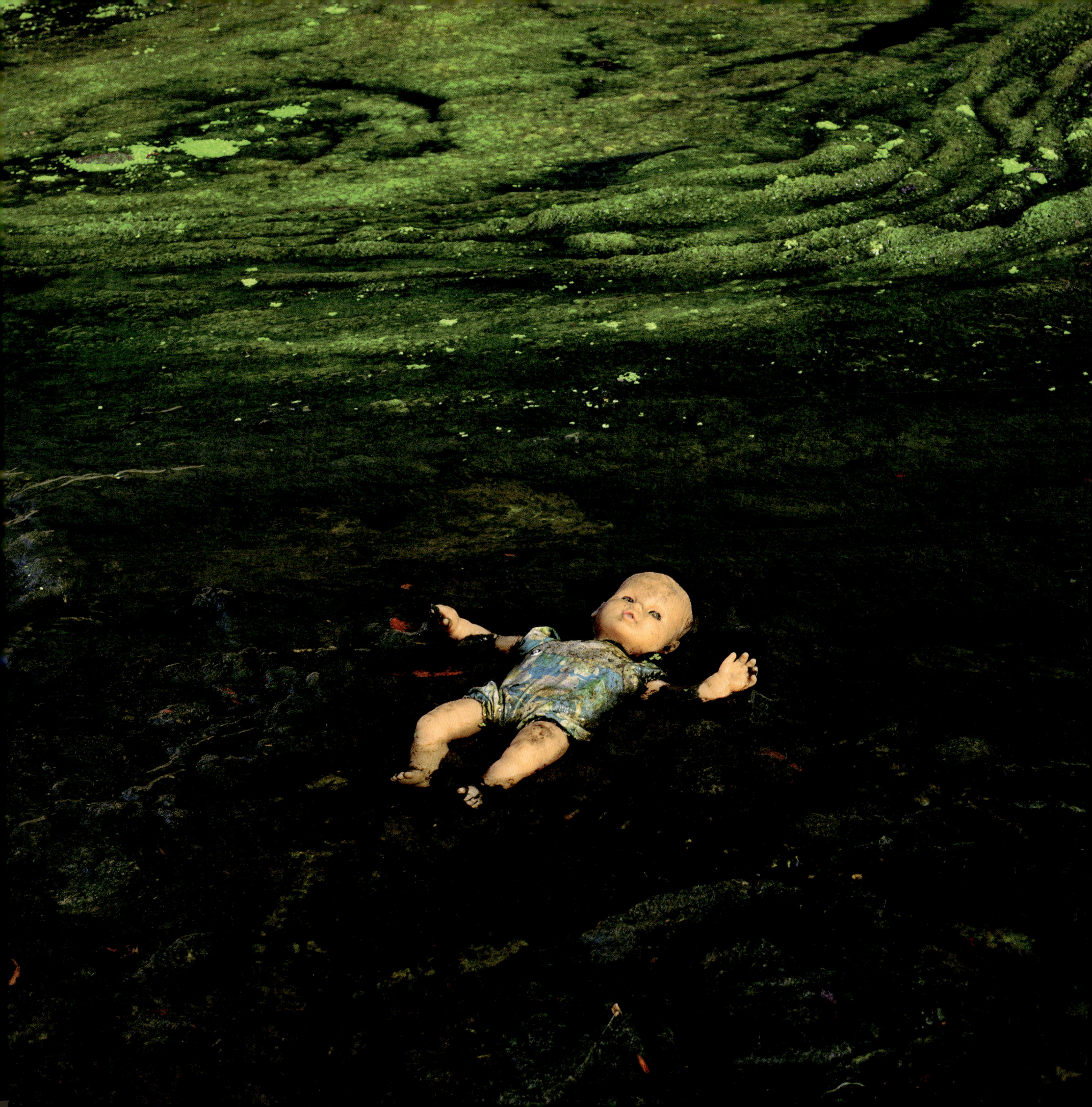

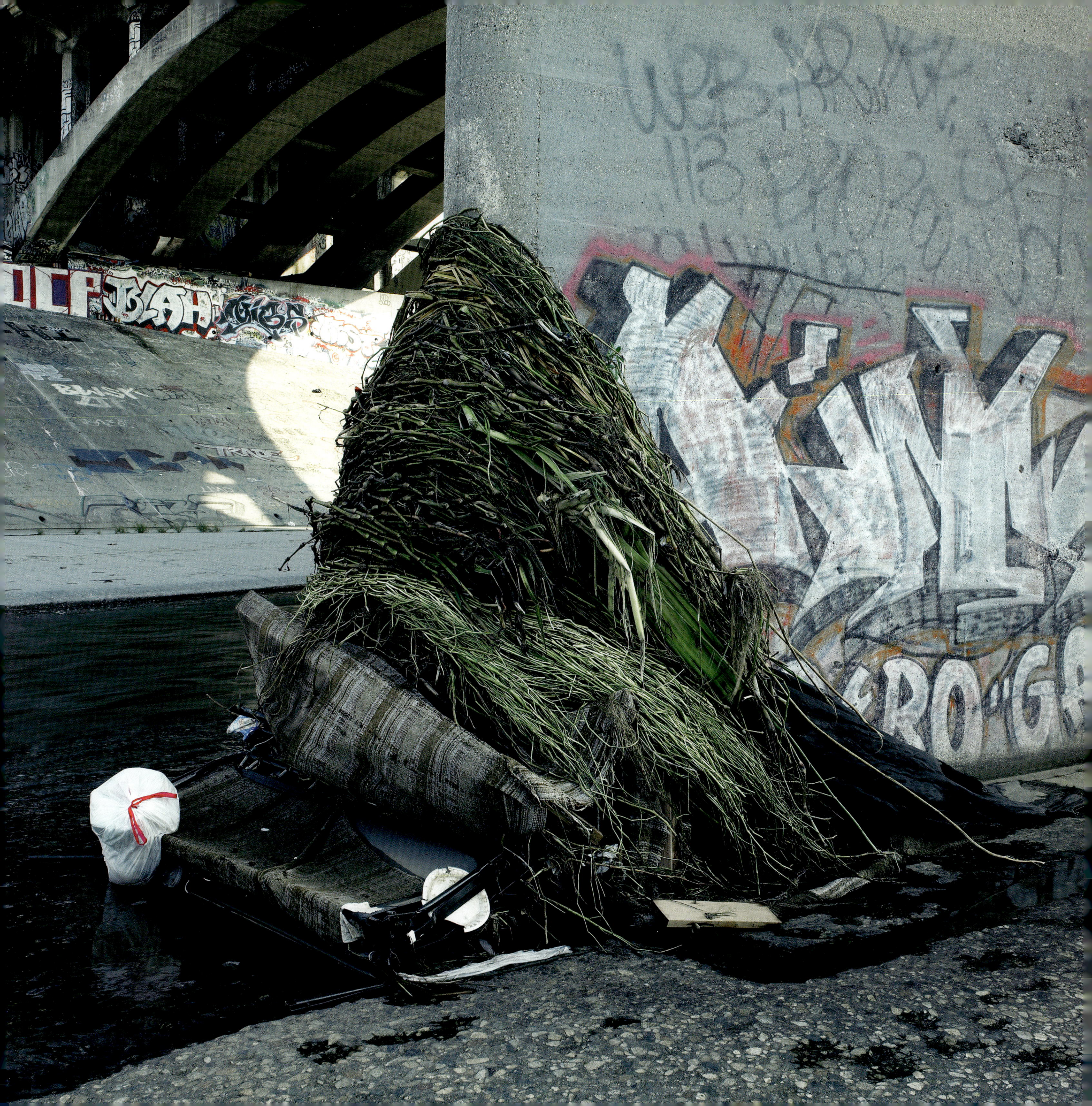

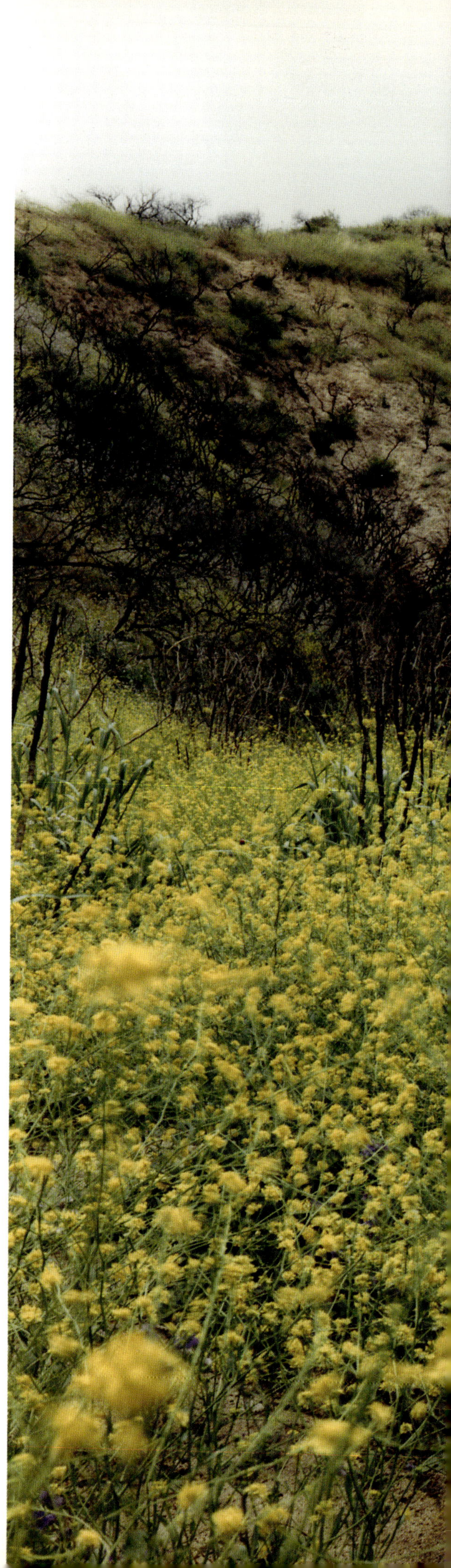

Kaucyila Brooke
Untitled (Griffith Park), 1998

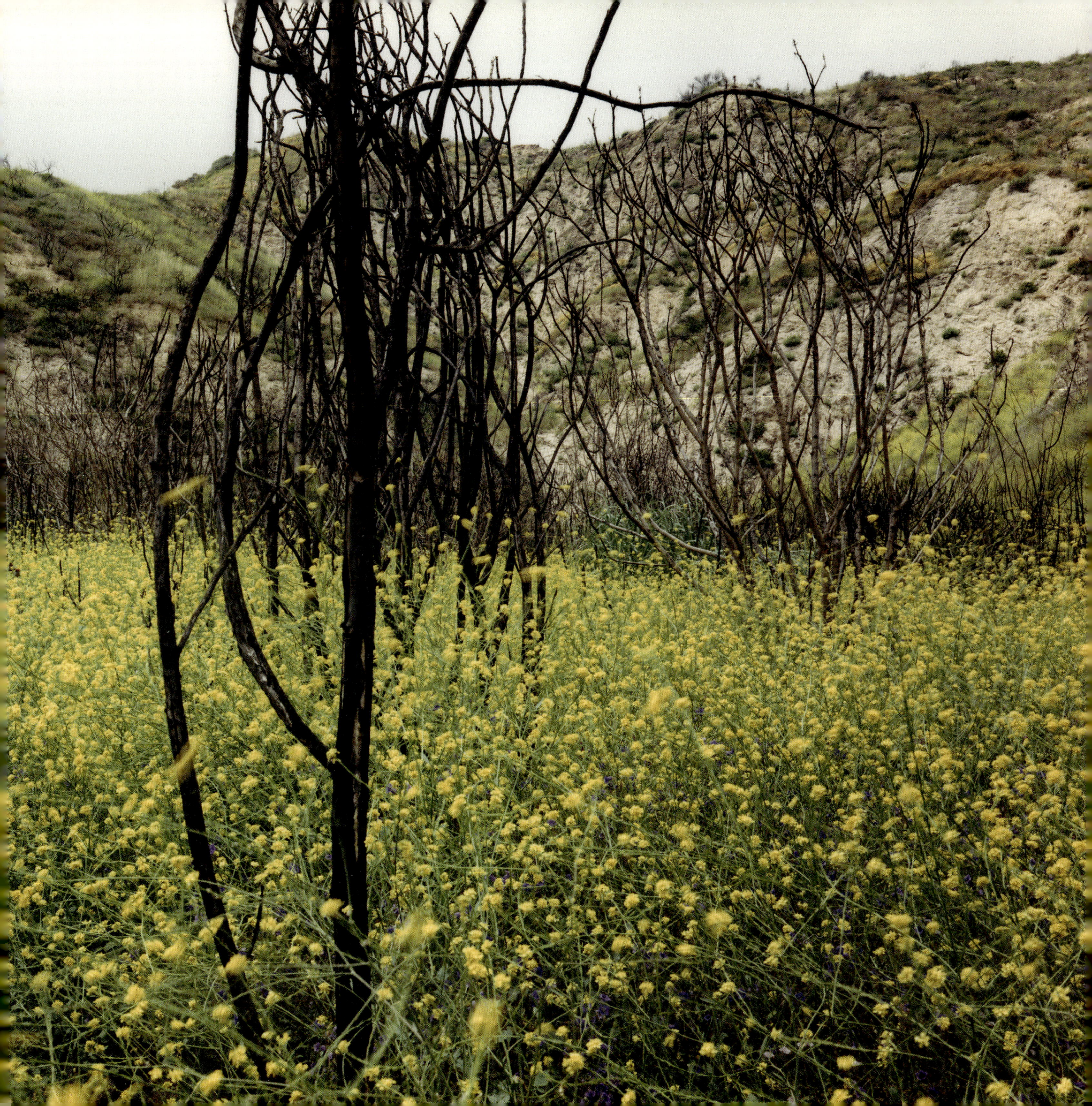

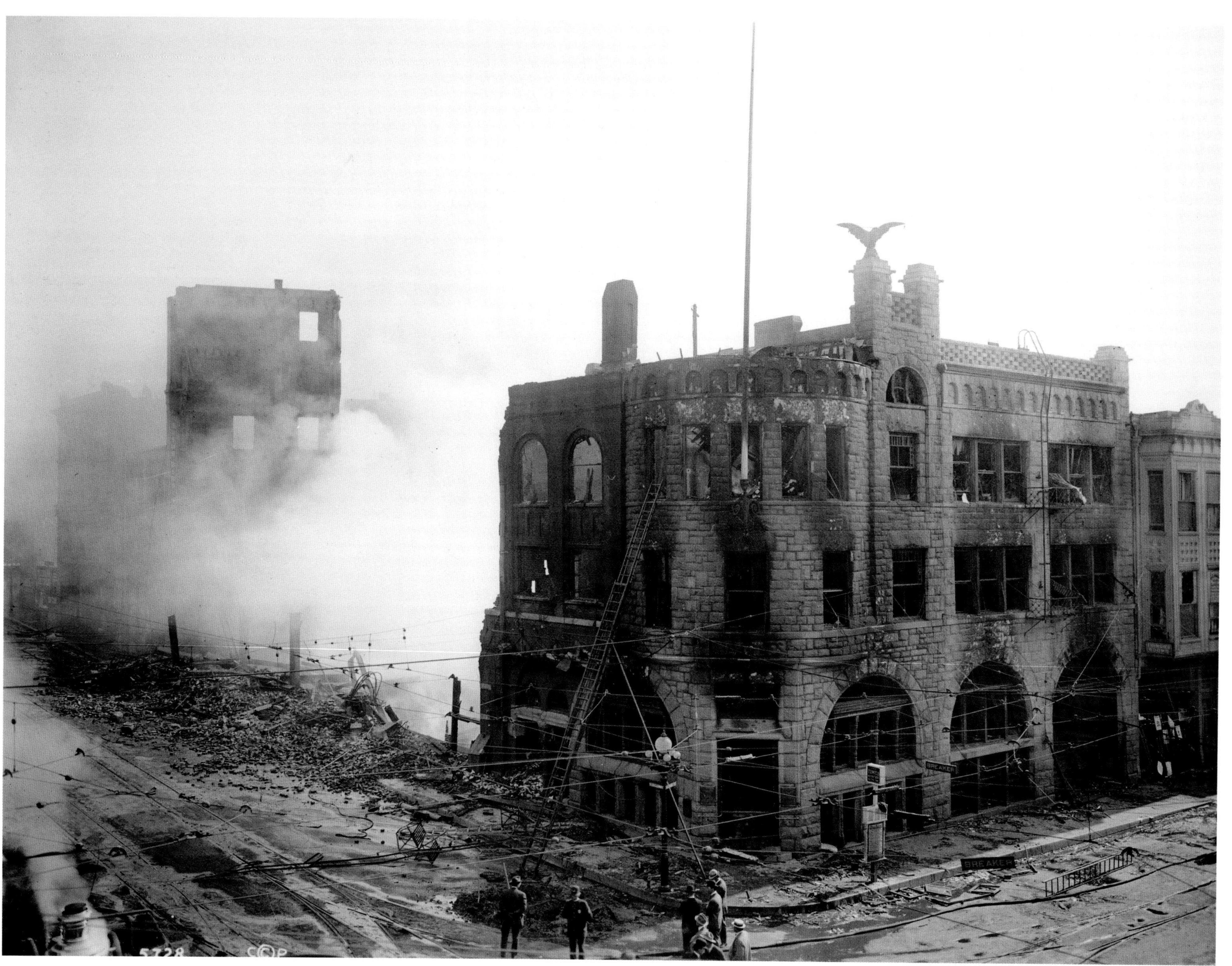

C.C. Pierce
Los Angeles Times Disaster,
October 1, 1910

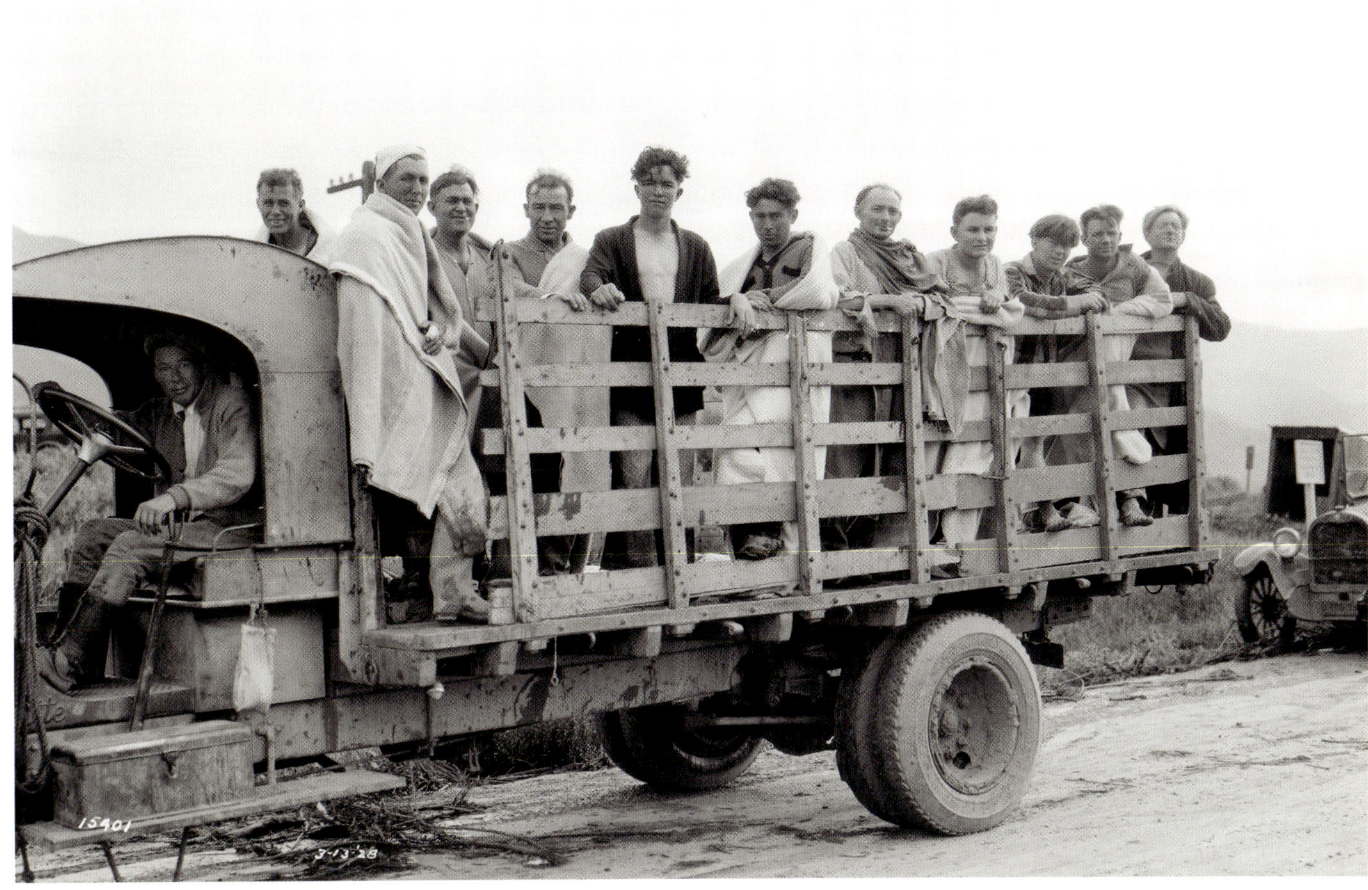

G. Haven Bishop
*Edison refugees from Kemp
Camp on back of truck at
seven o'clock the day after
the St. Francis Dam Disaster*,
March 13, 1928

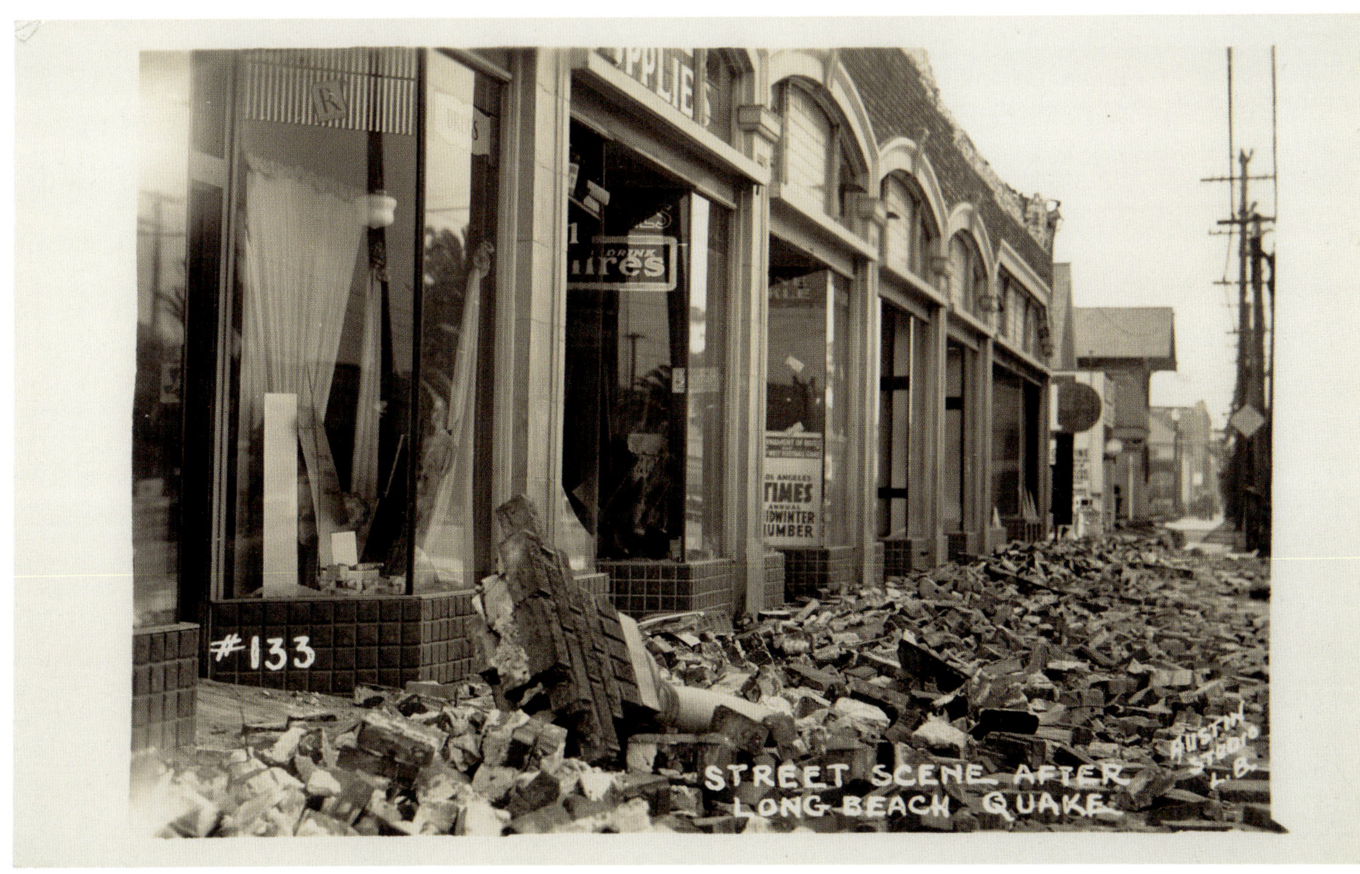

Austin Studio
*Street Scene After Long
Beach Quake*, 1933

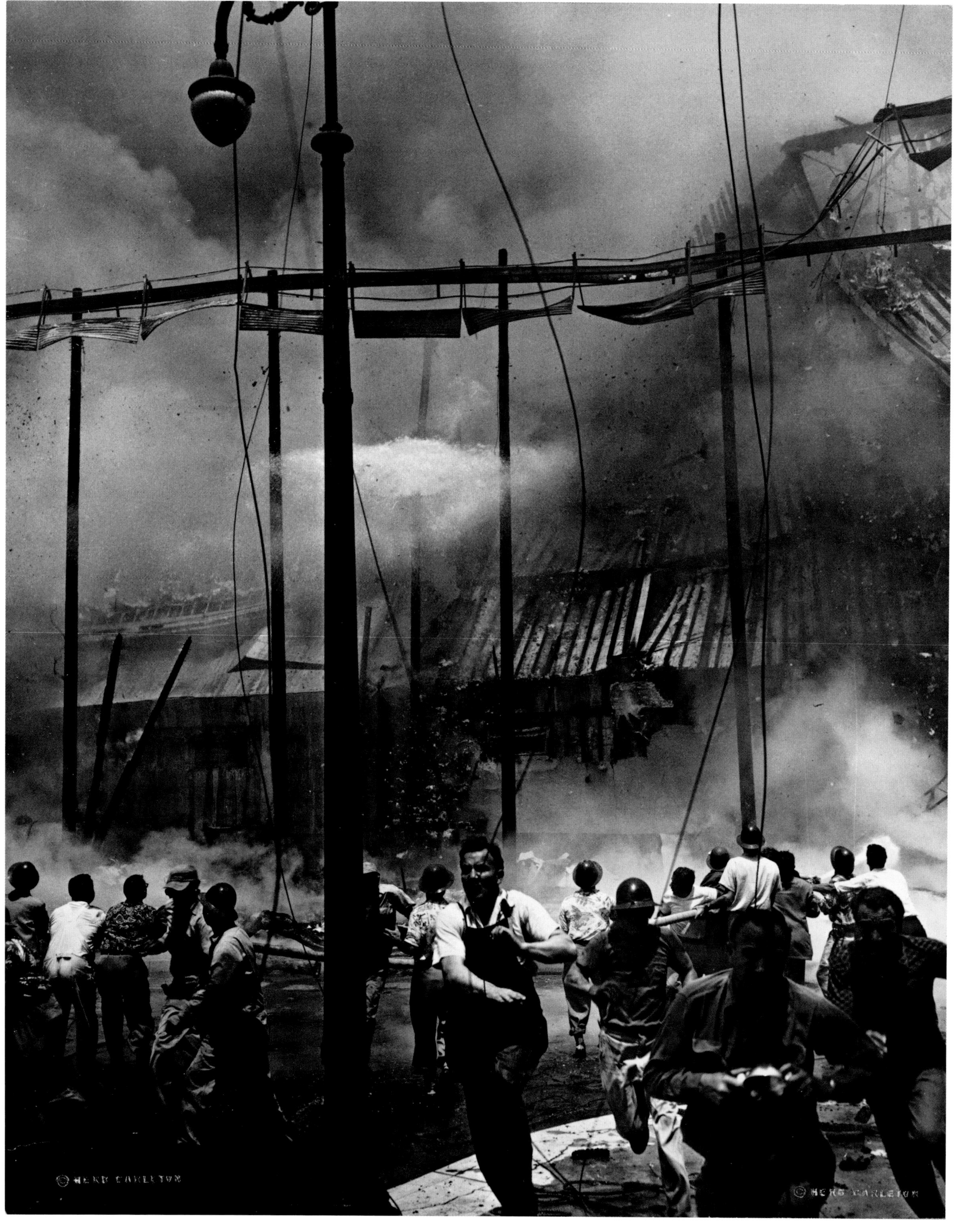

Herb Carleton
Studio Fire, Warner Brothers,
May 16, 1952

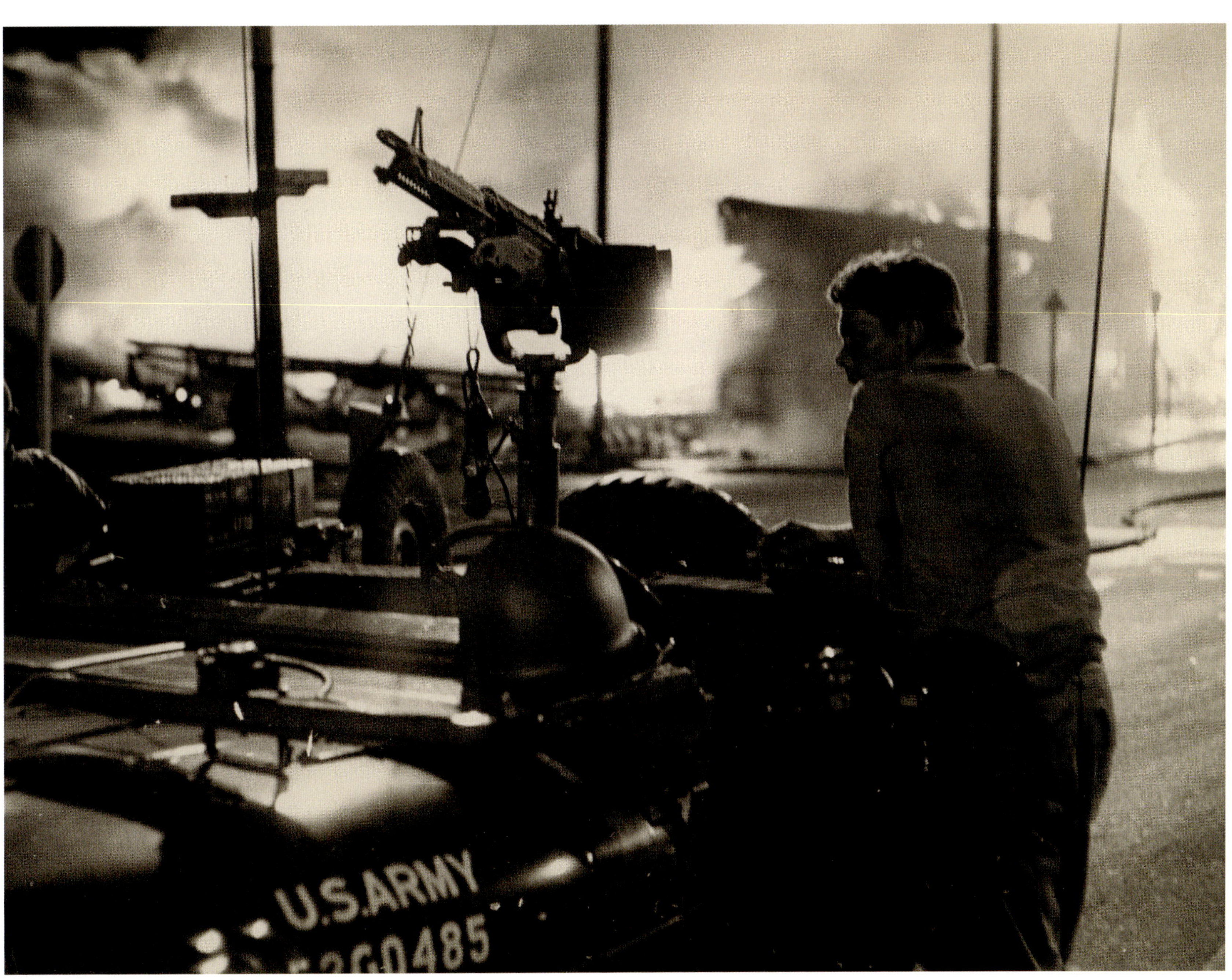

Robert Flora
Watts Riots—Army Jeep,
1965

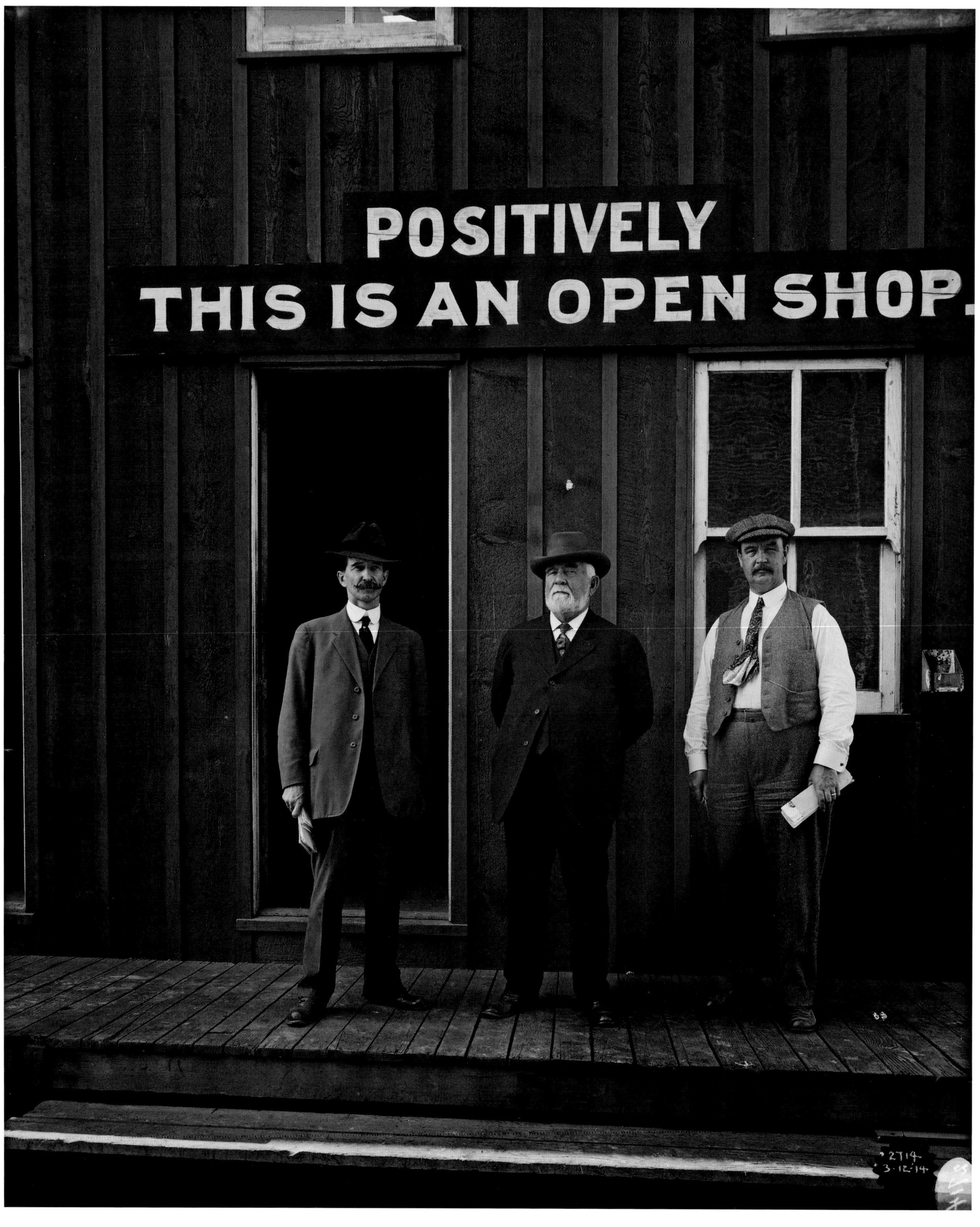

G. Haven Bishop
Craig Shipbuilding Plant with Mr. Craig Jr. and Sr., San Pedro, California, March 12, 1914

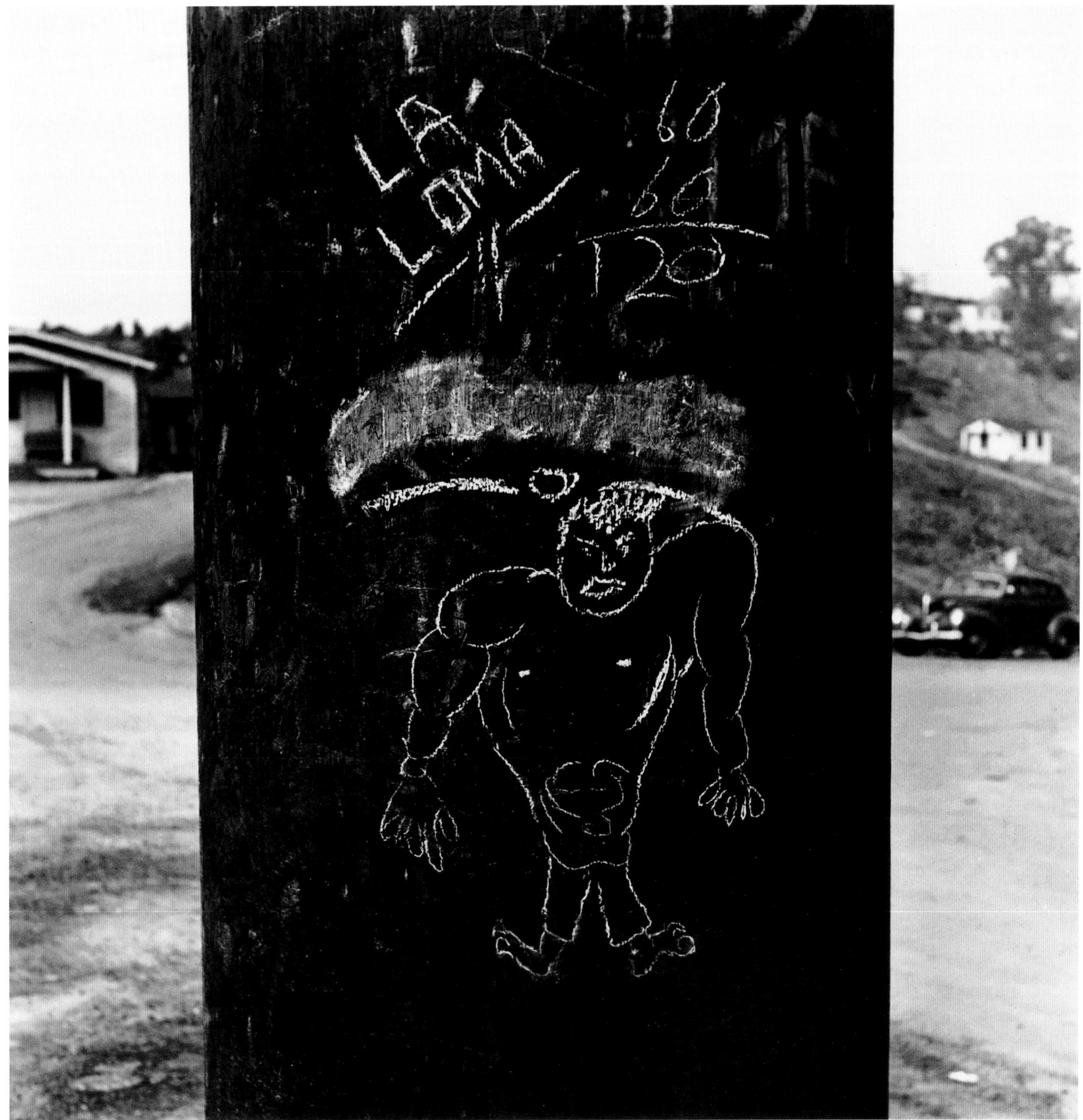

Don Normark
*Chalk Drawing on the
Water Tank—The Main
Meeting Place in La Loma,*
1949

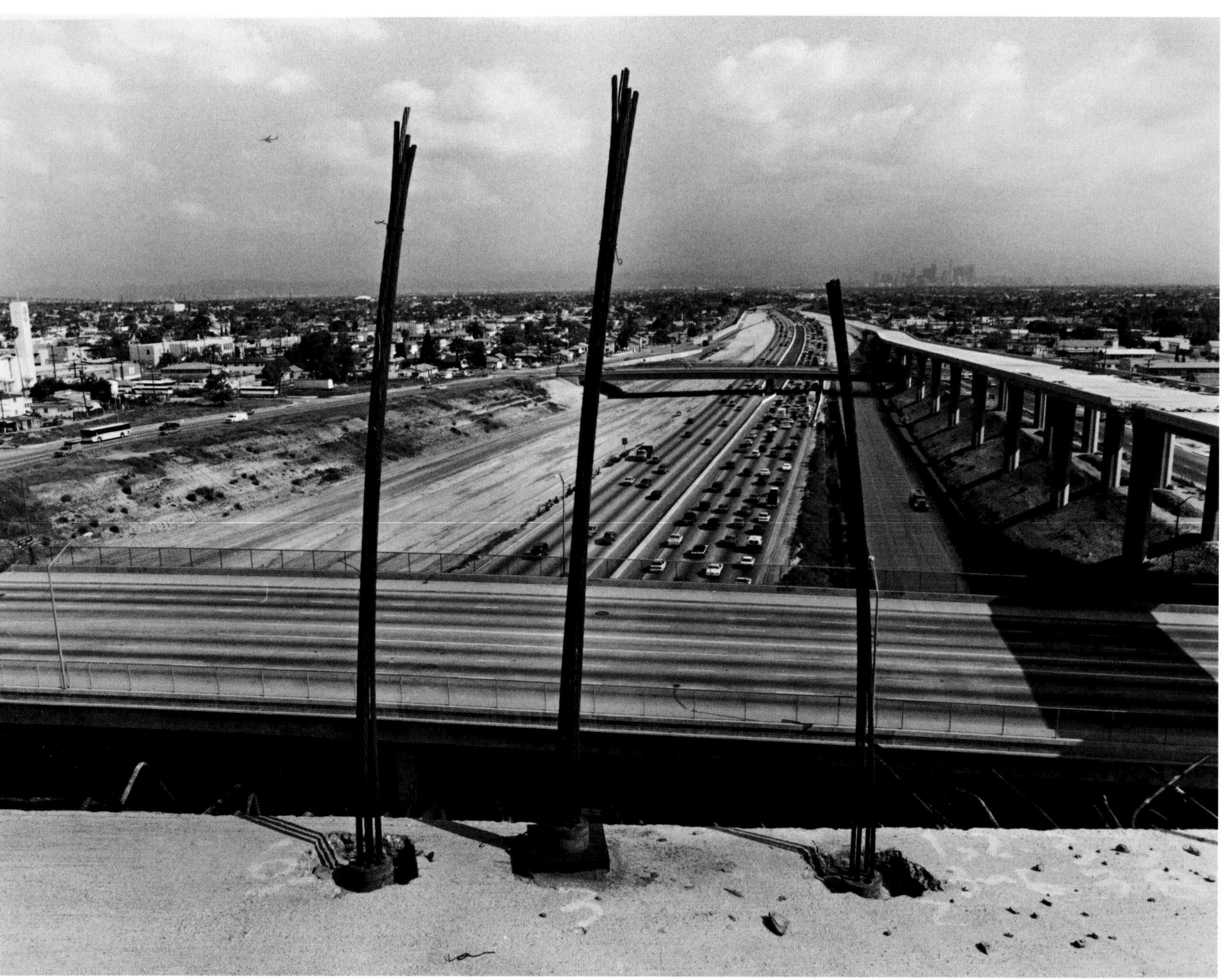

Jeff Gates
*Construction of the 105
Freeway, c. 1990–93*

Opposite
John Divola
*Los Angeles International
Airport Noise Abatement
Zone Exterior View B,*
1975

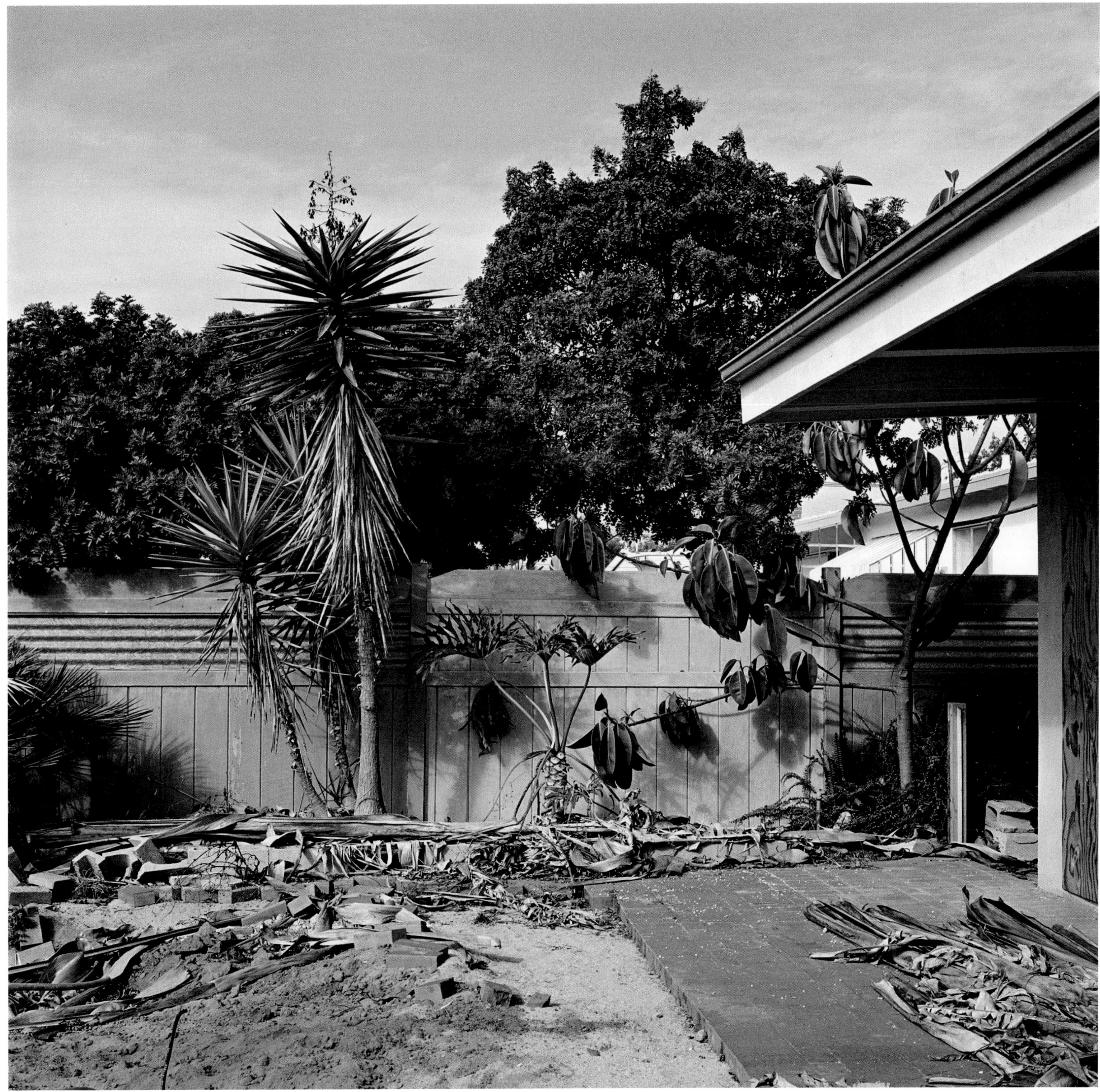

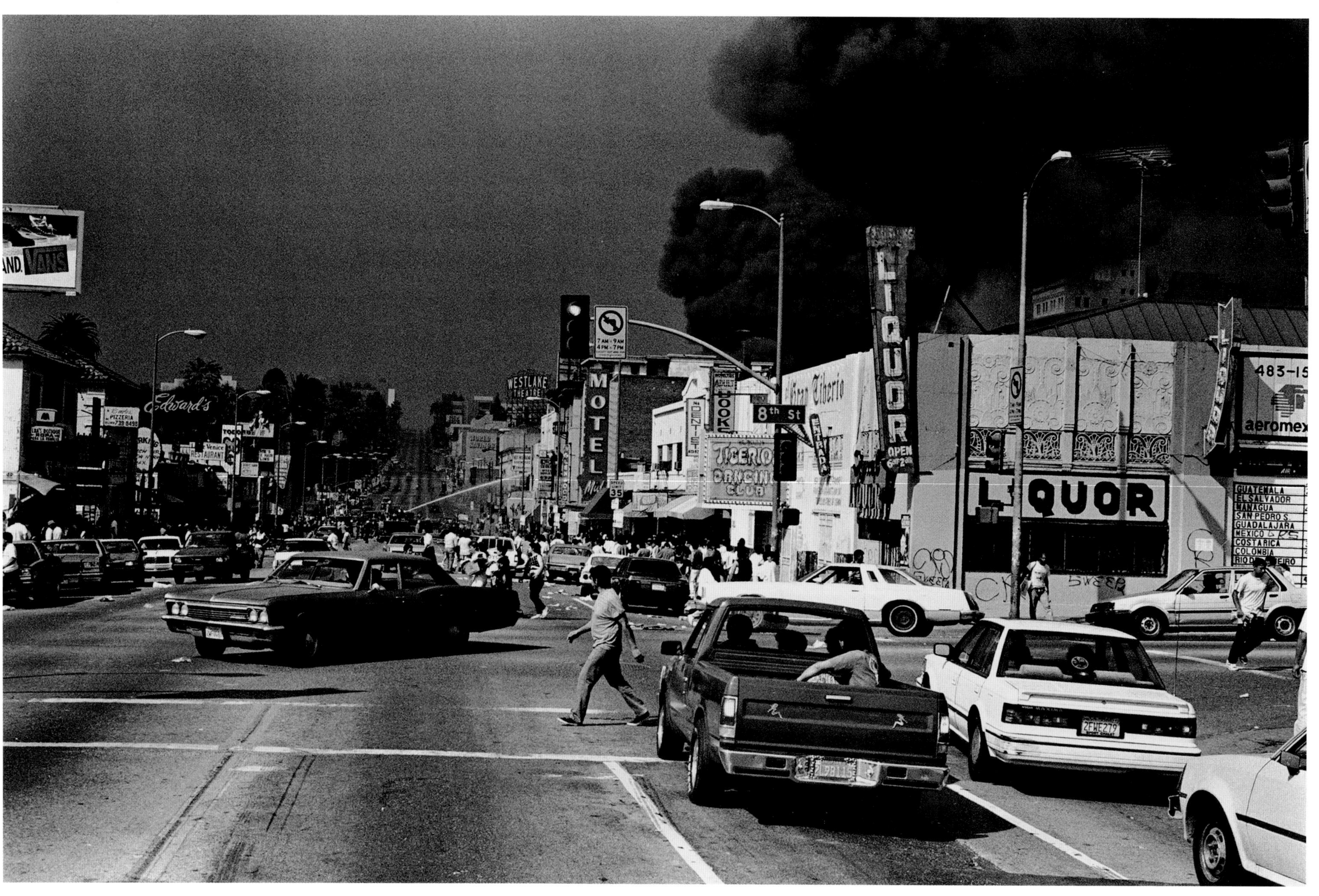

Gary Leonard
April 30, 1992, Los Angeles, California, 1992

Opposite
Willie Middlebrook
In His "Own" Image, 1992

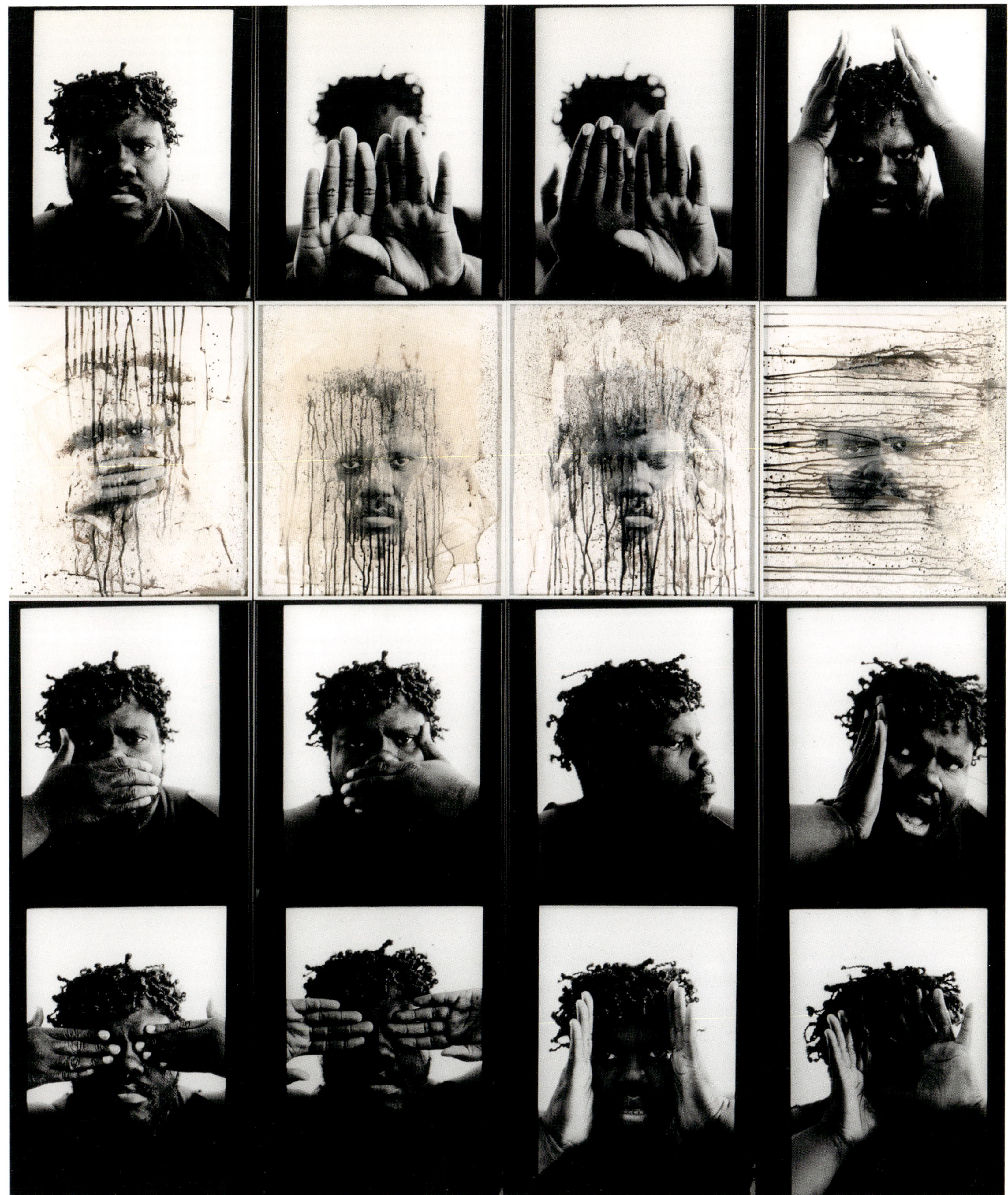

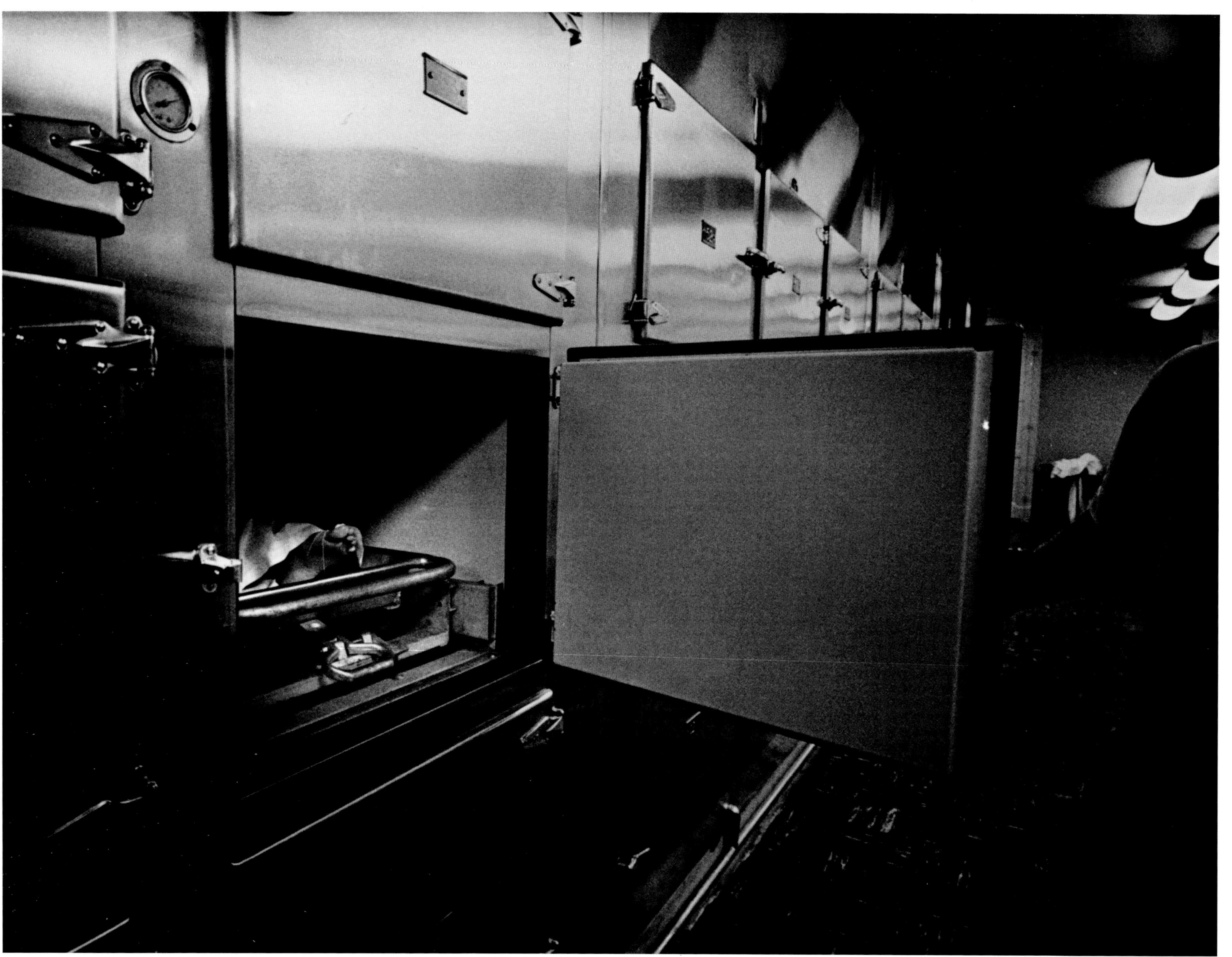

Leigh Wiener
Monroe: Los Angeles County Morgue, August 1962

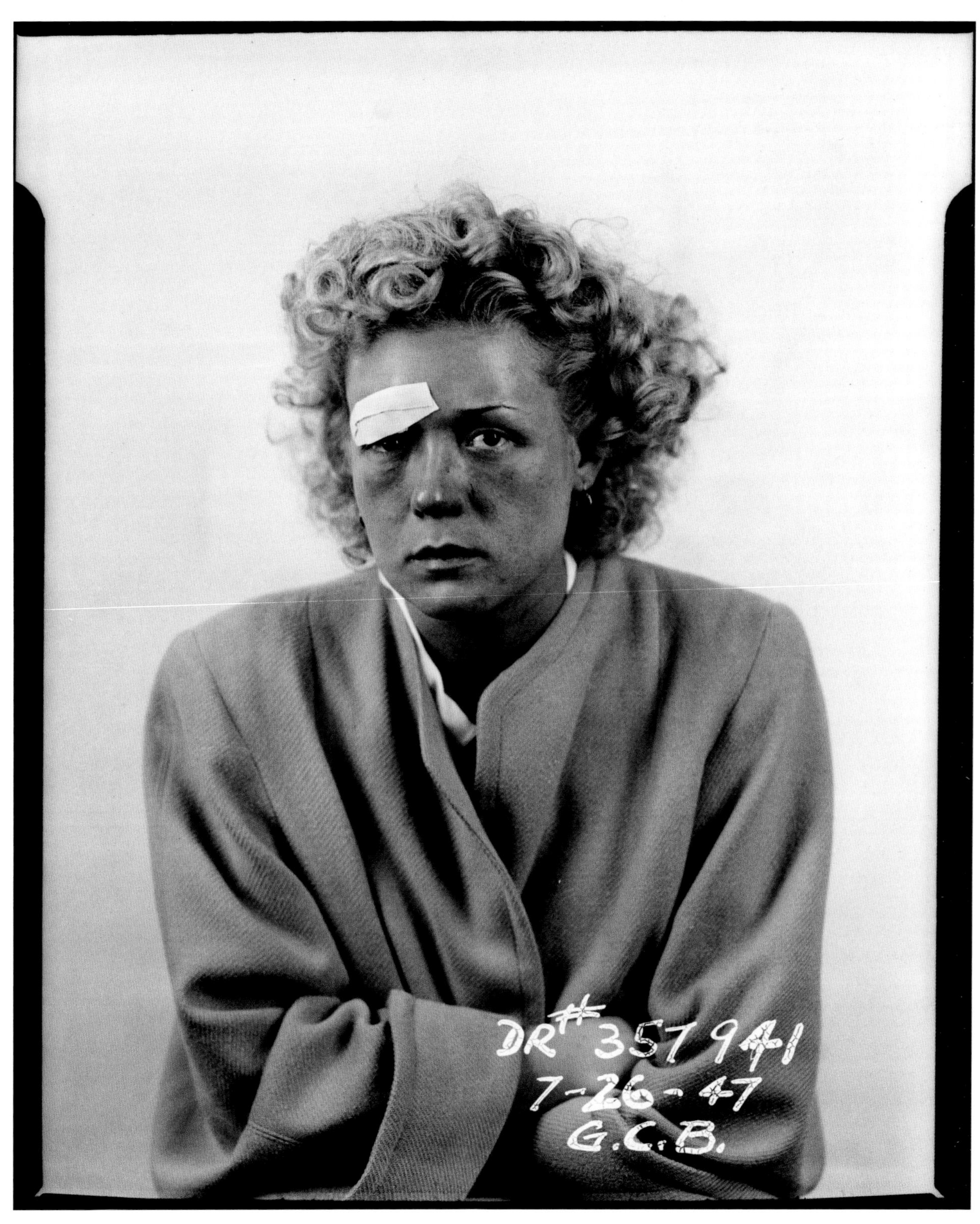

G.C. Babbit
*DR #357941, Domestic
Violence Victim,*
July 26, 1947

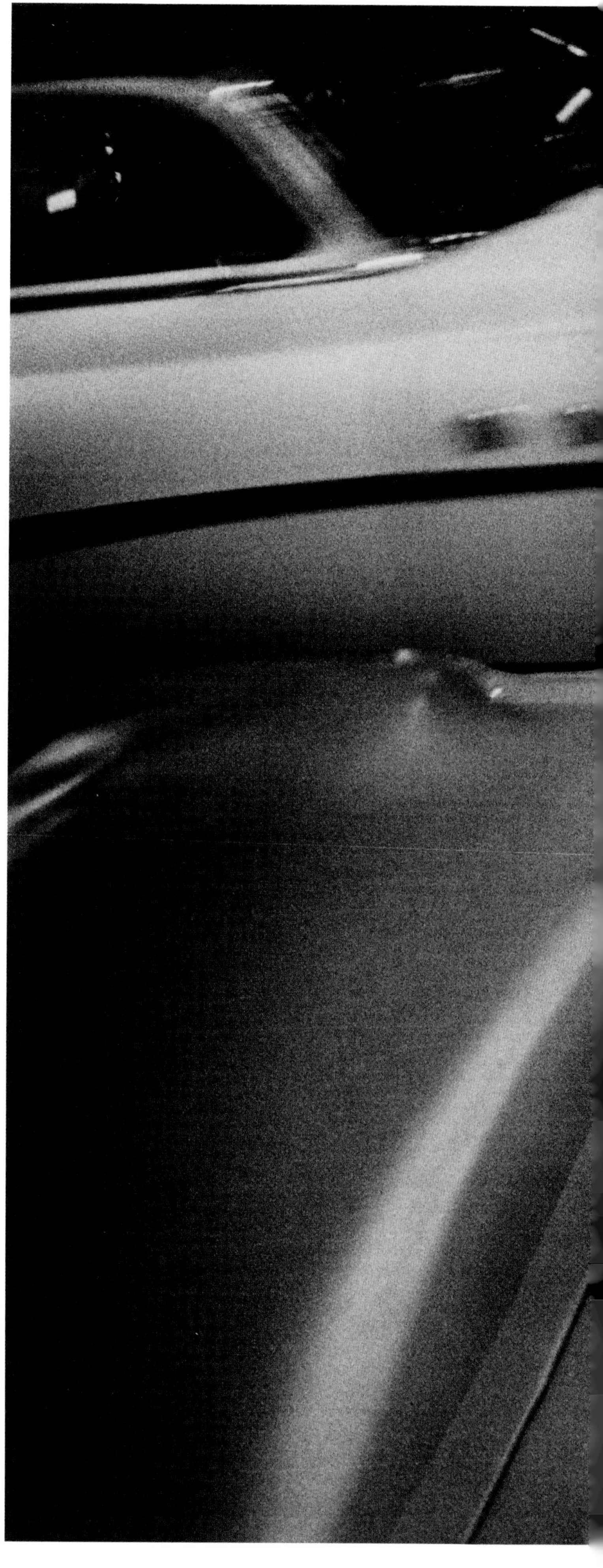

Garry Winogrand
Los Angeles, 1964

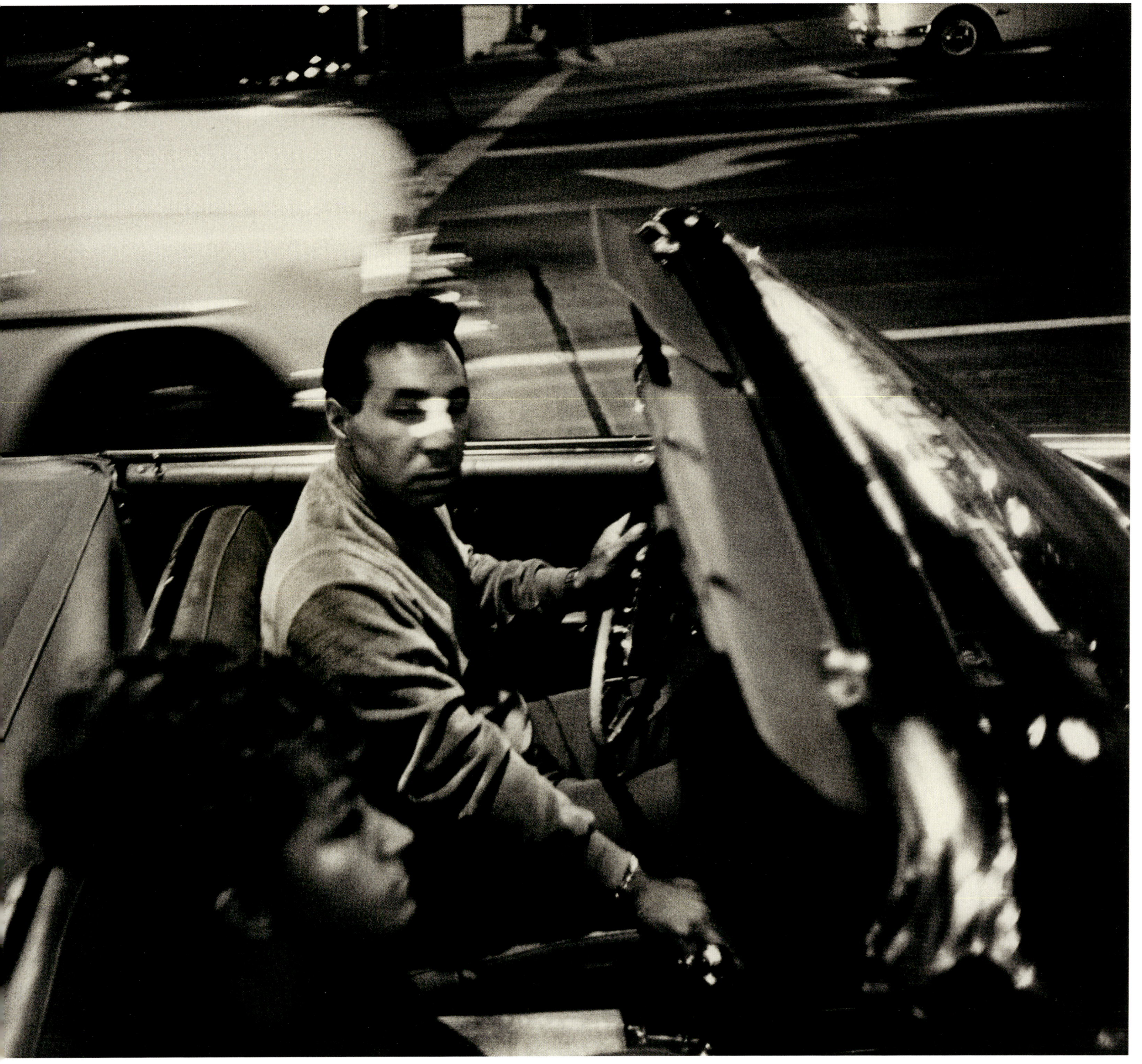

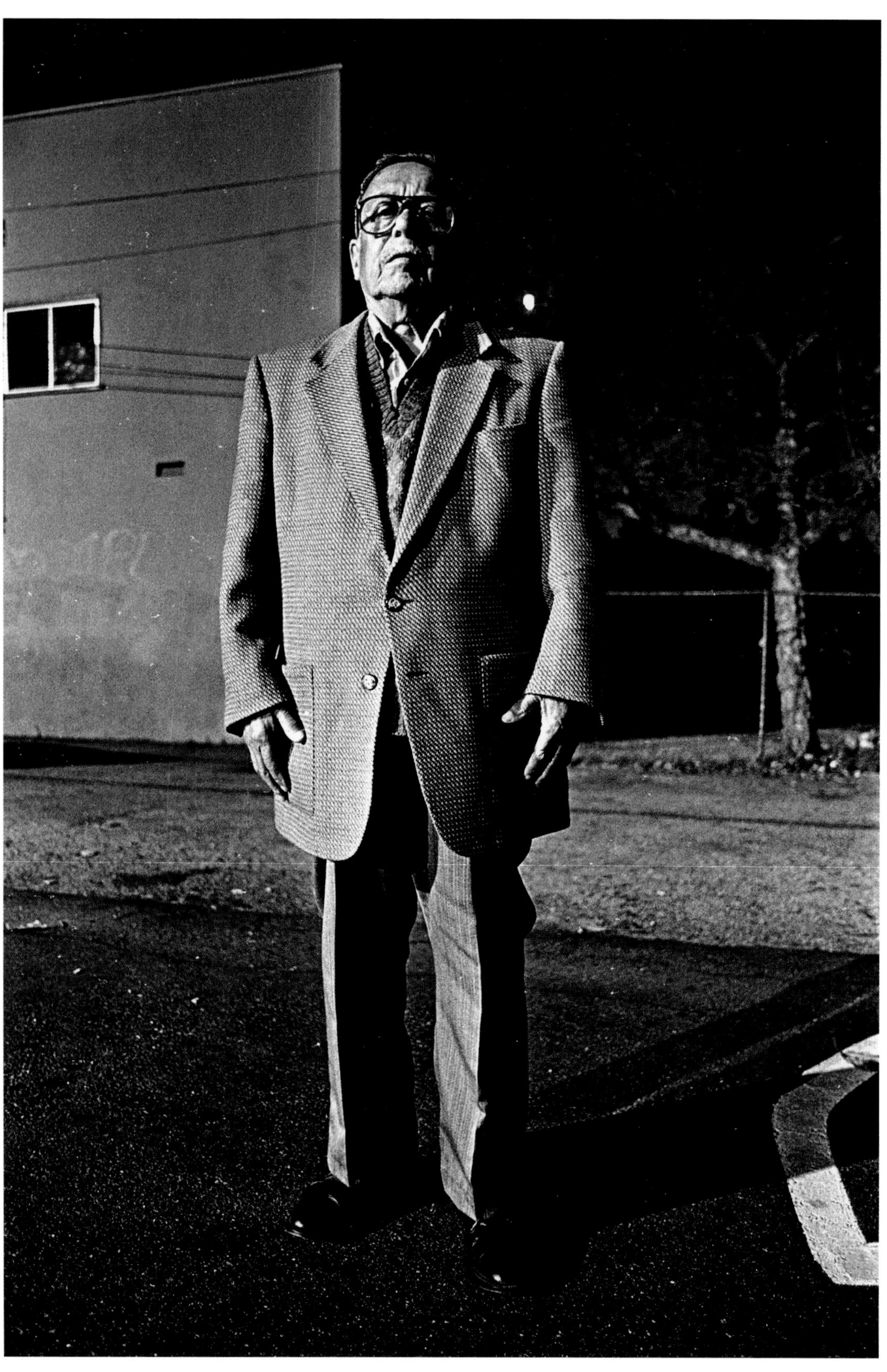

Harry Gamboa, Jr.
Harry T. Gamboa, Printer
(Retired), 1997

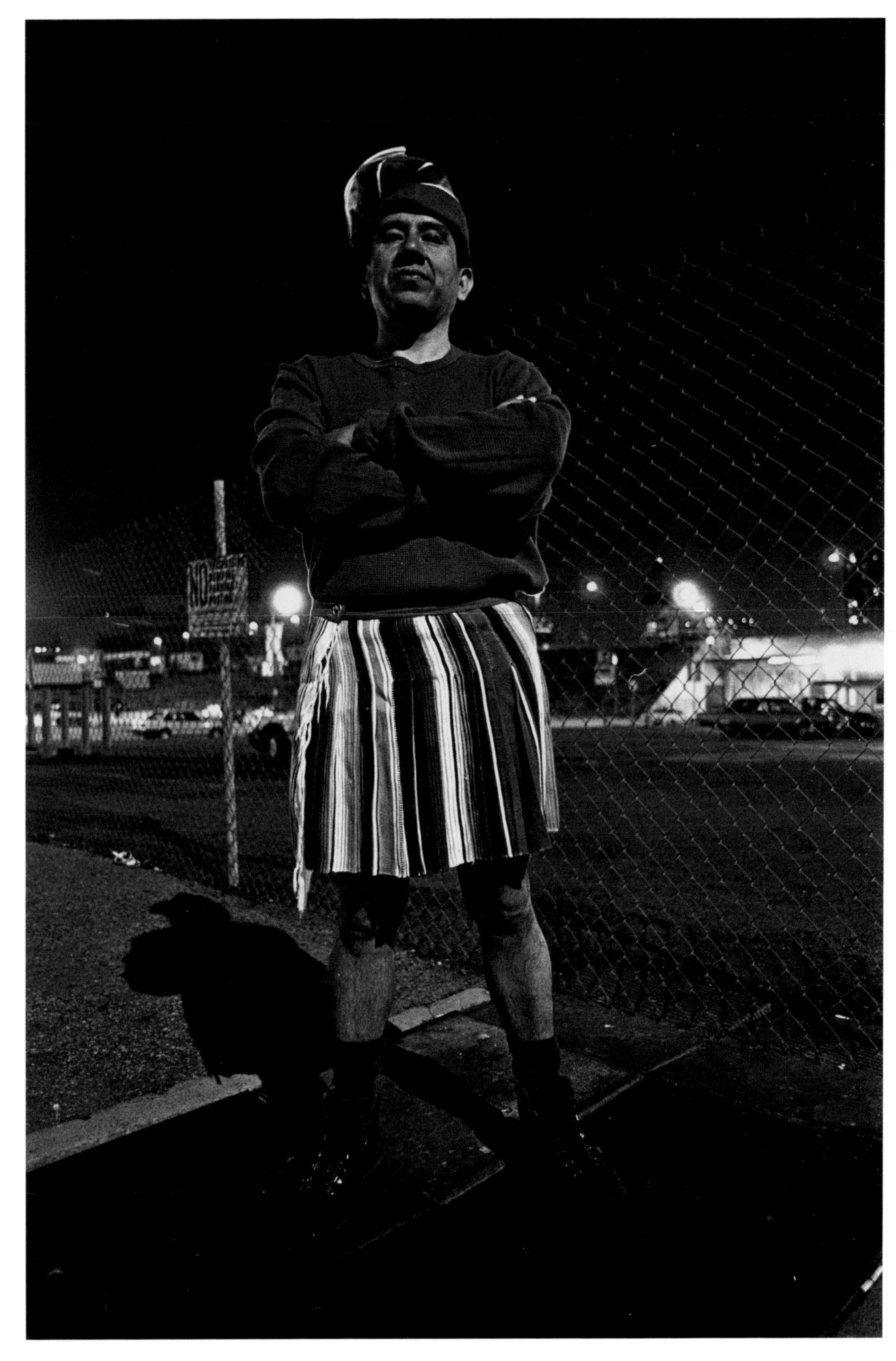

Harry Gamboa, Jr.
Roberto Bedoya, Poet, 1994

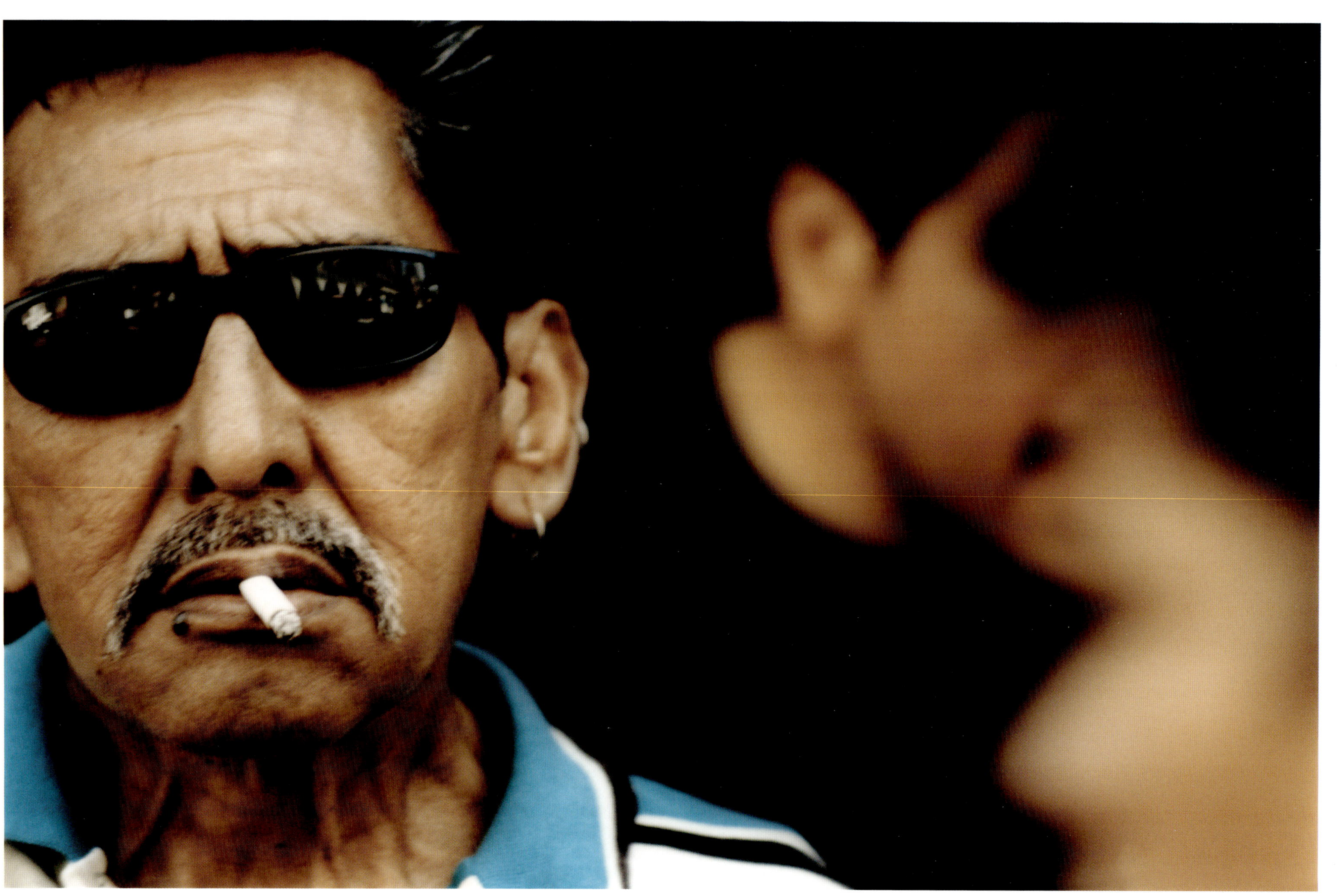

Gusmano Cesaretti
Beto, at Whittier and Lorena,
2001

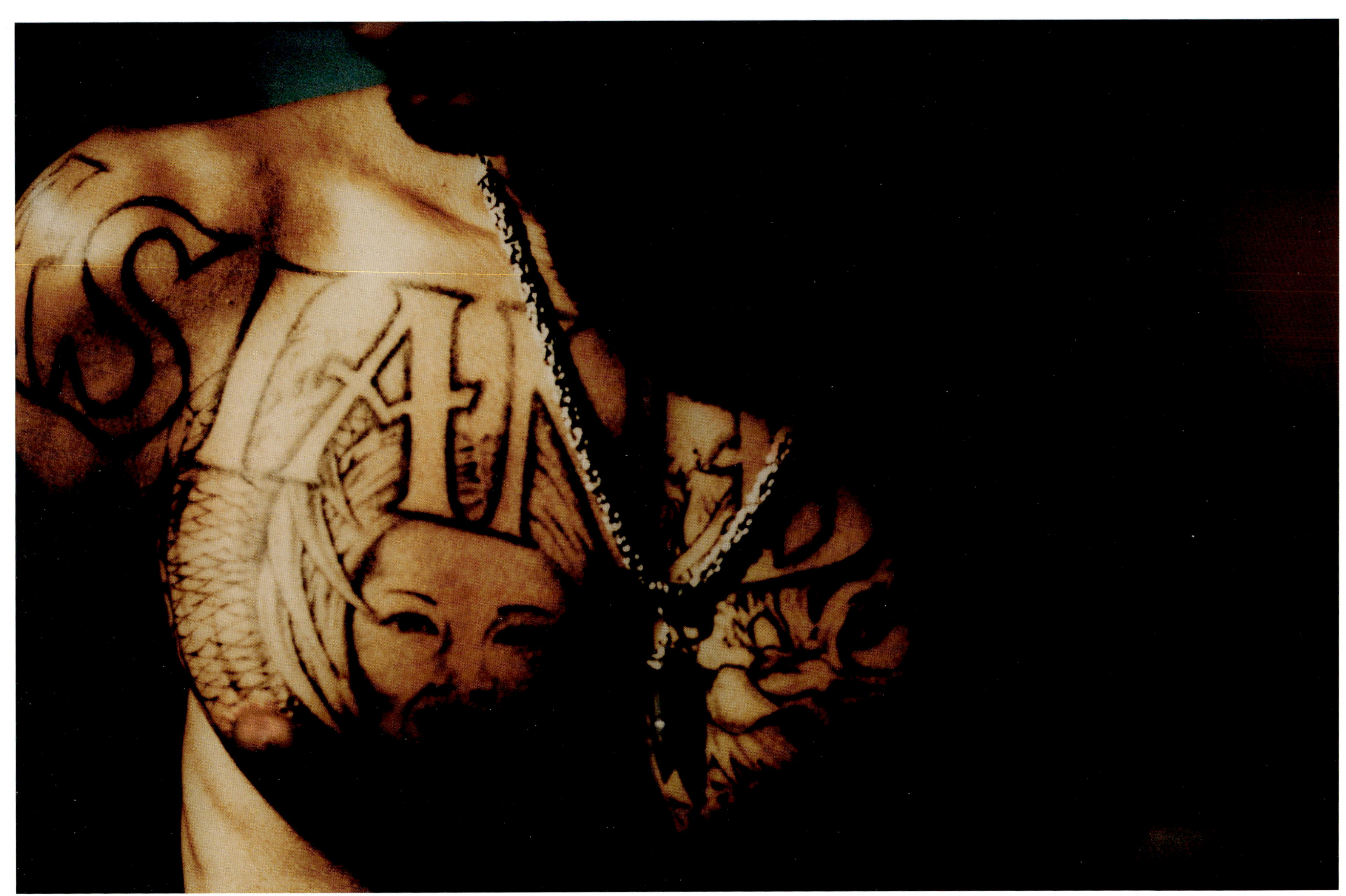

Gusmano Cesaretti
Bullet, 2004

DREAM

Wracked by floods, droughts, and earthquakes . . . it doesn't matter: nothing is as outrageous as a dream, and a city founded on dreams and scorning prudence is likely to endure forever.
Brendan Gill, architecture critic

That light: the late-afternoon light of Los Angeles—golden pink off the bay through the smog and onto the palm fronds.
Lawrence Weschler, writer

Los Angeles has always been a city of dreams and desires, envisioned, attained, or gone tragically haywire. It is a place where human hope flourishes, eternally and creatively linked to fulfilling one's personal destiny. Visions of the Pictorialist photographers of the 1910s and 1920s depict Southern California suffused with a hazy mist, softening reality's edges to suggest a dreamy incandescence. Other photographers, such as Max Yavno, William Claxton, and Michael Light, convey Los Angeles's penchant for dreams through subject matter, depicting the city at night, with mellow lights and neon signs glinting faintly in the distance. Anthony Friedkin's *Surfboard with Setting Sun, Santa Monica, California* from 1980 evokes the singular, ethereal beauty of outdoor life in the Southland, writ large on the infinite screen of the Pacific Ocean at sunset. Robert Weingarten's rose-colored sunrise and Hiroshi Sugimoto's blank movie screen emanate waves of preternatural light, as if creating planes upon which countless dreams might be projected.

"Few images telegraph the paradox of the American dream better than a drunk passed out in the shadow of Hollywood," observed one acerbic writer, insisting upon the intimacy of success and failure in Los Angeles. To be sure, Los Angeles is a dream factory of unprecedented reach and proportion, thanks largely to Hollywood's seductive promises of fame and fortune. But it is also home to ordinary millions whose lives and dreams belie the excessive grandeur of the film industry. As John Humble's photograph of a Venice Beach sunset reiterates, redemption in Los Angeles may result less from celebrity than from reverie.

John Humble
From Lifeguard Station 26 #15,
1999

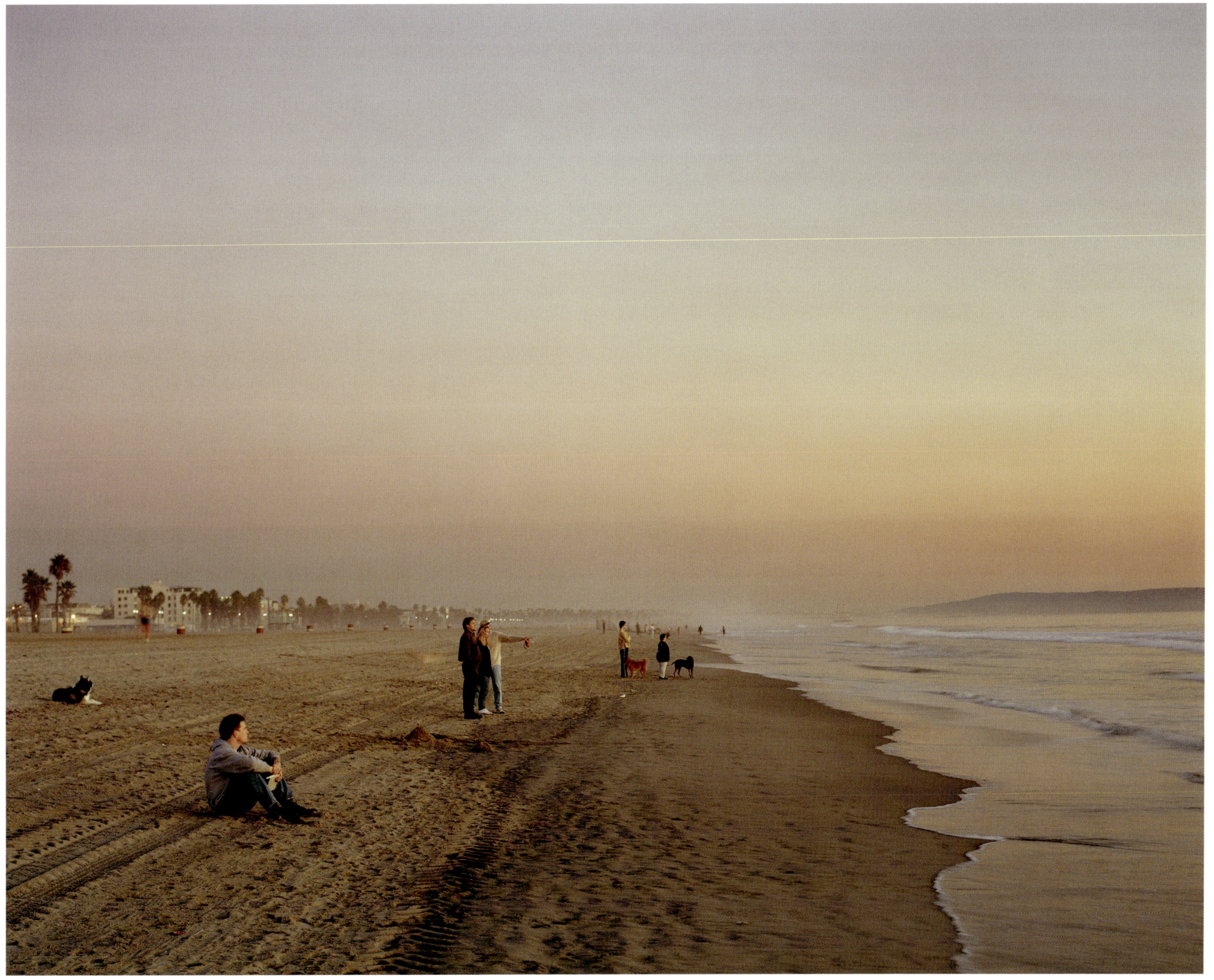

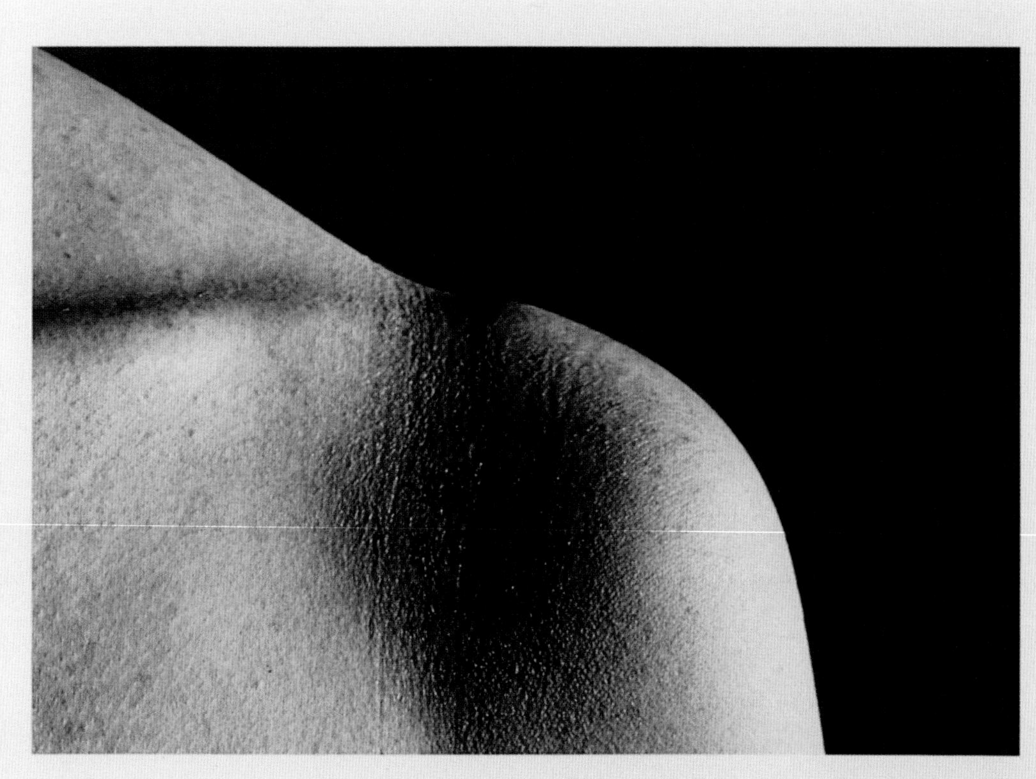

Eileen Cowin
Returning to Ordinary Life,
1997

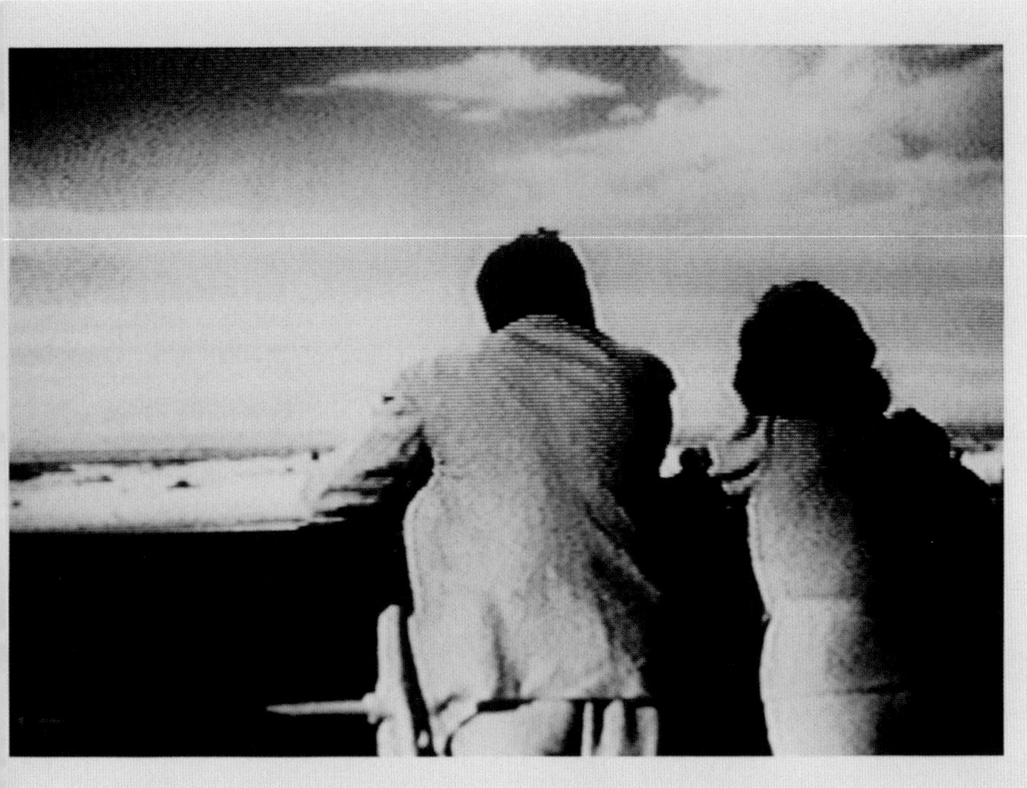 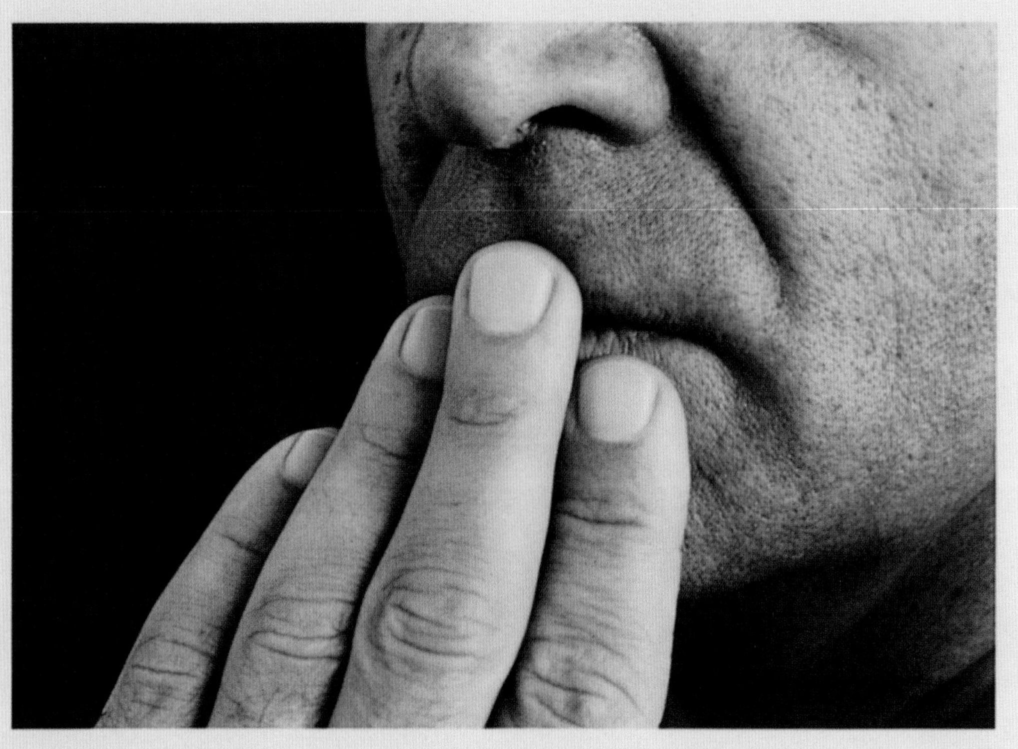

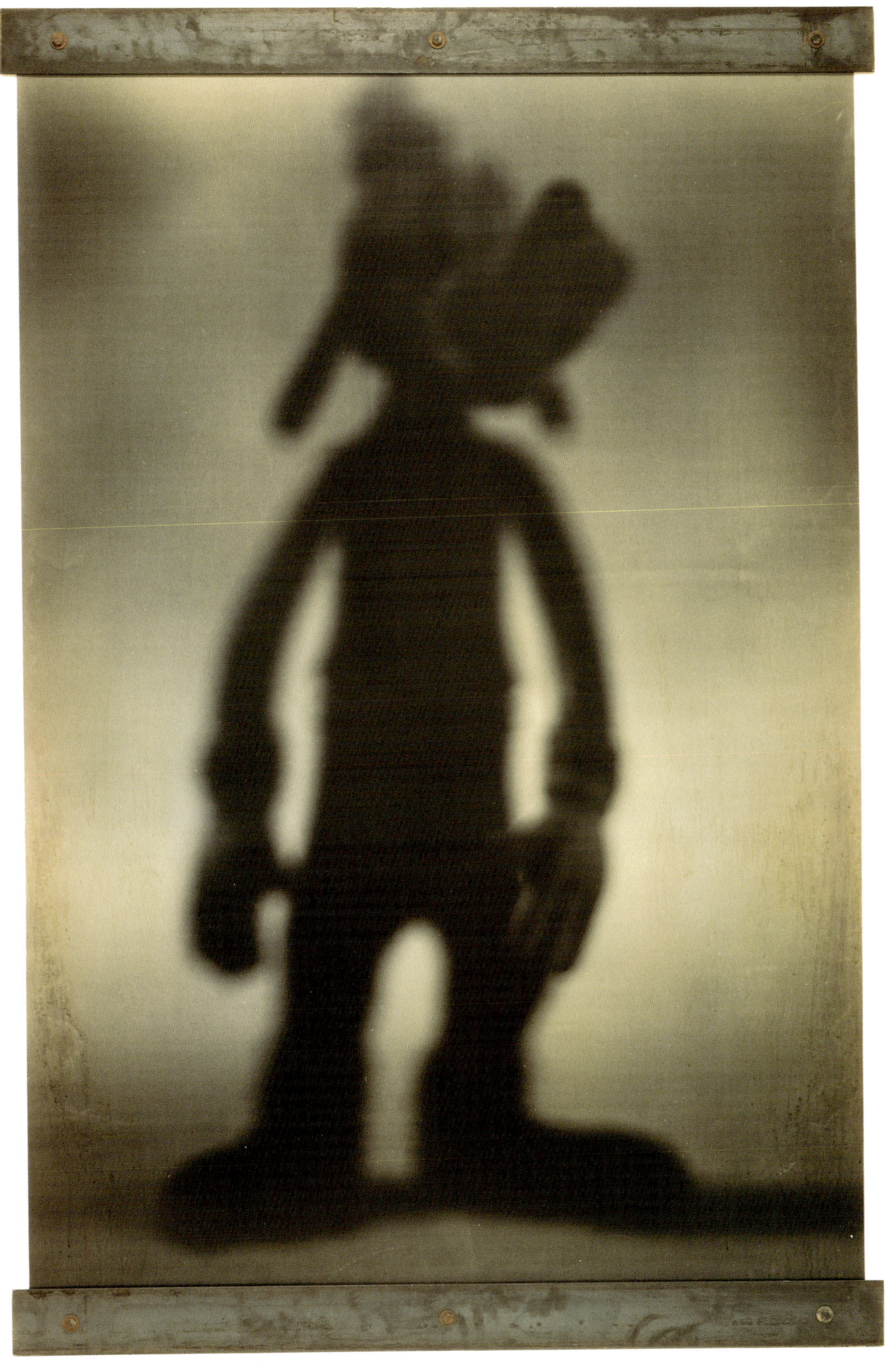

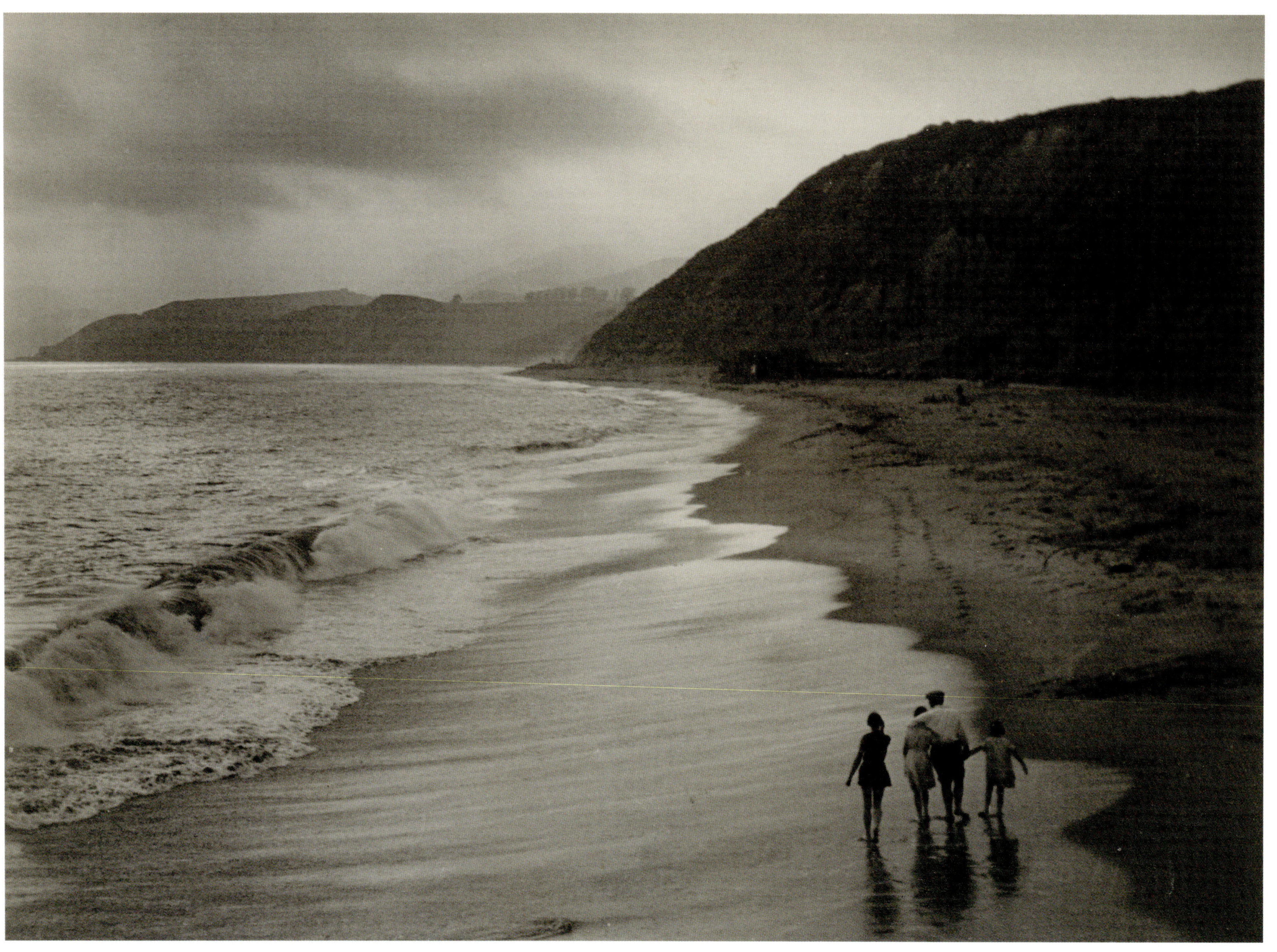

Marjorie Bentley
Strollers, 1929

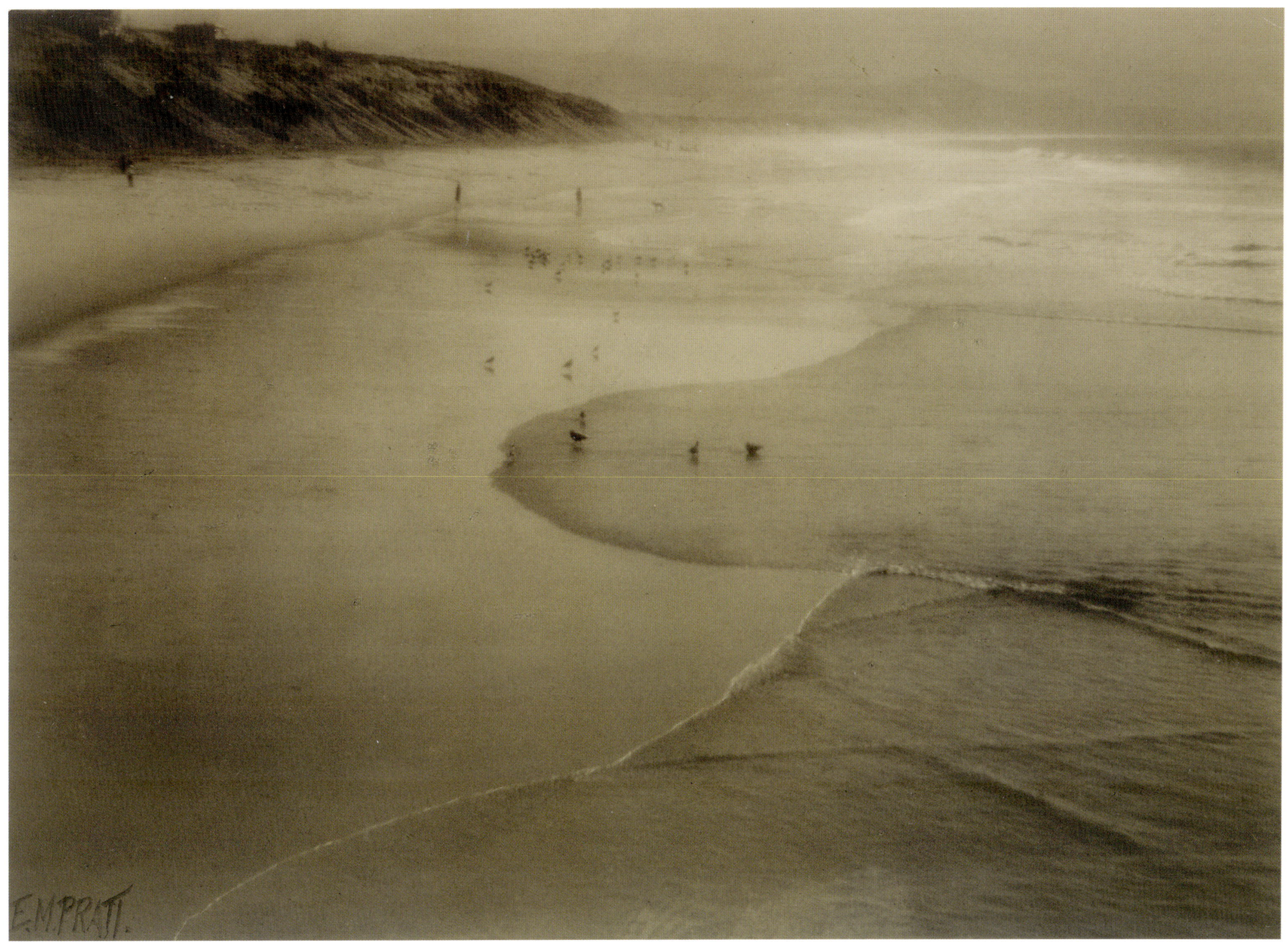

Ernest M. Pratt
Ebb Tide, c. 1925

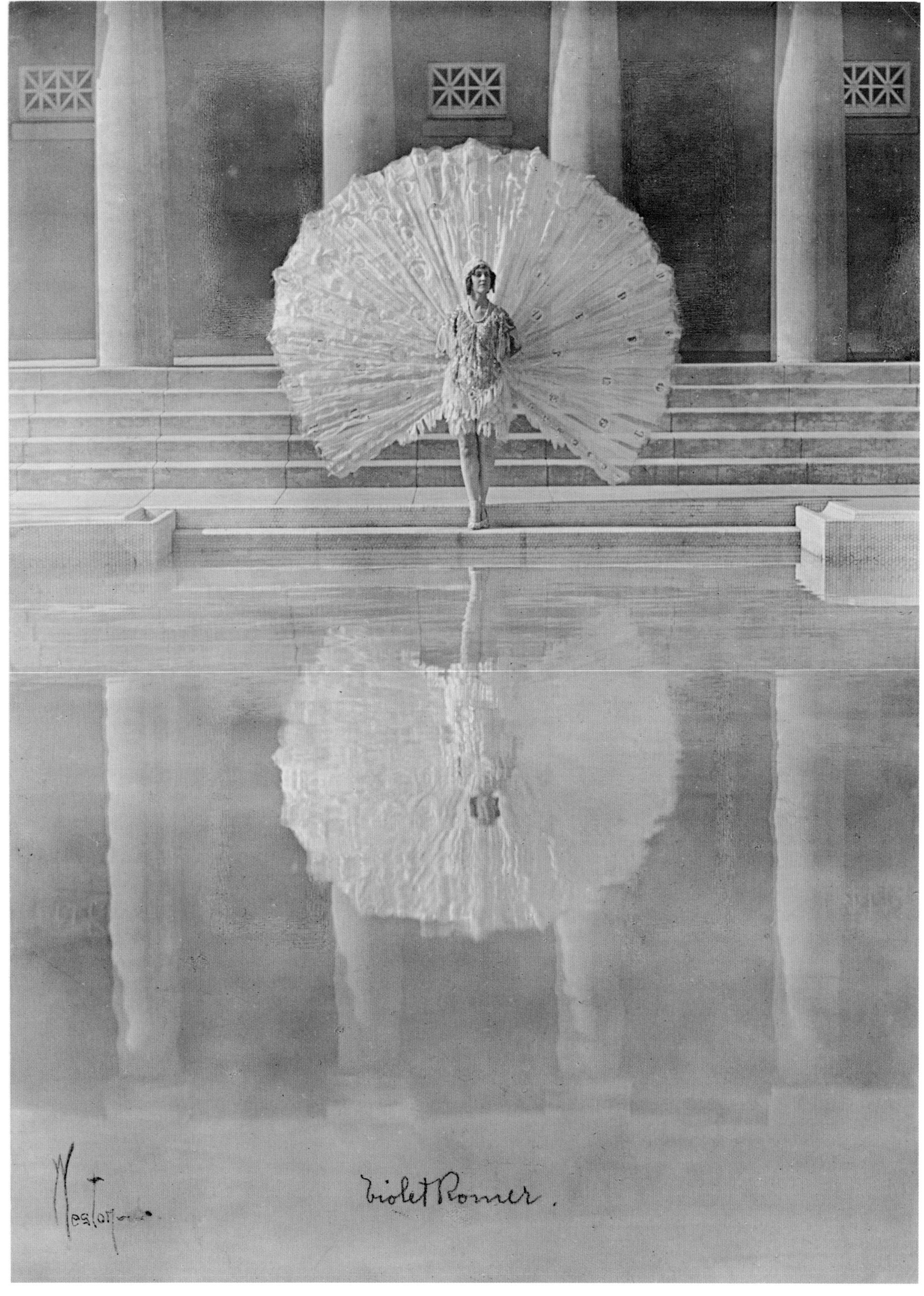

Edward Weston
Violet Romer, c. 1921

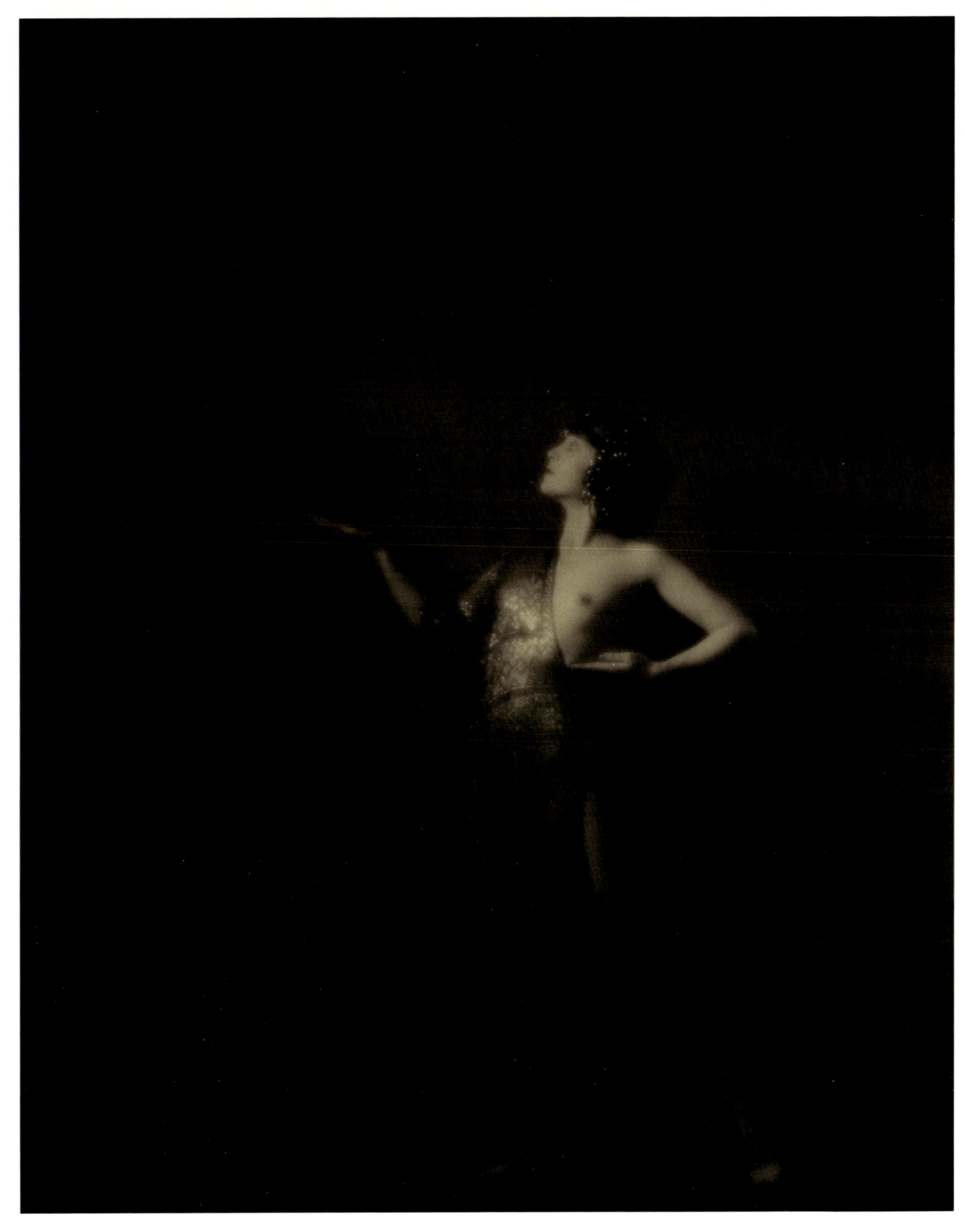

Arthur F. Kales
In the Temple of the Sun,
c. 1918

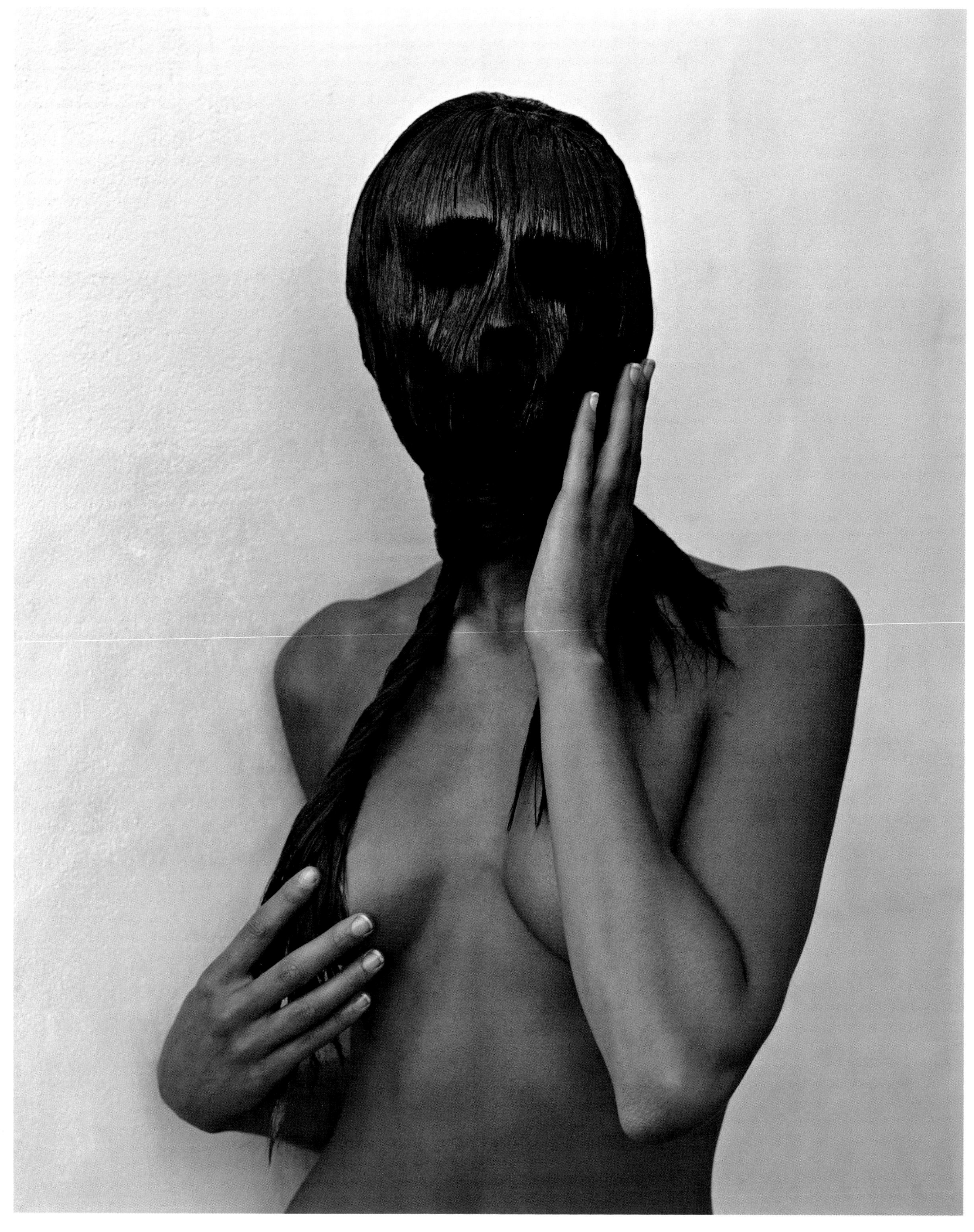

Herb Ritts
Mask, Hollywood, 1989

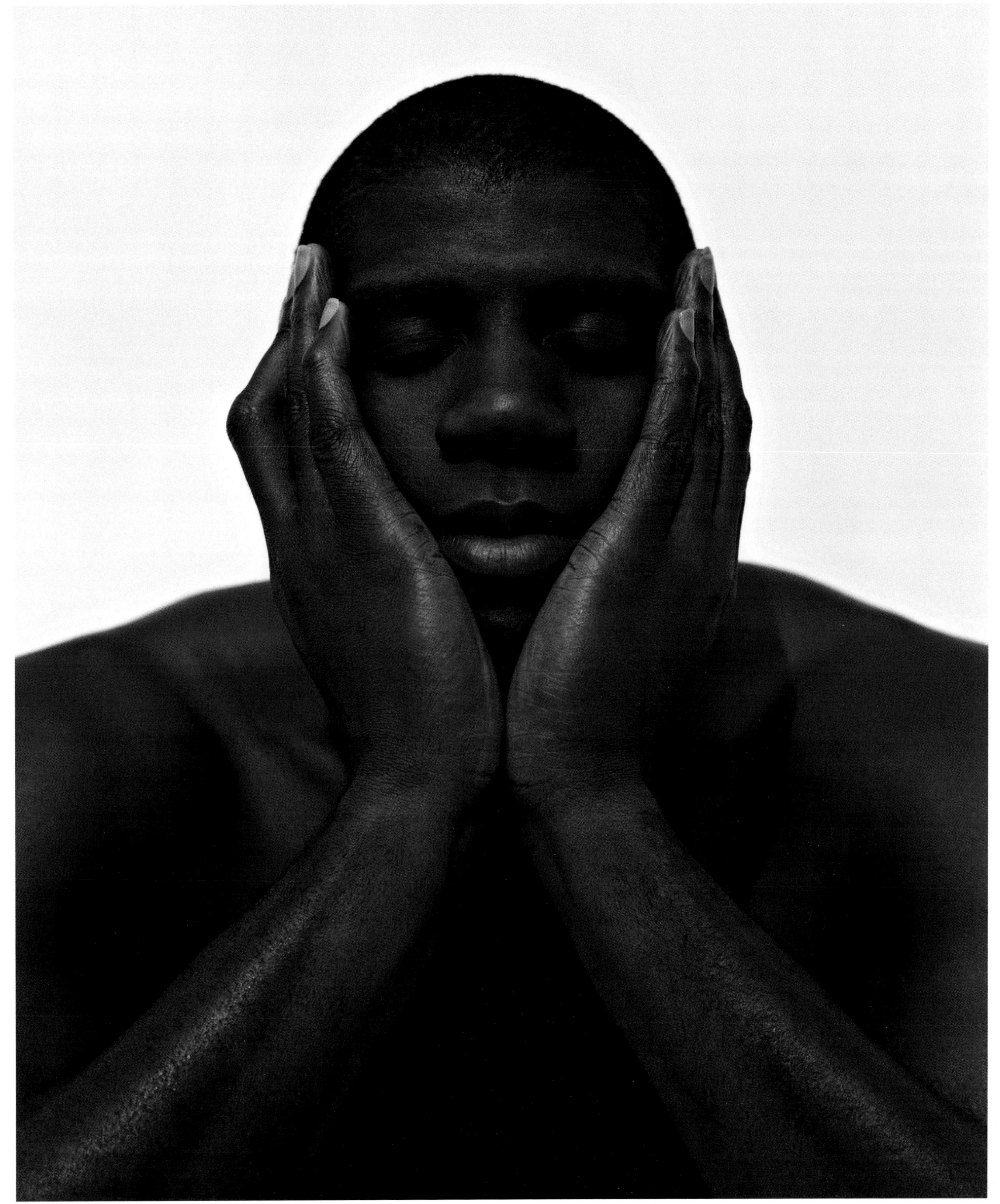

Herb Ritts
Earvin (Magic) Johnson,
Hollywood, 1992

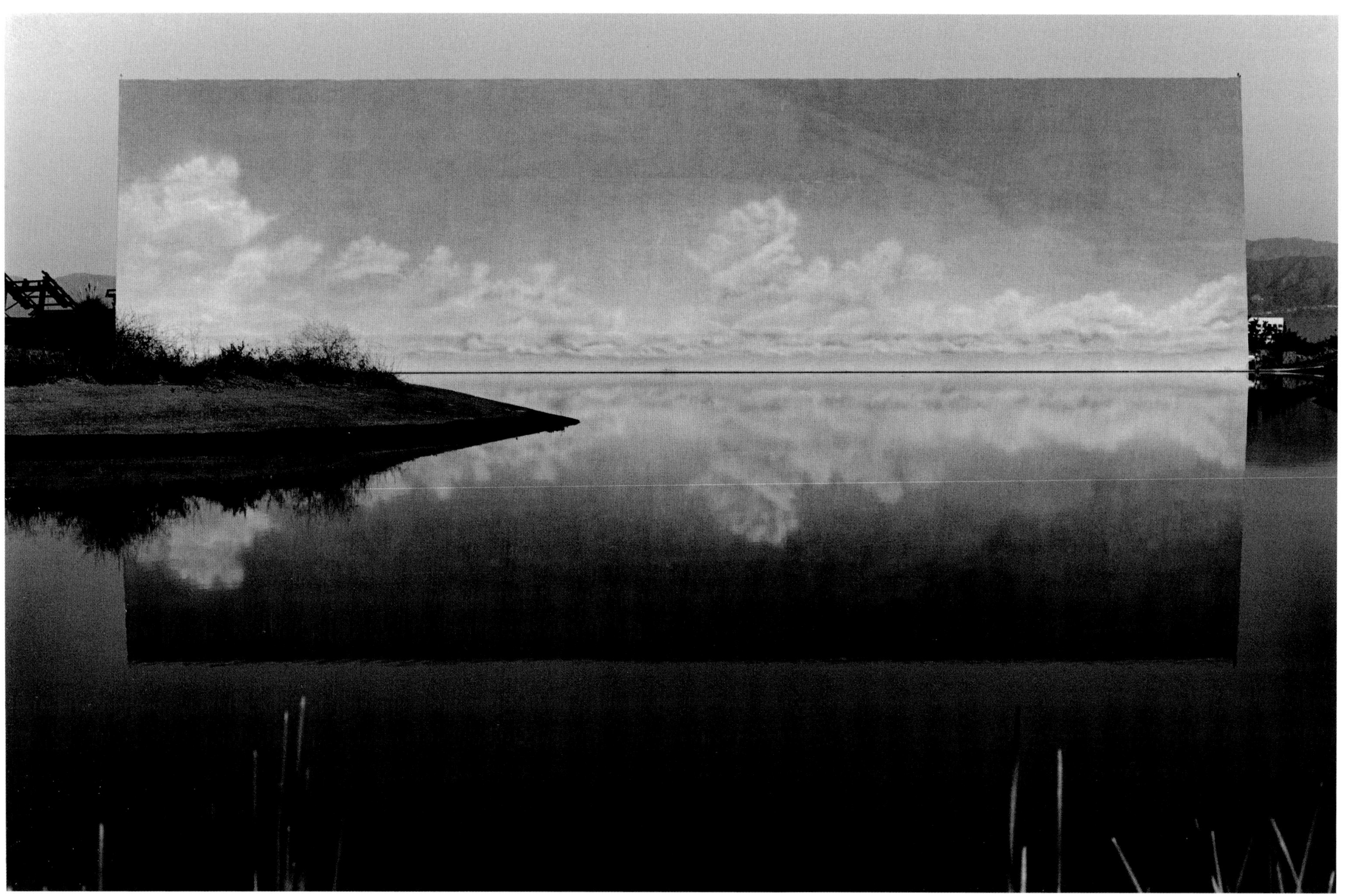

Anthony Friedkin
*Skyline and Lake, Universal
Studios, Hollywood*, 1989

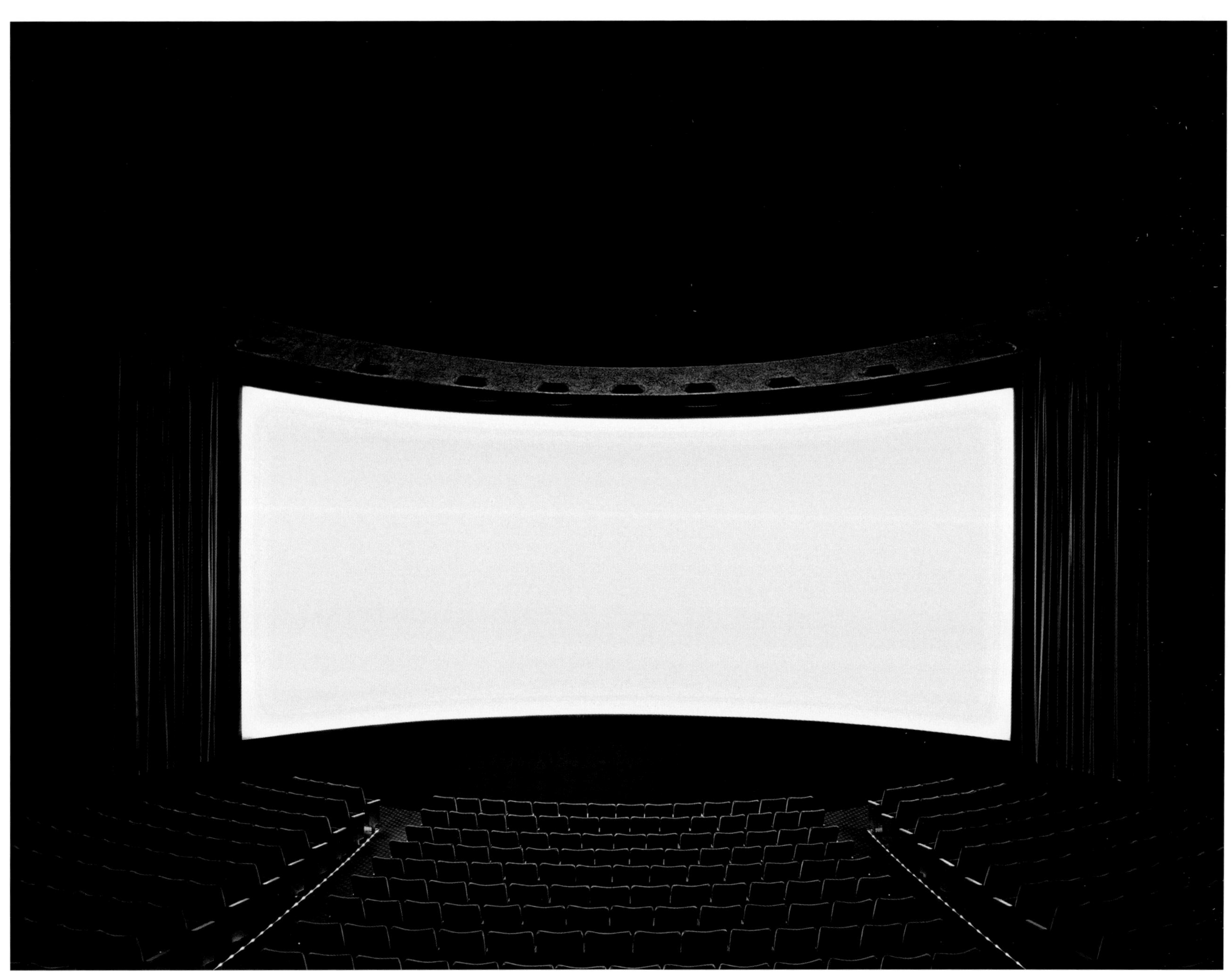

Hiroshi Sugimoto
Cinerama Dome, Hollywood,
1993

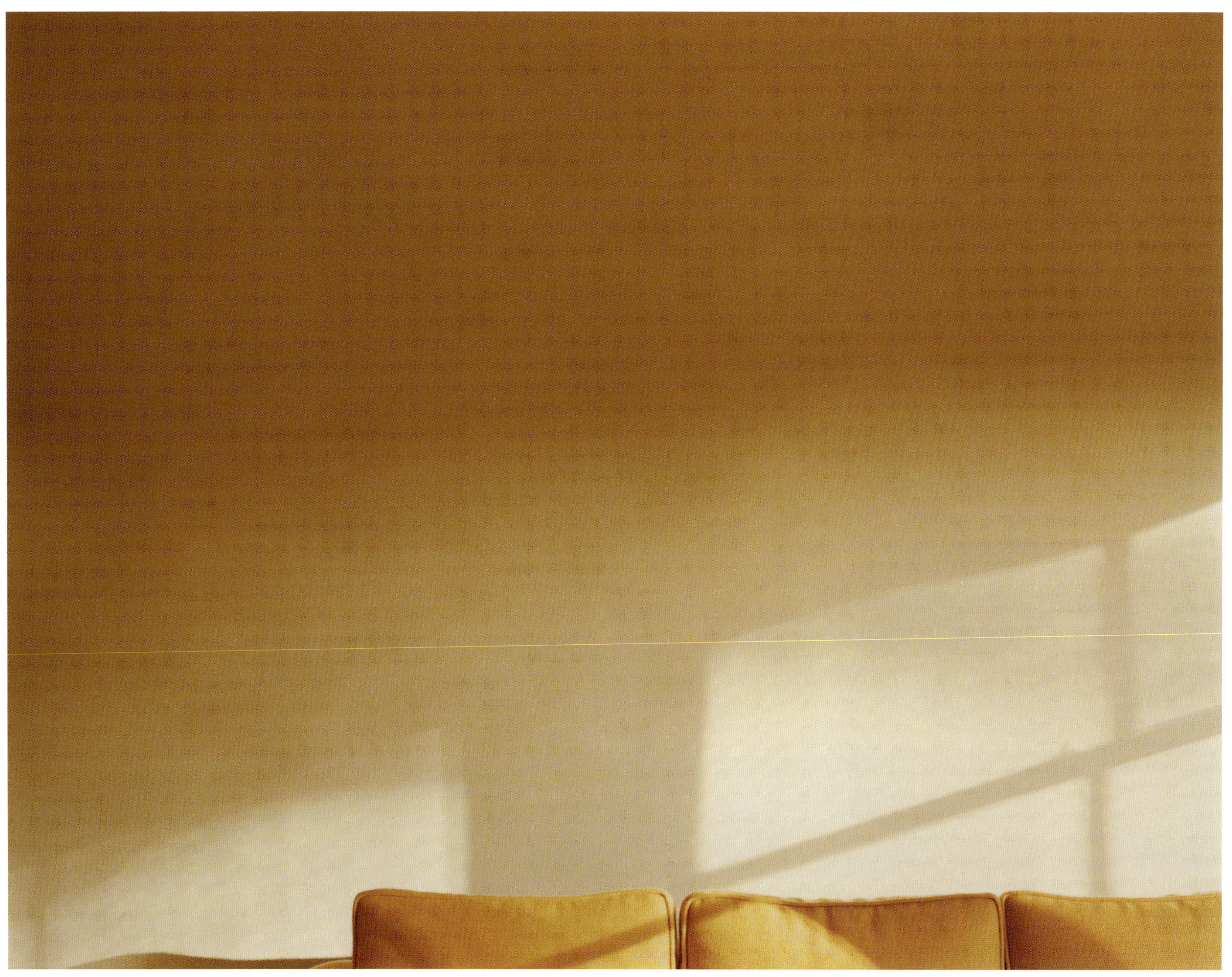

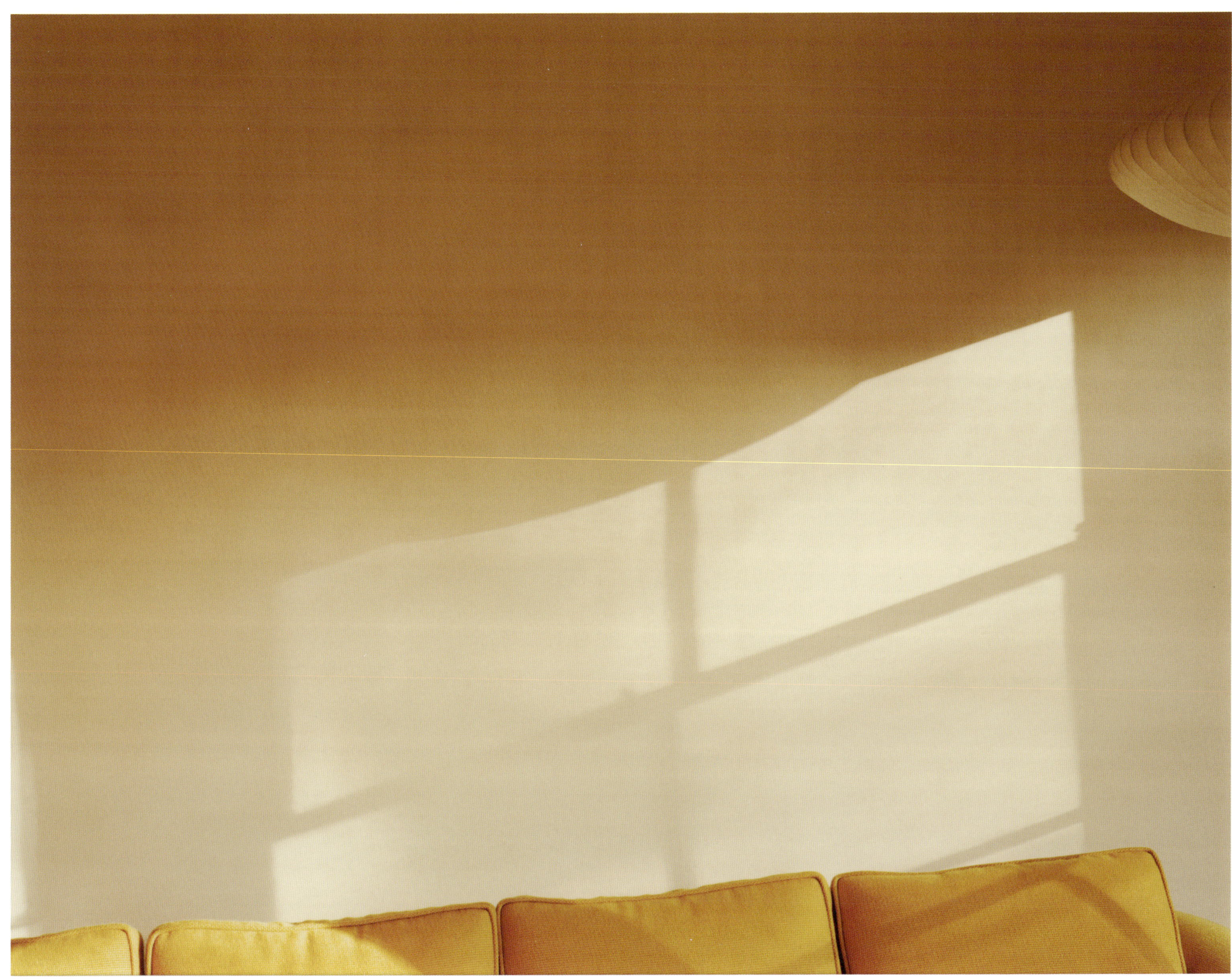

Anthony Friedkin
*Surfboard with Setting Sun,
Santa Monica, California*,
1980

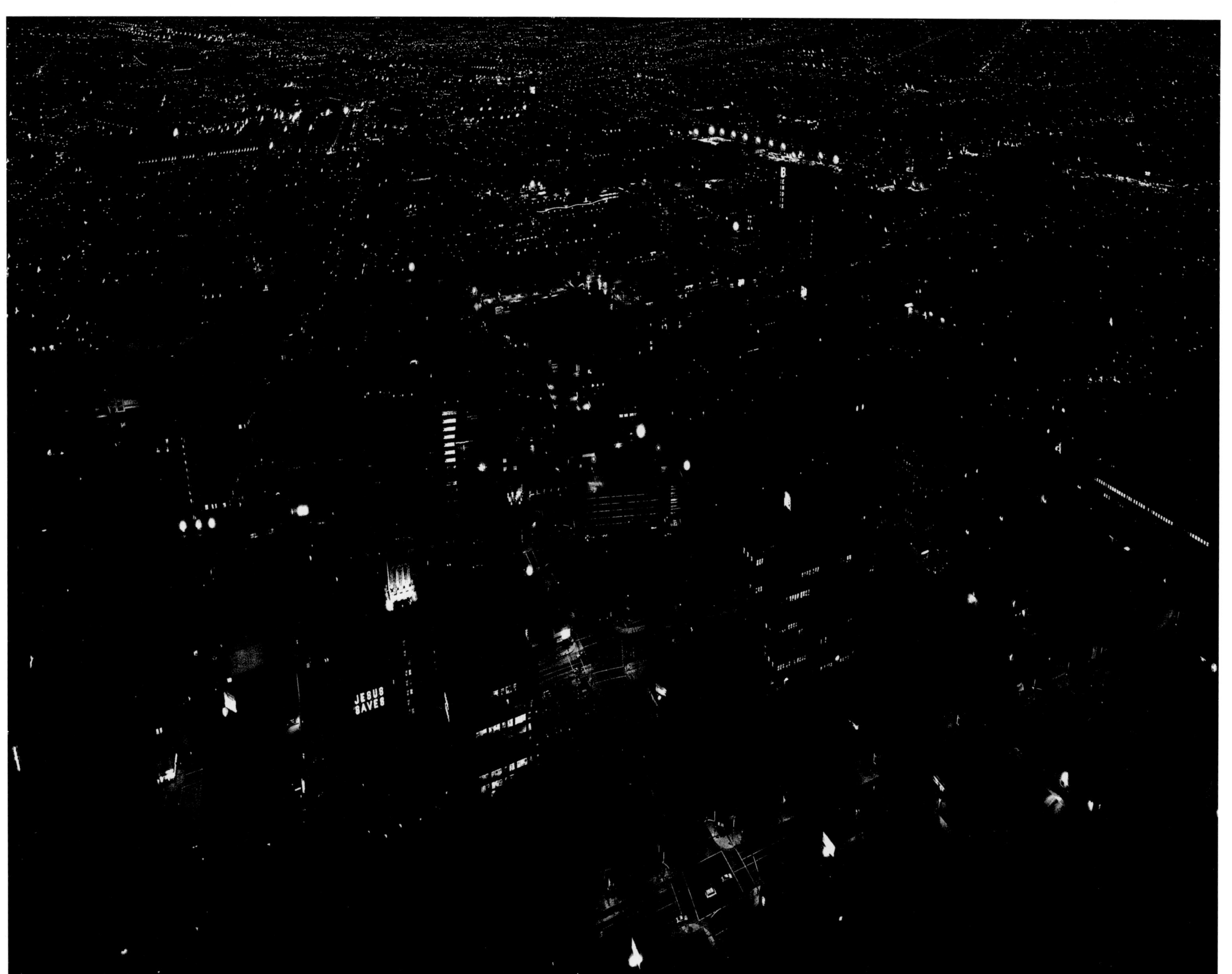

Michael Light
From Los Angeles 07.27.05,
Untitled/Jesus Saves,
2005

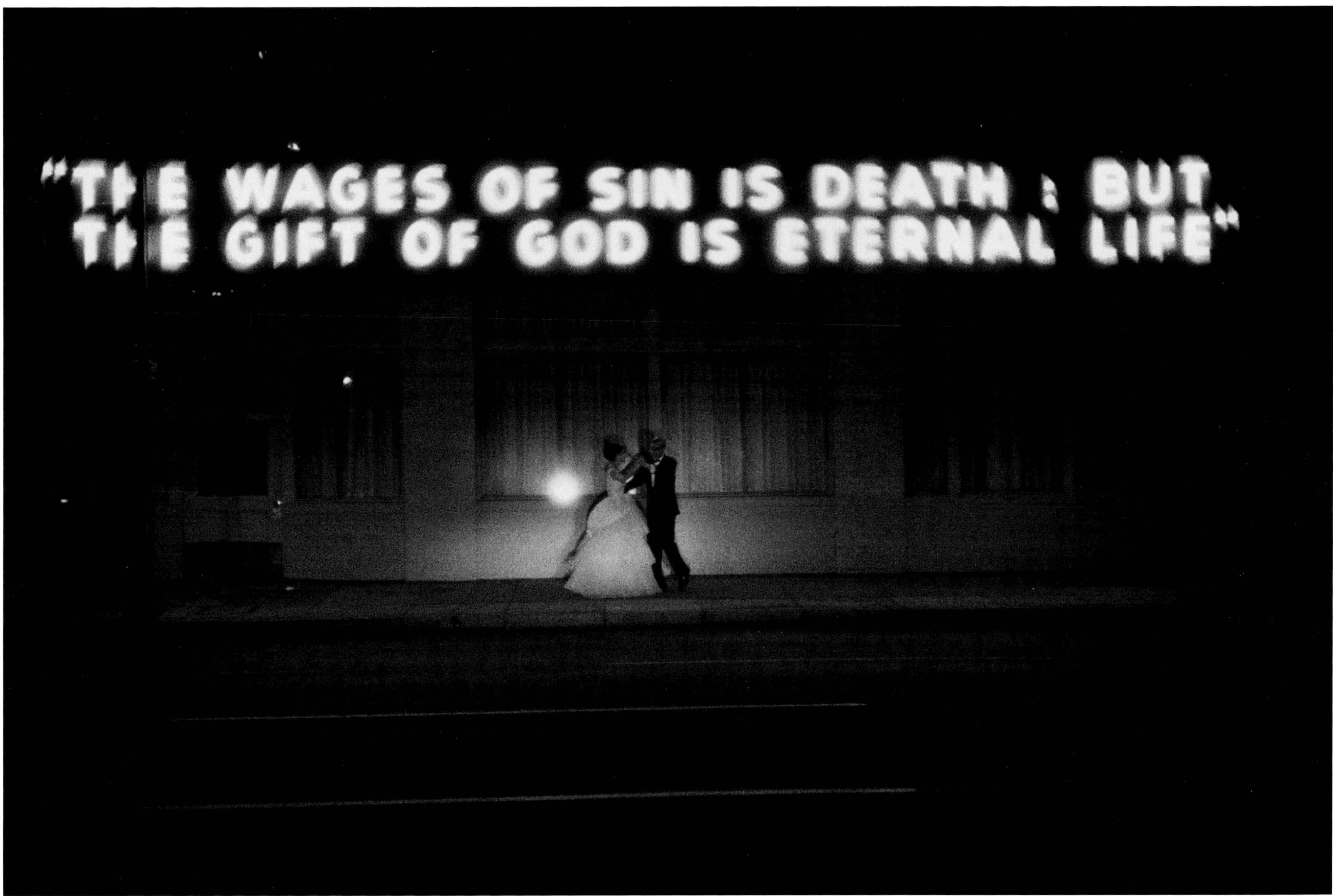

William Claxton
Wages of Sin, Los Angeles,
1961

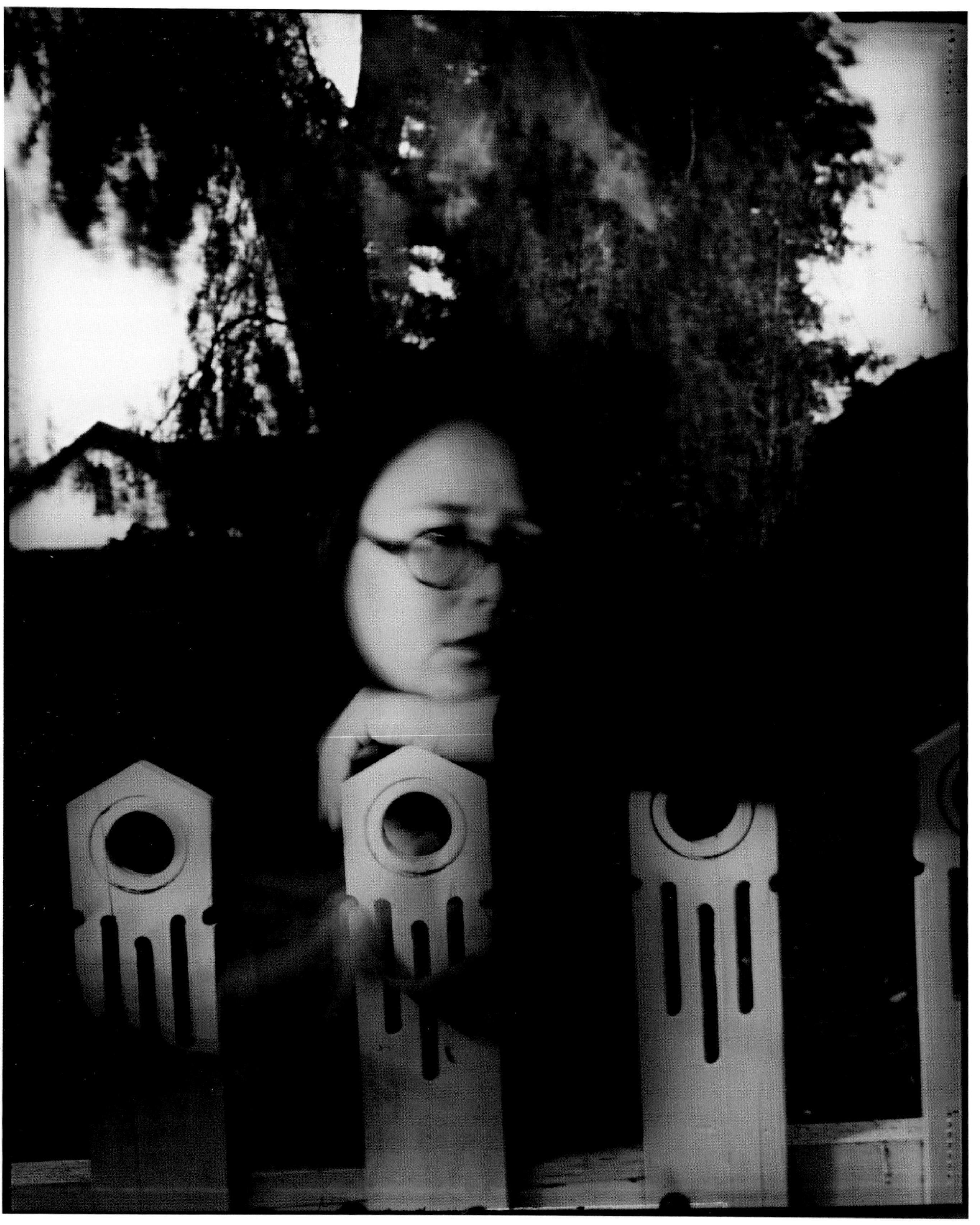

Ken Ohara
03:40pm – 04:40pm
2/8/1998, 1998

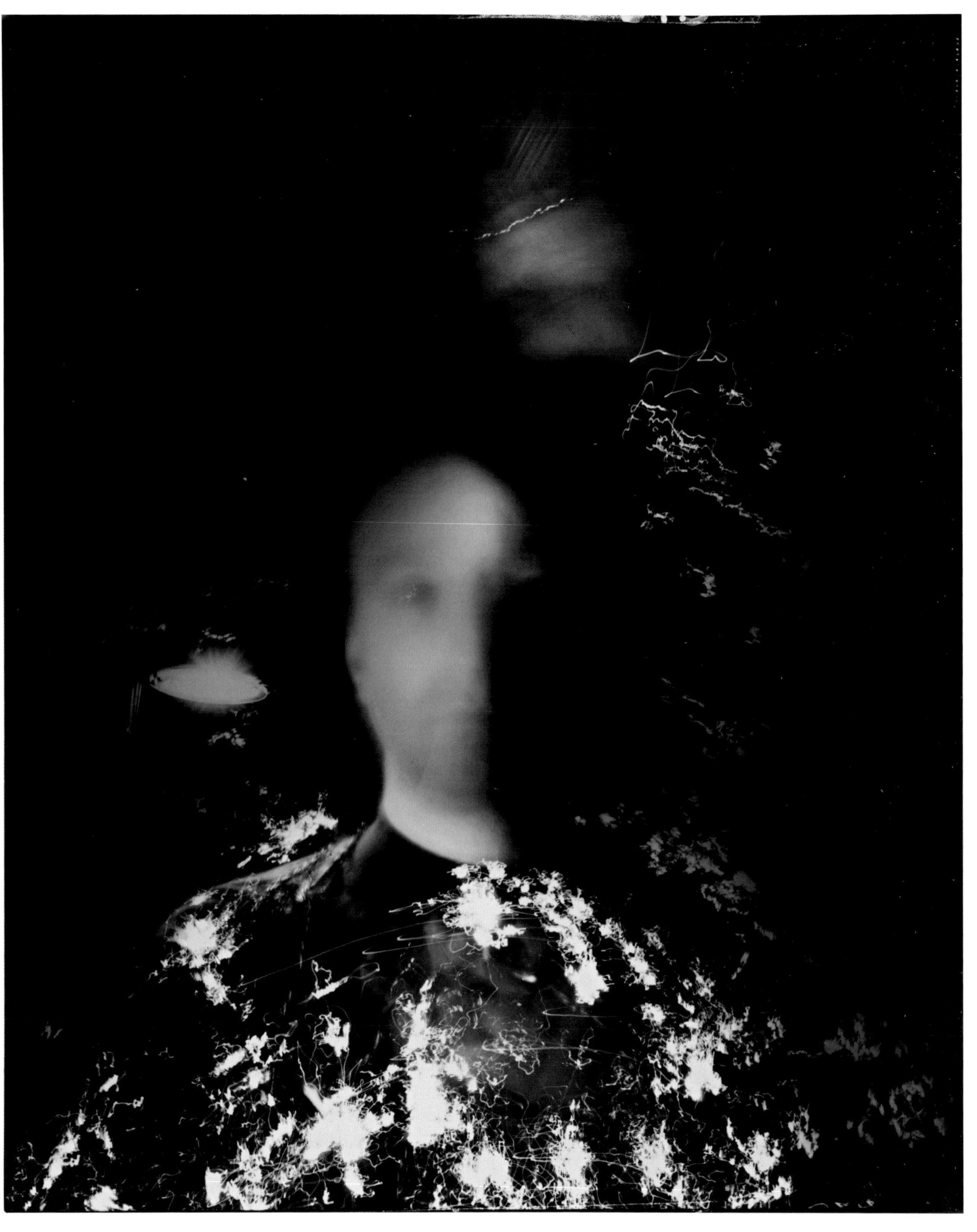

Ken Ohara
01:17pm – 02:17pm 2/28/1998,
1998

Robert Weingarten
6:30 a.m. #106 10/28/03,
2003

LIST OF WORKS

*Works marked with an asterisk (*)
are not included in the exhibition.*

Ansel Adams (1902–1984)
p. 144
*Mannequins, Columbia Movie Lot,
Los Angeles*, 1942
Gelatin silver print
13 ½ × 19 ¼ in. (34.3 × 48.9 cm)
© 1985 Ansel Adams Publishing Rights Trust
Center for Creative Photography, University
of Arizona

p. 43
Interchange, Los Angeles Freeway,
1967
Gelatin silver print
10 ½ × 9 ⅟₁₆ in. (26.7 × 23 cm)
© 1985 Ansel Adams Publishing Rights Trust
Center for Creative Photography, University
of Arizona

Harry Adams (1918–1988)
p. 173
*Black Dot McGee with Friends at
Pacific Town Club, Adams and 24th
Streets, Los Angeles*, 1955
Modern archival print from vintage
negative
11 × 14 in. (27.9 × 35.6 cm)
Black Photographers of California Archive,
California State University, Northridge

*NAACP Protest at Cadillac
Dealership, Los Angeles*, April 1962
Modern archival print from vintage
negative
14 × 11 in. (35.6 × 27.9 cm)
Black Photographers of California Archive,
California State University, Northridge

p. 76
*Evangelist at Shrine Auditorium,
Los Angeles*, n.d.
Modern archival print from vintage
negative
11 × 14 in. (27.9 × 35.6 cm)
Black Photographers of California Archive,
California State University, Northridge

Robert Adams (born 1937)
p. 27
Ontario, California, 1983
Gelatin silver print
14 ⅞ × 18 ¾ in. (37.8 × 47.6 cm)
© Robert Adams
The J. Paul Getty Museum, Los Angeles

Laura Aguilar (born 1959)
p. 19
In Sandy's Room, 1990
Gelatin silver print
40 × 51 in. (101.6 × 129.5 cm)
Courtesy of the artist and Susanne Vielmetter
Los Angeles Projects, Culver City, California

Clem Albers (c. 1903–1991)
p. 89
*The Nagamine residence prior to
evacuation of people of Japanese
ancestry from this area, Los
Angeles, California*, April 11, 1942
Modern archival print from vintage
negative
8 × 10 in. (20.3 × 25.4 cm)
Central Photographic File of the War
Relocation Authority, 1942–45, National
Archives and Records Administration,
Washington, D.C.

p. 57
**Burlington Hotel, "Little Tokio"
Closed, Los Angeles*, 1942
Digital image made from vintage
film negative
5 × 4 in. (12.7 × 10.2 cm)
Central Photographic File of the War Relocation
Authority, 1942–45, National Archives and
Records Administration, Washington, D.C.

Thomas Alleman (born 1958)
p. 2
Mount Hollywood, October 2004
(printed 2008)
Archival print from digital file
15 ¾ × 15 ½ in. (40 × 39.4 cm)
The Huntington Library, San Marino, California

Hollywood Freeway, January 2007
(printed 2008)
Archival print from digital file
15 ¾ × 15 ½ in. (40 × 39.4 cm)
The Huntington Library, San Marino, California

Austin Studio
p. 189
*Street Scene After Long Beach
Quake*, 1933
Gelatin silver photographic postcard
3 ½ × 5 ½ in. (8.9 × 14 cm)
The Huntington Library, San Marino, California

Richard Avedon (1923–2004)
p. 67
*Santa Monica Beach #4, September
30, 1963, Santa Monica, California*,
1963
Gelatin silver print
19 ¾ × 12 ¼ in. (50.2 × 31.1 cm)
© 2008 The Richard Avedon Foundation
Center for Creative Photography, University
of Arizona

G.C. Babbit
p. 199
*DR #357941, Domestic Violence
Victim*, July 26, 1947 (printed 2008)
Gelatin silver print from vintage
negative
14 × 11 in. (35.6 × 27.9 cm)
© City of Los Angeles
Courtesy of Fototeka Gallery, Los Angeles

James Baker (born 1953)
pp. 132–33
Home Sweet Home, 1999–2001
(printed 2007)
Light jet print
8 ¾ × 42 in. (22.2 × 106.7 cm)
Courtesy of the artist

John Baldessari (born 1931)
p. 172
Some Rooms, 1986
Gouache, black-and-white
photographs
96 ½ × 109 ½ in. (245.1 × 278.1 cm)
The Museum of Contemporary Art, Los Angeles

Lewis Baltz (born 1945)
p. 25
Claremont, 1973
From the *Prototype Work* series
Gelatin silver print
5 ¾ × 8 ½ in. (14.6 × 21.6 cm)
Courtesy of the Collection of Susanne Preissler
and Independent Media, Inc., Santa Monica,
California

Uta Barth (born 1958)
p. 220
. . . and of time, 2000
Light jet on Fujicolor paper,
laminated with a pressure-
sensitive adhesive onto Centra
35 × 45 in. (88.9 × 114.3 cm)
Courtesy of the artist

p. 221
. . . and of time, 2000
Light jet on Fujicolor paper,
laminated with a pressure-
sensitive adhesive onto Centra
35 × 45 in. (88.9 × 114.3 cm)
Courtesy of the artist

Adam Bartos (born 1953)
Ocean Drive, Manhattan Beach,
1979
Fuji crystal archive print
34 × 45 in. (86.4 × 114.3 cm)
Courtesy of the artist and RoseGallery,
Santa Monica, California

Marjorie Bentley
p. 212
Strollers, 1929
Toned gelatin silver print
9 ⅞ × 6 ⅞ in. (25.1 × 17.5 cm)
Touring Topics Collection, The Huntington
Library, San Marino, California

G. Haven Bishop (1879–1972)
p. 134
*Group Portrait of the E[lectric]
D[istribution] S[ystems] Gang in
Pomona*, September 3, 1912
Modern archival print from vintage
negative
8 × 10 in. (20.3 × 25.4 cm)
Southern California Edison Archive,
The Huntington Library, San Marino, California

p. 192
*Craig Shipbuilding Plant with
Mr. Craig Jr. and Sr., San Pedro,
California*, March 12, 1914
Modern archival print from vintage
negative
14 × 11 in. (35.6 × 27.9 cm)
Southern California Edison Archive,
The Huntington Library, San Marino, California

p. 181
*Street scene at night with
illuminated sign advertising the
Mission Play at the San Gabriel
Mission, Los Angeles*, April 12, 1915
Modern archival print from vintage
negative
28 ¾ × 23 in. (73 × 58.4 cm)
Southern California Edison Archive, The
Huntington Library, San Marino, California

*Wreckage After the St. Francis Dam
Disaster, Fillmore, California*, 1928
Modern archival print from vintage
negative
8 × 10 in. (20.3 × 25.4 cm)
Southern California Edison Archive,
The Huntington Library, San Marino, California

p. 189
*Edison refugees from Kemp Camp
on back of truck at seven o'clock
the day after the St. Francis Dam
Disaster*, March 13, 1928
Modern archival print from vintage
negative
8 × 10 in. (20.3 × 25.4 cm)
Southern California Edison Archive,
The Huntington Library, San Marino, California

E.A. Bonine (1843–1916)
Ornamental Hedge, Pasadena,
c. 1895
Albumen print
5 ¼ × 8 ⅜ in. (13.3 × 21.3 cm)
The Huntington Library, San Marino, California

Kaucyila Brooke (born 1952)
pp. 186–87
Untitled (Griffith Park), 1998
From the *Burned* series, 1998–99
Chromogenic print
40 × 50 in. (101.6 × 127 cm)
Courtesy of the artist and Michael Dawson
Gallery, Los Angeles

F.A. Bussey
*Fire Department After Earthquake,
Long Beach, Calif., March 10, 1933*,
1933
Gelatin silver photographic
postcard
3 ½ × 5 ½ in. (8.9 × 14 cm)
The Huntington Library, San Marino, California

Jo Ann Callis (born 1940)
p. 168
Man in a Tie, 1977
Dye transfer print
21 ¼ × 15 ½ in. (54 × 39.4 cm)
Courtesy of Andy Schwartz

Paul Caponigro (born 1932)
Huntington Botanical Garden, 2002
Gelatin silver print
5 × 7 in. (12.7 × 17.8 cm)
The Huntington Library, San Marino, California

Huntington Botanical Garden, 2002
Gelatin silver print
5 × 7 in. (12.7 × 17.8 cm)
The Huntington Library, San Marino, California

Herb Carleton (1927–1992)
p. 190
Studio Fire, Warner Brothers,
May 16, 1952
Gelatin silver print
13 ¼ × 10 ⅜ in. (33.7 × 26.4 cm)
Black Photographers of California Archive,
California State University, Northridge

Gusmano Cesaretti (born 1946)
p. 120
Whittier Boulevard, Night, 1975
Gelatin silver print
8 × 12 ¼ in. (20.3 × 31.1 cm)
Courtesy of the artist

p. 177
Alexandra Hotel, Klique Dance, 1976
Gelatin silver print
8 × 12 ½ in. (20.3 × 31.8 cm)
Courtesy of the artist

Intruder, Soto Street, 2000
Digital color print
13 × 19 in. (33 × 48.3 cm)
Courtesy of the artist

p. 204
Beto, at Whittier and Lorena, 2001
Digital color print
13 × 19 in. (33 × 48.3 cm)
Courtesy of the artist

Tokyo Night, 2002
Digital color print
13 × 19 in. (33 × 48.3 cm)
Courtesy of the artist

p. 205
Bullet, 2004
Digital color print
13 × 19 in. (33 × 48.3 cm)
Courtesy of the artist

Eighteen, 2004
Digital color print
13 × 19 in. (33 × 48.3 cm)
Courtesy of the artist

William Claxton (born 1927)
p. 175
Halima & Chet Baker, Redondo Beach, 1955
Gelatin silver print
16 × 20 in. (40.6 × 50.8 cm)
© William Claxton
Courtesy of Fahey/Klein Gallery, Los Angeles

p. 225
Wages of Sin, Los Angeles, 1961
Gelatin silver print
20 × 24 in. (50.8 × 61 cm)
© William Claxton
Courtesy of Fahey/Klein Gallery, Los Angeles

Will Connell (1898–1961)
p. 55
*Study in Diagonals, c. 1925
Bromide print
13 1/4 × 8 1/2 in. (33.7 × 21.6 cm)
Touring Topics Collection, The Huntington Library, San Marino, California

p. 111
Underpass, 1937
Gelatin silver print
7 5/8 × 9 1/2 in. (19.4 × 24.1 cm)
Courtesy of Will Connell, Jr.
Will Connell Papers, Department of Special Collections, Charles E. Young Research Library, University of California, Los Angeles

p. 94
L.A. Subdivision, 1939
Gelatin silver print
7 1/2 × 9 5/8 in. (19.1 × 24.4 cm)
Courtesy of Will Connell, Jr.
Will Connell Papers, Department of Special Collections, Charles E. Young Research Library, University of California, Los Angeles

Eileen Cowin (born 1941)
pp. 208–209
Returning to Ordinary Life, 1997
C-print
30 × 160 in. (76.2 × 406.4 cm)
Courtesy of the artist

Imogen Cunningham (1883–1976)
Spencer Tracy, 1932
Gelatin silver print
10 × 8 in. (25.4 × 20.3 cm)
Courtesy of Susan Ehrens and Leland Rice

Darryl Curran (born 1935)
p. 38
Before & After Delivery, 1968
Gelatin silver print, photographic glass plate, wood-and-metal frame
14 × 11 3/4 × 2 in. (35.6 × 29.8 × 5.1 cm)
Courtesy of the artist

This Sale Bowser, 1968
Gelatin silver print, litho film, Plexiglas, wood-and-metal frame
14 × 11 3/4 × 2 in. (35.6 × 29.8 × 5.1 cm)
Courtesy of the artist

Louise Dahl-Wolfe (1895–1989)
p. 147
Dolores Del Rio, Hollywood, 1938
Gelatin silver print
12 1/2 × 10 in. (31.8 × 25.4 cm)
© 1989 Arizona Board of Regents
Center for Creative Photography, University of Arizona

Joe Deal (born 1947)
San Fernando, California, 1978
Gelatin silver print
11 1/4 × 11 1/4 in. (28.6 × 28.6 cm)
Center for Creative Photography, University of Arizona

p. 26
Inglewood, California, 1979
Gelatin silver print
11 1/4 × 11 1/8 in. (28.6 × 28.3 cm)
Center for Creative Photography, University of Arizona

John Divola (born 1949)
p. 53
Untitled (Man Watering Lawn), 1971–73
Gelatin silver print
6 × 9 in. (15.2 × 22.9 cm)
Courtesy of the artist

p. 124
Untitled (Young Woman on Sidewalk), 1971–73
Gelatin silver print
6 × 9 in. (15.2 × 22.9 cm)
Courtesy of the artist

p. 195
Los Angeles International Airport Noise Abatement Zone Exterior View B, 1975 (printed 2006)
Archival pigment print
20 × 20 in. (50.8 × 50.8 cm)
Courtesy of the artist

p. 9
Zuma, #63, 1978 (printed 2006)
From the *Zuma* series, 1977–78
Archival pigment print
40 × 50 in. (101.6 × 127 cm)
Courtesy of the artist

Lemuel S. Ellis (1854–unknown)
*Skarf Street Between Adams Street and Ellis Avenue, Los Angeles, c. 1890
Albumen print
7 3/4 × 4 1/2 in. (19.7 × 11.4 cm)
The Huntington Library, San Marino, California

Christina Fernandez (born 1965)
pp. 140–41
Lavanderia #11, 2003
Color photograph
30 × 40 in. (76.2 × 101.6 cm)
© Christina Fernandez
Courtesy of Gallery Luisotti, Santa Monica, California

Judy Fiskin (born 1945)
Untitled #195, 1982
Gelatin silver print
2 3/4 × 2 3/4 in. (7 × 7 cm)
© 2007 Museum Associates/LACMA
Courtesy of the Los Angeles County Museum of Art, Los Angeles

p. 95
*Untitled, c. 1983
Gelatin silver print
2 1/2 × 2 3/8 in. (6.4 × 6 cm)
© 2007 Museum Associates/LACMA
Courtesy of the Los Angeles County Museum of Art, Los Angeles

p. 95
*Untitled, c. 1983
Gelatin silver print
2 3/4 × 2 3/4 in. (7 × 7 cm)
© 2007 Museum Associates/LACMA
Courtesy of the Los Angeles County Museum of Art, Los Angeles

W.[illiam] H.[enry] Fletcher (1838–1922)
*Junction of Main and Spring Streets, Los Angeles, Cal., c. 1885
Albumen print
5 1/4 × 8 1/2 in. (13.3 × 21.6 cm)
The Huntington Library, San Marino, California

p. 85
*Sonoratown, Los Angeles, c. 1885
Albumen print
5 1/4 × 8 1/2 in. (13.3 × 21.6 cm)
The Huntington Library, San Marino, California

p. 46
View of the Hills from Bunker Hill Avenue and Third Street, 1887
Modern print from glass plate negative
11 × 14 in. (27.9 × 35.6 cm)
The Huntington Library, San Marino, California

p. 84
Old Chinatown, Los Angeles, 1888
Albumen print
5 1/4 × 8 1/2 in. (13.3 × 21.6 cm)
The Huntington Library, San Marino, California

Robbert Flick (born 1939)
pp. 36–37
Manhattan Beach, Looking West from Vista, 1980
From *Sequential Views* series, 1979–90
Gelatin silver print
20 × 24 in. (50.8 × 61 cm)
The Huntington Library, San Marino, California

p. 54
Hollywood Blvd North and South, between La Brea and Cahuenga, 2001 (printed 2007)
From *L.A. Documents* series, 1990–2001
Light jet on Kodak Endura paper
35 1/2 × 67 1/2 in. (90.2 × 171.5 cm)
Courtesy of the artist

Robert Flora (1929–1986)
p. 191
Watts Riots—Army Jeep, 1965
Gelatin silver print
10 1/2 × 13 1/4 in. (26.7 × 33.7 cm)
The J. Paul Getty Museum, Los Angeles

Robert Frank (born 1924)
p. 176
Movie Premiere, Hollywood, 1955–56
Gelatin silver print
12 1/2 × 8 1/2 in. (31.8 × 21.6 cm)
© Robert Frank, from *The Americans*
Center for Creative Photography, University of Arizona

p. 34
Covered Car—Long Beach, California, 1956
Gelatin silver print
9 × 13 1/4 in. (22.9 × 33.7 cm)
© Robert Frank, from *The Americans*
The Museum of Contemporary Art, Los Angeles

Anthony Friedkin (born 1949)
Woman by the Pool, Beverly Hills Hotel, California, 1975
Gelatin silver print
16 × 20 in. (40.6 × 50.8 cm)
© Anthony Friedkin
Courtesy of the Stephen Cohen Gallery, Los Angeles

pp. 164–65
Clockwork Malibu/Rick Dano on the Highway, Malibu, California, 1977
Gelatin silver print
16 × 20 in. (40.6 × 50.8 cm)
© Anthony Friedkin
Courtesy of the Stephen Cohen Gallery, Los Angeles

pp. 222–23
Surfboard with Setting Sun, Santa Monica, California, 1980
Gelatin silver print
16 × 20 in. (40.6 × 50.8 cm)
© Anthony Friedkin
Courtesy of the Stephen Cohen Gallery, Los Angeles

p. 218
Skyline and Lake, Universal Studios, Hollywood, 1989
Gelatin silver print
16 × 20 in. (40.6 × 50.8 cm)
© Anthony Friedkin
Courtesy of the Stephen Cohen Gallery, Los Angeles

Lee Friedlander (born 1934)
pp. 40–41
Los Angeles, 1965
Gelatin silver print
7 1/2 × 11 1/4 in. (19.1 × 28.6 cm)
Center for Creative Photography, University of Arizona

Herve Friend (fl. c. 1860s–1890s)
p. 113
*Los Angeles, c. 1890
Albumen print
5 1/4 × 8 1/2 in. (13.3 × 21.6 cm)
The Huntington Library, San Marino, California

Harry Gamboa, Jr. (born 1951)
Alfred Arteaga, Poet, 1994
From *Chicano Male Unbonded* series, 1991–2007
Gelatin silver print
14 × 11 in. (35.6 × 27.9 cm)
Courtesy of the artist

p. 203
Roberto Bedoya, Poet, 1994
From *Chicano Male Unbonded* series, 1991–2007
Gelatin silver print
14 × 11 in. (35.6 × 27.9 cm)
Courtesy of the artist

p. 202
Harry T. Gamboa, Printer (Retired), 1997
From *Chicano Male Unbonded* series, 1991–2007
Gelatin silver print
14 × 11 in. (35.6 × 27.9 cm)
Courtesy of the artist

Max Benavidez, Writer, 1997
From *Chicano Male Unbonded* series, 1991–2007
Gelatin silver print
14 × 11 in. (35.6 × 27.9 cm)
Courtesy of the artist

Harry Ortiz Liflan, Artist, 2000
From *Chicano Male Unbonded* series, 1991–2007
Gelatin silver print
14 × 11 in. (35.6 × 27.9 cm)
Courtesy of the artist

Francesco X. Siqueiros, Master Printer, 2001
From *Chicano Male Unbonded* series, 1991–2007
Gelatin silver print
14 × 11 in. (35.6 × 27.9 cm)
Courtesy of the artist

Luis J. Rodriguez, Author, 2004
From *Chicano Male Unbonded* series, 1991–2007
Gelatin silver print
14 × 11 in. (35.6 × 27.9 cm)
Courtesy of the artist

Abel Correa, Student (UIUC), 2005
From *Chicano Male Unbonded* series, 1991–2007
Gelatin silver print
14 × 11 in. (35.6 × 27.9 cm)
Courtesy of the artist

William A. Garnett (1916–2006)
p. 59
Finished Housing, Lakewood, California, 1950
Gelatin silver print
7 3/8 × 9 1/2 in. (18.7 × 24.1 cm)
© Estate of William A. Garnett
The J. Paul Getty Museum, Los Angeles

p. 59
Foundations and Slabs, Lakewood, California, 1950
Gelatin silver print
7 1/2 × 9 3/8 in. (19 × 23.8 cm)
© Estate of William A. Garnett
The J. Paul Getty Museum, Los Angeles

Framing, Lakewood, California, 1950
Gelatin silver print
7 1/4 × 9 1/2 in. (18.4 × 24.1 cm)
© Estate of William A. Garnett
The J. Paul Getty Museum, Los Angeles

p. 59
Grading Lakewood, California, 1950
Gelatin silver print
7 1/2 × 9 1/2 in. (19 × 24.1 cm)
© Estate of William A. Garnett
The J. Paul Getty Museum, Los Angeles

Plaster and Roofing, Lakewood, California, 1950
Gelatin silver print
7 ¾ × 9 ½ in. (19.7 × 24.1 cm)
© Estate of William A. Garnett
The J. Paul Getty Museum, Los Angeles

Trenching Lakewood, California, 1950
Gelatin silver print
7 ¼ × 9 ½ in. (18.4 × 24.1 cm)
© Estate of William A. Garnett
The J. Paul Getty Museum, Los Angeles

Jeff Gates (born 1949)
p. 194
Construction of the 105 Freeway, c. 1990–93
From the *In Our Path* series, 1982–93
Gelatin silver print
11 × 14 in. (27.9 × 35.6 cm)
The Huntington Library, San Marino, California

William M. Godfrey (1825–1900)
p. 46
The Plaza, Los Angeles, c. 1862
Albumen print
2 ½ × 4 ¼ in. (6.4 × 10.8 cm)
The Huntington Library, San Marino, California

Sonoratown, Los Angeles, c. 1868
Albumen print
2 ½ × 4 ¼ in. (6.4 × 10.8 cm)
The Huntington Library, San Marino, California

Commercial St., Los Angeles, 1872
Albumen stereographic print
3 ⅞ × 6 ⅞ in. (9.8 × 17.5 cm)
The Huntington Library, San Marino, California

Bella Union Hotel, Los Angeles, c. 1869
Albumen stereographic print
3 ¼ × 6 ⅞ in. (8.3 × 17.5 cm)
The Huntington Library, San Marino, California

Downey's Old Block, Los Angeles, c. 1872
Albumen stereographic print
3 ¼ × 6 ¾ in. (8.3 × 17.1 cm)
The Huntington Library, San Marino, California

Scene of Chinese Riot, c. 1872
Albumen stereographic print
3 ⅞ × 6 ⅞ in. (9.8 × 17.5 cm)
The Huntington Library, San Marino, California

Jim Goldberg (born 1953)
p. 75
Dave Panhandling, Hollywood, 1988
From *Raised by Wolves*
Gelatin silver print
20 × 16 in. (50.8 × 40.6 cm)
Courtesy of Stephen Wirtz Gallery, San Francisco

Leroy Grannis (born 1917)
p. 155
Henry Ford, 22nd Street, Hermosa Beach, November 3, 1963, 1963 (printed 2006)
Gelatin silver print
30 × 30 in. (76.2 × 76.2 cm)
Courtesy of the artist and M + B, Los Angeles

p. 6
Hermosa Beach Strand, 1967 (printed 2007)
Chromogenic print
36 × 36 in. (91.4 × 91.4 cm)
Courtesy of the artist and M + B, Los Angeles

Todd Gray (born 1954)
p. 211
Goofy (Body) #6, 1993
Gelatin silver print, varnished, with metal bands
81 × 50 in. (205.7 × 127 cm)
© 2007 Museum Associates/LACMA
Courtesy of the Los Angeles County Museum of Art, Los Angeles

Lauren Greenfield (born 1966)
pp. 30–31
Lindsey at a Fourth of July party three days after the surgery, Calabasas, 1993
Cibachrome
16 × 20 in. (40.6 × 50.8 cm)
© Lauren Greenfield
Courtesy of Fahey/Klein Gallery, Los Angeles

John Gutmann (1905–1998)
p. 52
**Car Hops, Early Drive-In Restaurant, Hollywood*, 1935
Gelatin silver print
7 ½ × 8 ⅛ in. (19.1 × 20.6 cm)
© 1989 Arizona Board of Regents
Center for Creative Photography, University of Arizona

Philippe Halsman (1906–1979)
p. 151
Marilyn with Barbells, 1952
Gelatin silver print
10 × 13 in. (25.4 × 33 cm)
© Philippe Halsman estate
Center for Creative Photography, University of Arizona

Karen Halverson (born 1941)
pp. 108–109
Mulholland Near Skyline Drive, Los Angeles, 1993
Chromogenic print
17 × 51 in. (43.2 × 129.5 cm)
Courtesy of the artist

Lyle Ashton Harris (born 1965)
p. 169
Sisterhood, 1994
Ilfochrome print
14 × 11 in. (35.6 × 27.9 cm)
The Museum of Contemporary Art, Los Angeles

Robert Heinecken (1931–2006)
p. 39
Are You Rea #12, 1966
Gelatin silver print
10 ¾ × 8 in. (27.3 × 20.3 cm)
Center for Creative Photography, University of Arizona

Lingerie for a Feminist Sun Tan, #5, 1973
Photo emulsion on linen, chalk, and mixed media, in triptych format with hanger apparatus
21 ⅛ × 48 in. (53.7 × 121.9 cm)
Center for Creative Photography, University of Arizona

Anthony Hernandez (born 1947)
p. 125
Vermont and Wilshire Boulevard #11, 1979 (printed 2007)
Gelatin silver print
20 × 24 in. (50.8 × 61 cm)
The Huntington Library, San Marino, California

p. 93
Landscapes for the Homeless #38, 1990 (printed 2007)
Endura paper
48 × 47 ½ in. (121.9 × 120.7 cm)
Courtesy of Christopher Grimes Gallery, Santa Monica, California

p. 183
Everything #5, 2003–04
Chromogenic print
50 × 50 in. (127 × 127 cm)
Courtesy of Christopher Grimes Gallery, Santa Monica, California

Miyo Hernandez (born 1973)
Resurrection, 2008
C-print
14 × 98 in. (35.6 × 248.9 cm)
Courtesy of the artist

Douglas Hill (born 1950)
p. 185
First Street #23, 2005
From *Poured in Place: 72 L.A. River Bridges*
Archival pigment print
12 × 12 in. (30.5 × 30.5 cm)
Courtesy of the artist and Craig Krull Gallery, Santa Monica, California

Fourth Street from Under First Street, 2005
From *Poured in Place: 72 L.A. River Bridges*
Archival pigment print
12 × 12 in. (30.5 × 30.5 cm)
Courtesy of the artist and Craig Krull Gallery, Santa Monica, California

Dennis Hopper (born 1936)
p. 50
Double Standard, 1961 (printed later)
Gelatin silver print
16 × 24 in. (40.6 × 61 cm)
© 2007 Museum Associates/LACMA
Courtesy of the Los Angeles County Museum of Art, Los Angeles

John Humble (born 1944)
Back jacket (detail) and inside front flap
Selma Avenue at Vine Street, Hollywood, January 23, 1991, 1991 (printed 2008)
C-print
40 × 30 in. (101.6 × 76.2 cm)
Courtesy of the artist and Jan Kesner Gallery, Los Angeles

5602 Van Ness Avenue, South Central Los Angeles, August 2, 1991, 1991
Dye coupler chromogenic print
16 × 20 in. (40.6 × 50.8 cm)
Courtesy of the artist and Jan Kesner Gallery, Los Angeles

pp. 100–101
719 Lincoln Boulevard, Venice, May 13, 1995, 1995
Dye coupler chromogenic print
20 × 24 in. (50.8 × 61 cm)
Courtesy of the artist and Jan Kesner Gallery, Los Angeles

p. 207
From Lifeguard Station 26 #15, 1999
Dye coupler chromogenic print
20 × 24 in. (50.8 × 61 cm)
Courtesy of the artist and Jan Kesner Gallery, Los Angeles

George Hurrell (1904–1992)
Jean Harlow, 1933
Gelatin silver print
10 × 13 in. (25.4 × 33 cm)
Courtesy of Pancho Barnes Trust Estate Archive, Pasadena, California

p. 149
Carole Lombard, 1937
Gelatin silver print
14 × 11 in. (35.6 × 27.9 cm)
Courtesy of Pancho Barnes Trust Estate Archive, Pasadena, California

Shinsaku Izumi (1880–1941)
p. 55
The Shadow, c. 1931
Bromide print
10 ¼ × 13 ¼ in. (26 × 33.7 cm)
Courtesy of Dennis Reed and Amy Reed

William Henry Jackson (1843–1942)
pp. 82–83
The Raymond [Hotel], East Pasadena, California, c. 1889
Albumen print
17 × 54 ¾ in. (43.2 × 139.1 cm)
The Huntington Library, San Marino, California

Arthur F. Kales (1882–1936)
p. 215
In the Temple of the Sun, c. 1918
Bromide print
13 ½ × 10 ⅝ in. (34.3 × 27 cm)
Courtesy of Dennis Reed and Amy Reed

Bobby Klein (born 1943)
pp. 178–79
The Doors Performing on Stage, Los Angeles, c. 1967
Gelatin silver print
16 × 20 in. (40.6 × 50.8 cm)
© Bobby Klein
Courtesy of Fahey/Klein Gallery, Los Angeles

Gary Leonard (born 1951)
p. 196
April 30, 1992, Los Angeles, California, 1992
Sixteen gelatin silver prints
3 ½ × 5 ½ in. (8.9 × 14 cm) each
Courtesy of the artist

Neo-Nazis at Tom Bradley's Inauguration, 1992 (printed 2008)
Gelatin silver print
20 × 24 in. (50.8 × 61 cm)
Courtesy of the artist

Michael Light (born 1963)
p. 107
Highways 5, 12, 60, and 101 Looking West, L.A. River and Downtown Beyond, February 12, 2004
Archival pigment print
40 × 50 in. (101.6 × 127 cm)
Courtesy of the artist and Craig Krull Gallery, Santa Monica, California

p. 224
From Los Angeles 07.27.05, Untitled/Jesus Saves, 2005
Archival pigment print
40 × 50 in. (101.6 × 127 cm)
Courtesy of the artist and Craig Krull Gallery, Santa Monica, California

Los Angeles County Health Department
p. 91
Glendale, December 7, 1931
From *The Habitations of the Unemployed in Los Angeles County*
Gelatin silver print
5 × 7 in. (12.7 × 17.8 cm)
The Huntington Library, San Marino, California

Bandini, March 18, 1932
From *The Habitations of the Unemployed in Los Angeles County*
Gelatin silver print
5 × 7 in. (12.7 × 17.8 cm)
The Huntington Library, San Marino, California

Graham, March 18, 1932
From *The Habitations of the Unemployed in Los Angeles County*
Gelatin silver print
5 × 7 in. (12.7 × 17.8 cm)
The Huntington Library, San Marino, California

Mary Ellen Mark (born 1940)
p. 105
The Damm Family in Their Car, Los Angeles, California, 1987
Gelatin silver print
24 × 20 in. (61 × 50.8 cm)
© Mary Ellen Mark
Courtesy of Fahey/Klein Gallery, Los Angeles

Douglas McCulloh (born 1959)
Untitled [Actress on red carpet at Oscar ceremonies, Hollywood], 2005
RGB laser print on Fujicolor Crystal Archive paper
20 × 13 in. (50.8 × 33 cm)
Courtesy of the artist

Jerry McMillan (born 1936)
pp. 22–23
Five Boxes, 1965–67
Gelatin silver prints, Plexiglas boxes, mirror base
Photo boxes: 4 × 3 ¼ × 3 in. (10.2 × 8.3 × 7.6 cm) each
Plexiglas vitrine: 8 ¼ × 7 × 25 in. (21 × 17.8 × 63.5 cm)
Plexiglas base with mirror: 2 ¾ × 6 ⅞ × 21 ⅞ in. (7 × 17.5 × 55.6 cm)
© 2007 Museum Associates/LACMA
Courtesy of the Los Angeles County Museum of Art, Los Angeles

Willie Middlebrook (born 1957)
p. 197
In His "Own" Image, 1992
From the *Portraits of My People*
series, 1992
Sixteen gelatin silver prints
24 × 20 in. (61 × 50.8 cm) each;
96 × 80 in. (243.8 × 203.2 cm) overall
© 2007 Museum Associates/LACMA
Courtesy of the Los Angeles County Museum
of Art, Los Angeles

Don Milton
p. 66
Cyclists in Sunset Park, c. 1920s
Gelatin silver print
9 ¾ × 7 ⅝ in. (24.8 × 19.4 cm)
Eugene Swarzwald and "Pictorial California and
the Pacific" Collection, The Huntington Library,
San Marino, California

Robert Mizer (1922–1992)
p. 163
Jack Conant, 1949
Gelatin silver print
3 × 5 in. (7.6 × 12.7 cm)
© Reprinted courtesy of AthleticModelGuild.com
Courtesy of Sonsini-Barajas

Bob McCune, 1952
Gelatin silver print
5 × 3 in. (12.7 × 7.6 cm)
© Reprinted courtesy of AthleticModelGuild.com
Courtesy of Sonsini-Barajas

William Mortenson (1897–1965)
p. 13
Torse, c. 1935
Gelatin silver print
5 ¼ × 6 ½ in. (13.3 × 16.5 cm)
Center for Creative Photography, University
of Arizona

Karin Apollonia Müller (born 1963)
p. 90
Power Lines, 1997
C-print
30 × 30 in. (76.2 × 76.2 cm)
Courtesy of the artist and Karyn Lovegrove
Gallery, Los Angeles

Leonard Nadel (1916–1990)
311–313 N. Hewitt Street, June 12,
1952
Gelatin silver print
3 × 5 in. (7.6 × 12.7 cm)
The Getty Research Institute, Los Angeles

p. 57
Commercial and Alameda Streets,
June 12, 1952
Gelatin silver print
3 × 5 in. (7.6 × 12.7 cm)
The Getty Research Institute, Los Angeles

N. Hewitt and Turner Street,
June 12, 1952
Gelatin silver print
3 × 5 in. (7.6 × 12.7 cm)
The Getty Research Institute, Los Angeles

p. 99
First Street Before Demolition,
c. 1952
Modern archival print from vintage
negative
11 × 14 in. (27.9 × 35.6 cm)
The Getty Research Institute, Los Angeles

Don Normark (born 1928)
p. 193
*Chalk Drawing on the Water Tank—
The Main Meeting Place in La Loma*,
1949 (printed 1994–95)
Gelatin silver print
11 × 14 in. (27.9 × 35.6 cm)
Courtesy of the artist

p. 17
*Palo Verde Neighborhood with
Elysian Park Beyond*, 1949 (printed
1994–95)
Gelatin silver print
11 × 14 in. (27.9 × 35.6 cm)
Courtesy of the artist

Ken Ohara (born 1942)
10:39am – 11:39am 12/2/1997, 1997
(printed 1999)
From the *With* series, 1994–98
Gelatin silver print
20 × 16 in. (50.8 × 40.6 cm)
Courtesy of the artist

10:33am – 11:33am 2/1/1998, 1998
(printed 1999)
From the *With* series, 1994–98
Gelatin silver print
20 × 16 in. (50.8 × 40.6 cm)
Courtesy of the artist

p. 226
03:40pm – 04:40pm 2/8/1998,
1998 (printed 1999)
From the *With* series, 1994–98
Gelatin silver print
20 × 16 in. (50.8 × 40.6 cm)
Courtesy of the artist

p. 227
01:17pm – 02:17pm 2/28/1998, 1998
(printed 1999)
From the *With* series, 1994–98
Gelatin silver print
20 × 16 in. (50.8 × 40.6 cm)
Courtesy of the artist

Catherine Opie (born 1961)
p. 74
Self-Portrait, 1993
Chromogenic print
40 × 30 in. (101.6 × 76.2 cm)
© 2007 Museum Associates/LACMA
Courtesy of the Los Angeles County Museum
of Art, Los Angeles

p. 170
Oliver in a Tutu, 2004
C-print
24 × 20 in. (61 × 50.8 cm)
Courtesy of Regen Projects, Los Angeles

Pacific Electric Railway Company
p. 66
*Hikers Near Alpine Tavern,
Mt. Lowe*, 1932
Gelatin silver print
10 ⅛ × 8 in. (25.7 × 20.3 cm)
The Huntington Library, San Marino, California

p. 115
Main Street Station, Los Angeles,
1944
Gelatin silver print
8 ¼ × 10 in. (21 × 25.4 cm)
The Huntington Library, San Marino, California

p. 69
Lifeguard Surfing at Long Beach,
n.d.
Gelatin silver print
4 ¾ × 7 in. (12.1 × 17.8 cm)
The Huntington Library, San Marino, California

p. 156
Redondo Plunge Guard, n.d.
Gelatin silver print
10 × 8 in. (25.4 × 20.3 cm)
The Huntington Library, San Marino, California

*Sierra Madre Junction on Monrovia
Line, San Marino*, n.d.
Gelatin silver print
7 ⅞ × 9 ⅞ in. (20 × 25.1 cm)
The Huntington Library, San Marino, California

Marion Palfi (1907–1978)
Los Angeles, 1946–49
Gelatin silver print
10 ½ × 13 ½ in. (26.7 × 34.3 cm)
Center for Creative Photography, University
of Arizona

Maynard L. Parker (1900–1976)
p. 56
**Interior of Cecil J. Birtcher
Residence, Los Angeles*, 1945
Kodachrome transparency
5 × 7 in. (12.7 × 17.8 cm)
Maynard L. Parker Archive, The Huntington
Library, San Marino, California

p. 87
*House Beautiful Pace Setter House
Designed by Cliff May, Riviera Ranch
Subdivision, Los Angeles*, 1946
Modern archival print from vintage
Kodachrome transparency
11 × 14 in. (27.9 × 35.6 cm)
Maynard L. Parker Archive, The Huntington
Library, San Marino, California

*Mandalay, Residence of Cliff May,
Riviera Ranch Subdivision, Los
Angeles*, 1957
Modern archival print from vintage
Kodachrome transparency
11 × 14 in. (27.9 × 35.6 cm)
Maynard L. Parker Archive, The Huntington
Library, San Marino, California

*William Powell Residence, Beverly
Hills*, c. 1940s
Gelatin silver print
13 ¼ × 10 ¼ in. (33.7 × 26 cm)
James Dolena Architectural Collection, The
Huntington Library, San Marino, California

Petit's Studio
pp. 118–19
*Atlantic and Beverly Boulevards
Looking South and East*,
January 29, 1946
Modern archival print from vintage
negative
10 × 55 in. (25.4 × 139.7 cm)
Verner Collection of Panoramic Negatives,
The Huntington Library, San Marino, California

C.C. Pierce (1861–1946)
*Store on West Side of Castelar
Street, Between Ord and Alpine*,
c. 1895
Gelatin silver print
7 ⅞ × 9 ¾ in. (20 × 24.8 cm)
C.C. Pierce Collection, The Huntington Library,
San Marino, California

p. 135
Chinese Field Hands, 1898
Gelatin silver print
7 ⅞ × 9 ⅞ in. (20 × 25.1 cm)
C.C. Pierce Collection, The Huntington Library,
San Marino, California

p. 16
*Griffith Park and Los Angeles River
at the Source*, 1900
Gelatin silver print
8 × 10 in. (20.3 × 25.4 cm)
C.C. Pierce Collection, The Huntington Library,
San Marino, California

p. 131
*Harvesting Grain on Van Nuys
Lankershim Ranch*, c. 1905
Gelatin silver print
6 ⅜ × 8 ⅜ in. (16.2 × 21.3 cm)
C.C. Pierce Collection, The Huntington Library,
San Marino, California

Eagle Rock Valley, 1908
Nine gelatin silver prints
7 ¾ × 9 ½ in. (19.7 × 24.1 cm) each;
7 ¾ × 76 in. (19.7 × 193 cm) overall
C.C. Pierce Collection, The Huntington Library,
San Marino, California

p. 188
Los Angeles Times Disaster,
October 1, 1910
Gelatin silver print
7 ¾ × 9 ¾ in. (19.7 × 24.8 cm)
C.C. Pierce Collection, The Huntington Library,
San Marino, California

Los Angeles Times Disaster,
October 1, 1910
Gelatin silver print
7 ¾ × 9 ¾ in. (19.7 × 24.8 cm)
C.C. Pierce Collection, The Huntington Library,
San Marino, California

pp. 20–21
*North End of Cahuenga Pass, Los
Angeles*, 1910
Modern archival print from vintage
negative
10 × 55 in. (25.4 × 139.7 cm)
Verner Collection of Panoramic Negatives,
The Huntington Library, San Marino, California

p. 116
*Seventh and Broadway Looking
North*, 1925
Gelatin silver print
6 ¾ × 10 in. (17.1 × 25.4 cm)
C.C. Pierce Collection, The Huntington Library,
San Marino, California

pp. 138–39
Long Beach Oil Field, Signal Hill,
January 18, 1931
Modern archival print from vintage
negative
10 × 35 ½ in. (25.4 × 90.2 cm)
Verner Collection of Panoramic Negatives,
The Huntington Library, San Marino, California

*Making Adobe Brick at Casa
Verdugo*, n.d.
Gelatin silver print
9 ¾ × 7 ⅞ in. (24.8 × 20 cm)
C.C. Pierce Collection, The Huntington Library,
San Marino, California

Ernest M. Pratt (1876–1945)
p. 110
Mulholland Highway, 1925
Toned bromide print
7 ⅛ × 5 ½ in. (18.1 × 14 cm)
Touring Topics Collection, The Huntington
Library, San Marino, California

p. 213
Ebb Tide, c. 1925
Toned bromide print
6 × 8 ¼ in. (15.2 × 21 cm)
Touring Topics Collection, The Huntington
Library, San Marino, California

Charles Puck (1882–1968)
p. 114
*Buena Vista Street with City Hall in
the Distance, Los Angeles*, n.d.
Gelatin silver print
3 ½ × 4 ½ in. (8.9 × 11.4 cm)
Historical Society of Southern California
Collection, The Huntington Library, San Marino,
California

p. 114
*Wilshire Boulevard Looking West
with Bullock's Wilshire on Left*, n.d.
Gelatin silver print
3 ½ × 4 ½in. (8.9 × 11.4 cm)
Historical Society of Southern California
Collection, The Huntington Library, San Marino,
California

Putnam Photo (*fl.* 1891–1902)
*Southern California Packing
Company and Supt. Welch's
Residence*, c. 1895
Albumen print
7 × 9 ¼ in. (17.8 × 23.5 cm)
The Huntington Library, San Marino, California

Leland Rice (born 1940)
p. 103
*Tar Covered Vat and
Condominiums*, 1980
Color coupler print
14 × 17 ⅛ in. (35.6 × 43.5 cm)
Courtesy of Susan Ehrens and Leland Rice

Herb Ritts (1952–2002)
p. 32
Tony in White, Hollywood, 1988
Gelatin silver print
20 × 16 in. (50.8 × 40.6 cm)
Courtesy of The Herb Ritts Foundation,
Los Angeles

p. 216
Mask, Hollywood, 1989
Gelatin silver print
20 × 16 in. (50.8 × 40.6 cm)
Courtesy of The Herb Ritts Foundation,
Los Angeles

p. 33
Tatjana in Swimsuit, Hollywood,
1989
Gelatin silver print
20 × 16 in. (50.8 × 40.6 cm)
Courtesy of The Herb Ritts Foundation,
Los Angeles

p. 217
*Earvin (Magic) Johnson,
Hollywood*, 1992
Gelatin silver print
20 × 16 in. (50.8 × 40.6 cm)
Courtesy of The Herb Ritts Foundation,
Los Angeles

Allen Ruppersberg (born 1944)
Summer Days, 1971
Three gelatin silver prints
8 × 10 in. (20.3 × 25.4 cm) each
Three pieces of bond paper with text
11 × 8 1/2 in. (27.9 × 21.6 cm) each
Courtesy of Margo Leavin Gallery, Los Angeles

Edward Ruscha (born 1937)
p. 121
Shell, Daggett, California, 1962
(printed 1989)
Gelatin silver print
19 1/2 × 23 in. (49.5 × 58.4 cm)
The Museum of Contemporary Art, Los Angeles

Every Building on the Sunset Strip,
1966
Photomechanical reproductions
folded to form 53 leaves
7 × 254 5/8 in. (17.8 × 646.7 cm)
The Huntington Library, San Marino, California

J.T. Sata (1896–1975)
Untitled [Man walking], 1930
Bromide print
8 1/2 × 10 in. (21.6 × 25.4 cm)
The Japanese American National Museum,
Los Angeles

Julius Shulman (born 1910)
p. 69
*Sunday Trekkers on Mount
Hollywood*, 1933
Gelatin silver print
4 × 6 1/2 in. (10.2 × 16.5 cm)
Courtesy of the artist and Craig Krull Gallery,
Santa Monica, California

p. 137
*City Hall and Construction of Union
Terminal, Los Angeles*, 1934
Gelatin silver print
14 × 11 in. (35.6 × 27.9 cm)
© J. Paul Getty Trust. Used with permission.
Julius Shulman Photography Archive
Research Library at the Getty Research
Institute, Los Angeles

p. 29
*Case Study House #22, West
Hollywood*, 1960
Modern archival print from vintage
negative
16 × 20 in. (40.6 × 50.8 cm)
© J. Paul Getty Trust. Used with permission.
Julius Shulman Photography Archive
Research Library at the Getty Research
Institute, Los Angeles

Peter Stackpole (1913–1977)
p. 150
Extra Tryouts, 1938
Gelatin silver print
9 3/4 × 7 in. (24.8 × 17.8 cm)
Center for Creative Photography, University
of Arizona

Phil Stern (born 1919)
Pin-Up Girl for "Attack," 1947
Archival pigment print
28 3/4 × 40 in. (73 × 101.6 cm)
© Phil Stern
Courtesy of Fahey/Klein Gallery, Los Angeles

p. 153
Sammy Davis Jr., (Front Kick), 1947
Gelatin silver print
14 × 11 in. (35.6 × 27.9 cm)
© Phil Stern
Courtesy of Fahey/Klein Gallery, Los Angeles

Joel Sternfeld (born 1944)
p. 127
*The northwest corner of Florence
and Normandie Avenues, Los
Angeles, California, October 1993*,
1993 (printed 2005)
Chromogenic dye coupler print
18 1/2 × 23 1/2 in. (47 × 59.7 cm)
Courtesy of the artist and Luhring Augustine,
New York
The J. Paul Getty Museum, Los Angeles

Stiffler & Gill
*On Pasadena and Mount Wilson
Toll Road. Campers*, c. 1900
Gelatin silver print
6 1/2 × 8 1/2 in. (16.5 × 21.6 cm)
The Huntington Library, San Marino, California

Timothy Street-Porter (born 1939)
p. 81
Flintstones Set at Vasquez Rocks,
1994 (printed 2008)
Archival ink-jet print
20 × 24 in. (50.8 × 61 cm)
Courtesy of the artist

Hiroshi Sugimoto (born 1948)
p. 219
Cinerama Dome, Hollywood, 1993
Gelatin silver print
20 × 24 in. (50.8 × 61 cm)
© Hiroshi Sugimoto, courtesy of Fraenkel
Gallery, San Francisco
The Museum of Contemporary Art, Los Angeles

Larry Sultan (born 1946)
pp. 160–61
Chandler Boulevard, 2000
Chromogenic print
50 × 60 in. (127 × 152.4 cm)
Courtesy of the artist and Stephen Wirtz
Gallery, San Francisco

p. 63
Backyard, Woodland Hills, 2002
Chromogenic print
50 × 60 in. (127 × 152.4 cm)
Courtesy of the artist and Stephen Wirtz
Gallery, San Francisco

Front jacket
Woman in Curlers, 2002
Chromogenic print
60 × 50 in. (152.4 × 127 cm)
Courtesy of the artist and Stephen Wirtz
Gallery, San Francisco

John Swope (1908–1979)
p. 52
*Guides to the Stars, Sunset
Boulevard*, 1938
Gelatin silver print
4 × 5 in. (10.2 × 12.7 cm)
Courtesy of Craig Krull Gallery, Santa Monica,
California

Edmund Teske (1911–1996)
p. 129
Newspaper Vendor, Los Angeles,
1943
Gelatin silver print
8 1/16 × 7 5/8 in. (20.5 × 19.4 cm)
© Edmund Teske Archives, Laurence Bump/
Nils Vidstrand
The J. Paul Getty Museum, Los Angeles

Ramon, Los Angeles, 1943
Gelatin silver print
9 5/8 × 6 1/4 in. (24.4 × 15.9 cm)
© Edmund Teske Archives, Laurence Bump/
Nils Vidstrand
The J. Paul Getty Museum, Los Angeles

*Jane Lawrence with Mandrake
Root, Zuma Beach, California*, 1944
Duotone solarization print
8 1/2 × 11 in. (21.6 × 27.9 cm)
© Edmund Teske Archives, Laurence Bump/
Nils Vidstrand
Courtesy of Nils Vidstrand

p. 18
[Marc Rambeau], 1962
Gelatin silver print
12 3/4 × 8 7/8 in. (32.4 × 22.5 cm)
© Edmund Teske Archives, Laurence Bump/
Nils Vidstrand
The J. Paul Getty Museum, Los Angeles

Unknown
*Mexican School Children, San
Gabriel, California*, c. 1890s
Albumen print
5 5/8 × 8 1/4 in. (14.3 × 21 cm)
The Huntington Library, San Marino, California

p. 65
**Out-Doors in January. A 15-
months' old California Baby*, 1899
Halftone reproduction from *Land of
Sunshine*, September 1899
3 × 5 in. (7.6 × 12.7 cm)
The Huntington Library, San Marino, California

p. 136
*Construction View of Los Angeles
Railway Building, Los Angeles*,
November 1, 1920
Gelatin silver print
8 × 10 in. (20.3 × 25.4 cm)
Los Angeles Railway Collection, The
Huntington Library, San Marino, California

*Aiko Kuromi and Her Brother,
Isamu, Los Angeles*, 1925 (printed
2008)
Modern archival print
11 × 14 in. (27.9 × 35.6 cm)
Security Pacific Collection, Los Angeles
Public Library

p. 88
*Aileen Pringle in the Doorway at
722 Adelaide Place, Santa Monica*,
c. 1925
Gelatin silver print
10 × 8 in. (25.4 × 20.3 cm)
Eugene Swarzwald and "Pictorial California and
the Pacific" Collection, The Huntington Library,
San Marino, California

p. 71
**People at "The Cross," the
Boundary Between the Segregated
Sections of Santa Monica and
Venice Beaches*, c. 1925
Gelatin silver print
3 × 5 in. (7.6 × 12.7 cm)
Shades of L.A. Archives/Los Angeles
Public Library

p. 71
St. Francis Dam Disaster, Morgue,
March 13, 1928
Modern archival print from vintage
negative
8 × 10 in. (20.3 × 25.4 cm)
Los Angeles Times History Collection, The
Huntington Library, San Marino, California

*Western Union Operating on the
Street After Earthquake, Long
Beach, March 10, 1933*, 1933
Gelatin silver photographic
postcard
3 1/2 × 5 1/2 in. (8.9 × 14 cm)
The Huntington Library, San Marino, California

pp. 96–97
*Marlow-Burns Subdivision, Windsor
Hills, Los Angeles*, December 1938
Modern archival print from vintage
negative
10 × 53 in. (25.4 × 134.6 cm)
Verner Collection of Panoramic Negatives,
The Huntington Library, San Marino, California

p. 76
*Aimee Semple McPherson with
portion of congregation at Angelus
Temple*, 1942
Modern archival print from vintage
negative
11 × 14 in. (27.9 × 35.6 cm)
Los Angeles Times Collection, Department of
Special Collections, Charles E. Young Research
Library, University of California, Los Angeles

p. 73
*Members of the Hollywood Negro
Ballet in a Publicity Photograph for
Ebony Magazine*, November 1953
Modern archival print from original
gelatin silver print
16 × 20 in. (40.6 × 50.8 cm)
Joseph Rickard Papers, The Huntington Library,
San Marino, California

pp. 14–15
*San Fernando Valley from above
Chatsworth, looking toward Los
Angeles with E. John Brandeis's
estate in the foreground*, n.d.
Gelatin silver print
7 1/2 × 9 3/4 in. (19 × 24.8 cm)
Eugene Swarzwald and "Pictorial California and
the Pacific" Collection, The Huntington Library,
San Marino, California

R.L. van Oosting (1899–1938)
Becalmed, 1925
Bromide print
9 × 7 1/4 in. (22.9 × 18.4 cm)
Touring Topics Collection, The Huntington
Library, San Marino, California

Adam Clark Vroman (1856–1916)
p. 130
Men at Mission San Fernando, c. 1897
Modern archival print from vintage
glass negative
11 × 14 in. (27.9 × 35.6 cm)
The Huntington Library, San Marino, California

Carleton E. Watkins (1829–1916)
*Apiary at Sierra Madre Villa, San
Gabriel*, 1877
Albumen print
5 1/2 × 4 1/8 in. (14 × 10.5 cm)
The Huntington Library, San Marino, California

*Banana Trees, Mr. Wallace, San
Gabriel*, 1877
Albumen print
5 1/2 × 4 1/8 in. (14 × 10.5 cm)
The Huntington Library, San Marino, California

*Citrus Groves, Stoneman Ranch,
San Gabriel, Cal.*, 1877
Albumen print
5 1/2 × 4 1/8 in. (14 × 10.5 cm)
The Huntington Library, San Marino, California

*Distant View, S.P.R.R. Depot,
Los Angeles*, 1877
Albumen print
5 1/2 × 3 7/8 in. (14 × 9.8 cm)
The Huntington Library, San Marino, California

Indian Huts, San Gabriel, Cal., 1877
Albumen print
5 1/2 × 4 1/8 in. (14 × 10.5 cm)
The Huntington Library, San Marino, California

p. 45
Old Santa Monica, 1877
Albumen print
5 1/2 × 4 1/8 in. (14 × 10.5 cm)
The Huntington Library, San Marino, California

p. 45
The Pasadena, Near San Gabriel,
1877
Albumen print
5 1/2 × 4 in. (14 × 10.2 cm)
The Huntington Library, San Marino, California

Pico House, Los Angeles, 1877
Albumen print
5 1/2 × 3 7/8 in. (14 × 9.8 cm)
The Huntington Library, San Marino, California

The Plaza, Los Angeles, 1877
Albumen print
5 1/2 × 3 7/8 in. (14 × 9.8 cm)
The Huntington Library, San Marino, California

*R.R. Co.'s Works at Wilmington,
S.P.R.R.*, 1877
Albumen print
5 1/2 × 4 1/4 in. (14 × 10.8 cm)
The Huntington Library, San Marino, California

St. Charles Hotel, Los Angeles, 1877
Albumen print
5 1/2 × 4 in. (14 × 10.2 cm)
The Huntington Library, San Marino, California

Santa Anita Rancho, 1877
Albumen print
5 1/2 × 3 7/8 in. (14 × 9.8 cm)
The Huntington Library, San Marino, California

*Street View in Los Angeles
[Downey Block at North Main and
Temple streets]*, 1877
Albumen print
5 3/8 × 3 7/8 in. (13.7 × 9.8 cm)
The Huntington Library, San Marino, California

*View from Lake Vineyard, B.D.
Wilson's, San Gabriel*, 1877
Albumen print
5 1/2 × 4 1/4 in. (14 × 10.8 cm)
The Huntington Library, San Marino, California

[View of San Pedro, California],
1877
Albumen print
5 1/2 × 3 7/8 in. (14 × 9.8 cm)
The Huntington Library, San Marino, California

SELECTED BIBLIOGRAPHY

Abel, Emily K., *Suffering in the Land of Sunshine: A Los Angeles Illness Narrative*, New Brunswick, NJ (Rutgers University Press) 2006

Addison, Heather, *Hollywood and the Rise of Physical Culture*, New York and London (Routledge) 2003

Almaguer, Tómas, *Racial Fault Lines: The Historical Origins of White Supremacy in California*, Berkeley (University of California Press) 1994

Banham, Reyner, *Los Angeles: The Architecture of Four Ecologies*, Harmondsworth (Penguin Books) 1984

Barron, Stephanie *et al.*, eds, *Made in California: Art, Image, and Identity, 1900–2000*, Berkeley and Los Angeles (University of California Press and Los Angeles County Museum of Art) 2000

—— *Reading California: Art, Image, and Identity, 1900–2000*, Berkeley and Los Angeles (University of California Press and Los Angeles County Museum of Art) 2000

Baur, John E., *The Health Seekers of Southern California, 1870–1900*, San Marino, Calif. (The Huntington Library) 1959

Betsky, Aaron *et al.*, *Experimental Architecture in Los Angeles*, Los Angeles (Forum for Architecture and Urban Design in association with Rizzoli, New York) 1991

Blueprints for Modern Living: History and Legacy of the Case Study Houses, exhib. cat. by Elizabeth A.T. Smith, Los Angeles Museum of Contemporary Art in association with MIT Press, 1989

Bottles, Scott L., *Los Angeles and the Automobile: The Making of the Modern City*, Berkeley (University of California Press) 1987

Brodsley, David, *L.A. Freeway: An Appreciative Essay*, Berkeley (University of California Press) 1981

Cándida-Smith, Richard, *Utopia and Dissent: Art, Poetry, and Politics in California*, Berkeley (University of California Press) 1995

Christopher, Nicholas, *Somewhere in the Night: Film Noir and the American City*, New York (Free Press) 1997

Cole, Carolyn Kozo and Kathy Kobayashi, *Shades of L.A.: Pictures from Ethnic Family Albums*, New York (New Press) 1996

Cuff, Dana, *The Provisional City: Los Angeles Stories of Architecture and Urbanism*, Cambridge, Mass. (MIT Press) 2000

Dailey, Victoria *et al.*, *L.A.'s Early Moderns: Art/Architecture/Photography*, Los Angeles (Balcony Press) 2003

Davis, Mike, *City of Quartz: Excavating the Future in Los Angeles*, London and New York (Verso Press) 1990

—— *Ecology of Fear: Los Angeles and the Imagination of Disaster*, New York (Metropolitan Books/Henry Holt) 1998

Dear, Michael *et al.*, eds, *Rethinking Los Angeles*, Thousand Oaks, Calif. (Sage Publications) 1996

Deverell, William, *Whitewashed Adobe: The Rise of Los Angeles and the Remaking of Its Mexican Past*, Berkeley (University of California Press) 2004

Deverell, William and Greg Hise, eds, *Land of Sunshine: An Environmental History of Metropolitan Los Angeles*, Pittsburgh (University of Pittsburgh Press) 2005

Didion, Joan, *Slouching Toward Bethlehem* [1968], New York (Simon & Schuster) 1979

Dumke, Glenn S., *The Boom of the Eighties in Southern California*, San Marino, Calif. (The Huntington Library) 1944

Featherstone, Mike *et al.*, *The Body: Social Process and Cultural Theory*, London (Sage Publications) 1991

Fine, David M., *Imagining Los Angeles: A City in Fiction*, Albuquerque (University of New Mexico Press) 2000

Flamming, Douglas, *Bound for Freedom: Black Los Angeles in Jim Crow America*, Berkeley (University of California Press) 2005

Fogelson, Robert, *The Fragmented Metropolis: Los Angeles, 1850–1930*, Berkeley (University of California Press) 1993

Fusco, Coco and Brian Wallis, *Only Skin Deep: Changing Visions of the American Self*, New York (International Center of Photography) 2003

Gabler, Neal, *An Empire of Their Own: How the Jews Invented Hollywood*, New York (Crown Publishers) 1988

Gebhard, David and Harriette Von Breton, *L.A. in the Thirties, 1931–1941*, Salt Lake City (Peregrine, Smith) 1975

Gottlieb, Robert and Irene Wolt, *Thinking Big: The Story of the Los Angeles Times, Its Publishers and Their Influence on Southern California*, New York (G.P. Putnam's Sons) 1977

Groth, Paul and Todd W. Bressi, eds, *Understanding Ordinary Landscapes*, New Haven, Conn. (Yale University Press) 1997

Hayden, Dolores, *The Power of Place: Urban Landscapes as Public History*, Cambridge, Mass. (MIT Press) 1995

Heimann, Jim, *Car Hops and Curb Service: A History of American Drive-In Restaurants, 1920–1960*, San Francisco (Chronicle Books) 1996

—— *Sins of the City: The Real Los Angeles Noir*, San Francisco (Chronicle Books) 1999

Heimann, Jim and Rip Georges, *California Crazy: Roadside Vernacular Architecture*, San Francisco (Chronicle Books) 1980

Helter Skelter: L.A. Art in the 1990s, exhib. cat. by Paul Schimmel, Los Angeles Museum of Contemporary Art, 1992

Henstell, Bruce, *Sunshine and Wealth: Los Angeles in the Twenties and Thirties*, San Francisco (Chronicle Books) 1984

Hise, Greg, *Magnetic Los Angeles: Planning the Twentieth Century Metropolis*, Baltimore (Johns Hopkins University Press) 1997

Kampion, Drew, *Stoked: A History of Surf Culture*, Santa Monica, Calif. (General Publishing Group) 1997

Kaplan, Sam Hall, *L.A. Lost and Found: An Architectural History of Los Angeles*, New York (Crown Publishers) 1987

Karlstrom, Paul, ed., *On the Edge of America: California Modernist Art, 1900–1950*, Berkeley (University of California Press) 1996

Katzman, Louise, *Photography in California, 1945–1980*, New York and San Francisco (Hudson Hills Press in association with the San Francisco Museum of Modern Art) 1984

Kennedy, Marla Hamburg and Ben Stiller, eds, *Looking at Los Angeles*, New York (Metropolis Books) 2005

Klein, Norman, *The History of Forgetting: Los Angeles and the Erasure of Memory*, London and New York (Verso Press) 1997

Kobal, John, *The Art of the Great Hollywood Portrait Photographers, 1925–1940*, New York (Knopf) 1980

Krull, Craig, *Photographing the L.A. Art Scene, 1955–1975*, Santa Monica, Calif. (Smart Art Press) 1996

Kurutz, K.D. and Gary Kurutz, *California Calls You: The Art of Promoting the Golden State, 1870–1940*, Sausalito, Calif. (Windgate Press) 2000

Lippard, Lucy R., *The Lure of the Local: Senses of Place in a Multicentered Society*, New York (New Press) 1997

Loners, Mavericks, and Dreamers: Art in Los Angeles Before 1900, exhib. cat. by Nancy Dustin Wall Moure, Laguna Beach, Calif., Laguna Art Museum, November 1993–January 1994

Longstreth, Richard, *City Center to Regional Mall: Architecture, the Automobile, and Retailing in Los Angeles, 1920–1950*, Cambridge, Mass. (MIT Press) 1997

—— *The Drive-In, the Supermarket, and the Transformation of Commercial Space in Los Angeles, 1914–1941*, Cambridge, Mass. (MIT Press) 1999

Los Angeles, 1955–1985: The Birth of an Artistic Capital, exhib. cat. by Catherine Grenier, Paris, Centre Pompidou, March 8–July 17, 2006

Masters of Starlight: Photographers in Hollywood, exhib. cat. by David Fahey and Linda Rich, Los Angeles County Museum of Art, 1987

May, Kirse Granat, *Golden State, Golden Youth: The California Image in Popular Culture, 1955–1966*, Chapel Hill (University of North Carolina Press) 2002

May, Lary, *Screening Out the Past: The Birth of Mass Culture and the Motion Picture Industry* [1980], Chicago (University of Chicago Press) 1983

McClung, William A., *Landscapes of Desire: Anglo Mythologies of Los Angeles*, Berkeley (University of California Press) 2000

McCoy, Esther, *Modern California Houses: Case Study Houses, 1945–1962*, New York (Reinhold Publishing) 1962

McWilliams, Carey, *Southern California Country: An Island on the Land*, New York (Duell, Sloan & Pearce) 1946

Mirzoeff, Nick, *Bodyscapes: Art, Modernity, and the Ideal Figure*, New York (Routledge) 1995

Mitchell, W.J. Thomas, *Landscape and Power*, Chicago (University of Chicago Press) 2002

Pacific Dreams: Currents of Surrealism and Fantasy in California Art, 1934–1957, exhib. cat. by Susan Ehrlich, Los Angeles, Armand Hammer Museum of Art and Cultural Center at UCLA, 1995

Pictorialism in California: Photographs 1900–1940, exhib. cat. by Michael G. Wilson and Dennis Reed, Los Angeles, The J. Paul Getty Museum; San Marino, Calif., The Henry E. Huntington Library and Art Gallery, 1994

Pitt, Leonard and Dale Pitt, *Los Angeles A–Z: An Encyclopedia of the City and County*, Berkeley (University of California Press) 1997

Plagens, Peter, *Sunshine Muse: Contemporary Art on the West Coast* [1974], Berkeley (University of California Press) 2000

Proof: Los Angeles Art and Photography, 1960–1980, exhib. cat. by Charles Desmarais, Laguna Beach, Calif.,

Laguna Art Museum in association with the Fellows of
Contemporary Art, 1992

Reid, David, ed., *Sex, Death and God in L.A.*, Berkeley
(University of California Press) 1992

Roderick, Kevin, *Wilshire Boulevard: A Grand Concourse of Los
Angeles*, Santa Monica, Calif. (Angel City Press) 2005

Rose, Marla Matzer, *Muscle Beach: Where the Best Bodies in
the World Started a Fitness Revolution*, Los Angeles (LA
Weekly Books) 2001

Rubin, Barbara *et al.*, *L.A. in Installments: Forest Lawn*, Santa
Monica, Calif. (Westside Publications) 1979

Salas, Charles G. and Michael S. Roth, *Looking for Los Angeles:
Architecture, Film, Photography and the Urban
Landscape*, Los Angeles (The Getty Research Institute)
2001

Sander, Gloria Williams with Therese Mulligan, *The Collectible
Moment: Photographs in the Norton Simon Museum*,
Pasadena, Calif. (Norton Simon Art Foundation) 2006

Schwartz, Joan M. and James R. Ryan, *Picturing Place:
Photography and the Geographic Imagination*, New York
(I.B. Tauris) 2003

Scott, John Allen, *The City: Los Angeles and Urban Theory and
the End of the Twentieth Century*, Berkeley (University of
California Press) 1996

Shippey, Lee with Max Yavno, *The Los Angeles Book*, New York
(Houghton Mifflin) 1950

Sitton, Tom and William Deverell, eds, *Metropolis in the Making:
Los Angeles in the 1920s*, Berkeley (University of
California Press) 2001

Southern California Photography, 1900–1965, exhib. cat. by
Suzanne Muchnic, Los Angeles County Museum of Art,
December 18, 1980–March 15, 1981

Starr, Kevin, *Americans and the California Dream, 1850–1915*
[1973], New York (Oxford University Press) 1985

—— *Inventing the Dream: California Through the Progressive
Era*, New York (Oxford University Press) 1985

—— *Material Dreams: Southern California Through the 1920s*,
New York (Oxford University Press) 1990

—— *Endangered Dreams and the Great Depression in California*,
New York (Oxford University Press) 1996

—— *The Dream Endures: California Enters the 1940s*, New York
(Oxford University Press) 1997

—— *Embattled Dreams: California in War and Peace, 1940-1950*,
New York (Oxford University Press) 2002

—— *Coast of Dreams: California on the Edge, 1990–2003*,
New York (Knopf) 2004

Taylor, John Russell, *Strangers in Paradise: The Hollywood
Emigrés, 1933–1950*, New York (Holt, Rinehart & Winston)
1983

Thomson, David, *Beneath Mulholland: Thoughts on Hollywood
and Its Ghosts*, New York (Vintage Books) 1997

Ulin, David L., ed., *Writing Los Angeles: A Literary Anthology*,
New York (Library of America) 2002

Waldie, D.J., *Holy Land: A Suburban Memoir*, New York and
London (W.W. Norton) 1996

Whiting, Cécile, *Pop L.A.: Art and the City in the 1960s*,
Berkeley (University of California Press) 2006

Wilkman, Jon and Nancy Wilkman, *Picturing Los Angeles*,
Salt Lake City (Gibbs Smith) 2006

Wride, Tim *et al.*, *Scene of the Crime: Photographs from the
LAPD Archive*, New York (Harry N. Abrams) 2004

James Baker
Uta Barth
Black Photographers of California Archive/California State University, Northridge
Center for Creative Photography, University of Arizona, Tucson
Gusmano Cesaretti
Stephen Cohen Gallery, Los Angeles
Eileen Cowin
Darryl Curran
Michael Dawson Gallery, Los Angeles
Lou D'Elia
John Divola
Susan Ehrens and Leland Rice
Fahey/Klein Gallery, Los Angeles
Robbert Flick
Fototeka Gallery, Los Angeles
Harry Gamboa, Jr.
The J. Paul Getty Museum, Los Angeles
The Getty Research Institute, Los Angeles
Christopher Grimes Gallery, Santa Monica, California
Karen Halverson
Miyo Hernandez
Japanese American National Museum, Los Angeles
Jan Kesner Gallery, Los Angeles
Craig Krull Gallery, Santa Monica, California
Margo Leavin Gallery, Los Angeles
Gary Leonard
Los Angeles County Museum of Art, Los Angeles
Los Angeles Public Library
Karyn Lovegrove Gallery, Los Angeles
Gallery Luisotti, Santa Monica, California
M + B, Los Angeles
Douglas McCulloh
The Museum of Contemporary Art, Los Angeles
National Archives and Records Administration, Washington, D.C.
Don Normark
Ken Ohara
Susanne Preissler, Independent Media, Inc., Santa Monica, California
Dennis Reed
Regen Projects, Los Angeles
The Herb Ritts Foundation, Los Angeles
RoseGallery, Santa Monica, California
Andy Schwartz
John Sonsini
Timothy Street-Porter
Department of Special Collections, Charles E. Young Research Library, University
of California, Los Angeles
The Marjorie and Leonard Vernon Collection, Los Angeles
Nils Vidstrand
Susanne Vielmetter Los Angeles Projects, Culver City, California
Devik Wiener
Stephen Wirtz Gallery, San Francisco

First published 2008 by Merrell Publishers Limited

Head office:
81 Southwark Street
London SE1 0HX

New York office:
740 Broadway, Suite 1202
New York, NY 10003

merrellpublishers.com

in association with

The Huntington Library, Art Collections,
and Botanical Gardens
1151 Oxford Road
San Marino, CA 91108

huntington.org

Published on the occasion of the exhibition *This Side
of Paradise: Body and Landscape in Los Angeles Photographs*,
The Huntington Library, Art Collections,
and Botanical Gardens, San Marino, California,
June 14–September 14, 2008

A catalog record for this book is available from the Library
of Congress.

British Library Cataloguing-in-Publication data:
Watts, Jennifer A.
This side of paradise : body and landscape in Los Angeles
photographs
    1. Outdoor photography – California – Los Angeles –
    Exhibitions 2. Portrait photography – California – Los
    Angeles – Exhibitions 3. Los Angeles (Calif.) – In art –
    Exhibitions
    I. Title II. Bohn-Spector, Claudia III. Nickel, Douglas R.
    (Douglas Robert), 1961–
    770.9'79494'074

ISBN-13: 978-1-8589-4434-0
ISBN-10: 1-8589-4434-1

Printed and bound in Italy

Produced by Merrell Publishers Limited
Designed by Nicola Bailey
Copy-edited by Richard Dawes
Proof-read by Philippa Baker
Indexed by Hilary Bird